KAUTILYA
The True Founder of Economics

Balbir Singh Sihag, Ph D (MIT)

Vitasta
LET KNOWLEDGE SPREAD
www.vitastapublishing.com

Published by
Renu Kaul Verma
Vitasta Publishing Pvt Ltd
2/15, Ansari Road, Daryaganj
New Delhi - 110 002
info@vitastapublishing.com

ISBN 978-81-925354-9-4
© Balbir Singh Sihag
First Edition 2014
Third Reprint 2023
MRP ₹995

All Rights Reserved.

No part of this publication may be reproduced, stored in a retrieval system, or transmitted in any form, or by any means—electronic, mechanical, photocopying, recording or otherwise—without the prior permission of the publisher. The views and opinions expressed in this book are the author's own.

Typeset and Cover Design by Vitasta Publishing Pvt Ltd
Printed by Vikas Computer and Printers

To
My parents
Smt Nimbo Devi and Ch Munshi Ram Sihag,
Smt Prabhat Shobha Pandit and Prof Sher Singh
who taught me the value of learning, hard work and honesty.

Contents

Publisher's Note   *xi*
Forewords   *xiii*
Preface   *xvii*
Introduction   *xxiii*

ONE
Kautilya and His Times

1. **Prologue: Kautilya's Vision**   **3-17**
   1.1 Provision of Human Security
   1.2 Prevalent Views on Kautilya's Contributions
   1.3 Why Another Book on Kautilya?

2. **Society, Polity and Economy**   **18-28**
   2.1 Changes in Writing Styles over Time
   2.2 Socio-Religious-Political Conditions in 4th Century BCE

2.3 Economic Conditions, Markets and
Institutions in 4th Century BCE

TWO
Concepts, Methodology
and Tools of Analysis

3. **Origin, Scope and Methodology of Economics**   31-65
   3.1 Interpretation, Evaluation
   and Accreditation of Earlier Works
   3.2 Requirements for Establishing
   Origin of Economics
   3.3 Views on the *Wealth of Nations*
   3.4 *Arthashastra* on Definition
   and Scope of Economics
   3.5 Kautilya's Methodology:
   A Partial Equilibrium Approach
   3.6 Optimization Subject to Constraints
   3.7 Time-preference and
   Inter-temporal Arbitrage
   3.8 *Arthashastra* on Economics
   as a Separate Discipline

4. **A Forerunner of Neoclassical Price Theory**   66-85
   4.1 Anticipation of Ordinal Preferences
   4.2 Cost, Production and
   Substitution Possibilities
   4.3 Demand-Supply Apparatus

5. **Accounting Methods and Income Measurement**   86-96
   5.1 Accounting Methods
   5.2 Kautilya on the Scope and
   Methodology of Accounting
   5.3 A Forerunner of National Income Accounts

THREE
Ethical Foundation to Freedom from Wants

6. Foundational Role of Dharma   99-112
   6.1 Pre-Kautilyan Sages on the Foundational Role of *Dharma*
   6.2 Kautilya Followed the Indian Thought on the Role of *Dharma*
   6.3 Unique Contributions to Action-oriented Approaches

7. Ethical, Efficient and Energetic Decision-makers   113-123
   7.1 Conceptual Framework on Ethical Conduct
   7.2 Character-building of the Future King

8. Ethics and Economic Growth   124-142
   8.1 Creation of Good Institutions and Provision of Good Governance
   8.2 Capital, Labour and Land as Sources of Economic Growth
   8.3 Institutions, Governance and Risk-return Trade-off
   8.4 Interdependence of Knowledge, Governance, National Security and Economic Growth

9. Preventing Market and Government Failures   143-160
   9.1 Identification of Moral, Market and Government Failures
   9.2 Consequences of Market Failure
   9.3 Consequences of Government Failure
   9.4 Rules, Regulations and Organizational Design to Reduce Fraud

10. **Information, Knowledge, Wisdom and Management** — 161-173
    10.1 Bounded Rationality
    10.2 Wisdom-based Management and Economic Performance
    10.3 Trade-off between Pooling Knowledge and Confidentiality

11. **Labour Policy: Moral and Material Incentives and Effort** — 174-195
    11.1 Conceptual Framework on Incentives
    11.2 Matching Incentive-Type to Agent-Type
    11.3 Tailored Types of Material Incentives to Agent's Hierarchical Position
    11.4 Payment System Design to Alleviate Moral Hazard

12. **Taxation: Principles and Policies** — 196-213
    12.1 Origin of the Income Tax and the Institution of Kingship
    12.2 Principles of Taxation
    12.3 Anticipation of Dupuit-Laffer Curve by Kautilya
    12.4 Views on Other Related Concepts

13. **Kautilya on Famine and Freedom** — 214-224
    13.1 Kautilya's Conceptual Framework for Prevention of Famines
    13.2 Impact of Famines on Income and Freedom

14. **International Trade Policies** — 225-232
    14.1 Policies on Promotion of Imports
    14.2 Nature of International Trade in Ancient Times
    14.3 Theory of Gains from Trade

FOUR
Ethics and Freedom from Fear of Crime

15. Administration of Justice   **235-249**
    15.1 Corruption of Enforcers and Crime Deterrence
    15.2 Judicial Fairness and Minimization of Legal Errors
    15.3 The Optimum Level of Punishment
    15.4 Other Related Issues

16. Contract and Property Laws   **250-266**
    16.1 Contract Laws between Individuals & Government and Individuals
    16.2 Common Property and Protection of Private Property Rights

17. Penance, Penalty and Prevention of Torts   **267-288**
    17.1 Tort Laws before Kautilya
    17.2 Kautilya Proposed Penance-Penalty Mix for an Effective Deterrence
    17.3 Kautilya on Negligence-based Tort Law

FIVE
National Security

18. Defending Freedom by Every Means and at Any Cost   **291-301**
    18.1 Kautilya's Ideas on the Provision of Public Goods
    18.2 Kautilya on Relative Power Equation
    18.3 National Security and Kautilya's Relative Asset Hypothesis
    18.4 Kautilya on Invariance Hypothesis
    18.5 Kautilya's Hypothesis: Power Breeds More Power

19. Risk-return Analysis of Campaigns   302-311
  19.1 Risk-return Trade-off in Making Alliances
  19.2 Risk-return Trade-off in Acquiring Land
  19.3 Risk Reduction through Diversification
  19.4 Multi-Variable Approach
       to Success of a Campaign

**20. Time Inconsistency Problem
     and Asymmetric Information**   312-327
  20.1 Kautilya on Time Inconsistency Problem
  20.2 Kautilya on Asymmetric Information
  20.3 Kautilya on Bargaining
       with Private Information

**21. Epilogue:
     Kautilya's Place in Economic Thought**   328-336
  21.1 Recapitulation of Kautilya's Contributions
  21.2 Kautilya's Noteworthy Insights
  21.3 Giving Kautilya His Due Recognition as
       the Founder of Economics

Endnotes   *337-396*
References   *397-422*
Index   *423-429*
Conclusion   *431-432*
Acknowledgements   *433-436*
Afterword   *437-442*

Publisher's Note

Four years after Vitasta published Prof Balbir Sihag's book, *Kautilya*, we bring to our discerning readers another edition of this book, in changed economic conditions in India and globally. In today's fast paced world, four years is a long time in the economic time-scale. Today, even WTO norms are obsolete and no longer sacrosanct in trade, low cost does not necessarily sell, terms like social enterprise drives innovation and technology and the goals of capitalism have shifted from good of the individual to that of shared welfare of all. In India too, since 2014, economic policies have changed, decision-makers are revisiting the roots and *Arthashastra* is one such roadmap to a more equitable socio-economic order. The new edition with an insightful Introduction and Afterword, on the eve of another democratic general election, reveals a certain bias towards Eastern theories and concepts and Western reluctance to give due credit, though world economics is today driven by the East. Intellectual bias against India has become very visible in recent times with books like *How India Lost Her Freedom* and *An Era of Darkness*. It took many years for the West to concede that the 'zero' was an Indian concept and may take some more to acknowledge Kautilya's contribution to good economics and good governance. Nevertheless, we in India take pride in bringing to the world, what we call *Chanakyaniti* – economic policies for the greater good of all from the world's first economist.

Forewords

AN EFFICIENT WORLDVIEW

The opus *Arthas'astra* or the science of wealth or prosperity in Sanskrit is attributed to Kautilya, also known as Chanakya and Vishnugupta. Not much is known about him except the legend that the Nandas, then rulers of Pataliputra (modern Patna), insulted Kautilya who succeeded in uprooting them and installing the Mauryas in their place. Though the date of the opus is not known precisely, it is generally agreed that Kautilya completed it in the 4th century BCE. It was widely known primarily by references of others to it, a complete text was found only in 1905 by R Shamasastry of the Government Oriental Library in Mysore who published its first English translation in 1915. Many translations in English and other languages have appeared since then.

Kautilya seems to have intended *Arthas'astra* as a manual for the Mauryas on settling the land they acquired, building and administering their state efficiently, maintaining law and order, accumulating and sustaining wealth and defending themselves against enemies within and outside their state. The strategic aspects of the advice to the ruler in it have naturally lead many to compare it to Machiavelli's *The Prince* of vintage 1532 CE.

As its title suggests, the *Arthas'astra* as a manual of statecraft naturally had to deal with many economic matters such as raising revenue, paying civil servants, preventing corruption and many other issues. To be able to provide sensible advice on such matters, its author had to have an implicit or explicit economic theory as well as for law and economics. Professor Balbir Sihag, a PhD in economics from MIT, learnt his economic theory from giants like Paul Samuelson. He has chosen to examine the *Arthas'astra* with the tools and techniques of economic theory. Interestingly, he finds that Kautilya anticipated several centuries earlier many basic concepts and theories of modern economics. One does not have to agree with each and every attribution to Kautilya by Professor Sihag to appreciate the depth of his scholarship and careful scrutiny in doing so. I recommend this book to politicians, administrators, economists as well as curious lay readers.

— T N Srinivasan
Samuel C Park Jr, Professor Emeritus of Economics

OUTSTANDING CONTRIBUTION

Economic science based on ethics and good governance originated in India 2500 years ago when Kautilya wrote the *Arthashastra*, a scholarly comprehensive treatise on economic and political administration. Kautilya was instrumental in establishing a crime-free, prosperous and powerful empire by ousting the corrupt Nanda regime and installing Chandragupta Maurya on the throne.

Prof Sihag has made an outstanding contribution in creating awareness about Kautilya in the West where he had been either ignored or misunderstood. Prof Sihag has developed equations to analyse the principles and philosophy of Kautilya's economics for the first time, for better understanding of the scholars who believe that unless quantitative treatment is given to a discipline, it would not be acceptable. I recommend reading this new book on Kautilya to all those who wish to analyse critically the great contribution made by Kautilya.

— **Prof Lallan Prasad,**
Executive President, Kautilya Foundation, Delhi
Former Head and Dean, Department of Business Economics, University of Delhi

KAUTILYA'S *DHARMANOMICS*

Kautilya's *Arthashastra*, a 4th century BCE treatise on statecraft, has several remarkable features: its comprehensiveness and attention to details is mind boggling; it gives primacy to economic issues and policies in the perspective of larger purpose of life and projected in the totality of environment; it is based on sound economic principles and policies combined with righteousness and sensitivity towards the weak (termed *Dharmanomics* by Prof Sihag); it shows an in-depth understanding of the intricacies of human nature and conduct towards which policy responses are evolved; it keeps in view the dynamics of real situations; it favours nation-building sentiments, and it enunciates principles that carry universal relevance and applicability transcending time and space. Kautilya's genius lay in bringing together such multifarious aspects into a consistent whole. Prof Sihag has well grasped this yoga. With cogent logic and details, he has analyzed many of Kautilya's formulations and ideas that made use of the concepts of modern economics, which were subsequently developed by and credited to a number of different economists over the last few centuries. In establishing this and helping comprehension of Kautilya's ideas, Professor Sihag has applied standard mathematical and graphical techniques and has painstakingly reviewed related literature in economics and other social sciences.

Professor Sihag has done an excellent job in getting Kautilya recognized as the 'founder of economics' and has made his country proud. Hope this book will stimulate useful research in the field of history of economic thought besides being found of much interest by social scientists, policy makers and general readership.

— **Bhoopendra Pratap Sinha,**
Economist and Social Analyst,
Ex-Member, Indian Economic Service

Preface

I happened to own two copies of the English translation of Kautilya's *Arthashastra*. One late afternoon, I went to MIT to give one of them to my professor, Paul Samuelson, who had illuminated the horizon of economics for seven decades. To my surprise, he was in his office working hard, like an assistant professor seeking tenure. I presented the book to him. He looked into it for a while and asked me, 'Does it contain the concept of opportunity cost?' Since I had not read the book thoroughly at the time, I had to confess that I would have to ascertain this. But my curiosity was aroused and I read through the *Arthashastra* only to realize that not only did Kautilya use the concept of opportunity cost but also a number of current concepts that make up for the vastly enriched discipline of economics today. Indeed, here was a fascinating work awaiting a modern economist to discover how well Kautilya—also known as Chanakya—had, as early as in the

4th Century BCE, understood and used in his *magnum opus* many elements of modern economic analysis, as we know it.

There are several books on Kautilya's *Arthashastra*, as well as numerous references to it, in the literature on political science. However, there are only two books—and they too deal only briefly (each having just one chapter) with Kautilya's contributions to economics — Ajit K Dasgupta's *A History of Indian Economic Thought* (Routledge, 1993) and Joseph J Spengler's *Indian Economic Thought* (Duke University Press, 1971). They only scratch the surface and fall short in conveying Kautilya's enormous range and depth in the sphere of economics.

This book seeks to bring out the monumental contribution of Kautilya to economics and its practice. The *Arthashastra* is the first book that proposes *Yogakshema*, all round well-being of everyone, especially of the weak. It explicitly promotes the goals of both *artha* (material well-being) and *dharma* (righteous behaviour) as a consistent whole and repudiates any deviation from them. The ensuing framework and action-oriented approach relies on market mechanism, with government intervention limited to situations of emergency and excesses. Kautilya, thus, recommended a mixed economy in which the private sector has the predominant position while the public sector too has an active role in support of governance and in facilitating economic growth in the private sector. Kautilya identified increases in land, labour and capital as the sources of economic growth. He understood the concept of 'bounded rationality' and suggested cognitive division of labour for overcoming it and arriving at a better decision. This implied a much deeper understanding of the concept of division of labour since this has relevance to the creative economy of today. In comparison, Adam Smith's understanding of division of labour was limited to an assembly-line type of concept called 'Fordism' (making workers dull). The *Arthashastra*, thus, offers a more advanced theory of economic growth than provided by Adam Smith's *Wealth of Nations*.

One needs to read the whole of the *Arthashastra* and also has to understand its connection to Vedic literature, in order to appreciate its unique contribution whose outcome is an ethics-intensive economics that may be labelled as *Dharmanomics*, that is economics imbued with ethics. According to Kautilya, system-building (moral order) was essential to nation-building and, so, he postulated an ethical but demonstrably pragmatic approach to handle economic issues. He did not believe that there was any trade-off between ethics and efficiency. He did not consider following of *dharma* codes as constraints on economic well-being, rather as relaxing them by creating trust and cooperation and, thus, expanding the opportunity set. He recommended vaccinating children with a healthy dose of ethics to protect them and society against debilitating personal vices and social ills, and to maintain immunity throughout their lives through booster shots of ethics.

Kautilya also emphasized administration of justice. He advanced several cardinal principles of justice: that punishment must be certain, proportional to the crime and, above all, must be administered impartially.

Kautilya had a full grasp of the whole system and understood the interdependence between the 'freedom from wants' and 'freedom from fear' components of human security. The *Arthashastra* is, thus, a complete manual on how to make every citizen's life richer and fuller. He identified the sources of systemic risk and suggested measures to reduce it. He was an empiricist who did not believe in fate but understood the stochastic nature of variables.

Kautilya wholeheartedly embraced the Vedic philosophy: 'Live and help others live'. But while one could persuade the native king to be ethical and efficient one had no control over foreign kings. At that time, and to a large extent even today, there was no such thing as live-and-let-live type of understanding vis-à-vis foreign rule. It is doubtful that Alexander was sent an invitation to attack Egypt or India. Kautilya, therefore, in addition to the development of an exchange theory, also developed a conflict theory. He brought out the negative consequences of foreign rule since that would ruin the economy and the native culture. His advice to the native king was to destroy the aggressor at all cost and by every means. Unfortunately, though patently justifiable, this aspect of the *Arthashastra*, along with the imperatives to reliably know and monitor the ground reality for effective governance, even with the use of clandestine means and distrustful disposition, has attracted disproportionate attention.

Ancient India was an incubator of innovations. Atharvan Angiras was the world's first innovator, who produced *agni* (fire). Certainly, curiosity is part of the human DNA but, until that time, it was limited only to exploration. This discovery kindled the desire to undertake experimentation and that initiated the creation of a civilization. India produced Yagnavalkya, the world's first philosopher and system-giver, Sushruta, the world's first surgeon and sage Punarvasu Atreya, the world's first founder of medicine. The numeral/zero, trigonometry and even calculus had their origin in India.

No one should get surprised by the claim that Kautilya founded economics. Kautilya's genius has been recognized in India and Southeast Asia but very little is known or acknowledged about his contributions in the West. Surprisingly, there is not even a mention of his name in the literature on the history of economic thought, which, after a brief reference to the Greek masters, usually covers the conditions and thoughts in the post-Middle Ages in the western hemisphere. Even well-read and eminent economists display ignorance about Kautilya's contributions. In this book I have sought to present Kautilya's *Arthashastra* as objectively as possible. I was inspired by Professor Samuelson's work on Adam Smith and follow his 'rational reconstruction' approach to interpret Kautilya's *Arthashastra*. However, the 'historical reconstruction' approach cannot be used effectively in this case, since sufficient information for the purpose is not available for that period. Elementary graphs and charts have been used at some places to facilitate greater clarity in understanding.

Recently, Mattessich (2000, Chapter 6) finds that Luca Pacioli, the Italian mathematician, who is acknowledged as the founder of modern accounting, simply initiated the practice of double-entry book keeping, whereas Kautilya founded the theory of accounting itself. He concludes that Kautilya's *Arthashastra* is as important a contribution as Pacioli's *Summa*. It is claimed here that Kautilya's *Arthashastra* is as important a contribution as Adam Smith's *Wealth of Nations*. After going through this book, many open-minded readers might be convinced that Mattessich's above cited observation about Kautilya's contribution in the field of economics is an understatement.

Chronological priority has been the sole legal standard of proof/criterion to grant patent/copyright to an innovator/writer. My objective in writing this book is simply to get Kautilya his due recognition as the true founder of economics since he, indeed, accomplished much more than what Adam Smith did two thousand years later. Also, many unfounded distortions, both about Kautilya and Hindu culture, get corrected with this work. It is, indeed, extremely difficult for anyone to accept that he/she has been worshipping a wrong god or that his/her father is someone other than the one who he/she knows as his/her father. My purpose in writing this book is not to hurt or convert anyone. Still, it might not convince or it might even infuriate some guardians of the faith. Kautilya's *Arthashastra* is, indeed, a world heritage. It is a manual on how to achieve peace and shared prosperity. The world community could benefit by adopting Kautilya's ethical and practical approach. I hope this book initiates a constructive debate as to how to ensure that every citizen of every country enjoys a richer and fuller life.

Introduction

MY LEARNING CURVE

When I started reading the *Arthashastra* for the first time, my reaction was WOW! I was looking for the *opportunity cost* concept, but I found many other economic concepts. My interest got really heightened and initial embarrassment turned into a curiosity to learn more about it. I read it several times and wrote a non-technical paper. I tried to get it published but got rejected. I was at a loss. Almost two years went by. Then suddenly I experienced enlightenment (my Budhha moment). I realized that Adam Smith, Recardo and others had no clue about equations and graphs, but almost everyone uses these modern tools of analysis to express their ideas. Why can't I use them to express Kautilya's ideas, I told myself.

I was in business. I was reading *The Arthashastra* over and over and I started to see the links among various sectors. Very quickly I wrote about 12 chapters on Kautilya's various contributions. On my behalf, Prof Jagdish Bhagwati requested Dr Anand Chandavarkar to edit my manuscript. He did an excellent job and taught me how to write in this field.

Let me take this opportunity to throw some light on certain hidden practices of the West that are obstructions to the dissemination of ideas and historical facts. With Prof Jagdish Bhagwati's blessing, I submitted a draft of my manuscript (MS) entitled, *Kautilya's Arthashastra: The First Word on Economics* to a renowned university publisher in New Delhi on 28 November 2001.

The published manuscript entitled, *Kautilya: The True Founder of Economics* published in 2014, has a few additional chapters resulting from reorganization of the material, but has no additional economic concepts than those presented in the 2001 manuscript (*Kautilya's Arthashastra: The First Word on Economics*). Table 1 lists some of the concepts which were presented in the 2001 MS. First column lists references to *The Arthashastra*. The third column cites the references to the published version.

Table 1: **A Truncated List of the Concepts Developed and used by Kautilya**

Arthashastra (Book#, Chap.#)	Ideas/Concepts innovated and Used	Book (Chap.#)
(1.15), (9.4), (7.9)	Constrained Maximization, Inter-temporal Choice, Discounting	Chapter 3
(2.16), (7.17), (5.2), (2.6), (12.1)	Opportunity cost, Diminishing returns, Demand-supply apparatus, Liquidity,	Chapter 4
(8.2), (6.2), (3.11), (3.13), (2.12), (2.15)	Value added, Analysis of Variance, National income accounting	Chapter 5
(9.4), (7.11), (7.10), (3.11),	Sources of economic growth, Role of institutions and governance, Ethics not institutions as the deep determinant	Chapter 8

(4.1), (2.36), (2.9)	Market failure (regulation of monopoly and monopsony), Externality, and Government failure	Chapter 9
(1.7), (1.15)	Pooling of information and knowledge, Trade-off between Efficiency and Confidentiality	Chapter 10
(5.3), (10.3), (2.23), (2.9)	Efficiency wages, Moral and material incentives, Moral Hazard	Chapter 11
(2,21), (1.13), (2.1)	Producer surplus, Piece-wise Linear Income Tax	Chapter 12
(2.16), (8.4)	Risk Management, Self-protection, Self-insurance	Chapter 13
(2.16), (7.12)	Gains from trade, Economies of scale	Chapter 14
(3.11), (3.1)	Minimization of legal errors, Judicial Fairness, Optimal Level of Punishment	Chapter 15
(3.1), (2.1)	Externality, Labour theory of property	Chapter 16
(3.11)	Risk premium	Chapter 17
(7.14), (2.12),	Public goods, Power breeds more power	Chapter 18
(9.3), (2.6)	Loss-Aversion and Diversification	Chapter 19
(7.5), (7.11),	Time Inconsistency (credibility), Asymmetrical Information	Chapter 20

It is difficult to place Kautilya in terms of traditional classification of history of economic thought since some of his ideas reemerged only recently. The following table provides Kautilya's ideas in terms of a historical perspective:

Table II: **Concepts Developed and Applied by Kautilya**

Reemerged during the period	Concepts Originated and applied by Kautilya
1700-1850	Gains from trade, Diversification, Division of Labour, Inter-temporal choice, Labour theory of property, Law of diminishing returns, Moral hazard, Regulation of monopoly, Sources of economic growth, Principles of taxation
1850-1900	Distinction between short-run and long run, Efficiency Wages, Externality, Duipit-Laffer Curve, Demand-Supply Apparatus, Opportunity cost, Producer Surplus
1900-1970	Principal-agent problem, Liquidity, Mean-Variance approach, Non-cooperative game
1970-Present	Asymmetric information, Piece-wise Linear Income Tax, Loss-aversion, Information economics, Self-protection, Self-insurance, Time Inconsistency, Systemic risk

KAUTILYA OR ADAM SMITH?

Kautilya not only innovated the concept of opportunity cost but also a score of other key economic concepts. On the other hand, Adam Smith did not originate a single economic concept. Who has a better claim to be an Economist – Kautilya or Adam Smith? It is a standard practice in the West to undermine the works of non-western writers.

Spengler (1971) points out that Kautilya understood the important role of incentives. He (p 74) observes, 'His analysis, of course, was implicit, not explicit; it rested upon the assumption that individual behaviour could be controlled in large measure through economic rewards and penalties, particularly when these were commensurate with the action to be encouraged or discouraged.

Accordingly, while Kautilya looked at economic issues through the eyes of an economic administrator, he was aware that rules must fit man's economic propensities and foster rather than repress useful economic activity'.

He (1971, p 158) adds, 'Kautilya was, of course, familiar with the general nature of man's response to changes in price and income as well as to changes in the structure of rewards and penalties'. Clearly, Kautilya was an economist in the modern sense.

On the other hand, was Adam Smith an economist in the modern sense? Ruth Grant (2002, p 115) remarks, 'We are accustomed to believe that our thinking about political economy rests on the work of the likes of John Locke, Bernard Mandeville, Adam Smith, David Hume, Jeremy Bentham, James Mill, John Stuart Mill and the authors of the Federalist Papers. I believe that with one exception, "incentive" does not appear in any of their writings'. She (p 115, fn. 2) credits only J S Mill and Ricardo, *not* Adam Smith, implying that Adam Smith cannot be called a modern economist.

Almost all the western economists claim that economics originated with the publication of *The Wealth of Nations,* implying that no one before that can qualify to be an Economist. This is a patently false claim. There is almost a consensus that there is nothing original in *The Wealth of Nations*. Clearly, Adam Smith lifted economic ideas/concepts from various sources including *Kautilya's Arthashastra*. That means, those who created those economic ideas should be considered Economists.

THE DEBATE OVER KAUTILYA

In 2001, the university publisher sent the manuscript (MS) for evaluation to a Reviewer.

In my first submitted MS, I had said: *Kautilya's Arthashastra* asks a series of interesting questions. Can the economic claims in Kautilya's *Arthashastra* be analytically reconstructed in light of contemporary knowledge of economics and methods of formalization? The author's hope is that such reconstruction will establish Kautilya's credibility as *a serious economic thinker,* if not the founder of economics.

Following was one of the Reviewer's major comments: That Kautilya is a sophisticated practical thinker, often weighing alternative courses of action, assessing risk and so forth is beyond doubt. But can one interpret that this makes him an economic theorist?

The Reviewer had rejected my submission. I then revised the manuscript according to the referee/reviewer's wishes and resubmitted the manuscript. Yet again, the Reviewer rejected my claims that (i) Kautilya was an Economist in the modern sense and (ii) he understood and applied the concept of 'opportunity cost'.

Who is an Economist in the modern sense? Anyone, who practices modern economics. This leads to the question: what is modern economics? Myerson (1999) on the current definition of economics: A generation before, Nash could have accepted a narrower definition of economics as a specialized social science concerned with the production and allocation of material goods.

He adds, 'But today economists can define their field more broadly, as being about the analysis of incentives in all social institutions'. Similarly, Canice Prendergast (1999) remarks, 'Incentives are the essence of economics'. See Sihag (2014, Chap. 3, Fn. 2, pp. 340-342) for details on the evolution of the scope of economics.

KAUTILYA ON INCENTIVES

Kautilya wanted to accomplish with incentives what was accomplished earlier by coercion. He relied heavily on incentives and they are pervasive throughout *The Arthashastra*. But, he knew that incentives were a blunt instrument unless tailored to each person individually, that is, a matching of incentive-type to agent-type was critical for their effectiveness. He believed that violation of horizontal equity and reneging on a promised reward would result in a crowding-out effect. Most importantly, he considered material incentives as complementary to the moral incentives and not as substitutes. Let me just repeat a few applications of incentives (details are presented in Chapter 11). (Chap11, pp. 188-189)

Job Tenure: Kautilya (p, 281) stated, 'Those officials who do not eat up the king's wealth but increase it in just ways and are loyally devoted to him shall be made permanent in service (2.9).'

Promotion: Kautilya (p 284) suggested, 'An officer who accomplishes a task as ordered or better shall be honored with promotion and rewards (2.9).'

Reward for Extra and better Work by the Piece-rate Workers: Kautilya was aware of the fact that piece-rate workers paid less attention to quality. He recommended extra payments as an incentive to these workers so that they made products of better quality and also worked on holidays. He (p, 233) suggested: For better work [or greater productivity] women who spin shall be given oil and myrobalan cakes as a special favor. They shall be induced to work on festive days [and holidays] by giving them gifts. Weavers, specializing in weaving any fabrics of flax, dukula, silk yarn, deer wool and [fine] cotton shall be given gifts of perfumes, flowers and similar presents of encouragement (2.23). (Chap. 8, pp., 127-128)

Emphasis on Incentives to Encourage Capital Formation:
Kautilya suggests many policies to encourage capital formation. He (p 231) recommends

(i) **Tax Holidays**: Anyone who brings new land under cultivation shall be granted exemption from payment of agricultural taxes for a period of two years. Similarly, 'for building or improving irrigation facilities' exemption from water rates shall be granted (3.9).

(i) **Full Protection of Private Property Rights**: Water works such as reservoirs, embankments and tanks can be privately owned and the owner shall be free to sell or mortgage them (3.9)

(ii) **Concessionary Loans** (p 179): [On new settlements] the cultivators shall be granted grains, cattle and money which they can repay at their convenience (2.1).

(iv) **Duty Free Imports** (p 238): Any items that, at his discretion, the Chief Controller of Customs, may consider to be highly beneficial to the country (such as rare seeds) (2.21) are to be exempt from import duties.

One may wonder whether Adam Smith understood economics or an economic system. For example, he (1790) compares a system to a machine. He (p, 60) wrote, 'Systems in many respects resemble machines. A machine is a little system, created to perform, as well as to connect together, in reality, those different movements and effects which the artist has occasion for. A system is an imaginary machine invented to connect together in the fancy those different movements and effects which are already in reality performed'.

Such comparison is inappropriate since parts of a machine do not negotiate with each other the terms and conditions of engagement and similarly, no part of a machine ever displays moral hazard or strategic behaviour but people, who are the primary constituents of an economic system, do. Anyhow, such comparison was harmless, although inappropriate, to treat the baker, the barber and the butcher as parts of a machine *but now it could be disastrous since it diverts attention away from the source of systemic risk*. On the other hand, Kautilya believed that a kingdom or a system consisted of people (policy- makers and others) and things. Such characterisation of a system allows a more meaningful analysis of systemic risk.

KAUTILYA ON OPPORTUNITY COST

There are some concepts either one knows them fully or does not know them at all. 'Opportunity Cost' is one of them. Kautilya understands it fully in the modern sense. Kautilya applies the concept of Opportunity Cost throughout *The Arthashastra*. Let me present just one application. (see Chap. 4, pp. 70-74 for other applications).

Zero Opportunity Cost of a Useless Factor: Kautilya showed awareness of the advantages of bargaining with private information. One king knew the strengths and weaknesses of his sons and daughters, but the other king did not. Kautilya was aware of the opportunity cost of giving up a useless factor to be zero. He (p 599) stated, 'He who, gives a treacherous minister or a treacherous son or daughter as a hostage outmanoeuvres the other [the receiver]. The receiver is outmanoeuvred because the giver will strike without compunction at the weak point – i.e., the trust that the receiver has that the giver will let the hostage come to no harm (7.17).'

This is very significant since even the neoclassicals did not realize that a factor could have zero opportunity cost. Many such examples show that Kautilya fully understood and consistently and correctly applied the concept of opportunity cost throughout *The Arthashastra*.

The Reviewer Observed: '(On) p.10 it is clear that Kautilya endorses the generation of wealth; he also wants to remove all obstacles to increasing the revenue of the state. But does this amount to 'Capital Formation?'

My Answer: (Chap. 8, p 130): Kautilya on the Importance of Capital: Kautilya (p 637) argues, 'Man, without wealth, does not get it even after a hundred attempts. Just as elephants are needed to catch elephants, so does wealth capture more wealth. Wealth will slip away from that childish man who constantly consults the stars. The only [guiding] star of wealth is itself; what can the stars of the sky do? (9.4)'

Adam Smith makes a similar assertion in his *Wealth of Nations*. He (p 112) states that machines 'facilitate and abridge labour, and enable one man to do the work of many'

If we compare the above statements by Kautilya and Adam Smith, two points are clear: (i) Kautilya, like Adam Smith, points out that not a whole lot can be produced with bare hands. Adam Smith has been given credit for originating capital as a source of economic growth, then why not Kautilya?

(ii) Kautilya goes beyond Adam Smith in stating 'wealth captures more wealth'. Additionally, as mentioned above, Kautilya recommends several measures to promote capital formation.

Reviewer's Observation: Use of marginal analysis. All the quotes from Kautilya are sound advice. But really none of them establish the concept of marginal analysis.

My Answer: This is what I claim on marginal analysis. It is not claimed that Kautilya knew differential calculus, but he did understand discrete marginal changes (that is why I use the notation D, which is a standard notation for indicating discrete marginal changes) and their importance in making choices. These points are brought out on pages (Chap.3, pp. 52-54).

(PP. 53-54): (i) Kautilya (p 553) states, 'Applying these [active and passive policies] may result in any one of the following: decline, progress, or no change in one's position (6.2).' He (p. 553) proceeds to define these concepts as follows: A king makes progress by building forts, irrigation works or trade routes, creating new settlements, elephant forests or productive forests, or opening new mines. Any activity, which harms the progress of the enemy engaged in similar undertakings, is also progress. However, a king may ignore an enemy's progress if his own progress will be quicker or greater [than that of his enemy] or if there is a prospect of greater future gain. A king suffers a decline when his own initiatives are ruined or when the enemy's undertakings prosper. When there is neither progress nor decline, the situation is said to be one of 'no change' (7.1)

Thus, according to him, progress, and no change, may be indicated by $DY = [DY_d - DY_e]^3\ 0$ and a decline by $DY<0$, where DY_d and DY_e represent changes in domestic and enemy's incomes respectively.

This is further elaborated in my paper entitled, *Exploring the Origin of Mathematical Economics* (published in 2016, available on the web).

(1) **Loss-aversion**: Kautilya put heavier weight on a loss than on an equal size of gain when taking risky decisions. He (p 634) surmised, A small revolt in the rear outweighs a large gain in the front; for, when the king is not there, a small revolt in the rear may be worsened by the anger of the people or by traitors, enemies and jungle tribes. If this happens, a large gain in front, even if actually obtained, will be eaten up by the subjects, allies, losses and expenses. Therefore, a king shall not undertake a campaign when the gain in front is [less than] a thousand times the likely loss due to a revolt in the rear or, at least, a hundred times the loss. A well-known proverb is: 'Misfortunes are [in the beginning] no longer than the point of a needle' (9.3).

(2) **Emphasis only on Marginal Gains and Losses**: Kautilya considered power almost perfectly correlated with prosperity since he believed that a richer country could afford a stronger national security. He expected the king to be very vigilant and must keep parity with a potential adversary. He (p 554) explained, It is a decline for the conqueror if the enemy's undertakings flourish; conversely, the decline of an enemy's undertakings is progress for the conqueror.

Parity between the two is maintained when both make equal progress. A small gain for a large outlay is decline; the converse is progress. A gain equal to the expenditure on an undertaking means that the conqueror has neither progressed nor declined. Hence a conqueror shall seek to obtain a special advantage by undertaking such works [as building forts] which would produce a large profit for a small expenditure (7.12).

Kautilya's advice to the conqueror was to undertake such projects where the net gain (Revenue/Cost) was the largest. The above statement implies the following cases:

$R^0 = W_E / W_C$, (initial reference point)
- $R^1 = (W_E + DW_E)/ (W_C + DW_C)$
- $= R^0 + (DW_E - DW_C)/ (W_C + DW_C)$
- Case (i) If $DW_C = 0$ and $DW_E > 0$, it is a decline in the relative position of the conqueror.
- Case (ii) If $DW_C = 0$ and $DW_E < 0$, it is a progress in the relative position of the conqueror, that is, $R^1 < R^0$.
- Case (iii) If $DW_C = DW_E$, there is no change in the relative position of the conqueror, then $R^1 = R^0$.

Where R^0 = reference point (initial relative position), W_C = Conqueror's own wealth and W_E = enemy's wealth, DW_C and DW_E are the incremental changes in conqueror's and enemy's wealth respectively.

According to Kautilya, the king (conqueror) required $RP_1 < 1$ for maintaining sovereignty. Otherwise, there was always a risk of losing it. Kautilya (p 624) stated, The king may face dangers even from a trusted king of equal power, when the latter has achieved his objective. Even an equally powerful king tends to become stronger after the task is accomplished and, when his power has increased, becomes untrustworthy. Prosperity changes peoples' minds (7.5)"

Two things are obvious from the above statement: Initially, the ally was of equal power (i.e., $R^0 = 1$) and was trustworthy. But after the ally acquired additional power by winning a campaign, $R^1 > R^0$, according to Kautilya, he was likely to become untrustworthy. Why? Kautilya hypothesized that 'Prosperity changes peoples' minds', implying that the ally might not keep his promise not to attack the conqueror, that is, his preferences might change (time inconsistency problem) and also (ii) after accomplishing the task, his aspiration level was likely to rise (a new reference point) and his attitude towards risk-taking would change and was likely to become more assertive. Incidentally, according to the prospect theory, ally was to the left of his new reference point, more like in the domain of loss and would be risk-acceptant. If one looks at the past rulers, Alexander, Napoleon or any other ruler, each win made him more assertive and he kept on attacking other states until he met his Waterloo (losing the battle). It implies that Alexander most likely lost the battle and that is why decided to return back from the bank of the Indus.

Reviewer's Observation: Does the injunction 'No one shall throw dirt on the street or let mud water collect there' show that Kautilya has the concept of externality. Similarly, the concept of moral hazard.

My Answer: The words, such as *externality, moral hazard, market failure* etc. were not used by Kautilya or the classical economists. But that does not mean they did not know them. For example, Adam Smith did not use the word *'laissez faire'* still we associate this with his thinking.

Externality: When the actions of an individual have a positive or negative effect on others. Clearly, if a person throws dirt or mud on the road (like solid waste nowadays) it causes inconvenience to others. That is precisely the definition of an externality.

Moral Hazard:

Chapter 11 deals with this concept in full detail. Moral hazard is defined as: a person does not do what s/he is expected to do. The following two examples satisfy this definition of moral hazard.

Chapter 11, p 191: He (p 317) recommends, 'They (a herdsman, milker, a churner and a hunter-guard) shall be paid in cash, because if they are paid in milk or butter oil, they will starve the calves to death [by milking the cows dry, leaving nothing for the calves] (2.29).'

Chapter 11, p 177: 'The king shall have the work of Heads of Departments inspected daily, for men are, by nature, fickle and, like horses, change after being put to work.' Kautilya (p 283). Actually,

Kautilya offers a more effective way to tackle this problem.

[He shows awareness of the principal-agent problem and suggests at least one solution.} As pointed out in chapter 11, the word *Principal-agent* was coined only in 1973. Kautilya not only recognizes the problem of shirking but also offers the payment of efficiency wages to mitigate this problem. Kautilya has much deeper insight into the moral hazard problem than Adam Smith and should be given credit for this concept.

Reviewer's Observation: The central point is this: people can trade without having a theoretical idea of comparative advantage, they can weigh options without having a theoretical concept of opportunity cost etc. It seems that the transition from some idea implicit in a practice to that idea being a explicit theoretical concept is what is required for 'ecoomics' Dr Sihag has not satisfactorily proved that Kautilya makes these transitions. He gives a quote from Kautilya that refers to a practice and then he formalizes the implicit theory. This was my worry last time and it still remains so.

My Answer: Kautilya was a thinker and not a trader, farmer or an administrator. He wrote a theoretical treatise on economic issues. His *Arthashastra* is not a collection of some prevailing practices There is no reference even to emperor Chandragupta or to his kingdom Magadha in *The Arthashastra* since it was meant to be a theoretical treatise. Let me give a few examples.

Example (i) **(Chap. 18, p 293):** He **(p 658)** recommends to the king, 'If he lacks [physical] protection, he shall build an impregnable fort (7.14).' He adds, 'In times of trouble, the fort provides a haven to the people and the king himself (7.14).'

Kautilya as a Precursor of the Definition of Public Goods: It is obvious from the above statements that at that time, forts were a major part of national security both to the public and to the king. Thus, the statement 'haven to the people and the king himself' truly describes the pure public good nature (non-rivalry) of national security.

[There are two characteristics of a public good. Kautilya was the first one to identify one of them and that is why I claim him as a precursor of this concept. It may also be noted his advice to the king is based on sound analysis and there is no mention of any practice.]

Example (ii) **(Chap. 19, P 306:** Kautilya **(p 619)** states, 'As between land dependent on rain and land with flowing water [i.e. a river], a smaller tract with flowing water is preferable to a larger drier one because with flowing water, which is always available, the production of crops is assured.'

[There is no mention of any practice here. Kautilya advances the idea that both return and risk should be taken into consideration in the acquisition of an asset. Even Keynes, the father of macroeconomics did not understand it (see **Chap. 19, fn. 6, p 393**). I just use a graph to express it and claim that Kautilya could be called a forerunner of the portfolio-balance theory.]

Example (iii) **(Chap. 14, p. 228): A Mix of Riskless and Risky Products**: Kautilya (p 238) states, 'If the Chief Controller of State Trading sends a caravan by a land route, he shall choose a safe route. One quarter of the goods shall be of high value. Jungle chieftains, frontier officers and governors in the City and the countryside shall be contacted beforehand for assuring security. Steps shall be taken to ensure the protection of the members of the caravan and goods of high value (2.16).'

[Kautilya recommends diversification. Again, there is no mention of any practice. Therefore, no need for any transition.]

Example (iv) **(Chap. 20, p 312)**: 'No enemy shall know his secrets. He shall, however, know all his enemy's weaknesses. Like a tortoise, he shall draw in any limb of his that is exposed.' Kautilya **(p 177)**

(Chap. 20, p 320): Offering a lemon: (a) A King knows the quality of his land, which is poor, but the buyer of the land does not know any thing about its quality. Kautilya (p 621) states, 'If a settlement of a tract is likely to entail heavy losses or expenditure, a king shall first sell the land, with the intention of reacquiring it, to one who will fail in the attempt at settlement. Such agreements shall remain verbal (7.11).'

[Again, there is no mention of any practice, but the idea of asymmetrical information is advanced.]

Thus, it is clear from the above examples that Kautilya does not need the transition from a practice to an idea. In that sense *The*

Arthashastra is different from Adam Smith's *Wealth of Nations* and is more sophisticated and abstract (also practical). On the other hand, Adam Smith derives his famous invisible hand hypothesis from a practice. Smith (pp 477-78) writes, 'By pursuing his own interest he frequently promotes that of the society more effectually than when he really intends to promote it. I have never known much good done by those who affected to trade for the public good. It is an affection, indeed, not very common among merchants, and very few words need be employed in dissuading them from it.' Smith does mention a practice 'not very common among merchants'.

Kautilya does not need any transition and making a quote explicit, that is, its formalization is now a norm. (For example, Prof Paul Samuelson formalized Adam Smith's work. Forget Adam Smith, it is so mathematical even 99% of living economists do not understand it).

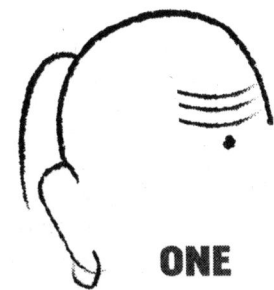

ONE

Kautilya and His Times

Kautilya set out to lay down the foundation, erect the necessary pillars and structures to build and sustain such an ideal economy. He believed that the establishment of rule of law, an impartial judicial system, private property rights, an incentive mechanism to ensure efficiency and honesty of government officials, and establishment of *dharma* through the moral and spiritual rules of human behavior, were the key ingredients for the creation of a prosperous economy.

Prologue
Kautilya's Vision

Kautilya's *Arthashastra* is comprehensive, internally consistent, original and wide in scope. It contains sufficiently large number of significant concepts and hypotheses that clearly establish Kautilya as the founder of economics.

Vishnugupta Chanakya (son of Chanaka), also known as Kautilya, wrote the *Arthashastra*, the science of wealth and welfare, during the latter half of the 4th century BCE. It has 150 chapters that are distributed subject-wise in fifteen books. Kautilya was addressed as an *Acharya* (professor) and a statesman. He has been credited with the destruction of the oppressive and corrupt Nanda Dynasty and installing Chandragupta Maurya (321-297 BCE) on the Magadha throne. Chandragupta Maurya considered him as mentor and sought his advice on both political and economic matters. Some writers incorrectly claim that he served as a Prime Minister to Chandragupta Maurya. Nehru (1946, p 123) describes their special relationship quite appropriately as: 'He sat with the reins of empire in his hands and looked upon the emperor more as a loved pupil than as a master. Simple and austere in his life, uninterested in the pomp and pageantry of high position.' Kautilya was an independent thinker and it would be incorrect to label him as an administrator only.

It may be reasonable to assume that he was older and undoubtedly wiser than Chandragupta Maurya. Kautilya was probably born around 360 BCE, was very influential during Chandragupta's rule (321-297 BCE), and might have lived beyond the latter date.

This implies that he was a junior contemporary of Aristotle (384-322 BCE). However, there is absolutely no evidence that Kautilya was aware of Aristotle's ideas. Moreover, Aristotle wrote very little (if any) on economics. Kautilya's *Arthashastra* was very widely referred to and was revered by scholars for more than a thousand years after its writing.[1]

There is no reference to the emperor Chandragupta Maurya or to his kingdom Magadha in the *Arthashastra* since it was meant to be a theoretical treatise designed to instruct kings everywhere and in all times.[2] Kautilya is also credited with two other works, *Chanakya Sutras* (Chanakya's Precepts) and *Chanakya Rajanitisastra* (Chanakya's Statecraft).

1.1 PROVISION OF HUMAN SECURITY

Kautilya had a grand vision of building an empire encompassing the whole of the Indian subcontinent, prosperous (free from wants), secure against foreign threats, crime-free (free from fear), internally stable and based on secular virtues such as non-violence, compassion, benevolence, truth and honesty. There was a big gap between Kautilya's ideal economy and the one actually prevailing at the time. His goal was to write a theoretical treatise for transforming the actual economy into an ideal economy and sustaining it. Kautilya's genius lay in developing a conceptual framework while anticipating various problems that might arise in the intended transformation, and devising appropriate policies to resolve them. The level of abstraction achieved in the *Arthashastra* is remarkable for his times.

Kautilya set out to lay down the foundation, erect the necessary pillars and structures to build and sustain such an ideal economy. He believed that the establishment of rule of law, an impartial judicial system, private property rights, an incentive mechanism to ensure efficiency and honesty of government officials, and establishment of *dharma* through the moral and spiritual rules of human behavior, were the key ingredients for the creation of a prosperous economy. He critically examined, extended and codified the existing rules and regulations to establish the rule of law. However, he believed that in the absence of moral anchoring, no amount of rules and regulations could prevent systemic risks.

Joan Robinson (1953) has observed that neoclassical thought paid too much attention to little issues like 'why does an egg cost more than a cup of tea' and ignored the big issues like growth and distribution, which were pursued by the classical economists. However, both classical and neoclassical economists ignored the systemic risk arising from moral decline, foreign aggression or calamities like famine. Kautilya's *Arthashastra* was quite concerned about the losses arising from such disruptions whereas now the sole emphasis is on losses resulting from the distortions (called deadweight loss). For example, understanding the distinction between disruptions and distortions is of paramount importance when the effects of a lump sum tax are compared to those of an income tax.

Accordingly, Kautilya formulated three kinds of policies:
- economic policies (*Arthaniti*) to promote economic growth and prevent natural and man-made calamities,
- a judicial fairness policy (*Dandaniti*) for administration of justice, and
- a foreign affairs policy (*Videshniti*) to help maintain independence and to expand the kingdom.

He put heavy emphasis on acquiring new territories, developing the land and building settlements. He invariably analyzed all the available alternatives and recommended the best one. He laid emphasis on having a diversified economy with good infrastructure and irrigation facilities. He formulated detailed outlines for the various government departments, spelling out responsibilities and salaries of the officers. It was in the pursuit of formulating these policies that Kautilya originated more than a score of fundamental concepts of economics.

A brief review of the existing views on Kautilya's *Arthashastra* is provided in Section 1.2. 'Why Another Book on Kautilya?' is explained in Section 1.3. Reasons for using Rangarajan's (1992) translation of the *Arthashastra* for the basis of this work are provided in the Appendix A.

1.2 PREVALENT VIEWS ON KAUTILYA'S CONTRIBUTIONS

Spengler (1971) and Dasgupta (1993) discuss Kautilya's *Arthashastra* in limited detail. Spengler presents a few but quite fundamental economic concepts contained in the *Arthashastra*. He (1971, p 158) observes: 'Kautilya was, of course, familiar with the general nature of man's response to changes in price and income as well as to changes in the structure of rewards and penalties.' Spengler (1971, p 74) explains: 'His analysis, of course, was implicit, not explicit; it rested upon the assumption that individual behavior could be controlled in large measure through economic rewards and penalties, particularly when these were commensurate with the action to be encouraged or discouraged. Accordingly, while Kautilya looked at economic issues through the eyes of an economic administrator, he was aware that rules must fit man's economic propensities and foster rather than repress useful economic activity.' Spengler acknowledges that Kautilya not only recognized the agency problems but also suggested many solutions befitting the contemporary situation.

On taxation, Spengler (1971, p 72) remarks, 'Kautilya's discussion of taxation and expenditure, apparently in keeping with traditional doctrine, gave expression to three Indian principles: taxation power is limited; taxation should not be felt to be heavy or excessive; tax increases should be graduated. One of his main concerns seems to have been the collection and expenditure of revenue in such ways as to build up the permanent revenue-yielding capacity of the economy. While he manifested little knowledge of tax shifting and incidence, he emphasized the long run, cautioned against too heavy taxation in the short run, and noted that a ruler could not tax at his pleasure, particularly in frontier regions whence disgruntled taxpayers could flee to neighboring countries.' This phenomenon is now called the Dupuit-Laffer Curve. In fact, as asserted below, a slightly differently shaped curve, which may be called the Kautilya Curve is discernible in his analysis.

On the concept of diminishing returns, Spengler (1971, p 71) observes, 'He does not explicitly recognize the tendency to Ricardian diminishing returns implicit in his account of the quite unequally colonisable and unevenly cultivable character of India's lands'. This is a very significant observation since it makes the debate over priority to Smith or Ricardo for diminishing returns irrelevant.

On factors of production, Spengler (p 75) notes that Kautilya understood the 'distinction' between 'interest' and 'profit'. Kautilya discussed wages and rent also. In fact, not only did Kautilya understand the distinction among different factors of production but also discussed how to maximize profits from public enterprises, adjust interest rate for risk premium, pay efficiency wages to reduce shirking and how to determine the circumstances under which to have a wage system or a sharecropping arrangement on Crown land. It is obvious that Spengler acknowledges Kautilya's understanding and his application of the most fundamental concepts in economics. Unfortunately, he explores only a few aspects of Kautilya's contributions to economic thought.

On the other hand, Dasgupta does not think much of the contributions of ancient writers to economic thought (including those of Kautilya). He (p 6-7) makes a sweeping observation, 'In my judgment, "analytic or scientific aspects of economic thought" of the kind Schumpeter was referring to in defining economic analysis, cannot be found in Hindu, Buddhist, or Islamic writings on economic topics; nor for that matter in their Greek, Roman, Jewish or Scholastic counterparts. A history of economic analysis in India would have to start sometime in the nineteenth century.'

The author strongly disagrees with Dasgupta's claims. Reference is made to a few of Kautilya's ideas to refute the prevalent myths about his *Arthashastra*. Chapters 3 to 20 contain Kautilya's treatment of several concepts which, it is hoped, provide sufficient evidence to correct the prevailing misrepresentations regarding his contributions and maturity of the Hindu civilization.

The most likely reason for the many important omissions by Spengler, Dasgupta and others seems to be that they overlooked the chapters relating to law and order and foreign affairs to which Kautilya applied many important economic concepts. Similar omissions in other works have also been endured for centuries. For example, an important omission regarding Adam Smith's knowledge of diminishing returns persisted for more than two centuries as Samuelson (1980) points out, 'Ricardo and his contemporaries may, however, be in no need of enemies if their defenders must write on their behalf that they missed what was in the *Wealth of Nations* because the relevant material was "scattered" and appears in out of the way chapters where such esoteric subjects as colonies are discussed.'

Evaluation of Kautilya's *Arthashastra* on Political Issues by Non-economists

In the literature on political science, Kautilya has been compared to Machiavelli and even to Plato and Aristotle. The author is not competent to comment on the relevance or nature of such comparisons. However, a summary of their conclusions is presented below. The reader interested in further investigations of this aspect may refer to Basham (1959), Drekmeier (1962), Kangle (2000, part III), Parmar (1987), Ray (1999) and Varma (1995-96).

It is not surprising that different commentators read Kautilya's *Arthashastra* differently. Some find it merely a synthesis, although brilliant, of existing ideas. For example, according to Kamandaka, who wrote *Nitisara* (a set of thoroughly proved policies) during 4th or 5th CE (see Karwal, 1966), Kautilya 'churned the nectar of the science of policy from the ocean of political sciences.' Others like Ghoshal (see Kangle, part III, p 56) find Kautilya's *Arthashastra* 'a virtual reconstruction of the science'. Kangle (Part III, p 55) concludes, 'It appears reasonable to suppose that except in those cases where divergent opinions are specifically attributed to Kautilya, the bulk of the teaching in this text is materially the same as he found it in the source-books on which he relied'. He (p 56) adds, 'It is, therefore, possible to say that the *shastra* as it emerges from Kautilya's hand is more sober, more rational and inevitably more advanced than was the case in the earlier writings.'

1.3 WHY ANOTHER BOOK ON KAUTILYA?

A serious attempt is made to revise the currently accepted history of economic thought. First, it is claimed that presentation of Kautilya's monumental contributions should succeed in dispelling the deep seated myth that economics originated during the eighteenth century and Adam Smith is the founder of economics.

A claim is only as good as the arguments it stands on. For the first time, strong arguments are provided why Kautilya should be considered as the founder of economics in the 4th century BCE. Secondly, it is argued that Kautilya's *Arthashastra* may be correctly designated as *Dharmanomics*: economics built on an ethical foundation, projecting economics and economic policy in a more meaningful and socially desirable perspective. Thirdly, it is shown that Hindu civilization is not averse to economic growth as an important goal. A brief overview is provided below.

Kautilya as the Founder of Economics

Kautilya provided consistent and coherent interpretations of more than a score of modern economic concepts. It is claimed that Kautilya pioneered political economy much before appearance of Adam Smith's *Wealth of Nations* (1776). Adam Smith came to be accepted as the founder of economics based on the arguments that (i) he was the first one to write a treatise on economics, and (ii) he synthesized brilliantly the existing ideas. Samuelson has added another argument that Smith was also a theorist, who made original contributions. It is shown in Chapters 3-20 that Kautilya was the first economist who accomplished all these feats two thousand years earlier than Adam Smith. Kautilya carved out economics as a separate discipline. Additionally, Kautilya's *Arthashastra* is much more sophisticated, both in method and content than Adam Smith's *Wealth of Nations*. In fact, based on the degree of sophistication of his analysis, it could be claimed that Kautilya was a neoclassicist well before the classicists came on the scene.

A strong critique of the prevailing orthodoxies regarding the origins of economics and Adam Smith being its founder is provided here. It is not claimed that Kautilya provided any formal proofs or that the *Arthashastra* as a book is as sophisticated as Samuelson's *Foundations*. It can thus be claimed that Kautilya's *Arthashastra* is, at least, as important a contribution as Adam Smith's *Wealth of Nations*. It is shown that despite the non-availability of the calculus and statistical methods, Kautilya's economic analysis was reasonably organized, adequately developed, and applied to a variety of problems. The following table provides an insight into Kautilya's contribution and genius.

Table 1.1: **A Partial List of Concepts Used by Kautilya**

Genesis of Concepts in the *Arthashastra* during 4th century BCE	Re-emergence of these concepts	
	Author	Year
Opportunity Cost	Wieser	1889
Demand-Supply Framework	Marshall	1870
Diminishing Returns	Turgot	1766
Liquidity	Keynes	1936
'All other things being equal'	D Bernoulli	1738
Marginal Analysis	Turgot	1766
Constrained Optimization	Walras, Slutsky	1874-7, 1915
Distinction between Short Run and Long Run	Marshall	1870
Moral Hazard	Adam Smith	1776
Linear Income Tax	Mirrlees	1971
Public Goods	Lindahl, Samuelson	1919, 1954
Producer Surplus	Marshall	1870
Importance of Capital Formation	Adam Smith	1776
Theory of Gains from Trade	Ricardo	1817

Contd...

Genesis of Concepts in the *Arthashastra* during 4th century BCE	Re-emergence of these concepts	
Crime and Punishment	Becker	1968
Efficiency Wages	Marx, Solow	1867, 1979
Risk-return Trade-off	Markowitz	1952
Asymmetric Information	Akerlof	1970
Time Inconsistency Problem	Kyland-Presscott	1977
Non-cooperative Game	Waldegrave, Nash	1713, 1951
Contingency Planning	H Stein	1996

It may be noted that the above illustratively enumerated twenty-one concepts, used in modern economic analysis, were already used and applied in Kautilya's formulations. Adam Smith has the credit for only two. Undoubtedly, the social, the political and the economic institutions and conditions prevailing at the time of Kautilya were markedly different from those of today. Yet, remarkably, almost all of his insights, concepts, and methodology are as relevant today in our industrialized and globalized world as they were in his times.

Kautilya's *Arthashastra* as *Dharmanomics*

Contrary to the now prevalent view, Kautilya placed a very heavy emphasis on ethical values. Ancient thinkers in India attached justifiable significance to keeping a proper balance between spiritual health and material health, and elaborated the former as the objective and the latter as an accompanying obligation on the public plane. Although ideas regarding attainment of *artha* at an individual level and complimentary and enabling public policy at the government's level, are said to have their origin between 650-600 BCE, it was Kautilya who elaborated on raising the standard of living to achieve the true balance between spiritual and material health. He proposed advancement of material wellbeing along the path of *dharma* (ethics). Significantly, he argued that prosperity, even if somehow attained was not sustainable in an unethical society. He strongly believed that *dharma* was the glue that held the society together. According to him, *dharma* was the source of joy, harmony and prosperity. He wanted a sage king (*Rajarshi*) at the helm of affairs, who could be a role model for his subordinates and the people. He maintained this theme throughout the *Arthashastra*. He, thus, performed a Vedic (pious, purposive, genuine and inseparable) marriage between ethics and economics.

Kautilya understood the principal-agent problem and the concept of efficiency wages and suggested both moral and material incentives to elicit optimum amount of effort. Apparently, according to Kautilya, it is better to pass on good values rather than ill-gotten wealth to the younger generation. He believed market failure is bad, government failure is worse but moral failure is the worst. No amount of rules and regulations, without ethical anchoring, could prevent systemic risk (like the financial meltdown of 2008). Thus, an ounce of ethics is better than a ton of rules and regulations.

Kautilya's Ideas on Economic Growth and the So-called Hindu Growth Rate

The analysis in Kautilya's *Arthashastra* dispels the myth that Hindu civilization is inimical to economic (material) growth and also provides some insights into assessing policies like the 'second generation' economic reforms of recent years in India. Kautilya argued that ethical conduct not only paved the way to heaven but also to prosperity. He identified land, labour and capital as sources of economic growth but believed that increases in these inputs depended largely on the quality of institutions and good governance, which in turn depended on ethical environment and ethical conduct of the decision makers. That is, according to Kautilya, ethics was the 'deep determinant' of prosperity and not institutions as such. One may call Kautilya's *Arthashastra* as the '*Wealth of Nations*' much before Smith's *Wealth of Nations*, since it displays a far deeper understanding of the nature and causes of *Wealth of Nations* than that provided by Adam Smith in his *An Inquiry into the Nature and Causes of the Wealth of Nations* in 1776.

Relevance of Kautilya for the Post-WTO World–the World Stage

The WTO has been working hard to open up world markets, both in products and services. Certainly, even before the emergence of mercantilism during the 14th century, sizeable international economic intercourse prevailed. However, Kautilya is the only known writer who strongly argued for promotion of imports, rather than for both import-substituting and export-promoting policies. The challenge for the world leaders is to bring back Kautilya's internationalism in the interconnected world. Significantly, even Adam Smith favoured domestic production over international trade (see below); similarly Ricardo was certainly against the Corn Laws but did not fault the creation of comparative advantage through 'artificial' factors.

Again, no one has ever applied the modern methods while interpreting the *Arthashastra*, whereas such techniques have been applied to improve understanding of Adam Smith's *Wealth of Nations* and David Ricardo's *Theory of Comparative Advantage*. Finally, Kautilya practiced clarity, consistency and simplicity in writing that has been most sincerely sought to be maintained here in interpreting his work.

The chapters in the book are organized into five parts. Part One provides introduction to Kautilya, his vision and genius and the contemporary economic and social conditions.

Sen (1987) believes that there are two origins of economics. He credits the Greek philosophers for the 'ethical' approach to economics. He points out that Kautilya's *Arthashastra* is the first book on the origin of the 'engineering approach' to economics but it, just like the modern economics, is devoid of any ethical content. He (1987, p 6) asserts, 'The motivations of human beings are specified by and large in very fairly simple terms, involving, *inter alia*, the same lack of bonhomie which characterizes modern economics. Ethical considerations in any deep sense are not given much role in the analysis of human behavior. Neither the Socratic question nor the Aristotelian ones figure in this other ancient document of early economics, by a contemporary of Aristotle'. In the above statement Sen (1987) makes the following claims:

- Logic-based (engineering) approach to modern economics was originated by Kautilya.
- Ethics-based approach to economics was originated by the Greek philosophers.
- Kautilya's *Arthashastra*, just like modern economics, does not contain moral content.

Sen does not provide any arguments or examples to justify either of his claims. In part Two, strong arguments are offered to justify the claim that Kautilya is the founder of the logic-based, that is, the 'engineering approach' to economics. This part contains the tools of analysis, concepts and methodology, which are discernible in the *Arthashastra* and are used in modern economics.

Kautilya's ideas on ethics and freedom from wants (economics) are presented in part Three. Strong arguments are provided to refute Sen's second and third claims. Kautilya, just like the Vedic sages before him, assigned a foundational role to *dharma*: if there was no *dharma* there was no society. It is indicated that the Socratic question was asked by the Vedic sages more than a thousand years earlier in India, and serious and systematic attempts were made to formulate rules of moral conduct to lead a virtuous life. Kautilya was a Vedic man and he enthusiastically embraced and promoted *dharmic* (ethical) values.

Kautilya understood not only the importance of ethical conduct to liberation from poverty and to lowering the systemic risk but also explored various ways to create an ethical society. He realized that unless the laws and policies were guided and informed by *dharma*, they might weaken the ethical foundations or crowd-out moral motivation. That meant, if the decision-makers were not ethical, both formulation of laws and policies and their implementation would be less than ideal. Some of the government employees might become corrupt and promote corrupt people. Therefore, he put heavy emphasis on ethical anchoring of the decision-makers—the king, his advisers and other employees—to prevent moral failure.

Thus, Kautilya's *Arthashastra* is also the original ethics-based approach to economics, since it has much more ethical content than the contributions of Aristotle or Adam Smith. For example, the commercial man of the *Wealth of Nations* and the benevolent man of *Theory of Moral Sentiments* deliberately avoid each other, and consequently never get acquainted with each other whereas Kautilya performed a holistic marriage between ethics and economics.

Part Four presents Kautilya's ideas on creating ethics-based and efficient laws for the removal of social thorns for providing safety to citizens. On the other hand, Kautilya's approach to safeguarding national independence was based primarily on prudence. He argued that for people, freedom from foreign rule was essential to achieving freedom from wants. Thus, protecting independence by using every possible means available to the state was recommended. His ideas on freedom from fear of an attack by a foreign king are covered in part Five.

Many of Kautilya's statements or comments therein, by experts or the author, have relevance for more than one context discussed at different places in this book. They are often reproduced, in part or full, to facilitate the reader to have a self-contained analysis. They may, therefore, not be taken as repetitions as such.

APPENDIX A
Choice between Clarity and Fidelity

Kautilya's *Arthashastra* was written in Sanskrit, but fortunately English translations are now available of which Kangle's translation of the *Arthashastra* is regarded as the most authentic. However, adhering strictly to the Sanskrit text in verses may sometimes involve sacrifice of clarity in understanding, especially if one is not sufficiently familiar with the ethos embodying the language of the authors. Rangarajan's translation is, in general, clearer than the others currently available. Therefore, (occasionally, Kangle's translation has been used here but) to a large extent the interpretations here are based on the version edited, rearranged, translated and introduced by L N Rangarajan (1992), although at some specified places, Kangle's translation has also been used. The page references correspond to Rangarajan's translation cited above but references to the original text wherever made have been specified. For example, (1.15) means Chapter Fifteen of Book One of the *Arthashastra*.

Rangarajan (p 24-25) provides a few comparisons (from Kangle's translation to his own) to show the enhanced clarity of his translation. Both Spengler (1971) and Dasgupta (1993) use Kangle's translation for their observations. The following quotes, which are taken from their works, also justify Rangarajan's claim of enhanced clarity without altering the meaning of the original Sanskrit verses.

A Few Comparisons of the Translations

- Original Reference (1.19.34) from the Sanskrit *shloka* (stanza) in Kautilya's *Arthashastra*. Spengler (p 64-65), 'In the happiness of the subjects lies the happiness of the king and in what is beneficial to the subjects his own benefit. What is dear to himself is not beneficial to the king, but what is dear to the subjects is beneficial (to him).'

Rangarajan (p 149): 'In the happiness of his subjects lies his happiness; in their welfare his welfare. He shall not consider as good only that which pleases him but treat as beneficial to him whatever pleases his subjects.'

- Original reference (1.19.35-36) from Spengler (p 64-65): 'Therefore, being ever active, the king should carry out the management of material well-being. The root of material well-being is activity, of material disaster its reverse. In the absence of activity, there is certain destruction of what is obtained and of what is not yet received. By activity reward is obtained, and one also secures abundance of riches.'

Rangarajan (p 149): 'Hence the king shall be ever active in the management of the economy. The root of wealth [economic] is activity and lack of it [brings] material distress. In the absence of [fruitful economic] activity, both current prosperity and future growth will be destroyed. A king can achieve the desired objectives and abundance of riches by undertaking [productive] economic activity.'

- Original reference (2.1.16) from Spengler (p 73): 'A king with a small treasury swallows up the citizens and the country people themselves (2.1.16).'

Rangarajan (p 253): 'A king with a depleted Treasury eats into the very vitality of the citizens and the country.'
- Original reference (2.21.13) from Spengler (p 75-76): 'If, through fear of a rival purchaser, a [trader] increases the price beyond the [due] price of a commodity, the king shall receive the increase in price, or make the amount of duty double.'

Rangarajan (p 342): 'Calling out too high a price at the gate [anticipating competitive bidding] penalty shall be [the] "differences between actual sale and the price originally called or double the duty."'
- Original reference (9.4.26-27) from Dasgupta (p 40): 'The object slips away from the foolish person who continuously consults the stars; for an object is the [auspicious] constellation for [achieving] an object; what will the stars do? Men without wealth do not attain their objects even with hundreds of efforts.'

Rangarajan (p 637): 'Wealth will slip away from that childish man who constantly consults the stars. The only [guiding] star of wealth is wealth itself; what can the stars of the sky do? Man without wealth does not get it even after a hundred attempts. Just as elephants are needed to catch elephants, so does one need wealth to capture more wealth.'

2

Society, Polity and Economy

The main objective of this chapter is to highlight the gap between the actual economy at the time of Kautilya (4th century BCE) that was stagnant and segmented, and the ideal economy envisaged by him—dynamic, open and efficient. The *Arthashastra* is an exhaustive treatise on anticipating and resolving possible problems, which might arise in bridging such a wide gap. The level of abstraction it achieves is the source of its timeless utility. Consequently, despite the absence of modern problems of pollution, population pressure and industrialization at that time, Kautilya's *Arthashastra* still provides useful insights into the challenges of today's world.

According to Knight (1947), differences in social, political or economic conditions may not matter much if the goal is simply to explain the most fundamental concepts in economics. He (p xlviii) observes: 'The more general principles of analytic economics are simply the principles of economic behavior, of the effective achievement of ends by use of means, by individuals and groups, irrespective of social or political forms. Even under a "pharaoh", combining absolute sovereignty with outright ownership of men themselves as well as the land and goods, much the same choices and decisions would have to be made to make activity effective rather than wasteful and futile.' Notwithstanding Knight's assertions, it is believed that a historical perspective is absolutely essential for understanding and appreciating the true contributions of ancient writings.

Over time, the writing style changes and even a great contribution made in not too distant a past may appear prototypical today and that should be kept in mind in evaluating the significance of the contributions of earlier writers. Additionally, over time, even important historical facts fade away from peoples' memory and tend to acquire the status of fiction. For example, John Craig (1699) attempted to model this phenomenon and apply it to the second coming of Christ. This issue is discussed in Section 2.1. The socio-religious-political conditions prevailing at the time are presented in Section 2.2. Section 2.3 offers some limited background of economic conditions at the time.

2.1 CHANGES IN WRITING STYLES OVER TIME

The fact that the *Arthashastra* is an ancient classic should be borne in mind. A truly historical perspective on the *Arthashastra* may be gleaned from the fact that it was written more than a thousand years before the *Magna Carta*, and almost two thousand years before the Scientific Revolution and the Industrial Revolution. The passage of time is likely to have, at least, two effects:
- a change in the writing style and
- the creation of skepticism regarding certain historical facts.

Writing Style: Writing style, at least in ancient India, was quite different from the one prevailing today. For example, Surendra Mital (2000, p 22-23) points out, 'On the basis of the opinions of Kautilya expressed in the third person, the view as put forward by Hillebrandt that it is not the work of Kautilya but of a school, and this is also the opinion of Keith and Winternitz. But Kane says: "In order to avoid looking too egotistical ancient writers generally put their views in the third person."'

Similarly, as time passes, language and style change and works, which may not be even hundred years old, may appear strange. Weintraub (1992, p 3) remarks, 'If one looks back to the 1930s from the present and reads in the major economic journals and examines the major treatises, one is struck by a sense of "the foreign."' Additionally, some of the theories, which were developed during the recent past, may appear prototypical or obsolete today. As Zingales (2000) observes, 'While the existing theories have delivered very important and useful insights, they seem to be ineffective in helping us cope with the new type of firms that are emerging.'

Skepticism: According to Stephen Stigler (1999), Craig (1699) pointed out that the passage of time might create doubts about the occurrence of past events, such as, the story of Christ. Or more recently, Einstein, in paying tributes to M K Gandhi at his death in 1948, stated, 'The world will scarcely believe that such a man as this ever, in flesh and blood, walked upon this earth'. It is incorrect, although understandable, that many historians of economics may find it hard to imagine that a seminal thinker like Kautilya ever lived and, that too in a now developing country like India. It is truly astonishing that even many well-read individuals are not aware of the fact that both China and India experienced innovative periods very early on, very similar to the Italian Renaissance. Alternatively, imagine what would be the status of the *Wealth of Nations* in the year 4076 (ie. 2300 years after its publication).

Date and Authorship of the *Arthashastra*: Quite unexpectedly, someone in 1904 handed over a manuscript to Dr R Shamasastry, who was then the Librarian at the Mysore Government Oriental Library. He published the first English translation of Kautilya's *Arthashastra* in 1915. Since then there have been controversies about the date and authorship of the *Arthashastra*. Many Western writers have advanced the hypothesis that it was not written during the 4th century BCE and that it was written not by one, but by many scholars. Recently,

Mital (2000) meticulously examined the methods and evidence used, particularly by Trautmann (1971), to test such hypotheses. Mital concluded that the methods used by Trautmann are arbitrary and often contradictory and, therefore, insufficient to prove his claims.

So far, absolutely no direct evidence has been found against Kautilya being the sole author of the *Arthashastra*. And there is no evidence that it was not written during the 4th century BCE. And the indirect evidence such as the writing style of various segments of the *Arthashastra* is inadequate to disprove the date of its writing or Kautilya being the sole author. In other words, at present, these are merely doubts just like the doubts that someone else might have written at least some of the plays attributed to Shakespeare.

Additionally, there is no contradiction or inconsistency regarding the use of any concept in the *Arthashastra*[1]. For example, whether discussing the economic policies or the foreign policy, the use of the opportunity cost is consistent throughout the *Arthashastra*. In general, the probability that a book would be internally consistent with multiple authors is very low. In fact, it is a challenge even for any writer to be internally consistent[2]. In the absence of any other evidence, Trautmann's hypothesis of multiple authors seems to be unjustifiable, given the impeccable internal consistency of the various concepts used in the *Arthashastra*.

The period from 7th century BCE to 4th century BCE may be described as India's dynamic period, as Drekmeier (1962) has asserted. He (p 35) observes: 'From roughly the 7th to the 4th century BC, India was the scene of the formulation and spread of a remarkable number of doctrines, pantheist and materialist, atheist and rationalist. Many asserted the complete freedom of the human mind from religious doctrine and were outspoken in their criticism of the *Vedas* and the Brahmanical system, going so far as to call the Vedic teachers imposters.' There were many other developments as mentioned below.

A Paradigm Shift in Attitude Towards Health Care

Sage Punarvasu Atreya initiated a well-organized study of medicine in India called Ayurveda (science of life) during the 7th century

BCE. This may be considered a paradigm shift in medicine since it was realized that good health and longevity depended on human efforts, and diseases were not caused by any supernatural powers and their appeasement through prayers was unnecessary. One of sage Atreya's students, Agnivesha, wrote a *Samhita* (compendium) on medicine. Sometimes later, the precise date is unknown, Charaka revised Agnivesha's *Samhita* (compendium), and now it is known as *Charaka Samhita*.

Sushruta also wrote a book called *Samhita* during the 6th century BCE. It contains 300 surgical procedures and 120 instruments. Sushruta is known as the 'father of surgery' and also as the 'father of plastic surgery' in India. Tiwari and Shukla (2005) state: 'Sushruta is the pioneer of reconstructive rhinoplasty. Cutting off the nose was a common punishment in ancient India and more than 15 methods of repairing such damage are mentioned by Sushruta, akin to most modern plastic surgery techniques.' Similarly, Kautilya realized the need to have tort laws related to malpractices. Kautilya also suggested replacing many physical punishments by monetary penalties.

2.2 SOCIO-RELIGIOUS-POLITICAL CONDITIONS IN THE 4TH CENTURY BCE

There is hardly any ancient work in India on political thought, sociology or economics, which does not use the two words: *Dharma* and *Shastra*. The word *dharma* in general means duty, and righteousness in personal and social conduct. Ray (1999, p 10) defines *dharma* as, 'It comes from the Sanskrit etymology *dhr*, meaning to hold. *Dharma* is that which holds a society together.' He (p 12) adds, 'It alone holds society together; violation of it shakes the society to its foundations and constitutes a mortal threat to its existence.'

Again, according to Ray (p 10), 'The term *shastra* means a systematic study of the general principles and detailed organization of a specific form of human activity. Thus *dharmashastra* refers to a systematic treatise on the general principles and detailed content of righteous conduct. Sometimes, the term *shastra* is interpreted as an authoritative text, and the principles and the rules laid down in a treatise are given the status of injunctions. Thus the principles and rules of *dharmashastra* are not merely analytical and explanatory but also authoritative and binding in nature. This additional connotation, however, is absent in other usages of the term. Thus the principles laid down in Bharat's *Natyashastra* and Kautilya's *Arthashastra* are largely elucidatory and, at best, advisory.'

According to the *Vedas* (Brahminism), the life span of an individual was divided into four stages, namely, *Brahmacharya*—the stage of learning and celibacy; *Grihastha*—the stage of family life; *Vanaprastha*—the stage of penance and looking inward, and *Sanyaasa*—renunciation of all worldly things and detachment. Each individual following the prescribed role at each stage of his or her life implied adherence to *dharma*. At that time, under the influence of Buddhism and Jainism, individuals were giving up their vocations. Kautilya was particularly concerned with the ramifications of this phenomenon. He (p 405) asserted, 'No man shall renounce his marital life [to become an ascetic] without providing for his wife and sons (2.1)'. In fact, he (p 411) prescribed a fine for such an act (definitely no tolerance for deadbeat fathers) (2.1).

The canons of Brahminism were challenged from two fronts which, according to Karwal (1966), had diagonally opposite views. Buddhism rebelled against the caste system and recommended a radical social reform: a casteless society. However, its economic vision was not conducive to economic progress since it recommended renunciation of all worldly things. Similarly, Jainism also recommended asceticism. The other challenge to Brahminism came from the school of Brihaspati, sometimes referred to as founder of the Charvaka philosophy, whose thrust is typically summed up in the maxim: 'eat, drink and be merry so long as life is there even if one has to borrow to consume *ghee*, because once this body is consigned to ashes (after death), there won't be any re-birth.' Further, there was no heaven and no God. The followers of Brihaspati thus advocated stark materialism. Apparently, there was a considerable amount of social disorder and confusion at the time of Kautilya.

Karwal (1966) notes that during the 4th century BCE, India was divided into petty kingdoms fraught with internal unrest and mutual distrust among the neighbourly rulers. He summarizes the pre-Kautilyan conditions as: 'Thus, there were chaos and confusion in every sphere. The need of the time was in the political sphere, integration and consolidation, in the socio-religious sphere, reconciliation of the sectarian and caste conflicts, and, in the economic sphere, the control of economic aggressivism. Kautilya voiced this need and Kautilyanism was intended to meet it.'[3]

It seems that at the time of Kautilya, the caste system was not that rigid. For instance, the *Sudras* had a wide variety of choices regarding their economic activities. Kautilya (p 577) stated, 'Envoys, therefore, speak as they are instructed to, even if weapons are raised against them. The *shastras* say that even if an envoy is an outcast, he shall not be killed (1.16).' Similarly, he (p 421) wrote, 'In case a *Brahmin* has only one son by a *Sudra* wife, that son shall have only one-third of the property (3.6).' It seems that inter-caste marriages were not completely prohibited, particularly, if the upper castes were involved and a capable individual even if an outcast, could become an envoy (honorable position). However, in later years, it again became rigid and *varnas* degenerated into different *jatis* or castes and sub-castes (for details see Deshpande, 2000). Adherence to one's assigned caste and performing the assigned role implied following his or her *dharma*.

2.3 ECONOMIC CONDITIONS, MARKETS AND INSTITUTIONS IN 4TH CENTURY BCE

Karwal (1966) remarks: 'Economically also, there were factors making for disintegration, partly due to the politico-socio-religious disorder and partly because the individualistic enterprise of the pre-Kautilyan period was giving way to capitalism. The free bargaining of that period was being replaced by bargaining through guilds. It was the age of guilds—guilds of artisans, of craftsmen, of labourers, of merchants and of even priests. They arbitrarily raised prices, wages, profit and interest, the merchants in particular resorting to cornering and profiteering.'[4]

Agriculture was the most important economic activity. Basham (1959, p 194) writes, 'The Greek travelers were most impressed by the fertility of India's soil and the energy and ability of her cultivators.'

Mining was particularly important for making weapons and coins for the state. The metals mined were gold, copper, lead, tin and iron. Metallurgy and manufacturing industries were getting established. Making weapons and salt, brewing liquor, weaving textiles and manufacturing jewellery were the main industries. Gambling and betting were the main service industries.

Product Markets: Merchants from foreign countries brought goods to the cities where the bidding took place. However, Kautilya was aware of the potential problems of monopoly and monopsony. He had no idea about the deadweight loss but equity considerations were emphasized.

Factor Markets: Wages, profit, interest and rent were recognized as distinct factor payments. Some individuals did work for the government in public enterprises and civil services. But a majority of the individuals were self-employed. However, Basham (1959, p 216) notes, 'Though the basis of ancient Indian industry was at all times the individual craftsman, aided chiefly by members of his own family, larger manufactories, worked chiefly by hired labour, were by no means unknown.' Further, 'We read here and there of private producers who had far transcended the status of the small home craftsman, and who manufactured on a large scale for a wide market. Thus, an early Jain text tells of a wealthy potter named Saddalaputta who owned 500 potters' workshops, and a fleet of boats which distributed his wares throughout the Ganges valley; there are a few other references, which confirm that large scale production for a wide market was not unknown in ancient India.' Basham points out that the existence of cooperatives of workmen were also common. He asserts, 'Their existence tended to encourage division of labour; thus one man would fashion the shaft of an arrow, a second would fix the flights, and a third would make and fix the point.'

Currency: There was no inside money. The king issued silver and copper coins. The highest value coin, called *pana*, was rectangular-shaped and was the medium of exchange and also the unit of account.

According to Kautilya (p 327), 'The Chief Master of the Mint shall be responsible for the minting of silver coins, made up of [an alloy consisting of] 11/16th part silver, 1/4th part copper and 1/16th part hardening metal (such as iron, tin, lead or antimony) in the following denominations—one *pana*, ½ *pana*, ¼ *pana* and 1/8 *pana* [the weight of each coin being proportional to its value] (2.12).' The king charged 8% fee for issuing currency and it appears that seigniorage was an important source of government revenue even at that time.

There was some borrowing and lending of money between individuals. Parmar (1987, p 131) states, 'No doubt, banking facilities in the modern sense were not available in Kautilya's time, but the use of credit and promissory notes was not unknown. Loans and credits were frequently given and a reasonable amount of interest was charged on them. The big merchants in the few large towns gave letters of credit to one another.'

Urbanization: Most of the population lived in the countryside. But there were a few fortified cities with modern amenities as well as incidence of crimes. Pataliputra was the capital of Chandragupta Maurya's kingdom. Seleucus Nikator (successor to Alexander) appointed Megasthenes as his ambassador to the court of Chandragupta Maurya and he remained there for some time. Basham (1959, p 198-199) states, 'Pataliputra in the time of Mauryas, according to Megasthenes, was a long narrow city, stretching nine miles along the bank of the Ganges, and reaching only one and a half miles inland.' According to Chandler (1987), it was the largest city in the world with a population of roughly over 200,000 in 300 BCE. Book II of Kautilya's *Arthashastra* has two chapters detailing the construction-design of a fortified city (some writers claim that this is the first datable book on civil architecture). According to Majumdar (1980, p 77), 'Kautilya divides the city into sixteen sectors with twelve gates by means of three royal highways running east to west and three running north to south. The city was to be well provided with water, drainage, and underground passages.' Kautilya recommended building codes to protect privacy, civic codes to maintain hygiene and cleanliness and setting up industrial zones to minimize fire hazards by limiting craftsmen to specified industrial areas.

International Trade: Certainly international trade was not an engine of economic growth. But perhaps it was not that insignificant either.[5] Parmar (1987, p 129) notes, 'In the days of Kautilya, international trade had acquired considerable importance; therefore, in his *Arthashastra*, he discusses the import and export trade also at length.' In fact, the concept of terms of trade is quite explicit in the *Arthashastra*.

Scarcity of Labour and Capital: It appears that at that time, the population was not growing much and labour and capital were more scarce than land. For example, Kautilya recommended to the king that he demand settled land as his share from a successful joint campaign since the affiliated labour and embodied capital would come with it. If the king did not get settled land, he should prefer very fertile virgin land so that less labour and less capital were needed to settle it. Kautilya (p 405) went as far as to suggest, 'No one shall induce a woman [still capable of bearing children?] into becoming an ascetic (2.1)', implying shortage of labour. Similarly, he was concerned with the saving of lives of ordinary people, implying shortage of manpower. He (p 130) recommended, 'Persons carried away by floods shall be rescued using gourds, skin bags, tree trunks, boats and thick ropes. Owners of canoes shall be punished if they do not try to save someone in danger (4.3).' He suggested that physicians 'be called upon to counteract diseases and epidemics affecting human beings.'

Immigration: Kautilya (p 178) suggested, 'The king shall populate the countryside by creating new villages on virgin land or by reviving abandoned village sites. Settlement can be effected either by shifting some of the population of his own country or by immigration by inducement or force (2.1).'

SUMMARY

It is obvious that the economy needed almost everything: law and order, a functioning judiciary, an efficient and honest bureaucracy, creation of markets, infrastructure, national security and maintenance of independence. Kautilya's goal was to create an ideal economy, progressive, fair, open and efficient. Perhaps, that is why the *Arthashastra* is so broad in scope and abstract in reasoning.

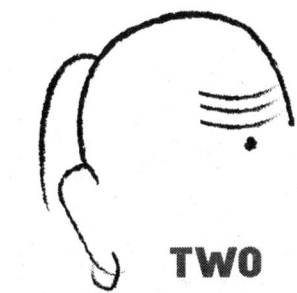

TWO

Concepts, Methodology and Tools of Analysis

In this part, arguments justifying the claim that Kautilya is the true founder of economics are provided. Kautilya's analysis is more rigorous, consistent, comprehensive and concise than that of Adam Smith. Kautilya surpasses Adam Smith in every category, viz., methodology, tools of analysis and innovation of concepts.

3
Origin, Scope and Methodology of Economics

> The history of economics as a science is, in my view, still waiting to be properly written.
> — *Redman (1997)*

What is a science? Is economics a science? Who should be given credit for founding it? Has there been progress in economic knowledge? Such questions may seem settled but in science nothing is ever settled for all times. Groenewegen (2002) considers the determination of the origin of economics very important and explores it in depth.[1] Similarly, Backhouse (1997) attempts to answer the questions related to the growth (or lack of it) in economic knowledge. Although economists seldom agree on an issue, it is amazing that for almost two hundred years, there has actually been a near consensus among economists that economics originated in the eighteenth century and that Adam Smith was its founder. This was accepted despite the fact that there has been no consensus regarding the requirements to be fulfilled for declaring someone to be a 'founder' of economics. However, in recent years, strong doubts have been raised on accepting Adam Smith as the one and only founder of economics.

Still, all these explorations have been limited only to Europe. Somehow, the Euro-centric mentality has not allowed any search or acknowledgement, for the fact that the non-Westerners, long before Adam Smith or anyone else in the West, might have founded economics as a separate discipline. Recently, Pack (2001, p 179) has remarked: 'There must be an Indian, a Chinese, Japanese, and other traditions of economic thought.' Indeed, India has an ancient tradition of appreciating and applying economic analysis to a wide range of problems. Sen (1987) believes that there are two ancient origins of economics: one ethics-based and the other technique-based, which he calls 'engineering'. He credits the Greek philosophers, particularly Aristotle, for originating the ethical approach to economics and Kautilya (in the tradition of Walras) for the engineering approach to economics. Part Three shows that Kautilya's *Arthashastra* actually has much more ethical content than the contributions of Plato, Aristotle or Adam Smith. Indeed, his work is also the original of the ethics-based approach to economics and came before all others. According to Sen, Kautilya's *Arthashastra* is the first book on the origin of the 'engineering approach' to economics. He (p 4) states: 'The "engineering" approach also connects with those studies of economics which developed from the technique-oriented analyses of statecraft. Indeed, in what was almost certainly the first book ever written with anything like the title "Economics", namely, Kautilya's *Arthashastra* (translated from Sanskrit, this would stand for something like "instructions on material prosperity"), the logistic approach to statecraft, including economic policy, is prominent.'

A justification for such an outstanding claim that Kautilya's *Arthashastra* is the first origin of the 'engineering approach' to economics was obviously beyond the scope of Sen's lectures in as much as the determination of the origin of economics as a science demands an involved discussion on three issues, viz.:

- interpretation of earlier, particularly, ancient writings
- the specification of the requirements for declaring economics as a science, and
- the definition, scope and methodology of economics

Section 3.1 offers the views of leading economists on how to interpret, evaluate and accredit earlier works. At present, there is no uniformity in the requirements to declare someone as founder of economics. In literature, at least three types of requirements have been advanced for determining the founder of economics:

(a) by whom and when was economics established as a separate or autonomous discipline
(b) by whom and when were a reasonable number of economic concepts and hypotheses developed, and
(c) who passed the Schumpeter's Test of displaying an understanding of the economy as a system of inter-dependent elements?

Almost invariably, these three types of requirements have been advanced as mutually exclusive but it seems that Schumpeter implicitly suggests requirements (b) and (c) as complementary in the determination of the origin of economics. Section 3.2 contains a discussion on the origin of economics and requirements for adjudging its founder. It is also indicated that Ekelund and Heberts' claim that microeconomics is of French origin falls far short of the requisites. Section 3.3 presents the views of a few prominent economists on Adam Smith as the founder of economics.

Kautilya specified a very broad scope for economics. He applied economic analysis not only to core subjects like taxation and economic growth, but also to other areas, such as law, war and peace. In fact, economics might have acquired the status of an imperial science during his time, the 4th century BCE. After a lapse of two millennia, economics re-emerged. Initially its scope was limited primarily to economic growth. However, from the latter half of the nineteenth century, its scope has been increasing steadily and it has been colonizing other disciplines.[2, 3] In Section 3.4, Kautilya's views on the scope of economics are discussed. In Section 3.5, Kautilya's methodology, which is very similar to Marshall's, is offered. Kautilya adopted a partial equilibrium approach and very frequently but implicitly, used phrases similar to the phrase 'all other things being equal'. Also, he implicitly used the discrete marginal analysis. A few examples are presented to illustrate Kautilya's partial equilibrium approach. Applications of the methodology of constrained optimization and an inter-temporal analysis by Kautilya are discussed in Sections 3.6 and 3.7, respectively. In Section 3.8, Kautilya's *Arthashastra* is examined against the most stringent requirements for declaring it as the first origin of the engineering approach to economics and it comes out faring far better than Adam Smith's *Wealth of Nations* or the contributions of Dupuit and the other French econo-engineers.

3.1 INTERPRETATION, EVALUATION AND ACCREDITATION OF EARLIER WORKS

How does one interpret or evaluate earlier works? Should one use today's beliefs and standards for evaluation, or those prevailing at the time? At present, there is no consensus that any specific method or approach is superior to the others. To a large extent, it depends on the purpose of the study, availability of the appropriate material and the competence or the comfort level of a researcher with the particular approach. For example, Grampp (2000) is concerned about the possibility of excessive imagination on the part of some researchers in interpreting earlier writers. Accordingly, he lays some ground rules to avoid such tendencies. He proposes: 'A way to get things straight about Smith or anyone else. It is to begin by distinguishing between (a) what the author actually said, (b) what is implied by what he said, (c) what can reasonably be inferred from it, (d) what we may conjecture he meant, (e) what he conceivably could have meant, and (f) what it would be convenient to believe what he meant. The next step is to stay as close as possible to points (a) and (b), to know that about point (c), the operative word is "reasonably", and to move as far as point (d) only when all else fails, or never at all. Distinctions (e) and (f) are left to those who, to paraphrase George Stigler, make the study of economic ideas a work of the imagination.'

Backhouse (1997) adds another perspective to the interpretation of the works of earlier writers. He remarks, 'This debate has centered on whether it is appropriate to read the past from the perspective of present-day ideas. The opponents of "Whig" history argue that it is important to read past writings against the contexts in which they were written, and the concerns of past economists, their presuppositions and beliefs may be very different from those of present-day economists. In its most extreme form, this position denies that there can be progress in economic thought: there are merely changes in the questions'.

Blaug (2001) labels this controversy as 'rational reconstruction' *versus* 'historical reconstruction'. Essentially, the rational reconstruction approach involves the use of modern methods and concepts to interpret earlier writings. Its proponents believe that it adds rigor to the analysis and helps in making any inconsistencies or implicit assumptions in the older writings explicit. On the other hand, the historical reconstruction approach consists of going back to the time of the writer under consideration, construct a picture of his time and interpret his writings in terms of what he meant and not what we think he meant. For example, Tribe (1999) asks: 'Is there any real point in laboriously excavating, cleaning down, and presenting a newly restored "Adam Smith", whose features would have been recognizable to few of his contemporaries, and a diminishing series of successors?' Blaug, Tribe and others who advocate the historical reconstruction approach strongly defend such an undertaking and deplore the rational reconstruction approach.

Blaug, however, concedes, that while 'rational reconstruction makes past thinkers appear to be a bit more like us than they were; historical reconstruction make them out to be a little less like us than they were.' It is obvious that these approaches are not substitutes, but rather complements of one another, meaning that the pursuit of both approaches helps in the reconstruction of a more complete picture of the past. However, sometimes, rational reconstruction approach is possible whereas the historical reconstruction approach is likely to fail due to lack of supporting writings.

Limiting the Role of Hindsight: Walker (1999) notes: 'The activity of describing, interpreting and evaluating past theory is undertaken under the powerful influence of current economic thought.' That is, knowledge of current theories and the availability of mathematical and statistical tools do help in a better understanding of past theories. However, one should guard against two possible pitfalls in the interpretation or evaluation of past contributions.

First, De Long (2000) points out, 'In Patinkin and Johnson's view, Old Chicago Monetarism was a retrospective construction by Milton Friedman (1956). In their view, Friedman used "Keynesian" tools and insights to provide a retrospective *post hoc* theoretical justification for policy recommendations that had little explicit theoretical base at the time, and to construct for himself some intellectual antecedents'.

A second pitfall may arise due to the failure to distinguish the current state of our knowledge from what existed in the earlier times. Thaler (2000) advances the hypothesis that 'Once we know something, we can't imagine ever thinking otherwise.' It means that if this hypothesis is valid, then the answer to Blaug's (2001) question that 'given the fact that texts must be reconstructed, the question is how are we to do so: in the light of all that we now know or as faithfully as possible to the times in which they were written?' — is not possible, implying that the historical reconstruction cannot be differentiated from the rational reconstruction.

Use of Modern Methods to Interpret Earlier Writers: Those who adopt historical reconstruction approach try to steer clear of mathematical and statistical tools, which is unfortunate since these modern tools are used as complements, and not as substitutes, to insight or intuition. Commenting on Samuelson (1978), Hollander (1980) advised economic historians to get acquainted with modern methods. He remarked, 'It is probable that Professor Samuelson's statement of the "canonical classical model of political economy" will become the *locus classicus* for the next generation of textbook writers; teachers of the history of thought would be advised to familiarize themselves with the ingenious diagrams in particular.'

Accreditation: Schaffer (1996, p 14) quotes Brannigan (1981, p 90) when he states, 'Events are discoveries not in virtue of how they appear in the mind, but how they are defined in and by a cultural criterion.' He (p 19) remarks, 'Much recent work on discovery and invention in the sciences demonstrates that retrospection and celebration play key roles in the production of discovery. Because discoveries acquire their status as the result of subsequent work within the relevant community, the 'fetishism' of discovery is therefore the consequence of the whole process through which change is analyzed, debated and assessed.' It may be pointed out that Adam Smith was declared founder of economics without going through such a process.

There is a major difference of opinion between the philosophers and the sociologists in this regard. Philosophers, like Kuhn, discuss the paradigm-shifts and attribute those to certain individuals. Sociologists believe that 'it is not the genius who creates the paradigm, but the paradigm that creates the genius who gives expression to it.' An old and popular saying in India captures this point of view: 'The origination of the River Ganges was inevitable, but Bhagiratha was credited with its origination.'

Sociologists concentrate on social factors and stress that a discovery is not a discovery unless authorized by the community. And there is a lengthy process of review before authorship is granted. Schaffer (p 43) notes that according to Gooding (1985, p 234), 'Herschel wrote, "He who proves, discovers."' However, this standard of accreditation has not been used in economics. If economists had used such a standard, Adam Smith, for example, could not be given credit for the Invisible Hand Theorem, not because it was already in the air, but because of the fact that he merely stated it and did not prove it. As Rosenberg (1998) remarks: 'Walras's Theorem that a general market clearing equilibrium exists, that it is stable and unique, follows from the axioms of microeconomic theory. Walras offered this result in 1874, as a formalization of Adam Smith's conviction about decentralized economies, but he was unable to give more than intuitive arguments for the theorem. It was only in 1934 that Abraham Wald provided an arduous and intricate satisfactory proof, and much work since his time has been devoted to producing more elegant, more intuitive, and more powerful proofs of new wrinkles on the theorem.'

Similarly, Adam Smith discussed the regulation of monopolies and provision of public goods by the government but he did not label them as 'market failures'. He was not aware of the concept of the deadweight loss. Therefore, the undesirability of monopoly, as argued by Adam Smith was not based on the ground that it created a deadweight loss, but it was considered oppressive. Economists still credit him for recognizing these problems. The point is that if an earlier writer recognized a problem and suggested a reasonable solution, later-day economists have given him credit for its origination. As another illustration, during the 1860s, Scottish chemist Peter Tait simply started cataloging knots. He could not imagine that today, the Knot theory would be one of the hottest topics in mathematics and might be useful in understanding DNA and making computers more efficient. Just to emphasize the point, if an earlier writer initiated and advanced a concept further than Tait (ie. beyond making a classification) and well short of our current understanding, he would be given credit for originating that concept. This methodology is followed in the author's evaluation of Kautilya's work. In other words, economists do follow a very liberal approach in evaluating earlier writings but it does not imply, for example, that Aristotle should get credit for originating the concept of the 'law of gravitation', based on his argument that a stone falls to the ground since it has a tendency to return to its natural resting place.

The interpretations in this work are confined to Grampp's points (a) and (b) and only occasionally, with recourse to point (c), but points (d), (e) and (f) are avoided altogether. In other words, interpretations are limited to what Waterman (1999) calls 'can be found—or read into'. Secondly, the origin of a concept is attributed to Kautilya only if he provided at least as much substantive material on it as Adam Smith did. The work is undertaken as a challenge to minimize the pitfalls of hindsight.

The narrative highlights only the salient and seminal ideas initiated by Kautilya, provides some details on the re-emergence of these ideas since Adam Smith, and the current state of our knowledge on them. Every important concept, which has been used by Kautilya in various contexts, for example (i) opportunity cost (Chapter 4), is discussed and then a history of its re-emergence is provided in the end notes. Currently, the credit for originating the concept of opportunity cost goes to Wieser in 1876—implying that Kautilya was way ahead of the classicists. Second example: (ii) Kautilya was acutely aware of the time inconsistency problem (Chapter 20) and the credit for the revival of this concept goes to Keyland and Prescott in 1977. This methodology keeps the discussion focused, brief and informative and helps in easy placement of Kautilya's ideas since it is difficult to give him a single label, such as classical, neoclassical or postmodern.

3.2 REQUIREMENTS FOR ESTABLISHING ORIGIN OF ECONOMICS

Questions, such as what is a science? Is economics a science? These are not questions of major concern in this book. No economic historian, who has explored the origin of economics, has made any distinction between establishing of economics as a science and economics as a separate discipline and that practice is followed here also. According to Schumpeter (1954), it is futile to search for the origin of economics. He (p 9) remarks: 'As regards economics, bias or ignorance alone can explain such statements as that A Smith or F Quesnay or Sir William Petty or anyone else "founded" that science, or that the historian should begin his report with one of them.'

On the other hand, Groenewegen (2002) argues, unlike Schumpeter, for dating the emergence of economics as a science. However, Spiegel hints at some arbitrariness in the search for the origin of economics. He (1991, p xxii) remarks, 'Where should a history of economics start? Often the nationality of an author makes him inclined to open up the discussion with the contributions of fellow nationals. Even in the absence of an explicit claim the whole matter then appears to be part of the national heritage, perhaps even a national invention—thus French historians of economics are apt to open up the story with the Physiocrats, while the English may prefer the mercantilists or the classics.'

The above remark by Spiegel may be interpreted in more than one way. Since it may mean that the requirements to declare economics as a science/separate discipline either are not standardized regarding its definition, scope and method, inconsistently followed or have been changing over time.[4] Any one of these possibilities could allow some arbitrariness in determining the origin of economics as a science but in this case all of the above seem to hold. For example, Groenewegen (2002, p 49) observes, 'A study of the literature of the history of economics quickly reveals that the question of the emergence of economics as a science has been treated in different ways, and that these different ways not infrequently can be explained by differences in the scope, subject matter and objectives of economics accepted by the historian. Hence there is a strong relationship between the treatment of the emergence of economics as a science, and the definition of economics as a science, different definitions generally, but not always, leading to different periods of time, and to different individuals or groups to whom or to which the emergence can be assigned.'

There are indeed no uniform standards. For example, (a) Spiegel emphasizes only the autonomous aspect, and (b) Ekelund and Hebert (1999) concentrate only on the development of a reasonable number of concepts. However, (c) Schumpeter is much more demanding as to the requirements although he himself is inconsistent in their applications.[5] According to him, the author, who understood the economy as a system of inter-dependent elements should be acknowledged as the founder of economics as a science. These requirements are discussed in turn. It may be added, however, that Alfred Marshall (1920) singles out only the writing of a treatise on economics, while Barber (1967), Landreth and Colander (1994) consider only the providing of a brilliant synthesis as the requirements for declaring an author (in this case, Adam Smith) as the founder of economics.[6]

Economics as an Autonomous Discipline: Spiegel (1991, p xxiii-xxiv) asserts: 'Economics as an autonomous and systematic science is of comparatively recent origin; it arose as part of the science of man in the seventeenth and eighteenth centuries. Before that time, economic ideas were presented in the context of philosophy in classical Greece, in the context of theology during the Middle Ages, and again in the context of philosophy, but at times in the somewhat more emancipated form of separate essays, during the era of Locke and Hume. The economic thought of the mercantilists may have been autonomous—that is, independent of religion and philosophy—but it touched only certain aspects of economics and did not cover the entire field in systematic fashion. The same can be said of the Physiocrats. With Adam Smith economics became established as an autonomous and systematic field of study.'

According to Spiegel, establishment of economics as an autonomous discipline—independent of religion and philosophy—is the only requirement and Adam Smith was the first one, who accomplished this during the eighteenth century. As explained below, this is neither necessary nor sufficient to declare economics as a science. Also, at that time, economics was still not separated from political science. But more important, Adam Smith not only made economics independent of religion and philosophy, but also of ethics and thus the *Wealth of Nations* is solely responsible for causing 'the lack of bonhomie' in modern economics. The commercial man of the *Wealth of Nations* never met the benevolent man of the *Theory of Moral Sentiments*.

Development of a Reasonable Number of Concepts: Ekelund and Hebert (p 6) quote Dupuit: 'All sciences undergo a period when they are considered mere practice. A few sparse principles based on observation or reason do not constitute a science. For a science to merit its title, its principles must be numerous and sufficiently well established to explain a particular order of phenomenon. Therefore, each science undergoes a period of gestation before its birth; but little by little, through successive discoveries, a more or less comprehensive body of doctrine is formed. This body of doctrine, accepted by all those adept in the field, constitutes the science's lifeblood. It is the unanimous consent of the scholars in the field that imposes itself on the public (1863b, p 238).' And (p 7), 'Then, one glorious day the new principle is demonstrated through observation or reason.'

Several remarks are in order. According to Dupuit, the true criterion to be a discipline (or science) is that it must have 'numerous and sufficiently well established' principles. The word 'numerous' is a little vague since it does not specify a lower limit on the required number of principles. The phrase 'sufficiently well established' is used by Dupuit to indicate that a principle must be demonstrated by 'observation or reason' and must be 'accepted by all'. However, if unanimous consent were used as a criterion to declare a body of knowledge as a separate discipline, economics, most likely, would not qualify to be a discipline. Moreover, the phrases 'little by little' and 'accepted by all' together imply that probably more than one founder would be needed to establish a discipline. Therefore, the only meaningful requirement to be called a new discipline may be whether there is a distinctly identifiable core consisting of, at least, a respectable number of basic concepts and testable hypotheses. The expressions 'respectable number' and 'distinctly identifiable core' too need some explanation.

An Evaluation of Dupuit's Contributions: Some of the contributions of Dupuit and the French engineers are quite remarkable.[7] However, the claim by Ekelund and Hebert 'that microeconomics, as we know it today, is uniquely of French origin' is not justified. Since Dupuit's contributions, both in terms of depth and breadth, are far too insubstantial to bestow him with the fatherhood of microeconomics.

Schumpeter's Test for Declaring Economics as a Science: According to Schumpeter (p 7), 'A science is any kind of knowledge that has been the object of conscious efforts to improve it. Such efforts produce habits of mind, methods or "techniques"—and a command of facts unearthed by these techniques which are beyond the range of the mental habits and the factual knowledge of everyday life. Hence we may also adopt the practically equivalent definition: a science is any field of knowledge that has developed specialized techniques of fact-finding and of interpretation or inference (analysis).' He (p

173) adds that one has to 'show how they hang together and how they determine each other, which is where scientific economics begin.' That is, until the economy was seen as a system consisting of inter-dependent elements, economics would remain in the pre-scientific stage.

It may be pointed out that although Schumpeter specified a rigorous standard for a body of knowledge to qualify as a scientific discipline, he himself did not follow it. It should also be noted that Schumpeter's requirements as to what is scientific are much different than those prevalent during the eighteenth century. For example, Redman (1997, p 104) remarks, 'I have said that doing science, or philosophy, in the eighteenth century meant systematic inquiry. What exactly did this entail? For the Scots, science was a body of coherent knowledge organized around a few simple principles of explanation.' In other words, according to the Scots, science was concerned with systematic analysis, and not with systemic analysis as required by Schumpeter.

3.3 VIEWS ON THE *WEALTH OF NATIONS*

Each economist has his/her own view of the *Wealth of Nations*, implying that there may be thousands of them. It is impossible and unnecessary to accommodate all of them. The only reasonable thing to do is to ignore the outliers like the views of Dugald Stewart and George Stigler on one side and those of Murray Rothbard and Schumpeter on the other. Still, it is not claimed that the selection here is based on any random sampling.

How Adam Smith Came to be Known as the Founder of Economics: Schumpeter (1954, p 194) explains, 'But outside of England, most economists were not quite up to Ricardo, and Smith continued to hold sway. It was then that he was invested with the insignia of "founder"—which none of his contemporaries would have thought of bestowing on him—and that earlier economists moved into the role of "precursors" in whom it was just wonderful to discover what nevertheless remained Smith's ideas.'

Traditional Views on Adam Smith: Three kinds of arguments have been advanced to accredit Adam Smith as the founder of economics. The first is that he wrote the first treatise on economics—*Wealth of Nations*; secondly, he provided a brilliant synthesis of existing ideas in economics, and thirdly, upon a closer examination, he was also a theoretician who made original contributions. Obviously, so considered, if Adam Smith is accepted as the founder of economics, then the study and formulation of economic thought in a systematic manner could not have begun much earlier than the eighteenth century.

Samuelson (1962) remarks, 'Past experience at these annual gatherings of the sons and daughters of Adam Smith suggests that the popular subject of discussion among economists is not so much economics as economists.' In fact, at least from Ricardo onwards, Adam Smith has been declared as the founder of economics, which various prominent writers at different times have reaffirmed. A representative listing of their views is provided below. Ricardo (1821) in the preface to his *Principles of Political Economy and Taxation* states, 'The writer, in combating received opinions, has found it necessary to avert more particularly to those passages in the writings of Adam Smith from which he sees reason to differ; but he hopes it will not, on that account, be suspected that he does not, in common with all those who acknowledge the importance of the science of Political Economy, participate in the admiration which the profound work of this celebrated author so justly excites.'

Deane (1978, p 3-4) asserts, 'It was not until the eighteenth-century philosophers—primarily the Physiocrats and Adam Smith—began systematically, and not merely incidentally, to apply to economic phenomena their theories of natural order underlying the real world that economic theory began to develop into a unified system of explanation, a definitive technique of analysis.' She (p 6) adds, 'Karl Marx too had no doubt where modern economics effectively began. Adam Smith "must be given credit", he wrote, "for having closely determined the abstract categories and for having securely labeled the differences analyzed by the Physiocrats."'

Samuelson (1980) provides a different perspective in evaluating the contributions of earlier writers. He observes, 'Every historian of science appreciates how vague are the brilliant perceptions of the earliest writers and how constructive is the achievement of later writers in synthesizing and clarifying ideas.' He emphasizes originality, rather than the synthesis in Smith's work. In fact, Samuelson (1977, 1978, and 1980) has attempted to establish Adam Smith as a theorist, contrary to the traditionally established view that he was merely a synthesizer of ideas. It is beside the point that if Adam Smith were to read the interpretation of his own work by Samuelson, being a humble Scotchman (having completed the evolution from 'savage to Scotchman'), he would declare Samuelson to be the father of economics and agree with Wordsworth that 'child is the father of man'.

Recent Revisions of the Initial Views on Adam Smith: Miller (1997) points out that the classical economists before J S Mill did not consider economics as a separate discipline and the style was non-technical. He remarks, 'From Adam Smith until the middle of the nineteenth century, leading social thinkers made little distinction between their economic and political writing. The methods of analysis were similar, using largely verbal arguments dominated by normative concerns.' Similarly, Redman (1997, p 4) observes: 'Binding the eighteenth and early nineteenth-century thinkers was a belief in a common method for the social sciences. This strand of thought stops, however, with J S Mill, who developed the idea of political economy as a separate science.' It is obvious from the above assessments by Miller and Redman of Adam Smith's work that he alone really did not establish economics as a separate discipline, implying that he cannot be declared as the sole founder of economics.

Ekelund and Hebert (1999, p 1) asserts, 'The popular wisdom is that classical economic inquiry, which extends from Adam Smith to John Stuart Mill, is focused on macroeconomics, whereas neoclassical economic inquiry, which begins with William Stanley Jevons and Carl Menger and culminates with Alfred Marshall, centered on microeconomics.' That is, they believe that the classical economists may be declared as the founders only of macroeconomics. But they (p 2) claim 'that microeconomics, as we know it today, is uniquely of French origin.'

Joan Robinson (1953) did remark that neoclassical thought paid too much attention to little issues like 'why does an egg cost more than a cup of tea' and ignored the big issues like growth and distribution, which were pursued by the classical economists. Stewart (1986, p 23-24) while commenting on the *Wealth of Nations*, remarks, 'Yet, despite its great sweep, and its pre-eminent concern with what we would now call "economic growth", the book contains no real discussion of why the level of employment is what it is. Clearly, this was not a question which interested the author; indeed it probably never occurred to him.'

Deane also wonders about the recognition of Adam Smith as the founder of macroeconomics. She (p 5-6) states, 'The case for beginning a study of the evolution of economic ideas with Adam Smith rather than with the Physiocrats does not rest, however, either on the innate superiority of his analytical framework, or on his claims to chronological priority in the unified methodological approach which both shared. No doubt Francois Quesnay has as much right as Adam Smith to be regarded as the founder of modern political economy. Indeed his concept of a circular flow of incomes and his *Tableau Economique*, which can be interpreted as kind of input-output table, will strike economists used to operating with social accounting tools of analysis as more relevant to modern macroeconomics than any part of mainstream classical political economy from Smith onwards.' Thus, according to Deane, the credit for originating macroeconomics, if at all, should go to Francois Quesnay but definitely not to Adam Smith.

Rationality Assumption: The current methodology of economics also would be foreign to Adam Smith. For example, Redman (p 234) remarks, 'Unlike twentieth-century usage, Smith's self-interest is not rooted in a concept of rationality. He did not believe that reason should be the primary guide of human destiny; in *The Theory of Moral Sentiments* he asserts nature implants a consciousness in the human breast that is wiser than reason, for nature intends the good of the species and endows people with social sentiments (1976b: p80).'

Optimization Assumption: Similarly, according to Redman, Adam Smith was averse to the assumption of optimization, which is the underlying foundation of all economic decisions. She (p 218) asserts, 'Smith was not interested in optimization problems, "which offer an irresistible invitation to mathematical treatment" (Spiegel 1976:p487).' She continues, 'Thus, the many modern interpretations of Smith's theory that mathematize and axiomatize his theory are not Smith at all but a transformation of Smith.'

Absence of Marginal Analysis and *Ceteris Paribus* from Adam Smith's Analysis: However, a few observations regarding Adam Smith's methodology may be added here. First of all, he did not use the marginal analysis and 'all other things being equal'. Regarding the marginal analysis, Redman (fn. 24, p 217) quotes Worland as stating, 'Adam Smith did not appreciate the difference between the value of a variable, and the rate of change in the value, and his economic theory suffers for it.' Marshall (p 37) notes, 'Adam Smith and many of the earlier writers on economics attained seeming simplicity by following the usages of conversation, and omitting conditioning clauses. But this has caused them to be constantly misunderstood, and has led to much waste of time and trouble in profitless controversy; they purchased apparent ease at too great a cost even for that gain.'

Core of Economic Knowledge Offered by Adam Smith: Deane (1978, p 11) asserts: 'If we were to define a theoretical science as a set of "general laws which can serve as instruments for systematic explanation and dependable prediction" and a scientific methodology as a technical apparatus for logically or empirically verifying these laws it would be too much to say that Adam Smith had founded a science of economics. But it is reasonable to claim that he had at any rate made the first steps in this direction by devising a system and testing it. By postulating a logical system of economic relationships based on an underlying law of human nature (analogous to Newton's law of gravity), he set the course of the theoretical political economy towards a system-building discipline.' She adds, 'However, what accounted for the tremendous impact that this book had on economic thought was not its components which, taken out of context, are easily criticized, but the way it built up into a logically interdependent whole, the first unified socioeconomic model.' Thus, Deane specifies the requirements for the establishment of a new discipline but she is not sure whether Adam Smith fulfilled those requirements. Essentially, her conclusion is similar to that of Miller and Redman that Adam Smith is one of the founders of economics since he just initiated the discussion but did not develop the required set of general principles.

3.4 ARTHASHASTRA ON DEFINITION AND SCOPE OF ECONOMICS

The word *Arthashastra* is a combination of two words: *Artha* and *Shastra*. Kautilya uses the word *Artha* (p 100) as 'wealth' and (p 145) as 'material well-being'. There is no ambiguity regarding the word *Shastra*: it means science. As Varma (p 583) observes, 'The name of the book is *shastram*, which means a philosophical and theoretical exposition and not a historical presentation.' However, in later periods, the original meaning of the word *Shastra* got diluted and sometimes came to be used to denote less theoretical works as well, actually to heap significance on them.

According to Deane (1983), the social needs of the time should determine the scope of a discipline. She states, 'The scope and method of our discipline needs at all times to be described in relation to the social problems which give purpose to it and there is room for more than one progressive research program in operation at the same time.' I believe that in addition to the social needs, the progress in other fields and the capabilities of its practitioners may also be important determinants of scope and method of a discipline.

Kautilya on the Scope of Economics: Kautilya (p 99), with characteristic Indian humility, described his work thus: 'This *Arthashastra* is a compendium of almost all similar treatises, composed by ancient teachers, on the acquisition and protection of territory. Easy to grasp and understand, free from verbosity, Kautilya has composed this treatise with precise words, doctrines and sense (1.1).' It has 150 chapters distributed among 15 books. Books 1, 2 and 8 deal primarily with economic policies and economic administration, Books 3 and 4 discuss crime and punishment, and administration of justice, Books 6, 7, 9, 11 and 12 primarily deal with foreign policy and Books 10 and 13 deal with issues related to war. Interestingly, 'The Method of Science', is placed at the end rather than in the beginning of the *Arthashastra*.

Kautilya covered a wide range of topics, such as economic growth, taxation, government expenditure, administration, crime and punishment, property laws, consumer protection laws, labour laws, foreign trade, war and peace, principal-agent problem, diversification to reduce risk and many others. Essentially, anything related to the wealth and welfare of citizens is covered in the *Arthashastra*. He (p 100) summarizes the scope of the *Arthashastra* as: 'The science by which territory is acquired and maintained is *Arthashastra*—the science of wealth and welfare (15.1).' Ray (1999) believes that Kautilya's *Arthashastra* may be considered as the first treatise on conceptualizing a state based on *Loksamgraha* (welfare of all and performed in a manner that would be worthy of emulation by others). He (p 108) observes, 'Another element which was important was the motive. Since we do not have any control over outer conditions, we are permitted to act according to time, place and circumstances so long as our motive, over which we have absolute control, is clear, transparent; so long as we are inspired by the idea of the welfare of all (*Loksamgraha*) and not personal gratification, we are permitted everything. In formulating the entire statecraft on this principle, his system has not been superseded by any subsequent thinker. This was no doubt a departure from popular notions but in the time in which the idea of *Loksamgraha* was expressed, it had surely radical implications, decisively influencing the organization of the central state in India during the Mauryan and Gupta periods.'

Similarly, Drekmeier (1962, p 76) states, 'Now the king must concern himself directly with the common good, an idea anticipated in the *Arthashastra*.' Thus, according to Kautilya, the scope of economics is more like that of the contemporary economics, that is, it is limited only by one's imagination. However, it took more than two thousand years to restore its original scope.

3.5 KAUTILYA'S METHODOLOGY: A PARTIAL EQUILIBRIUM APPROACH

> Adhishthanam tatha karta, karanam cha prithagvidham,
> vividhashcha prithakcheshta, daivam chaivaatra panchamam
> — *Bhagawat Gita (2nd BCE, Chapter 18, Verse 14)*

> अधिष्ठानं तथा कर्ता करणं च पृथग्विधम्
> विविधाश्च पृथक्चेष्टा दैवं चैवात्र पंचमम्
> — *Bhagawat Gita (Ch 18, Verse 14)*

(The Base, the Doer, the different Equipments, different types of Efforts, and also Destiny.)

> शरीरवाङ्.मनोभिर्यत्कर्म प्रारब्धते नरः
> न्याय्यं या विपरीतं वा पंचैते तस्य हेतवः
> — *Bhagawat Gita (Ch 18, Verse 15)*

(Whatever actions, just or perverse, are performed by a person with his body, speech or mind, these five are always their causes.)

> Success (output) depends on five factors: initial conditions, doer (labour), tools (capital), managerial efforts and random variables (luck).
> — *Bhagawat Gita (Ch 18, Verse 14)*

Kautilya on the Role of Methodology: At the time of Kautilya, and also that of Adam Smith, there were no theoretical models, as we know them today.[8] There were just statements of hypotheses, and no formal proofs were offered. Also there were no tools available to test acceptance or rejection of these hypotheses. There are only verbal arguments in Kautilya's *Arthashastra*. Surprisingly, Book 15, which is the last one in the *Arthashastra*, has just one chapter and it deals exclusively with methodology adopted in writing it. Kautilya (p 101) stated, 'Thirty-two stylistic and logical devices are used in this work.' Some of them are just stylistic rules like the ones in the 'University of Chicago Manual of Style'. But others are more substantive, such as stating a hypothesis, a verbal (non-technical) reasoning to prove it, a conclusion and a recommendation.

Kautilya (p 101) explained, 'A statement is used to describe a conclusion or a rule. For example, {1.4.16}: The people of the four *Varnas* and the four walks of life follow their own *dharma* and pursue with devotion their occupations if they are protected by the king and the just use of *danda.*' That is, he puts forward the hypothesis that the maintenance of security and law and order is essential for people to pursue their occupations. He (p 103) stated, 'Reasoning is used to prove an assertion. In asserting [in {1.7.7}] that *artha* alone is supreme, the reason is given: "because *dharma* and *kama* depend on *artha*."' According to Kautilya, a poor person did not have the resources to enjoy life or to share with other needy people. He wrote, 'An analogy is used to establish an unknown with the help of the known. [For example, {2.1.18}:] "(the king) should treat leniently, like a father would treat his son, those settlers whose exemptions from taxes have ceased to be effective."' Kautilya's goal in establishing methodological rules was not to accelerate the creation of knowledge, rather to ensure that the reader understands him clearly. The sentence 'Easy to grasp and understand, free from verbosity, Kautilya has composed this treatise with precise words, doctrines and sense' reflects simplicity of expression as his overriding concern. Occasionally, he used historical facts to support his arguments.[9]

Usages of the Phrase 'Ceteris Paribus' ('Other Things Being Equal'): Whitaker (1987, Vol 1, p 396-397) distinguishes among its three different usages.
- The validity of a theory must assume the stability of a model's structure, viz., the quote from Gita uses this phrase in this sense, that is, no change in background conditions, particularly the place of operation
- constancy of certain exogenous variables, and
- assumptions regarding certain endogenous variables. The usage in this sense has three interpretations:
  ⇨ use of a partial equilibrium analysis as an approximation,
  ⇨ as a transitional step to a general equilibrium, and

⇨ 'experiments as heuristic aids sustaining general equilibrium theory'.

Implicit Use of 'Other Things Being Equal' by Kautilya: The use of this phrase has been more widespread than acknowledged by the modern writers. Kautilya was possibly the first economic thinker who implicitly used phrases similar to the phrase 'all things being equal' in economics. Two examples from his Book 7 are presented to support this claim.[10]

Kautilya (p 665) suggested (to the king), 'Where there is a choice between kings equally immune to the diplomacy of the aggressor, the weak king shall seek the protection of one who has better counselors and who surrounds himself with wise elders. When there is a choice between kings equally immune to the diplomacy and might of the aggressor, the one who had made more extensive preparations for war shall be preferred. When there is a choice between kings equally immune to the diplomacy, might and energy of the aggressor, he who has battlefields favorable to him shall be preferred; among those having equally favorable battlefields, he who can fight at a time suitable to him shall be preferred; among those equal in place and time of war, he who has better weapons and armor shall be preferred (7.15).'

A few points may be noted. Kautilya is engaged in thought experiments as to how a weak king should explore his choice set. He first compares two kings in terms of just two variables, adds the third variable while holding the other two variables constant and so on. This is essentially Whitaker's case two in which only certain exogenous variables are held constant, that is, Kautilya adopts a partial equilibrium approach. According to him, a weak king seeking protection should compare the relative physical might, intellectual power, war preparedness, weapons and other factors of all the kings under consideration. Formally, this may be expressed as:

$$U = f(\Delta M, \Delta H, \Delta R, \Delta W...)$$

Where U= a weak king's utility; the difference between the strengths of two other kings, $\Delta M = M^1 - M^2$; the difference between their intellectual powers, $\Delta H = H^1 - H^2$; the difference between their readiness for war, $\Delta R = R^1 - R^2$; and the difference between the quality of their weapons, $\Delta W = W^1 - W^2$. Since Kautilya assumes $\Delta M = \Delta I = \Delta R = 0$. Then, Kautilya's analysis implies that the partial derivative $\partial U / \partial W > 0$.

In other words, if two kings were equal in might, intellectual powers and readiness for war (this amounts to the Marshallian phrase 'all other things being equal'), and $\Delta W > 0$ (ie. the quality of weapon of king one was better than that of king two), then the weak king should seek protection from the first king. Thus, his analytical approach is identical to that of Marshall.

Kautilya (p 609) wrote, 'When, among a group of allies, many give equal help in terms of manpower, it is specially advantageous to get the troops from one whose troops are valorous, able to tolerate hardship, loyal and versatile (7.9).' Formally this may be specified as:

$$U = U (\Delta L, \Delta V)$$

Where $\Delta L = L_1 - L_2$, $\Delta V = V_1 - V_2$, L and V indicate manpower and valor, respectively.

According to Kautilya, if $\Delta L = 0$ (ie. the two kings supplied the same number of soldiers), $\partial U / \partial V > 0$ implying that the soldiers with a higher level of valor should be preferred. There are many additional situations to which this methodology that 'all other things being equal' was used by Kautilya.

Use of Marginal Analysis by Kautilya: Kautilya implicitly used discrete marginal analysis.[11] It is shown in the three examples from Books 2, 6 and 7, which are also related to foreign policy.

Kautilya (p 259) stated, 'With increased wealth and a powerful army more territory can be acquired, thereby further increasing the wealth of the state (2.12)'. Two points are in order. First, he was referring to a dynamic process, and secondly, to increments in wealth, army and territory.

Kautilya (p 553) stated, 'Applying these [active and passive policies] may result in any one of the following: decline, progress, or no change in one's position (6.2).' He (p 553) proceeded to define these concepts as follows: 'A king makes progress by building forts, irrigation works or trade routes, creating new settlements, elephant forests or productive forests, or opening new mines. Any activity, which harms the progress of the enemy engaged in similar undertakings, is also progress. However, a king may ignore an enemy's progress if his own progress will be quicker or greater [than that of his enemy] or if there is a prospect of greater future gain. A king suffers a decline when his own initiatives are ruined or when the enemy's undertakings prosper. When there is neither progress nor decline, the situation is said to be one of "no change" (7.1).' Thus, according to him, progress, and no change, may be indicated by $\Delta Y = [\Delta Y_d - \Delta Y_e] \geq 0$ and a decline by $\Delta Y < 0$, where ΔY_d and ΔY_e represent changes in incomes of domestic and enemy's economies respectively.

Kautilya (p 565) argued, 'When the degree of progress is the same in pursuing peace and waging war, peace is to be preferred. For, in war, there are disadvantages such as losses, expenses and absence from home (7.2).' Kautilya clearly emphasized the concept of additional net gain in making comparisons between choices. Interestingly, in calculating the net gain, he netted out the disutility of staying away from home. Thus, according to Kautilya, a king should not wage a war unless the net gain from a war ($\Delta Y_w - C$) was greater than that in pursuing peace (ΔY_p), that is, unless ($\Delta Y_w - C$) > ΔY_p, where C=loss of men, material and disutility of staying away from home.

3.6 ON OPTIMIZATION SUBJECT TO CONSTRAINTS

At present, utility maximization by the consumer, subject to his budget constraint or output maximization by a firm subject to its resource constraint or some other optimization problem subject to constraints, is a well-established practice. However, its re-emergence is not that old. Allingham (1987, p 883) points out, 'The wealth constraint first appears explicitly in the writings of the neoclassical school, and particularly in the work of Walras (1874-7). However, it is first made use of rigorously by Slutsky (1915) and then Hicks (1946).'

Kautilya (p 115) explained, 'If only one method is recommended, it is defined as 'placing a restriction', if a choice is suggested, it is an 'option' and if two or more are to be used together, it is a 'combination' (9.7)'. He used optimization subject to resource constraints. He (p 199-200) suggested, 'The five aspects of deliberating on any question are: (i) the objectives to be achieved; (ii) the means of carrying out the task; (iii) the availability of men and material; (iv) deciding on the time and place of action; and (v) contingency plans against failure (1.15).'

Specification of an objective and the phrase *'availability of men and material'* clearly establish optimization, subject to constraints. Of course, the non-availability of calculus or the method of Lagrange multipliers would not allow him to undertake any formal analysis. Kautilya (p 166) explained the phrase *'means of carrying out'* as 'Of the four means of dealing with dangers, [conciliation, placating with gifts, sowing dissension and use of force], it is easier to employ a method earlier in the order (9.6).'

Another insight in formulating a policy may be noted. According to Kautilya, a contingency planning against unexpected outcomes was an essential ingredient of a sound policy. Stein (1996) points out about the Council of Economic Advisers (CEA) does not undertake any contingency planning. He remarks, 'The CEA, like the government as a whole, is deficient in contingency planning. I think the council has been good about giving the President a fair picture of his options. It has been less good about preparing him for the possibility that the option he selects turns out not to have the expected consequences.'

3.7 TIME-PREFERENCE AND INTER-TEMPORAL ARBITRAGE

> A pigeon today is better than a peacock tomorrow.
> — *Kautilya (Subramanian 2000, p 60)*

Usually, the credit for inventing the inter-temporal choice goes to John Rae (1834).[12] Apparently, Kautilya also offered many applications involving inter-temporal choices. Similarly, the credit for making the distinction between short-run and long run is given to Marshall.

Although, Kautilya did not analyze the short-run and long run cost curves like Marshall, but he was aware of the analytical relevance of such a distinction. A few instances from the *Arthashastra* would clarify the position:

There are at least two places in the *Arthashastra* where intertemporal arbitrage is discernible. Kautilya (p 635), while defining various kinds of gains whether they were temporary, permanent, safe, righteous, growing or great, wrote, 'A great gain is a substantial gain available immediately (9.4).' He (p 636) suggested, 'When the gains from two campaigns are equal, the king shall compare the following qualities and choose the one which has more good points: place and time; the power and the means required to acquire it; the pleasure or displeasure caused by it; speed or slowness of getting it; the proximity or distance, the immediate and future consequences; its high value or constant worth; and its abundance or variety (9.4).' According to him, if the gains from two campaigns were the same, the one, which had a stable worth, and was available quickly was preferable. Incidentally, the phrase *'speed or slowness of getting it'* indicates that he had some idea of discounting and the phrase *'the immediate and future consequences'* indicates that he also made a distinction between short-run and long run. It is obvious that he initiated the discussion on making inter-temporal choices.

Similarly, Kautilya (p 617) asked, 'Which is preferable—an immediate small gain or a large gain in the future?' According to him, the answer depended on two factors: 'A large gain in the future is preferable if it is like a seed [yielding fruit in the future] and if it is not likely to disappear [before fruition]. Otherwise, [if there is no growth and if there is a danger of it not fructifying] the small immediate gain is preferable (7.9).'

He explained that the choice between accepting a small gain immediately and a large gain in the future depended on two factors. First, what was the nature of the gain? Was it like a seed, which had a potential for growth? Secondly, how certain it was? Was it likely to disappear before it materialized?[13] He would have preferred the gain available at time G^t, if its discounted value were higher than that of the gain available immediately G^0.

Kautilya (p 158) stated, 'A king shall employ, without hesitation, the methods of secret punishment against traitors in his own camp and against enemies; but he should do so with forbearance keeping in mind the future consequences as well as immediate results (5.1).'

He discussed the immediate and future impacts of several policies. For example, he (p 642) wrote, 'helping a neighbour on the flank of the enemy with money or troops [without asking for payment; immediate loss of money or troops but long-term gain]' (9.7). That is, the immediate effect was negative but long-term impact might be positive.

Kautilya (p 594) asserted, 'A king may agree to forego a large immediate gain and seek [only] a small future benefit if he intends to use again the partner who is being helped (7.8)'. Along with the distinction between short-run and long run, it is also apparent that Kautilya believed in reputation building.

3.8 *ARTHASHASTRA* ON ECONOMICS AS A SEPARATE DISCIPLINE

As mentioned earlier, guidelines provided by Grampp are strictly followed in making the interpretations of Kautilya's *Arthashastra*. Ultimately, for Kautilya's *Arthashastra* to qualify as the first word on economics and Kautilya its founder, it has to cross the high bar set by Schumpeter (1954).

Economics as a Separate Discipline: According to Kautilya (p 105-106), 'traditionally, philosophy, the three *Vedas*, economics and the science of government are considered to be the four branches of knowledge. However, the followers of the *Arthashastra* of Prachetasa Manu say that there are only three branches— the three *Vedas*, economics and the science of government. For [to them,] philosophy is only a special branch of Vedic studies. The school of Brihaspati considers only economics and politics to be true branches of knowledge; [they argue that] those experienced in the ways of the world use the *Vedas* only as a cover [in order to avoid the accusation of being materialistic atheists]. The school of Ushanas maintains that politics is the only science; because, they say, it is in that science all other sciences have their beginning and end. Kautilya holds that there are, indeed, four branches of knowledge. Because one can know from these four branches, all that is to be learnt about *dharma* [spiritual welfare] and *artha* [material well-being] they are called 'knowledge'. Philosophy is the lamp that illuminates all sciences; it provides the techniques for all action; and it is the pillar, which supports *dharma*. Further, 'Samkhya, Yoga and atheistic are the three schools of philosophy. One should study philosophy because it helps one to distinguish between *dharma* and *adharma* [evil] in the study of the *Vedas*, between material gain and loss in the study of economics and between good and bad policies in the study of politics. [Above all] it teaches one the distinction between good and bad use of force. When the other sciences are studied by the light of philosophy, people are benefited because their minds are kept steady in adversity and prosperity and they are made proficient in thought, speech and action (1.2).'

The above statements make it clear that Kautilya identified economics as a separate discipline. It is claimed, as explained below, that Kautilya carved out the very first inter-disciplinary matrix.

Table 3.1: **Kautilya's Inter-Disciplinary Matrix**

	Political Science	Economics	Vedas	Philosophy
Political Science	A_{11}	A_{12}	A_{13}	A_{14}
Economics	A_{21}	A_{22}	A_{23}	A_{24}
Vedas	A_{31}	A_{32}	A_{33}	A_{34}
Philosophy	A_{41}	A_{42}	A_{43}	A_{44}

Interdependence among Different Disciplines: A discipline contributes in three ways. Ideas in a discipline may provide the seeds to create more ideas in its own field, in other disciplines and may help in developing better public policies or better products. It may be noted that the elements of this matrix could be matrices themselves. Kautilya established economics as a separate discipline. However, according to Kautilya, establishment of economics as a separate discipline did not mean its independence from other disciplines. That is, economics could provide and receive inputs from other disciplines.

Economics and Political Science: Kautilya's inter-disciplinary matrix is essentially hierarchical. Economics does provide inputs to political science but it does not receive any direct input from political science. For example, the king is supposed to carry out the cost-benefit analysis before undertaking a project, that is, economic concepts are used to improve the functioning of the government. Clearly, economics has been colonizing the other disciplines since antiquity.

Economics and *Vedas*: According to Kautilya, unless the survival of the state is threatened, ethical values should set the boundaries for all endeavours including economic ones. He (p 107) emphasized the basic *dharmic* (moral) duties of individuals as 'Duties common to all: Ahimsa [abstaining from injury to all living creatures]; Satyam [truthfulness]; cleanliness; freedom from malice; compassion and tolerance (1.3)'. Independence of economic thought from religion in itself was not a small feat since, even almost two thousand years after the Vedas, Galileo, who only indirectly challenged religion, was faced with Inquisition.

Anviksiki (Philosophy) and Economics: Kautilya believed that philosophy was 'privileged knowledge', and was an input to all other branches of knowledge. According to him, philosophy provided the reasoning in distinguishing between good and bad and between ethical and unethical actions. Also the line 'it provides the techniques for all action' is noteworthy; it implies that philosophy sheds light on methodological issues in all branches of knowledge including economics. Kautilya dedicated his work to Om (God or moral values) and Brihaspati and Sukra (political thinkers and gurus), implying that his goal was to strike a proper balance between material and spiritual well-being of the people.

Economic Knowledge and Public Policy: Marshall (1920, p 757), while acknowledging the contributions of the Physiocrats asserted, 'They thus gave to economics its modern aim of seeking after such knowledge as may help to raise the quality of human life.' Regarding the aim of the *Arthashastra*, Kautilya (p 100) wrote, 'By following [the principles set out in] this treatise one can not only create and preserve *dharma* [spiritual good], *artha* [material well-being] and *kama* [aesthetic pleasures] but also destroy [their opposites, ie.] unrighteousness, material loss and hatred. It is a guide not only for the acquisition of this world but also the next (15.1).' Thus, contrary to Marshall's assertion, the above statement by Kautilya and the presentations of his views on various public policies in other studies, indicate that such a change in the goals of economic knowledge had occurred much earlier than the Physiocrats.

Concepts Originated by Kautilya: Some of the concepts may be as old as mankind. Therefore, the critical question is: how did Kautilya use these concepts? And was he coherent in their use? Kautilya referred to eleven schools of thought before him.[14] It indicates that he could access the earlier works in physical form or through the practice of oral transmission from teacher to disciple or a combination of the two. These schools existed at different times and there were no 'competing research programmes' at one single time. Rangarajan (the editor of the *Arthashastra*) observes (p 817), 'The subjects on which Kautilya disagrees with earlier teachers are not many: the nature of the sciences, the number of ministers, the process of deliberation, fines for erring officials, the punishments for perjury and robbery, and calamities, including the discussion on anger and lust, are the more important ones. Most of the disagreements with the unidentified teachers are concentrated in the books on calamities and foreign policy.'

Two points are worth noting. First, it is important to point out that Kautilya originated several of the important concepts in economics while discussing calamities (Book 8) and foreign policy (Books: 6, 7, 9, 11, and 12). Secondly, what matters are the method, coherence and level of reasoning and not on how many topics Kautilya differed on from his predecessors. He did not accept any point without sound reasoning. His scientific methodology blended with rich content set him apart from his predecessors. Kautilya's *Arthashastra* has many concepts, which may be classified into two categories: (i) those originated by pre-Kautilyan writers and he refined and adapted them and (ii) those originated by Kautilya himself.

Refinements of the Existing Concepts by Kautilya: Some concepts, like 'bounded rationality', were advanced by Kautilya's predecessors as the primary reason for the establishment of a bureaucratic set-up. However, Kautilya elevated the discussion to a higher level by adding the importance of designing a bureaucratic system, which minimized the possibilities of conflict of interest. The identification of wage, rent, profit and interest as different factor payments by his predecessors was remarkable. But Kautilya saw the role of land, labour and capital as sources of economic growth and thus provided a modern interpretation. Finances were always critical to the maintenance of any kingdom and, therefore, some fiscal issues were discussed by his predecessors. However, Kautilya extended that in two directions, viz.: (i) there were limits to taxation and (ii) that tax revenue be directed to the provision of infrastructure, which increased income and consequently to more tax revenue; that is, instead of increasing the tax rate, he suggested enlarging the tax base. Similarly, law and order issues were considered critical to the stability of the kingdom and, therefore, reducing criminal activity through punishment was discussed by pre-Kautilyan writers. But Kautilya (p 377) qualified, 'It is the power of punishment alone, when exercised impartially in proportion to the guilt, and irrespective of whether the person punished is the king's son or an enemy, that protects this world and the next.' Kautilya's predecessors understood the logic of backward induction but Kautilya added the role of asymmetric information in bargaining and the time inconsistency problem. There are numerous other extensions and refinements undertaken by Kautilya.

Creation of a Core of Economic Knowledge by Kautilya: First, it may be noted that most of the words we use today, such as, principal-agent, asymmetric information, time inconsistency have been coined only very recently. But that does not mean that the earlier writers did not understand them or use them. In fact, Kautilya initiated the exploration of 'science of man'. For example, he (p 283) suggested, 'The king shall have the work of Heads of Departments inspected daily, for men are, by nature, fickle and, like horses, change after being put to work (2.9).' Secondly, as discussed above, the origin of a concept is attributed to Kautilya only if it can be 'found or read into' the *Arthashastra*, has a reasonably substantive discussion and correct application. Based on these criteria, more than a score of basic ideas in economics can be found in Kautilya's *Arthashastra*.

A partial list of some important concepts contained in The *Arthashastra* is: (i) opportunity cost, (ii) basic demand and supply apparatus, (iii) the law of diminishing returns, (iv) externalities, (v) undesirability of monopoly and monopsony and need for regulation, (vi) moral hazard, (vii) role of law and order, (viii) public goods, (ix) Kautilya-curve (nowadays called Dupuit-Laffer curve), (x) producer surplus, (xi) importance of human and physical capital accumulation to economic growth, (xii) role of infrastructure in economic growth, (xiii) theory of gains from trade and terms of trade, (xiv) principal-agent problem, (xv) efficiency wages (xvi) specification of explanation and prediction as the goals of an economic inquiry, (xvii) role of asymmetric information in bargaining, and (xviii) time inconsistency problem. Kautilya synthesized and refined the existing ideas at his time. But his true genius lay in innovating the novel concepts, such as, the optimization principle (see the next chapter for its exposition). Kautilya (p 609) stated, 'When equal monetary help is given, it is specially advantageous to get it from one who readily complies with requests, is generous, gives continuously and without much effort (7.9).'

A Set of Hypotheses Proposed by Kautilya: He advanced several hypotheses. A few of them may be listed here: (i) human effort and capital accumulation were the sources of economic growth; (ii) heavy taxation lead to the erosion of tax base; (iii) 'prosperity changes peoples' minds'; (iv) information was the key to better decision making; (v) justice and rule of law were the pre-requisites for economic growth, and (vi) consumer durable goods faced unstable demand.

Schumpeter's Test: The Vedic sages, much before Kautilya, had realized that system-building was essential to peace and harmony and suggested *dharmic* virtues to ensure its creation (presented in Chapter 6). Kautilya expanded the role of system-building further to nation-building. He developed the concept of systemic risk, identified its sources and suggested effective measures to lower it (systemic-risk arising from a famine is presented in Chapter 13). He conceptualized the whole system and how its different components interacted with each other. For example, he understood how growth in income affected governance and national security and how, in turn, it got affected by them (see details in Chapters 8 and 18).

In summary, Kautilya's *Arthashastra* does contain what Schumpeter (p 248) called a 'theoretical skeleton' and thus it cannot be labelled pre-scientific. The above analysis establishes that Kautilya's *Arthashastra* declares economics as a distinct discipline and thus satisfies the first requirement to declare it as the first origin of economics. It is also indicated that the *Arthashastra* considers economics as the 'science of man' and contains a logically consistent and adequate core of economic knowledge. These concepts, at least in some moderate detail, are presented in other chapters establishing that economics originated as a separate discipline for more than two millennia ago. The analysis in Kautilya's *Arthashastra* dispels the myth that Hindu civilization is inimical to economic growth and also sheds some light on issues like 'second generation' economic reforms in India, since it is essentially a treatise on the imperative of economic growth. Otherwise also, as per the core Hindu thought to which Kautilya subscribed, pursuit of *artha* (material well being) is regarded as one of the four *purusharthas* (human enterprise worth pursuing).

SUMMARY

Kautilya specified a very broad scope of economics, more like in the post-modern era with some imperialistic tendencies of colonizing other disciplines. His methodology is essentially Marshallian: the use of partial equilibrium approach and the making of a distinction between the short-run and the long run. Kautilya recommended the use of optimization, subject to constraints methodology. But the mode of implementing this methodology was beyond his capabilities. Also, discrete marginal analysis is discernible from his analysis. Contrary to the claim by Ekelund and Hebert, Dupuit was not the first one to use *ceteris paribus* clause or the marginal analysis. Besides Kautilya,

Bernoulli also used the *ceteris paribus* clause earlier than Dupuit. On the other hand, despite the availability of calculus, Adam Smith did not use either the marginal analysis or the *ceteris paribus* clause.

The following table provides a summary of the contributions of Kautilya, Adam Smith and Dupuit regarding the scope and methodology etc. of economics.

Table 3.2: **A Summary of Requirements & Origins of Economics**

Requirements Proposed by	Characterization of Economics as a Science	Kautilya's *Arthashastra* Fourth Century BCE	Adam Smith's the *Wealth of Nations* 1776	Dupuit and other Engineers 1830-1870
Groenewegen	Definition	Broad like today	Narrow	Narrower
	Scope	Broad like today	Narrow	Narrower
Spiegel	Separate	Yes	No	
Marshall	Writing a treatise	Yes	Yes	No
Barber, Dupuit, Landreth and Colander	Number of concepts	Reasonable	Reasonable	Very Few
	Original	Many	Just one or two	A few
	Synthesis	Yes	Yes	No
	Consistent	Yes	Not always	Yes
Schumpeter	Economy as a system	Yes	Yes	No
	Method or tooled knowledge	Scientific	Pre-scientific	Scientific

Groenewegen (2002) identifies three origins of economics based on the definition of economics: (i) at the end of the 17th century, if application of scientific method to economic phenomenon is considered its definition, (ii) to the third quarter of the 18th century if its subject matter consists of production and distribution of wealth, and (iii) at the end of 19th century if Robbins' definition of economics is taken (ie. allocation of scarce resources among alternative uses). Actually, Kautilya's *Arthashastra* is broader in scope than Robbins' definition of economics and, therefore, qualifies to be the true origin of the engineering approach to economics.

Kautilya was the first one, who wrote a treatise on economics, carried out brilliant synthesis of existing ideas, originated more than a score of basic concepts in economics, provided coherent interpretations and most importantly, understood economy as an interdependent system of various elements and thus clearing the high bar set by Schumpeter. Long before Adam Smith, Kautilya had founded economics to provide human security to every citizen.

4

A Forerunner of Neoclassical Price Theory

> Merchants who were authorized to sell Crown commodities, at prices fixed by the Chief Controller, had to compensate the government for the loss sustained in forgoing the profit that would have been made, had the goods sold through Crown outlets.
>
> —*Kautilya (p 266)*

Recently, Manski (2000) identified preferences, expectations, constraints and equilibrium as the core concepts in economics. These concepts may be relevant for providing some broad guidelines for keeping the analysis focused. However, this apparent parsimony of concepts is illusory since each one of these concepts may contain more unknowns than a Pandora's box. Moreover, some concepts may appear fundamental at a particular time in the evolution of a discipline but then become trivial or are dropped completely. During the classical period, concepts like centre of gravity, and normal price were considered central to economic analysis but neoclassical analysis made them obsolete. Similarly, thanks to the information revolution, even the fundamental theorems of welfare are not that fundamental any more. Many other concepts like competition and equilibrium have evolved into something much different.

However, at least, opportunity cost, demand and supply apparatus, diminishing returns and the rationality axioms are still considered fundamental. Also, by putting some of these basic concepts at one place, their unnecessary repetition is avoided. The objective is to place Kautilya's contributions in terms of the historical development of such core concepts in economics subject to two caveats. First, ideas do not originate in finished form ready to be used. This is not uncommon in the history of thought.[1] Secondly, the originator of an idea may not understand its full potential. For example, Edgeworth conceived the concept of indifference curves but did not appreciate its significance. As Samuelson (1983, p 206) remarks, 'To a man like Edgeworth, steeped as he was in the Utilitarian tradition, individual utility—nay social utility—was as real as his morning jam.' Therefore, one should be liberal in interpreting earlier writers or allowing what Samuelson calls 'a little charity' to the earlier writings, without which even Adam Smith would not be what he has been claimed to be.

Many modern concepts, such as ordinal preferences and isoquants are implicit and can be constructed from Kautilya's analysis but he did not use them to derive the demand or supply curves. Similarly, the law of diminishing returns can be established from the statements contained in the *Arthashastra*. Discussion related to these concepts is provided in Sections 4.1 and 4.2. Adam Smith (also Ricardo) identified just one point and a maximum possible stretch of imagination is required to construct a demand or supply schedule from it. It is claimed that with very little imagination, demand and supply schedules can be constructed from Kautilya's analysis. Section 4.3 contains his understanding of the demand-supply apparatus but it is not claimed that Kautilya had a fully developed Marshallian cross.

4.1 ANTICIPATION OF ORDINAL PREFERENCES

Ordinal Preferences: Obviously, individuals made decisions relating to work and consumption of various goods and services before Bentham's (1789) measurement of utility or disutility from pain and pleasure.[2] Kautilya's ideas shed some light on the debate on cardinal versus ordinal approaches to the utility theory since he could not have foreseen it.[3] Throughout the *Arthashastra*, decisions are based on comparisons between different alternatives and it seems that the ordinal approach is more natural than the cardinal approach.

The Axiom of Comparison: It should be noted that despite the fact that Ricardo and many others never conceived the indifference curves, isoquants and production possibility frontier, it has become a well-accepted practice to use such modern tools to express their ideas. These modern tools can be used to express Kautilya's ideas even if he was unaware of them. However, the rationality axioms of comparison and consistency are discernible in Kautilya's analysis. For example, he (p 609) stated, 'When equal monetary help is given, it is specially advantageous to get it from one who readily complies with requests, is generous, gives continuously and without much effort (7.9).' Figure 4.1 is used to express this comparison.

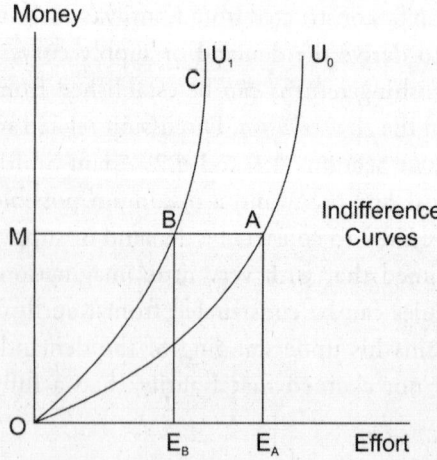

Figure 4.1: U_0 and U_1 are the indifference curves representing the various combinations of effort and money. Point B on indifference curve U_1 indicates (OM, OE_B) combination of money and effort and point A on indifference curve U_0 indicates (OM, OE_A) combination of money and effort.

A Forerunner of Neoclassical Price Theory

Kautilya is comparing two bundles consisting of money and effort. Point B with less effort and the same money is preferred to point A with same money but more effort. It is quite revealing that he assigned disutility to effort. Interestingly, in comparing the two bundles, say A and B, he considered the ranking of the choices, such as, B was preferred over A, but left out the ranking regarding indifference between them. That is, he did not compare points like B and C on the same indifference curve U_1, implying that he did not trace the whole indifference curve (may be choices like C were not available). However, Schumpeter did not know the existence of the *Arthashastra* and, instead, gave credit to Senior for introducing the axiomatic approach. He (p 575) states, 'To Senior belongs the signal honor of having been the first to make attempt to state, consciously and explicitly, the postulates that are necessary and sufficient in order to build up—it is misleading to say to "deduce"—that little analytic apparatus commonly known as economic theory, or, to put differently, to provide for an axiomatic basis.'

The Axiom of Consistency: A fort was built to protect lives and property. Kautilya ranked different forts in terms of providing protection. He (p 622) stated, 'Among forts of different types — a land fort, a river fort or a mountain fort— one later in the list is preferable to one earlier [ie. order of ascending importance] (7.12).'

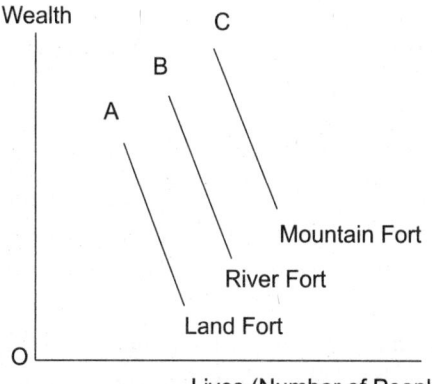

Figure 4.2: Indifference curves A, B and C represent the various combinations of wealth and lives saved by having a land fort, a river fort or a mountain fort, respectively. Alternatively, the indifference curves could be considered as the combinations of probability of protecting wealth and the probability of protecting lives.

He ranked the various forts according to the level of security provided by them. He believed that a mountain fort was likely to protect more lives and more property than a river fort, which was likely to protect more than a land fort implying that a mountain fort was preferred to a land fort. His analysis was probably confined to the comparisons of points A, B and C and clearly he preferred C to B, B to A implying C to A, that is, he fully understood the axiom of consistency.

Slope of the Indifference Curves: Kautilya (p 137) stated, 'Making enemies is worse than losing one's wealth; the latter only causes financial distress while the former endangers life itself (8.3).' He (p 664) added, 'It is life that is worth preserving not wealth which, being impermanent, can be given up without regrets (12.1).' This statement implies almost vertical indifference curves: giving up all the wealth to save a life. Apparently, he fully understood the axiom of consistency. But he did not see the need, or was unable to appreciate the significance of the ranking of being indifferent between choices. Surprisingly, despite the incomplete ordering, he extensively and correctly used comparisons in choosing between alternatives. Therefore, he has a serious claim to be a forerunner of the concept of ordinal preferences.[4]

4.2 COST, PRODUCTION AND SUBSTITUTION POSSIBILITIES

Definition of Opportunity Cost[5]: According to Buchanan (1987, p 719), 'Opportunity cost is the evaluation placed on the most highly valued of the rejected alternatives or opportunities.' He (p 721) concludes, 'Opportunity cost is a basic concept in economic theory.'

Application of Opportunity Cost by Kautilya: There are numerous applications of this concept in the *Arthashastra*, but only a few of them are presented to support this claim. It is significant that, in each application, Kautilya emphasized what Buchanan calls 'choice-influencing rather than choice-influenced' property of the opportunity cost and 'the *ex ante* or forward-looking property that cost must carry in this setting'. It may be mentioned that the frequency of use of the words 'ca' and 'va' in different chapters of the *Arthashastra* has been adopted by Trautmann (1971) to test its internal consistency, ie. to test whether it was written by one author, an approach challenged by Mital (2000). On the other hand, a more reliable indicator of an internal consistency may be to find out whether or not a concept has been used consistently in various contexts. It is shown below that there is an internal consistency in the use of the concept of opportunity cost in the formulation of economic policies, foreign affairs and other applications throughout the *Arthashastra*. This fact alone should be sufficient to exclude the possibility of multiple authors.

Compensation for the Profit Foregone: Kautilya proposed a mixed economy in which the state had a monopoly in the manufacture of certain goods. According to him, the Director of Trade should evaluate what would be the loss to the state, should he authorize private traders to sell such products rather than selling those through the state's own outlets? Kautilya (p 266) determined the loss as: 'Merchants who were authorized to sell Crown commodities, at prices fixed by the Chief Controller, had to compensate the government for the loss sustained in foregoing the profit that would have been made had the goods sold through Crown outlets (2.16).' The word 'foregoing' is noteworthy and compensation for the loss was not demanded after making the decision, ie. the state did not have to authorize private traders if they were not willing to compensate the state for the anticipated loss of profits.

Opportunity Cost of Giving up a Factor of Production: Negishi (1989, p 26) notes, 'The significance of the utility theory of value is much greater, unlike in the case of Walras, for the Austrian school of Menger and his followers. They developed the concept of the opportunity cost—that cost is nothing but the utility lost—and considered that values of the factors of production are imputed from the utility values of consumers' goods.' Kautilya did not specify the opportunity cost of giving up a factor of production in terms of utility lost or income foregone. Rather, it was expressed as a combination of both.

Ranking the Opportunity Costs of Various Choices: He discussed the terms and conditions of a peace treaty between two kings in which, reneging by the other one on a commitment was a strong possibility. Usually in such situations, a hostage was demanded to serve as a shield against aggression by the other. He offered some guidelines to a king as to who should be given as a hostage, such that if need be, he could break his commitment at the lowest possible cost. He evaluated and ranked the opportunity costs of alternative choices related to hostage giving.

Kautilya believed that the power of sound analysis and judgment enhanced economic development directly as well as indirectly by strengthening national security, which was considered as a prerequisite for economic development which, in turn, enhanced the power of the army through increases in tax revenue, and also won public support. Accordingly, he (p 600) suggested in the context of providing a hostage, 'When there is choice between a wise son and a brave son, it is better to give the brave son, who though valorous, lacks wisdom. For, a wise son, though timid, uses his intelligence in his endeavours; like the hunter outwitting the elephant, the intelligent outwit the brave (7.17).' [If a king was forced to give up a son, he should give a brave son as a hostage.] Since the opportunity cost in terms of loss in national security and economic growth of giving up a wise son, who

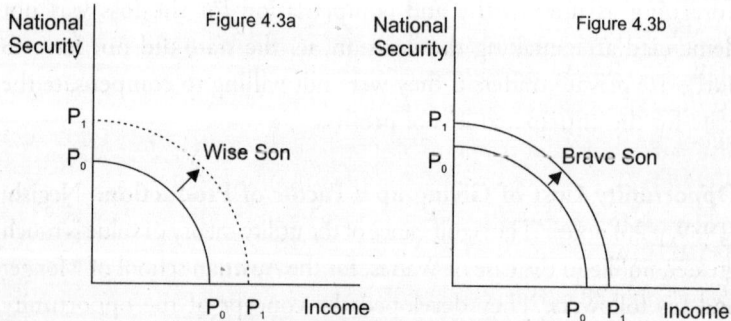

Both in **Figure 4.3a** and **Figure 4.3b** P_0P_0 is the initial production possibility frontier (PPF) representing the various combinations of income and national security. The larger shift in the PPF from P_0P_0 to P_1P_1 in Figure 4.3a represents the potential contribution of a wise son and the relatively smaller shift from P_0P_0 to P_1P_1 in Figure 4.3b represents the contribution of a brave son.

'uses his intelligence in his endeavours' was much higher than that of a brave son. The above figures may be used to express these ideas.

Opportunity Cost of a Wise Son: According to Kautilya, a wise son (a future king) could help much more than a brave son in enhancing national security and income than a brave son (ie. the shift in the production possibility frontier was much larger). The shift in the production possibility frontier in Figure 4.3a captures the opportunity cost in terms of enhanced national security and income of giving up a wise son.

Opportunity Cost of Giving-up a Brave Son: The shift in the production possibility frontier in Figure 4.3b provides a measure of the opportunity cost of a brave son. Usually, opportunity cost is calculated on the same production possibility frontier by shifting inputs from production, say of butter, to the production of gunpowder, that is, how many pounds of butter have to be given-up to get an extra pound of gunpowder. In the current example, the opportunity cost was measured in terms of giving up national security and prosperity by giving a son as a hostage. This is like asking today: what would be the opportunity cost of a scientist if he/she moves from a developing country to a developed country? There are two ways to measure it: (i) How much of something else could have been produced by the resources used to ᴛᴀin the scientist? Or (ii) how much the scientist could contribute to the developing country over his/her lifetime? Kautilya seems to adopt the second method of measuring opportunity cost, which is the appropriate and forward-looking one for such a purpose.

Zero Opportunity Cost of a Useless Factor: Another insight may also be noted. Kautilya showed awareness of the advantages of bargaining with private information. The king knew the strengths and weaknesses of his sons and daughters but the other king did not. Kautilya was aware of the zero opportunity cost of giving up a useless factor. He (p 599) stated, 'He who, gives a treacherous minister or a treacherous son or daughter as a hostage outmanoeuvres the other [the receiver]. The receiver is outmanoeuvred because the giver will strike without compunction at the weak point— ie. the trust that the receiver has that the giver will not let the hostage come to harm (7.17).' This is very significant since even the neoclassicals did not realize that a factor could have zero opportunity cost.[6] These examples show that Kautilya fully understood and consistently and correctly applied the concept of opportunity cost throughout the *Arthashastra*.

Law of Diminishing Returns: Regarding Kautilya's knowledge of the concept of diminishing returns, Spengler (1971, p 71) observes, 'He does not explicitly recognize the tendency to Ricardian diminishing returns, implicit in his account of the quite unequally colonizable and unevenly cultivable character of India's lands.' This is a very significant observation since it makes the debate over priority to Smith or to Ricardo for diminishing returns irrelevant.[7] However, Spengler's observation may demand some justification.

Kautilya understood that the yield from a piece of land depended on its quality along with other inputs. He discussed at length the varying quality of land (just like Ricardo) and suggested putting taxes (to replenish the treasury) corresponding to the yield from them. He (Kangle, part II, p 296) recommended to a king, 'He should demand a third or a fourth part of the grains from a region, whether big or small in size, that is not dependent on rains and yields abundant crops; from a middling or inferior one, according to yield (5.2).' Apparently, tax was imposed according to the yield, which depended on the quality of land and the best land was the one that had a permanent source of water ('yields abundant crops').

Similarly, according to Kautilya, in planning joint campaigns with other kings, a king should try to negotiate for land of superior quality. He (p 619) stated, 'As between land dependent on rain and land with flowing water, a smaller tract with flowing water is preferable to a larger drier one because with flowing water, which is always available, the production of crops is assured. As between two rain-fed tracts, that which is conducive to the growth of both early and late crops and which requires less labour and less rain for cultivation is preferable (7.11).' He (p 621) added, 'If settlement of a tract is likely to entail heavy losses or expenditure, a king shall first sell the land, with the intention of reacquiring it, to one who will fail in the attempt at settlement (7.11).'

It is apparent from the above statements that Kautilya ranked different tracts of land according to their quality: (i) a dry tract of land (C), which permitted two crops (ie. higher yield) with 'less labour and less rain'. (ii) The next best was a dry tract of land (B), which permitted only one crop and also needed relatively larger amounts of labour and rain compared to case (i), and (iii) at the bottom of the list was quite inferior land (A), which required excessive amount of expenditure to settle it. He implicitly displayed knowledge of three important concepts: the trade-off between risk and return, the law of diminishing returns (and rent), and the production function. These ideas may be illustrated by Figure 4.4.

Diminishing Returns: Kautilya explicitly mentioned that as the quality of land decreased from type (i) to (iii), increasing amounts of labour (and also rain in some cases) were required to produce a given amount of output. More specifically, the production of output, Y would require increasing amounts of labour, L_C, L_B, and L_A on

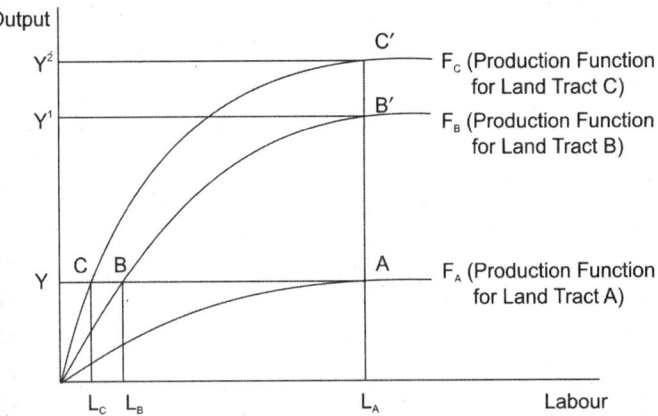

Figure 4.4: F_A, F_B and F_C are the production functions for the poorest quality Land Tract A, middle quality Land Tract B and the best quality Land Tract C, respectively, and L_A, L_B, and L_C are the respective amounts of labour required to produce Y amount of grains. Output $Y^1 Y^2$ represents the rent on Land Tract C and $Y Y^1$ is the loss on Land Tract A.

land tracts C, B and A, respectively. It is apparent that Kautilya's understanding of diminishing returns is at par with that of the classicists Adam Smith and Ricardo.

Rent: Alternatively, Labour, L_A can produce output Y on land tract A, output Y^1 on land tract B, and output Y^2 on land tract C implying that tract C is preferable to tract B, which is preferable to tract A. Thus output $Y^1 Y^2$ may be defined as rent on tract C, there is no rent on tract B and tract A 'is likely to entail heavy losses or expenditure' that is, there is a loss of $Y Y^1$.

Production Function: Kautilya did not provide any formal definition of a production function.[8] In fact, Atkinson (2002) points out that a mathematical definition of a function itself is relatively of recent origin. Use of the phrase 'requires less labour and less rain' by Kautilya indicates that he was aware of the relationship between inputs and output. Similarly, his (p 622) statement, 'Whoever gets an impregnable fort built on a place best suited for it at less cost and labour is said to outmanoeuvre the other (7.12)' reflects an understanding of such a relationship. It is also obvious that he emphasized efficiency (use of the word 'less') in all activities.

Proposed Complementary Relationship between Labour and Capital: In today's terminology, labour and capital are complements to each other means, an increase in capital leads to a shift in the marginal product of labour curve to the right or that both the factors are needed for obtaining a positive level of output. Kautilya (p 637) asserted, 'Man, without wealth, does not get even after a hundred attempts. Just as elephants are needed to catch elephants, so does wealth capture more wealth (9.4).' He believed that very little, if any at all, could be accomplished with labour alone implying that he understood the complementary nature of labour and capital.

Considered Land and Labour as Complements: Kautilya (p 619) stated, 'The value of land is what man makes of it (7.11).' He treated land and labour as complementary.[9] The following statement also implies the complementary nature of their relationship. He (p 620) stated, 'It is the people who constitute a kingdom. Like a barren cow, a kingdom without people yields nothing (7.11).'

Substitution Possibilities: Whether it is the choice of techniques in the production of a given level of output or the choice of goods and services in the consumption basket, the concept of substitution is at the heart of optimization of output or utility. However, in this context Kautilya was much more sophisticated than the classicists.[10] Since he was aware of the concept of substitution in its widest sense, and not just between labour and capital. He (p 609) argued, 'An ally who helps monetarily is preferable because one can always use money but troops only sometimes; and with money one can acquire troops and anything else one wants (7.9).'

Given the context, perhaps 'anything else' meant armament. In Figure 4.5, with troops, only point A is available whereas with money any point on line AB, like point E, which is on a higher isoquant allowing conquest of more land or enhanced national security, is

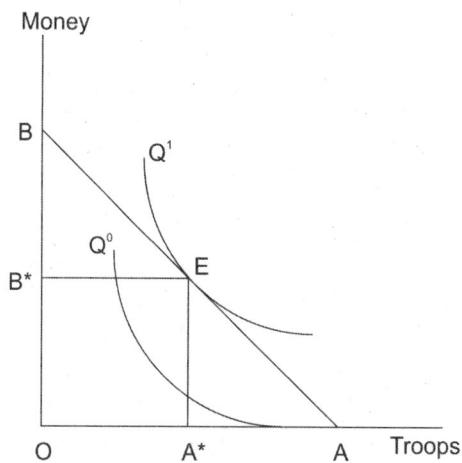

Figure 4.5: Isoquant Q^0 indicates the level of national security that could be achieved by troops only, and isoquant Q^1 indicates level of national security that could be achieved through various combinations of Troops and Money (by buying armour).

available. Thus, he was aware of the substitution possibilities along the line AB. He provided other examples, also related to substitution possibilities. For example, he (p 665) suggested, 'When there is a choice of forts, [some teachers think that] one with a better stock of materials shall be preferred. Kautilya is of the view that a fort with men, as well as stocks, is preferable (7.15).' Similarly, he (p 685) stated, 'Some teachers say that among *Brahmin, Kshatriya, Vaishya*, and *Sudra* troops, a higher *varna* force shall be mobilized before a lower one because the higher the *varna* the more the spirit. Kautilya disagrees. An enemy may win over *Brahmin* troops by prostrating himself before them. It is better to have either an army composed of *Kshatriyas* trained in the use of weapons or a *Vaishya* or *Sudra* army with a large number of men (9.2).' He understood the substitution possibilities between trained and untrained soldiers and perhaps also understood that training was labour-augmenting. The context has changed but the above examples indicate that Kautilya fully understood the significance of the concept of substitution.

A Map of Isoquants: He argued that it would be much harder to capture a king from a river fort than from a land fort. He (p 618-619) argued, 'As between a king entrenched in a land fort and one in river fort, seizing the land from the former is preferable. A land fort is more easily besieged, stormed and captured along with the enemy in it. Capturing a river fort is doubly difficult—the besieger has to cross the water while the besieged gets water and other necessities from it.'

Then he argued that capturing a king from a mountain fort would be much harder than from a river fort. He explained, 'As between a king entrenched in a river fort and one in a mountain fort, seizing the land from the former is preferable. A river fort can be assaulted using elephants, wooden bridges, earthworks or boats; a river does not have deep water all the year round and the water in it can be diverted. On the other hand, a mountain fort is protected by the mountain itself and, therefore, not easy to breach or ascend; even if one part is breached, everyone inside is not destroyed; and there is great loss to the besieger due to the rocks and trees thrown from above (7.10).' The above statements are captured in Figure 4.6.

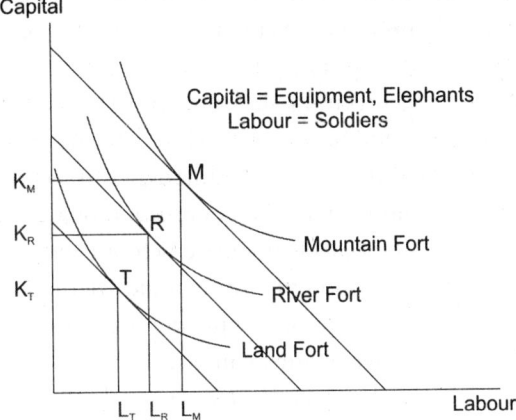

Figure 4.6: The isoquants labeled Land Fort, River Fort and Mountain Fort indicate the various combinations of capital and soldiers required to capture each one of them respectively.

According to Kautilya, for example, a combination of capital (elephants, armament) and labour (soldiers) (K_T, L_T) might be sufficient to capture a land fort whereas their higher levels (K_R, L_R) to capture a river fort and their much higher levels (K_M, L_M) were required to capture a mountain fort.

4.3 DEMAND-SUPPLY APPARATUS

Demand-Supply Mechanism: Significantly, Kautilya exhibited a workable knowledge (in fact more sophisticated than Adam Smith's or Ricardo's) of the demand-supply framework to determine the price of a product.[11] There were a few implicit applications of the demand-supply apparatus by Kautilya and these could be used for constructing demand and supply schedules. According to Spengler (1971), Kautilya distinguished between competitive markets and non-competitive markets. Spengler (p 74) states, 'Prices reflected actual or potential scarcity (4.2; 2.21.7-14) as well as the presence of monopolistic arrangements (2.6.10; 4.2.18-19, 28-30).' Kautilya (p 267) stated, 'Merchants selling foreign goods were to call out price three times, after paying duty. Likewise, owners of property were to call out the price of whatever property they were selling three times. If, due to competition among buyers, the goods or the property was sold at a higher price, the difference between the sale price and the call price had to be paid into the treasury (2.21).' Apparently, competition existed at least in some products. Although it is not known with certainty as to the motivation of the suggestion by Kautilya (p 236) that 'Commodities and products [of the countryside] shall not be sold in the places of their production [but sold only at the designated markets or brought into the city and sold after payment of duty] (2.22),' but its unintended consequence would have been the creation of competitive markets.

Demand Schedule: Kautilya discussed price stabilization by creating buffer stocks in periods of surplus and selling out of stocks during lean years. He (p 336) proposed, 'When there is an excess supply of a commodity, a buffer stock shall be built up by paying a price higher than the prevailing market price. When the market price reaches the support level, the buying price shall be changed according to the situation (2.16).'

The above statement indicates that he understood the impact of purchases by the government on price: the supply of the product was reduced, consequently its market price rose, and the gap between the support price and the market price decreased implying that the adjustment took place along the demand curve. Such an adjustment took place in a single season and not by decreases in production over time, as the one discussed by Adam Smith and Ricardo. Kautilya's ideas may be expressed by Figure 4.7.

Where S_G and S_B were the outputs in a good year and a bad year, respectively, and if left to the market, P_G and P_B could be the corresponding market prices, and P_S was the support price. As government bought a commodity, its supply in the market declined and price moved up from P_G to P_S and the segment GE could be traced. Similarly, Kautilya recommended that in a bad year, government should sell from its stocks, implying that price declined from P_B to P_S and the segment BE could be traced. Thus, a negatively sloped

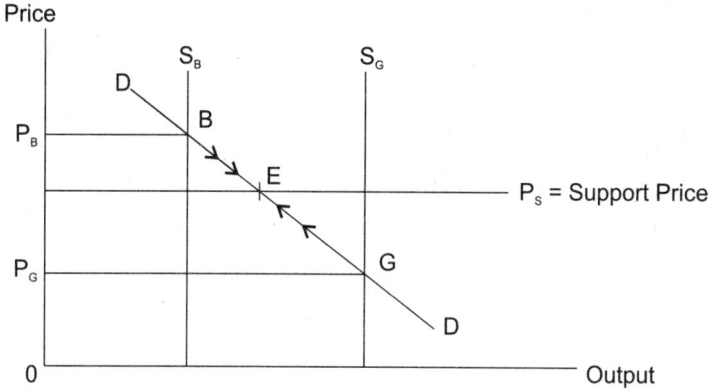

Figure 4.7: S_G and S_B were the respective output levels and P_G and P_B were the corresponding prices during good and bad crop periods. The line PS indicated the support price level fixed by the government. In a good period the movement was from point G to point E and during a bad crop year movement was from point B to point E.

demand curve was implicit in Kautilya's policy recommendation related to price stabilization.

Negotiating a Treaty Such That Total Revenue was Maximized: Second example relates to sharing the gains from successful joint programmes between two kings. Kautilya (p 623) stated, 'Some teachers say that a small production of high value minerals is preferable [to a large production of inferior products] because valuable products (such as diamonds, precious stones, pearls, corals, gold and silver) are worth much more than a large amount of inferior products. Kautilya disagrees. Buyers of high-valued products are rare and are found after a long search; there are many buyers and a steady demand for products of small value (7.12).'

In the above paragraph, Kautilya hinted at several important ideas. First, he pointed out that the total expenditure on a valuable item, say like a diamond, $P_e Q_e$ was likely to be less than that on an inexpensive item, $P_i Q_i$. Secondly, the costs of transportation and marketing varied from product to product and could be significant for some items (diamonds, pearls). Thirdly, instability of demand for durable consumer goods (diamonds etc.) was an issue even at that time. Fourthly, larger the number of customers for a product, the more outward would be its demand curve, ie. as the number of consumers increased, the demand curve shifted to the right. Fifth, he understood the forces of market demand and supply, and also that there was the absence of 'water-diamond paradox'.

Illiquidity: Finally, according to Kautilya, the 'Buyers of high-valued products were rare and were found only after a long search'. He revisited the liquidity issue again. He (p 669) stated, 'If peace is sought on condition of paying money, the weak king shall give articles of high value for which there are no buyers, or forest produce that is unfit for use in war (12.1).' He clearly understood the distinction between liquid and illiquid assets, since he pointed out the transaction cost as well as the lapse of time as important factors in selling an asset. The essence of these statements may be captured by Figure 4.8.

Although there was no derivation of a demand curve from optimization conditions, but a negatively sloped demand curve was implicit in Kautilya's policy statements.

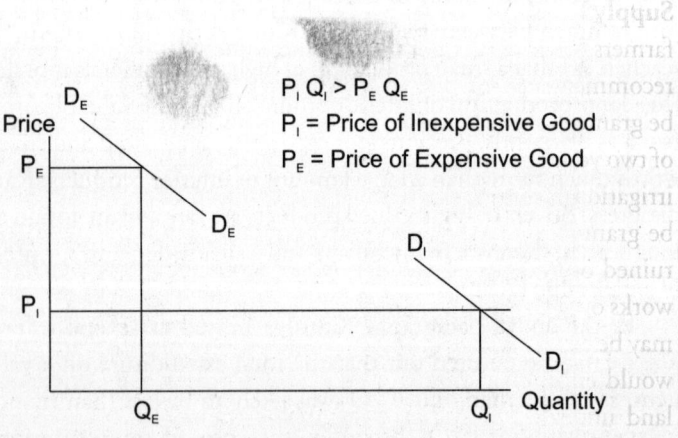

Figure 4.8: $D_E D_E$ and $D_I D_I$ are the respective demand curves and P_E, Q_E and P_I, Q_I are the respective prices and quantities for expensive and inexpensive goods.

Supply Schedule: Again, there is no explicit discussion on a supply schedule but it can be derived from his policy recommendations. Kautilya understood that a profit margin or loss depended on the strength of demand, which implies the existence of a supply curve, ie. shifts in the demand curve tracing a supply curve.

He (p 240) stated, 'An agent selling goods on behalf of someone else, at the right time and place [ie. realizing the best price], shall hand over to the owner of the merchandise the price as received (the cost price plus the profit made) [less their commission]. If the price realized is lower because of missing the best opportunity for sale, the agent shall pay the owner the cost of the goods at the time he received them and the normal profit. If it is so agreed upon beforehand between the two, the retail seller may pay to the wholesaler, whenever no profit is made, only the price of the goods. If the price falls [between the time of entrusting the goods and the time of sale], only the lower price [actually realized] shall be payable (3.12).'

A vertical supply curve is implicit in the above statements and the market price depended on the location of the demand curve. That is, price was determined where the demand curve intersected the vertical supply curve.

Supply Response to a Subsidy: Kautilya proposed incentives to the farmers for bringing additional land under cultivation. He (p 231) recommended, 'Anyone who brings new land under cultivation shall be granted exemption from payment of agricultural taxes for a period of two years (3.9).' Similarly, he suggested, 'For building or improving irrigation facilities, the following exemptions from water rates shall be granted: new tanks and embankments for five years; renovating ruined or abandoned water works for four years and clearing water works over-grown with weeds for three years (3.9).' These suggestions may be expressed by Figure 4.9. Kautilya believed that tax exemptions would encourage supply of agricultural products by bringing more land under cultivation and increasing the use of other inputs like water. The implication is that tax exemptions would shift point A to point B, or point E to point F and so on. By joining points A, E, etc. (or B and F) a supply curve can be derived implicitly.

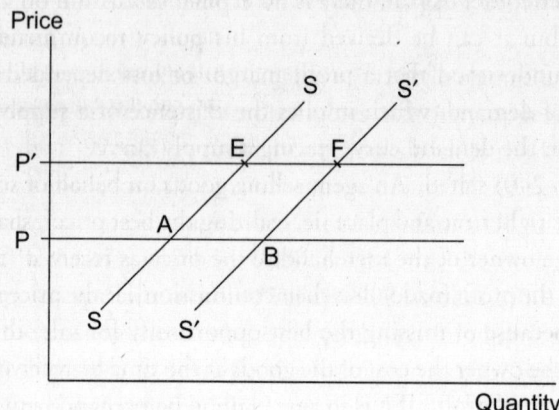

Figure 4.9: SS is the initial supply curve and it shifts to S'S' due to a tax subsidy.

Labour Supply Schedule: Kautilya discussed the effects of incentives on labour supply, also implying a positively sloped supply curve. He (p 233) suggested, 'For better work [or greater productivity] women who spin shall be given oil and myrobalan cakes as a special favour. They shall be induced to work on festive days [and holidays] by giving them gifts. Weavers, specializing in weaving fabrics of flax, *dukula*, silk yarn, deer wool and [fine] cotton shall be given gifts of perfumes, flowers and similar presents of encouragement (2.23).'

He made two points. First, spinners should be paid according to their contribution made both in terms of quality and quantity of output. Secondly, the spinners and weavers should be paid over and above their regular wages, W as an incentive to work on holidays (ie. W + cake or other gift). These statements may be expressed by Figure 4.10.

It is not claimed that Kautilya had a fully developed neoclassical demand-supply framework. Although Parmar (1987, p 253) remarks, 'Kautilya formulates a theory of demand and supply and plans production accordingly', what is claimed is that his framework is a genuine contender to be accepted as the forerunner to the neoclassical price theory, as compared to the one advanced by Adam Smith or Ricardo.

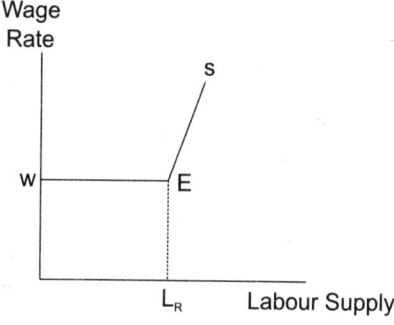

Figure 4.10: WES is the labour supply curve and L_R indicates the regular hours of work and W indicates the regular wage. The positively sloped segment ES shows that a higher than the regular wage, W, is required to induce higher than the regular hours of work, L_R.

Trade in Futures: Understandably, there were no financial derivatives at the time. But surprisingly, Kautilya mentioned trades in futures. He (p 337) stated, 'Fix prices for trade in futures (ie. for goods to be received at a future date or at a different place) after taking into account the investment, the quantity to be delivered, duty, interest, rent and other expenses (2.16).'

SUMMARY

Pre-Kautilyan writers had identified the four factors payments (wage, interest, rent and profit) separately, and were somewhat aware of the law of diminishing utility. However, Kautilya's *Arthashastra* is a landmark contribution in terms of both method and content. His understanding of the law of diminishing returns is at par with the classicists. His applications of concepts like opportunity cost, and of demand and supply framework, are closer to those of the neoclassicals. He comes out on the side of the ordinal approach, which seems more natural. His understanding of the rules (axioms) of comparison and consistency and the exploration of substitution possibilities is way ahead of the classicists. Thus, Kautilya's original contributions could be identified as: opportunity cost, basic demand-supply apparatus, law of diminishing returns, rent, demand instability for durable goods, discounting, liquidity and the importance of substitution possibilities.

5

Accounting Methods and Income Measurement

Mattessich [1998] identifies elements of modern principles of accounting in Kautilya's *Arthashastra* and shows that it contains more accounting theory than in Pacioli's *Summa*. Mattessich deserves credit for offering ingenious interpretations of Kautilya's implicit analysis. He makes insightful and bold observations, noting that many studies in accounting history focused too narrowly in searching for the origin of double-entry bookkeeping. He places Kautilya's *Arthashastra* at par with Pacioli's *Summa*. He (2000, p 205) concludes, 'These four items appear to be reason enough to put Kautilya's *Arthashastra* beside Pacioli's *Summa*, and revere both of them as the most crucial landmarks in the early history of our discipline.'

A brief introduction to Kautilya's contributions related to systematic record keeping, periodic accounting, budgeting, and independent auditing is provided in Section 5.1. His ideas on the scope and methodology of accounting are presented in Section 5.2. It is argued that he did not recommend separating accounting from economics, proposed testable hypotheses and thus implied that accounting has an equal claim to using the scientific method. He was preoccupied with the goal of achieving rapid economic growth, which implies that he must have had, at least some vague idea of the concept of national income accounts. Mercantilists emphasized the contribution only of trade and the Physiocrats only of agriculture in augmentation of national wealth/income. However, Kautilya recognized the importance of contributions from all industries, implying that he was ahead of the classical school of economic thought by almost two thousand years. His pioneering ideas regarding national income accounts are presented in Section 5.3.

5.1 ACCOUNTING METHODS

During the 4th century BCE, there were, of course, no multinationals, stock market, financial analysts, or pension funds. There were no external uniform standards or requirements for detailed bookkeeping. Mattessich [1998] notes that, yet, Kautilya developed several principles of modern accounting. However, he expresses his curiosity as 'One may even raise the question of why the *Arthashastra* concerns itself, at least to some extent, with accounting issues, while the even more comprehensive writings of Aristotle (despite revealing an awareness of economic issues) are silent about accounting theory.' Kautilya had a grand vision for building an empire, one that was prosperous, secure, stable, and based on fairness. He realized that the attainment of prosperity required not only human effort, but also accumulation of capital and maintenance of a systematic record of inflow and outflow of public funds etc. which was not possible without the development of some accounting methods and practices.

According to Kautilya, the level of net worth and its growth were of critical importance. Therefore, statements of revenues and expenditures of public enterprises and of the state budget were needed to monitor the growth in net wealth. He developed the necessary apparatus and financial rules and regulations to achieve the goal of sound financial health. He devised a reasonable system of (a) bookkeeping rules, and (b) financial rules or codes of conduct to manage the financial affairs of the state.

Bookkeeping, Maintenance of Records and Periodic Accounting: Kautilya developed a format for 'recording, classifying and summarizing' data on financial variables. He suggested a comprehensive approach to maintaining accounts for revenue, expenditures and net balances for each department. According to him, the Comptroller and Auditor should maintain detailed accounts. He (p 225) suggested, 'The Closing Day for the Accounting Year shall be the full moon day of the month of Asadha [June/July], the year consisting of 354 days (according to the lunar calendar) with a separate book for the intercalary month (2.7).'

Financial Rules for Appropriate Conduct: He specified many accounting rules. (i) Proper Maintenance of Accounts: He (p 278) stated, 'All accounts shall be maintained in the proper form and legibly written without corrections. Failure to do so shall be a punishable offence (2.7.35).'

Timely Submission of Accounts: He suggested, 'Day-to-day accounts [to be submitted once a month] shall be presented before the end of the following month and late submission shall be penalized (2.7.26, 27).' He instructed the accounts officers, 'Not [to] lie about the accounts and not try to interpolate an entry as if it was forgotten (2.7).' (iv) He (p 279) added, 'High officials shall be responsible for rendering the accounts in full for their sphere of activity without any contradiction in them. Those who tell lies or make contradictory statements shall pay the highest level standard penalty (2.7.25).'

The above statements indicate that he developed a comprehensive system of accounting, including bookkeeping rules, periodic accounting, preparing and reporting of income statements and independent audits to monitor, manage and assess financial status.

5.2 KAUTILYA ON THE SCOPE AND METHODOLOGY OF ACCOUNTING

> The use of science is the sight of truth.
> —*Kautilya's Sutras*

Cushing (1989) observes: 'Contemporary academic accountants have not deserted science, but they have in a fundamental sense deserted accounting. The majority of the research in today's leading academic accounting journals applies the research paradigms of economics and psychology within the institutional setting of accounting.' He calls this a crisis in accounting and suggests that one of the ways it may be resolved is by simply redefining the scope of accounting. He concludes, 'Accounting may be redefined in scientific terms as the science that attempts to explain and predict the economic performance of individuals or groups responsible for the utilization of economic resources.'

However, according to Kautilya, explanation and prediction were the key goals for any objective inquiry into accounting. This means that by applying scientific methods, contemporary accountants are not abandoning accounting; rather they are restoring its original status and ready to realize its full potential. This is contrary to Cushing's assertion since this is not a new paradigm, or an indication of a crisis in accounting.

Apparently, the prerequisites for the establishment of the discipline of accounting already existed in India. Kautilya used fractions, percentages, summation and subtraction operations, and even combinations quite extensively, displaying sufficient knowledge of arithmetic. Not surprisingly, he developed not only bookkeeping rules but also the procedures for periodic income statements, independent audits and budgeting. Ifrah's (2000) findings also support the existence of the required capabilities in arithmetic to support a separate discipline of accounting. He (p 434) writes, 'Before the beginning of the 5th century BCE, all the necessary "ingredients" for the creation of the written place-value system had been amassed by the Indian Mathematicians.'

Kautilya did not see the need for separating accounting from economics and believed that any demarcation of the boundary between them would be arbitrary. He considered accounting an integral part of economics, whereas, he explicitly treated Political Science and Philosophy as separate disciplines. This view is supported by the fact that the role of accounting is embedded within the set of economic policies. It is shown that Kautilya followed 'explanation and prediction' as the true objectives of a scientific inquiry and applied these to analyze the impact of various policies on the creation of wealth. He used these objectives, both explicitly and implicitly, to inquiries related to accounting. This leads to the conclusion that explanation and prediction lie within the rightful domain of accounting.

He advanced the hypothesis that the pursuit of productive activities was the key to stabilization of the current income and its rapid growth in the future. Obstruction, misuse of government property and false accounting by government servants lead to a reduction of wealth (2.8.4). He added, 'Calamities to the treasury can be any internal or external action which has the effect of reducing the revenue. Financial health can be affected by misappropriation by chiefs, remission of taxes, scattered collection, false accounting and looting by enemies and tribes before the revenue reaches the Treasury (8.4.49).'

Two observations are in order. First, according to him, 'false accounting' could be a serious threat to the creation of wealth. Secondly, this warning was incorporated in the heart of the set of core economic policies, such as, an economic growth policy, a sound fiscal policy, and a labour management policy. He discussed each of these means of creating wealth and preventing loss by developing accounting methods.

Importance of Financial Health: He emphasized the financial health of the state and understood that a sound treasury was a prerequisite to accomplishing other goals. He (p 253) stated, 'All state activities depend first on the Treasury. Therefore, a king shall devote his best attention to it. A king with a depleted Treasury eats into the very vitality of the citizens and the country (2.8.1-2).' In fact, according to him (p 147), a king should start his day by receiving 'reports on defense, revenue and expenditure'. He (p 255) added, 'If receipts and expenditure are properly looked after, the king will not find himself in financial difficulties (5.3.45).' According to him, therefore, a king must carefully manage the financial affairs of the state.

Explanation and Prediction: Stigler (1986) points out that the progress in statistical methods has been very challenging and painfully slow.[1] Undoubtedly, the marriage of economics and statistics during the twentieth century has been mutually beneficial. Progress in statistical methods (and econometrics) is a pre-requisite for progress in applied economics. Kautilya did not have to worry about the distinction between what McCloskey and Ziliak (1996) call 'economic significance and statistical significance' since there were no regression models available at the time. However, his insights are remarkable.

Evaluation of a Policy: Kautilya (p 544) evaluated a policy as follows: 'Events, both human and providential, govern the world (and its affairs). Acts of God are those which are unforeseeable and whose origin is unknown. If the cause is knowable and, hence, foreseeable, its origin is human. If an act of God results in (helping) the achievement of one's objective, it is good fortune; otherwise, it is misfortune. (Likewise,) any human action which increases one's wealth is a good policy; otherwise, it is a bad policy.'

Analysis of Variance: The above statement amounts to the specification of a regression model and separating the total variation (in the dependent variable, wealth) into explained and unexplained (random) components. According to Kautilya, a policy should not get credit for positive changes in wealth if that was due to random factors (he called them 'good fortune'). Similarly, a policy should not be blamed if there were negative changes in wealth due to unfavorable random variables. It implies that Kautilya's goal was to explain and predict the changes in the dependent variable. It may be noted that the evaluation of a policy depends on the ability to explain and predict. Indeed, according to Kautilya, explanation and prediction were the most important values of a discipline.

Thus, his implicit regression model may formally be specified as:

$$W = X\beta + \varepsilon. \qquad (5.1)$$

Where, W =wealth, the dependent variable, X= exogenous policy variables, which may be used to acquire wealth, ε = random error (the acts of God). Incidentally, the most important assumption of regression analysis — that the error terms are independent of the right hand side variables, X, that is, Cov (X, ε) = 0, is clearly satisfied in the above statement. Additionally, the Covariance $(\varepsilon_t, \varepsilon_{t-1}) = 0$ since acts of God are likely to be independent of each other across different years. It is not claimed that he knew the implications of these assumptions.

His analysis shows that the application of scientific methodology in accomplishing the objectives of 'explanation and prediction' is imbedded in accounting. His analysis implies that innovations of accounting methods were just like the innovations of writing, printing, steam-engine, the electric dynamo and computer microchips, as a general-purpose technology (GPT), which improves the efficiency of the whole economy (see Lipsey *et al* 1998 for a discussion on GPT).

5.3 A FORERUNNER OF NATIONAL INCOME ACCOUNTS

An exposition of Kautilya's ideas on national income accounts are collected in Section 5.3. According to the Mercantilist school, economic surplus was generated only through 'trade (exports),' while the Physiocratic school ascribed it only to 'agriculture'. It was eventually the Classical school, which generalized the concept of the economic surplus by pointing out that it emanated from all sectors, and this has since stayed. Kautilya's position on this issue is identical to that of the Classical school, since he also emphasized agriculture, industry, and trade.

Importance of Agriculture: Kautilya (Kangle part II, p 9) stated, 'Agriculture, cattle rearing and trade—these constitute economics, [which are] beneficial, as they yield grains, cattle, money, forest produce and labour (1.4).' The word 'economics' in this context stands for economic activities. He (p 619-620) elaborated, 'To begin construction of forts and other defensive works, grains are a prerequisite. However, land with mines is superior when the products of mines are in great demand (7.11).'

Importance of Mining and Manufacturing: Kautilya (p 304) asserted, 'The source of the financial strength of the state is the mining and metallurgical industry; the state exercises power because of its Treasury. With increased wealth and a powerful army, more territory can be acquired, thereby further increasing the wealth of the state (2.12).'

Importance of Trade: Kautilya (p 237-38) suggested (about the duties of Chief Controller of State Trading), 'He shall, in general, trade with such foreign countries as will generate a rate of profit; he shall avoid unprofitable areas. If no profit is likely to be made, he shall keep in mind the economic, political, or strategic advantages in exporting to or importing from a particular country (2.16).'

Mattessich (2000, p 203) remarks, 'Kautilya's *Arthashastra* is not merely significant for only for business accounting but also government accounting, with some stretch of imagination it may be regarded as a forerunner of national income accounting since the ultimate purpose of Kautilya's work was to strengthen the economy of the entire nation.' Indeed, if one collects all the elements, which are scattered throughout the *Arthashastra*, and allows only a little stretch of imagination, or Samuelson's charitable interpretation, a workable national income accounts can be constructed. In fact, the various approaches to the estimation of national income are implicit in his *Arthashastra*.

The Income Approach: Surprisingly, even before Kautilya, wage, rent, profit and interest had been identified as separate factor payments. It is also remarkable that there is absolutely no confusion between stocks and flows in the *Arthashastra*. Kautilya considered wealth as a stock and return (fruits) from it as a flow. According to him (p 639), 'Wealth is like a tree; its roots are *dharma* and the fruit is pleasure. Achieving that kind of wealth which further promotes *dharma*, produces more wealth and gives more pleasure is the achievement of all gains (*sarvarthasiddhi*) (9.7.81).'

Wages: Kautilya (p 450) recommended, 'The agreement between a labourer and the one hiring him shall be made in public. Labourers shall be paid wages as agreed upon. If there is no prior agreement, the labourer shall be paid in accordance with the nature of the work and the time spent on it at customary rates (3.13).'

Interest Rate: To a large extent, the interest rate was negotiated between the parties. He (p 425) stated, 'No one shall recover interest without agreeing on the rate with the debtor at the time of making the loan. Once agreed upon an interest rate shall not be changed during the course of the loan (3.11).'

Rent: He discussed payment of rent on leases of Crown land, mines and saltpans. He (p 259) fixed land rent on Crown land as 'State's share ¾ or 4/5 if lessee provided only labour; ½ if lessee provided seeds and implements as well as labour (2.15).' He (p 260) set rent on leased mines as: 'Lease payment, either a share of the ore recovered or payment of a fixed royalty (2.12).' Similarly, according to him (p 261), 'Lease rent on salt pans, (paid either as a share of the salt produced or as a fixed quantity) received in kind and sold to the public (2.12).'

Profits: He emphasized the maximization of profits from public enterprises. He (p 259) defined profits from the direct cultivation of Crown Land as: 'Net revenue to state was equal to value of production less expenditure on seeds, labour etc. (2.15).' Similarly, he (p 260) defined profit from manufacturing of textiles as: 'Realization from sale of textiles and products less cost of raw materials and wages (2.23).'

Moreover, according to him (p 220), 'Records of the inhabitants shall also be kept under the following headings: (i) the *varna* (ii) occupation (such as farmer, cowherd, trader, craftsman, labourer or slave) (iii) the number of males and females as well as the number of children and old people, their [family] history, occupation, income and expenditure (iv) livestock and poultry owned (v) the amount of tax payable in cash or in free labour and (vi) tolls and fines that may be due (2.35).' However, he did not take the final step of adding these factor payments (or the personal incomes of the households) to arrive at the national income.

Output Approach: He recommended an income tax rate of 1/6th on the agricultural output, which being the primary source of national output at the time. He (p 218-219) suggested the creation of the Office of a Chancellor, who was responsible for: 'The collection of revenue from the fortified towns, the country-side, the mines, the irrigation works, forests and trade routes; and the preparation of the budget and maintenance of detailed accounts of revenue and expenditure as prescribed (2.6).' He insisted on detailed record keeping. He recommended a stable tax structure. It is not known whether the agricultural output from different farmers was added up or not, but the revenue collected from those farmers was definitely added up and it would be a simple exercise to estimate national output from the collected tax revenue.

In fact, he fully understood the one-to-one relationship between income and the tax revenue. For example, he (p 116) suggested, 'In the interests of the prosperity of the country, a king should be diligent in foreseeing the possibility of calamities, try to avert them before they arise, overcome those which happen, remove all obstructions to economic activity and prevent loss of revenue to the state (8.4).' Clearly, he believed that only by preventing a loss in income, one could prevent a loss in revenue. He (p 255) added that the various means of increasing the state revenue (in addition to reducing fraud etc.) were 'ensuring the prosperity of state activities, increasing agricultural production and promoting trade' (2.8). Spengler (1971, p 72) also notes, 'One of his main concerns seems to have been the collection and expenditure of revenue in such ways as to build up the permanent revenue-yielding capacity of the economy.'

Value-added Approach: Kautilya was aware of the concept of value added. He (p 231) stated, 'A loss of [ripe] crops is worse than a loss of seedlings, because, with grown crops, the labour put in is also lost (8.2).' Similarly, he (p 230) explained, 'Sugarcane is very difficult to grow being susceptible to diseases and requiring much more expenditure (2.24).' Thus, it would be really odd that Kautilya, who was so concerned not only with growth in income but also with a reduction in its variability, did not seem to have had any idea of its estimation.[2]

SUMMARY

Kautilya specifically emphasized innovations in accounting methods along with accumulation of capital. Mattessich (1998) concludes that the origin of accounting principles found in Kautilya's *Arthashastra* and his ingenious interpretations of Kautilya's great work place it on a par with Pacioli's *Summa*. It is claimed that Kautilya viewed accounting as an integral part of economics, with explanation and prediction within its rightful domain, implying that the scope and methodology of accounting encompass much more than double-entry bookkeeping and auditing. His initiation of the process of innovations in accounting methods may be put at par with the innovations of writing and printing, which are identified as a general-purpose technology.

It is truly astounding that an Indian guru, more than a millennium before Pacioli's *Summa*, could initiate the process of genuine innovations in accounting methods, assign a central role to accounting for promoting economic development, and display a modern perspective on the scope and methodology of accounting.

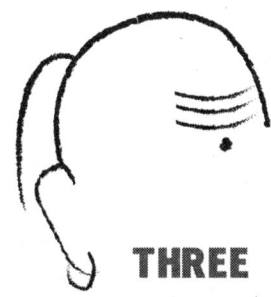

THREE

Ethical Foundation to Freedom from Wants

Kautilya was the high priest, who performed a holistic marriage between *artha* (economics) and *dharma* (ethics) as equal /made for each other partners. Chapters 6-13 present Kautilya's ideas on the integration of ethics into economic issues. He argued that unless decision-makers were ethical, the quality of institutions and governance could not be assured. It is shown that Sen's (1987) claim that Aristotle originated the ethics-based approach to economics is unsustainable. Kautilya originated both the engineering-based and the ethics-based approaches to economics. It is proved beyond any reasonable doubt that Kautilya's *Arthashastra* may rightfully be called [Kautilya's] *Dharmanomics*.

6

Foundational Role of Dharma

> Only small men discriminate saying: One is a relative; the other is a stranger. For those who live magnanimously the entire world constitutes but a family.
> — *Maha Upanishad (Chapter 6, Verse 72)*

Thinkers in ancient India considered financial wellbeing, spiritual wellbeing, enjoyment of art and music and good physical health as essential to a long and happy life on earth.[1] They understood backward induction. They reasoned that an individual could enjoy life to the fullest only if peace and harmony prevailed in society. They developed the concept of *dharma* to justify and enable creation of such a society. They firmly believed that if there was *dharma* [righteousness; observance of moral codes] there would be social order, that is, they assigned a foundational role to *dharma*. The emphasis on the foundational role of ethics was truly a unique insight since Aristotle emphasized only the remedial role of ethics and Adam Smith also gave up on its foundational role.[2]

Pre-Kautilyan sages emphasized the role of ethics in creating a joyous, peaceful and harmonious social order by motivating the individual to follow *dharma* for attaining bliss. These ideas on the foundational role of ethics are presented in Section 6.1. Kautilya enthusiastically accepted his predecessors' ideas on ethics. Section 6.2 shows that Kautilya was truly a Vedic Man.

Kautilya's most important insight was to link ethics to prosperity. He thus argued that ethics was also essential to salvation from poverty. He explained that ethical decision-makers would establish and maintain good institutions and provide good governance. They would formulate economic policies to advance the common good and implement them effectively. They would strengthen ethical values and help in creating an ethical environment and thus help in maintaining peace and harmony and law and order. Essentially, his *Arthashastra* may be correctly termed as *dharmanomics*, that is, economics wedded to *dharma* and propounding ethical foundation to prosperity. These ideas are discussed in detail in Section 8.4 of Chapter 8.

The ancient Greek philosophers and the Chinese philosopher, Confucius, emphasized only the virtue ethics. On the other hand, Han Feitzu (280-233 BCE) advanced only the legalistic approach to ethics and discarded the moralistic approach of Confucius.[3] Kautilya, just like the sages in ancient India, emphasized [the virtue] 'ethics' and its role in building of good character. He believed that moral individuals were likely to behave ethically, even if they had the opportunity to behave otherwise. However, he was not naïve and did not believe that everyone would be ethical even in a healthy society. According to him, given the opportunity, some amoral and immoral individuals might behave unethically. His second important insight was to propose complementing the virtue—ethics—with an action-oriented approach, such as, advocating the Silver Rule (viz., not doing unto others what one would not like to be done to him), designing a sound organizational structure and having *dharma-based* laws, rules and regulations. Kautilya's ideas on these issues are presented in Section 6.3.

6.1 PRE-KAUTILYAN SAGES ON THE FOUNDATIONAL ROLE OF *DHARMA*

ज्ञान्ति: सर्व ॰

> May there be peace throughout the world
> — *Yajur Veda (Chapter 36, mantra 17)*

Sages and seers in ancient India carried a vision in which each individual realized one's full potential and enjoyed life to the fullest. They understood the concept of backward induction and logically traced the steps, which could help the individual in living accordingly.

First, they reasoned that enjoyment of a richer and fuller life on earth was possible only if a peaceful and harmonious social system existed. Secondly, they proceeded to explore the requirements to create such a social system, that is, essentially for creating a heaven on earth. They developed the concept of *dharma* which, if followed, would create a trusting, caring, peaceful and harmonious social system. As pointed out earlier, *dharma* literally means behavior that holds the society together, that is, something foundational. They identified *dharmic* (ethical) values of non-violence, compassion, truthfulness, honesty and tolerance as basic to such a social order. They also believed that every individual, who practiced these virtues, created large positive externalities. For example, *Rig Veda* (10-65-11) contains the following statement: 'The godly people spread divine virtues on the earth.' These virtues are considered eternal and no further trial and error is required.[4] Also there is no circularity involved in defining them.[5]

The final step in the logical chain was motivating the individual to voluntarily practice *dharma*. Ancient thinkers understood human nature with all its appetites, emotions, passions and weaknesses. Keeping this in view, they devised the concepts of heaven and hell to motivate the individual to follow *dharma* for securing heaven and working for the eternal bliss. Their message was very clear—that unless an individual contributed to the creation of heaven on earth, s/he could not go to heaven after death. Essentially, their goal was to align private and social interests. Therefore, they emphasized roles of ethics both at the micro and macro levels.[6] (i) At the micro level, the practice of *dharma* helped in self-improvement by performing good deeds, controlling destructive emotions and living piously for breaking the birth-death-rebirth cycle, that is, achieving inner peace of mind (steady state or eternal bliss and essentially removing the 'depressive and euphoric' cycles of life). (ii) At the macro level, *dharma* was considered essential to system-building, that is, it was considered foundational in establishing the social order. These are presented below.[7]

Self-improvement (Spiritual Upliftment): The Vedic emphasis on *dharmic* values was pursued by the writers of the *Dharmasutras* also. For example, sage Apastamba (Olivelle, 1999, p 34) provided a detailed list of virtues and vices. He urged each individual to follow *dharmic* values and to control vices. He wrote, 'Refraining from anger, excitement, rage, greed, perplexity, hypocrisy, and malice, speaking the truth; refraining from overeating, calumny, and envy; sharing, liberality, rectitude, gentleness, self-control, amity with all creatures...benevolence and contentment.' The following Hindu proverb summarizes the self-improving role of ethics as: 'There is nothing noble about being superior to some other man. The true nobility is in being superior to your previous self.'

Each individual was urged to accumulate moral capital by undertaking virtuous deeds, particularly making charitable donations and also uplift oneself through prayers, meditation, reflection, contemplation and yoga. All these practices were recommended to motivate the individual to ensure an end to the birth-death-rebirth cycle, that is, the attainment of eternal bliss and in attaining the union of the *atman* (individual soul) with the *paramatman* (Supreme-Being).

System-building: Ancient sages identified cardinal *dharmic* values of non-violence, tolerance, compassion, truth, honesty and cleanliness for creating a peaceful, harmonious and caring society. Virtue of non-violence means not to hurt anyone physically, emotionally or financially. That means this virtue is incompatible with anger, greed, jealousy and lust. It also means that any kind of injustice arising from oppression, infringement, subjugation, discrimination and deprivation would be incompatible with the virtue of non-violence, that is, in an ethical society, justice would automatically be served.

Michael Sandel (2009, p. 187) explains, 'For Aristotle, justice means giving people what they deserve, giving each person his or her due. But what is a person due? What are the relevant grounds of merit or moral desert? That depends on what's being distributed. Justice involves two factors: "things, and persons to whom things are assigned."' He adds, 'Suppose we're distributing flutes. Who should get the best ones? Aristotle's answer: "the best flute players." However, according to the sages in ancient India, that would be an incomplete answer because the issue would be how the person who had the authority to decide the best players, was selected? Moreover, if this person was not ethical, he might declare even the worst player to be the best one. Ultimately, administration of justice depends on the morality of a particular society.'

Two thousand years later, Adam Smith (1790/1982, Part II. ii. 3.4) argued, 'Justice, on the contrary, is the main pillar that upholds the whole edifice. If it is removed, the great, the immense fabric of human society,..., must in a moment crumble into atoms'. A few remarks are in order. First, the pillar must be standing on the solid rock of *dharma*, otherwise it would be unstable. That is, justice in an unethical society is unattainable. Secondly, if justice has to serve as the main pillar, then it must be strong enough to support the edifice. However, it will not be strong unless it is constructed with the bricks and mortar of *dharmic* values. Finally, it appears as if the pillar and the edifice are two separate entities and not components of one system. Every society decides both the pillar and the edifice together, but Adam Smith's approach does not allow any possible interaction or interdependence between them.

A genuine question arises: has the emphasis on the concept of justice been misplaced? More than two thousand years of debate has not succeeded in removing its ambiguity since, in the absence of ethical grounding, each person possesses his/her own concept of justice. Clearly, the preoccupation with the concept of justice has done more harm than good since focus on foundational virtues has been neglected. It is perhaps time to deemphasize this concept and focus on ethical grounding, since manifestation of injustice is just a symptom of moral degradation.

Similarly, the virtue of tolerance is incompatible with arrogance, pride and pathological ego. The virtue of compassion is incompatible with large inequalities. As a result, there is heavy emphasis on charity. The virtues of truth and honesty are essential to the creation of trust, which is essential for all interpersonal dealings. That is, trust is a *dharma*-intensive concept. Cleanliness was equally important for enjoying a healthy life.

System-building through Individual-upliftment (Spiritual Wellbeing): Ancient thinkers understood the distinction between internal restraints, such as through self-discipline and external constraints, such as compliance through enforcement of laws. They emphasized internal restraints since those were considered more effective for system-building. Therefore, they put heavy emphasis on instilling moral values into young children through education. The teachers, parents and elders were assigned this important task. As adults, they were encouraged to undertake moral reflection freely and critically on moral issues. Their approach was not focused merely on dos and don'ts but on internalization of *dharmic* virtues and controlling of vices, such as anger, greed, lust, arrogance, jealousy, ego, attachment and pride. Since these were regarded destructive impulses for the individual as well as for the community, the sages urged the need to develop internal control over them. The following table captures their insights:

Table 6.1: **Ancient Thinkers on Creating Heaven on Earth through** *Dharma*

Type of Individual	Description of Characteristics	State of Individual's Well-being	State of Social Order
Dharmic	Practicing of *dharmic* values: Non-violence, freedom from malice tolerance, honesty, truthfulness, cleanliness, compassion	Happiness and bliss in the present life and emancipation (*moksha*) after death	Peace and harmony= heaven on earth
Self-disciplined	Controlling of vices: Anger, greed, lust, jealousy, arrogance, attachment, ego		

Contd...

Type of Individual	Description of Characteristics	State of Individual's Well-being	State of Social Order
Adharmic	Does not practice *dharmic* values	Unhappy in the present life and after death	Hellish conditions on earth
Indisciplined	Has no control over vices		

They prescribed four ends of a productive and happy life: *dharma, artha, kama* and *moksha*. According to them, an individual should accumulate moral capital (*dharma*) by doing good deeds and both *artha* and *kama* be guided by *dharma* (ethics). Bansi Pandit (2009, p 141) explains Vedic ethics aptly as: 'Man is born to give and not to grab.'[8]

6.2 KAUTILYA FOLLOWED THE INDIAN THOUGHT ON THE ROLE OF *DHARMA*

> Greed clouds the intellect. Another's wealth, even if it be husk, should not be stolen. One can conquer the worlds with righteousness. Righteousness is the root of happiness.
> —*Kautilya's Sutras*

Alexander the Great invaded northern India around 325 BCE, and after much difficulty, won one battle against a very small kingdom. Discouraged and facing revolt from his army, he left India and died around 323 BCE on his way back to Greece. Because Aristotle was Alexander's teacher, is it possible that he left impressions of Greek culture behind? Could Kautilya have been influenced by Aristotle's ideas on ethics? Based upon the historical evidence, it is doubtful that Kautilya would have benefited from Aristotle's ideas on ethics even if we assume that he had access to them. The intellectual pursuits leading to the development of philosophy and religion were initiated much earlier and were far richer in content in India than in Greece.[9] Kautilya was a Vedic man and he strictly adhered to Indian thought.

Kautilya believed in character-building (see the next chapter). He (p 107) listed ethical values as: '*Ahimsa* [abstaining from injury to all living creatures]; *satyam* [truthfulness]; cleanliness; freedom from malice; compassion and tolerance'. In fact, these values have not changed ever since they were enshrined in the *Vedas* and have been considered universal. Kautilya wholeheartedly and enthusiastically embraced and promoted the prevailing roles of *dharma*: (a) that it was a source of joy and attainment of eternal bliss (salvation from the birth-death-rebirth cycle), and (b) was essential to holding society together, that is, its foundational role and also in reducing the systemic risk.

According to Kautilya, *Vedas*, the Hindu religious scriptures and philosophy were the two primary sources of values. Kautilya (Subramanian, p 68) stated: 'There is no righteous duty, not specified in the learned scriptures.' He seemed to have a very broad concept of rationality, which included not only the usual axiomatic rationality but also self-discipline to check impulses of excessive greed, anger and lūst. He followed the *Atharva Veda* both in letter and spirit. He (p 106) wrote, '[The observance of] one's own *dharma* leads to heaven and eternal bliss. When *dharma* is transgressed, the resulting chaos leads to the extermination of this world.' He (p 180) added: 'For, when *adharma* overwhelms *dharma*, the king himself will be destroyed.' Figure 6.1 captures his ideas.

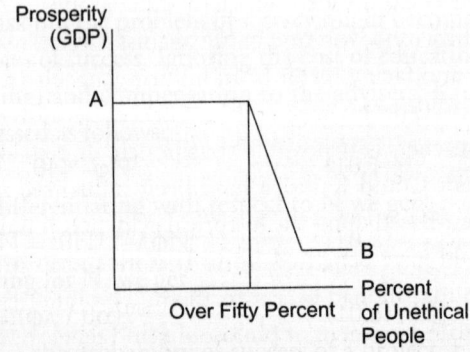

Figure 6.1: Curve AB indicates the relationship between prosperity (GDP) and the percentage of unethical people. GDP falls rapidly as the percentage of unethical people exceeds fifty per cent of the population.

According to Kautilya, there would be total anarchy if unethical people acquired a majority. Political instability would ruin prosperity and people would merely be surviving. He (p 177) summarized his advice to the king as: 'Ever victorious and never conquered shall be that *Kshatriya*, who is nurtured by *Brahmins*, made prosperous by the counsels of able ministers and has, as his weapons, the precepts of the *shastras* (1.9.11).' He (p 141) added, 'A king who flouts the teachings of the *Dharamshastras* and the *Arthashastra*, ruins the kingdom by his own injustice (8.2).'

Compassion and Tolerance: Kautilya advised the king to show compassion and tolerance. According to him (p 741), the king, 'Shall adopt the way of life, dress, language and customs of the people [of the acquired territory], show the same devotion to the gods of the territory [as to his own gods] and participate in the people's festivals and amusements. He shall ensure that devotions are held regularly in all the temples and ashrams. The ill, the helpless and the distressed shall be helped (13.5).' Incidentally, the use of the word 'tolerance' is significant since John Locke (1689) is usually given the credit for emphasizing its virtue.[10] The king was persuaded on moral grounds to make sacrifices, such as to be charitable, and show compassion and tolerance.

Prevention of Moral Decline: According to Kautilya, knowledge helped in developing self-discipline and logical abilities to foresee the harmful consequences of vices. He (p 137) explained, 'Vices are due to ignorance and indiscipline; an unlearned man does not perceive the injurious consequences of his vices (8.3).' He (p 144) stated, 'The sole aim of all branches of knowledge is to inculcate restraint over the senses (1.6.3). Self-control, which is the basis of knowledge and discipline, is acquired by giving up lust, anger, greed, conceit, arrogance and foolhardiness. Living in accordance with the *shastras* means avoiding over-indulgence in all pleasures of [the senses, ie.] hearing, touch, sight, taste and smell (1.6.1,2).'

6.3 UNIQUE CONTRIBUTIONS TO ACTION-ORIENTED APPROACHES

The Greek philosophers discussed the principle of virtue-ethics but did not discuss any action-oriented principles of ethics. They emphasized the building of a person's good character and believed that good conduct would naturally follow. According to both Chang (1987) and Choi (1989), Han Feitzu (280-233 BCE) advanced the legalistic approach to ethics but he discarded the moralistic approach of Confucius.[11] Carroll and Buchholtz (2003, p 212) explain the virtue ethics, 'Action-oriented principles focus on doing. Virtue ethics emphasizes being.' The assumption, of course, is that the actions of a virtuous person will also be virtuous. Traditional ethical principles such as utilitarianism, rights, and justice focus on the question, 'What should I do?'

Combined Moralist and Action-oriented Approaches: Kautilya believed that these approaches were complementary and not substitutes. He emphasized the role of the moralist approach in character building. However, Kautilya was not naïve to ignore the possibility that some people might not follow *dharmic* values voluntarily. He suggested action-oriented approaches, such as, (i) adopting legalistic approach, that is, having contract and property rules (see Chapter 16), tort laws and traffic codes (discussed in Chapter 17), accounting rules and regulations (see Chapter 9), and having rewards and punishments for better compliance (Chapter 11 provides an in-depth analysis), (ii) devising an organizational design that reduced scope for conflict of interest situations (see Chapter 9). The following table captures his ideas:

Table 6.2: Dharmic (Ethical) and Action-oriented Approaches

	Happy and Productive Life			
	Moksha= Individual's Upliftment (System-building)		Freedom from Wants (*Artha*)	Freedom from Fear
Dharma-based Approach (Internal Restraints)	Encouraging virtues: non-violence, compassion, tolerance, honesty, truthfulness and cleanliness	Developing internal controls over system destroying vices: greed, anger, lust, ego, attachment, jealousy	Fosters trust and cooperation, lowers systemic risk, reduces shirking, improves productivity and reduces transaction costs	Helps in maintaining law and order, reduces violence and business risk
Legalistic Approach (External Constraints)	Ethics-based laws (so that they did not weaken ethical values)	Punishment for resorting to violence, intolerance (hate crimes), fraud	Enforcement of contracts, property rules and tort laws	Punishment for non-compliance
Organizational Design			Increases accountability and reduces scope for conflict of interest situations	

Limitation of Auditing, Rules and Regulations in Checking Fraud: It may be pointed out that Kautilya was fully aware of the limitations of rules, regulations and auditing in preventing corrupt practices. He recognized that a good system of bookkeeping and auditing was necessary but not sufficient in ensuring ethical practices. In other words, an accounting method, no matter how good it is (even GAAP, Generally Accepted Accounting Principles), will not defeat 'aggressive and creative' (another name for unscrupulous) accounting practices.

He believed that not only were the principles of accounting important but also the ethics of those who practice them. That is, principles were only as good as the people who practiced them. He (p 133-134) stated: 'Some teachers say that oppression by the Treasurer is worse because he harasses by finding fault with whatever is done and levies fines [which he pockets?]. The Chancellor, on the other hand, cannot do much harm since he is supervised by a [audit] bureau and can enjoy only what is legitimately assigned to him (8.4).'

Kautilya disagreed. He explained, 'The Treasurer can only appropriate what is brought into the treasury by others. But the Chancellor collects his own revenue first and then he may collect the king's revenue or even let it go to ruin; he can do as he pleases with other people's property (8.4).'

These statements imply that Kautilya believed that independent audits were necessary but were not sufficient in eliminating financial misappropriations. He noted that the Chancellor, who was responsible for collecting revenue from the countryside, was audited and yet could cause a lot more financial loss than the Treasurer who was not audited. He urged the king to make every effort to appoint incorruptible individuals to such key positions.

He (p 286) identified several kinds of officials who may cause loss to the Treasury. Two types may provide some glimpse into the depth of his insights. According to him, an official who caused loss might be arrogant 'about his learning, his wealth or the support he gets from highly placed persons'. The phrase 'support he gets from highly placed persons' implies the potential for abuse from undue access to high officials. This is indeed an old problem. Similarly, an official may have greed, 'which prompts him to use false balances, weights or measures, or to make false assessments and calculations.'

He developed contract and property rules and tort laws, which did not weaken ethical conduct. Among other recommendations proposed were measures covering the royal succession, and laws against sexual harassment and child labour.

There are a few noteworthy points. First, *dharma*-based approach was considered the most efficient for bringing peace and prosperity. He believed that even the most comprehensive set of rules and regulations were not enough in checking greed and eliminating the potential for fraudulent practices. Secondly, all these approaches/ measures were considered as complements to ethics-based approach and not substitutes. He warned that if a majority of the people became unethical, no other measure would work and the system would collapse. Thirdly, Kautilya insisted on having laws that were ethics-based and promoted ethical conduct.[12] Kautilya's contributions are truly unique among the ancient thinkers.

SUMMARY

Socrates asked the question 'how should a man live?' but neither he, nor Plato or Aristotle, offered any substantive or satisfactory answer to that. Adam Smith was certainly a sophisticated thinker, but his ideas were based more on feelings than on any deep theory of choice.[13] Despite having strong intentions, Adam Smith died before he could accomplish the task of any meaningful intersection of ethics and economics. His commercial man of the *Wealth of Nations* and the benevolent man of *The Theory of Moral Sentiments* never came in contact with each other.

Not only was the Socratic question asked more than a thousand years earlier in India, but also were the virtues of truthfulness, compassion, tolerance and non-violence identified and recommended to create heaven on earth.[14] Detailed list of moral codes was formulated to help the individual lead a happy and virtuous life.[15] Kautilya was way ahead of the Greeks and Adam Smith in offering both morality-based and action-oriented approaches for eliciting desirable social conduct. Moreover, he believed that ethical conduct promoted prosperity whereas the Greeks thought that prosperity was a threat to the ethical fabric of a society. However, according to Kautilya, no amount of rules and regulations or auditing can prevent unethical behaviour. He suggested many other policies, which, although not explored here, also reflect his concern for ethical values. For example, he (p 321) wrote, 'Village headman shall be responsible for preventing cruelty to animals (3.10).'

7

Ethical, Efficient and Energetic Decision-makers

> The virtuous one despises prosperity attained through ignominy. The bounds of good conduct should never be crossed. Truth and charity are the roots of righteousness. Righteousness is the ornament of all.
>
> — *Kautilya's Sutras*

Traditionally a king was like a paid public servant. It was considered his moral duty to enrich the people, administer justice, formulate sound policies and ensure their effective implementation. This, in turn, required that all the decision makers—the reigning king, his advisers and other public servants—must be ethical. Kautilya (p 119-123) described the constituent elements of a state and argued that the king was the most important element of a state. If the king was ethical and energetic, other constituents and public were likely to acquire the same attributes.

Kautilya expected the king to behave like a father towards his people. He should enrich them and protect them. The king should be a loyal servant to his royal public. He argued that freedom from foreign rule was absolutely essential to prosperity and, therefore, a king must use every means to protect independence. He provided detailed instructions to the king as to how he should manage internal and external affairs. He advised the king to be benevolent to his public but must be prudent in dealing with other nations. These are discussed in Section 7.1. He advised the reigning king that he should make sure that his successor was also ethical. He specified an elaborate and rigorous ethical education programme for the prince. This is presented in Section 7.2. Conclusion is provided in Section 7.3.

7.1 CONCEPTUAL FRAMEWORK ON ETHICAL CONDUCT

Kautilya broadened the practice of ethics from what was good or bad (for an individual) to what was in public interest vis-à-vis private interest. He assigned ethics the key role of facilitating liberation from poverty, along with the traditional one of salvation, from the birth-death-rebirth cycle. He changed the focus of ethical debates from right and wrong to allow discussion on conflicts of public and private interests. He was a sophisticated thinker as noted by Ray. He (1999, p 107-108) remarks, 'We must also not forget the context in which the *Arthashastra* was written. Kautilya was trying to create, almost single-handedly, "order out of chaos, peace out of war, a public state out of a corrupt one". That is why his ideas were extremely complex. On the one hand, he had suggested the use of all evil, cruel and wicked methods, while on the other, he was obsessed by the idea of creation of a clean administrative system.'

Referring to the king, Kautilya observed: 'In the happiness of his subjects lies his happiness; in their welfare his welfare. He shall not consider as good only that which pleases him but treat as beneficial to him whatever pleases his subjects (1.19)'. The above statement contains the following four possibilities:
- If the policies/activities served both the public interest and the

king's interest, then there was no conflict and king should pursue such activities.
- If the activities were against both public interest and the king's interest, then too there was no conflict and the king did not face any dilemma.
- Some of the policies/activities might be in public interest but against the king's interest. There was conflict of interest but he advised the king to protect/promote public interest and sacrifice his own interest.
- If the policies/activities were not in public interest but were in the king's interest. There was a conflict of interest and the king was advised not to pursue his own interest at the expense of public interest.

Kautilya maintained that, to a large extent, there was no conflict between a king's own interest or his moral duty and public interest since he considered the king's happiness and those of his subjects as perfect complements. However, if there was any conflict among them, public interest should take precedence over his own interest. Kautilya kept the traditional moral and immoral distinction. He was aware of various combinations in this regard. His conceptual framework, which is implicit in his *Arthashastra*, has the following eight possible cases.

Table 7.1: **Moral, Immoral, Private and Public Interests**

	Moral (M)		Immoral (M^C)	
	S	S^C	S	S^C
P	Case I: $M \cap S \cap P$	Case III: $M \cap S^C \cap P$	Case V: $M^C \cap S \cap P$	Case VII: $M^C \cap S^C \cap P$
P^C	Case II: $M \cap S \cap P^C$	Case IV: $M \cap S^C \cap P^C$	Case VI: $M^C \cap S \cap P^C$	Case VIII: $M^C \cap S^C \cap P^C$

M=*Dharmic* (Moral), M^C=*Adharmic* (Immoral), S=Public interest, S^C=Against public interest, P=private interest and P^C=against private interest.

Kautilya divided these eight cases into two broad groups: actions which promoted public interest (Cases I, II, V and VI) were to be encouraged and actions, which harmed public interest (Cases III, IV, VII and VIII) even if sanctioned on religion-based moral grounds, were to be discouraged. The above framework helps in shedding light on some of the debates on Kautilya's ideas relating to ethics.

Case 1: M∩S∩P = King's Moral Duty and His Own Interest Coincide with Public Interest. Kautilya advised the king to promote the well being of his subjects since that fulfilled his (a) moral duty as well as served (b) his self-interest.

King's Moral Duty: Kautilya (p 145) stated, 'A *rajarishi* [a king, wise like a sage] is one who: has self-control, having conquered the [inimical temptations] of the senses, cultivates the intellect by association with elders, is ever active in promoting the security and welfare of the people, endears himself to his people by enriching them and doing good to them and avoids daydreaming, capriciousness, falsehood and extravagance (1.7).' He added, 'A *rajarishi* shall always respect those councilors and *purohitas* who warn him of the dangers of transgressing the limits of good conduct, reminding him sharply (as with a goad) of the times prescribed for various duties and caution him even when he errs in private (1.8).' He (p 142) asserted, 'Government by Rule of Law, which alone can guarantee security of life and welfare of the people, is, in turn, dependent on the self-discipline of the king (1.5).'

Leadership: Kautilya wanted the king to be a role model, earn respect and rule through leadership and not through authority. He (p 147) wrote, 'If the king is energetic, his subjects will be equally energetic. If he is slack and lazy in performing his duties the subjects will also be lax and, thereby, eat into his wealth. Besides, a lazy king will easily fall into the hands of his enemies. Hence, the king should himself always be energetic (1.19).' He (p 121) stated, 'A king endowed with the ideal personal qualities enriches the other elements when they are less than perfect (6.1).' He (p 123) added, 'Whatever character the king has, the other elements also come to have the same (8.1).' Thus, according to Kautilya, a king must have a good knowledge of philosophy but should not be an idle philosopher or a dictator and rather, should be an impartial, benevolent, far-sighted, disciplined and energetic doer.

Moderation: Kautilya did not mention Aristotle's golden mean, but he and many thinkers before him did suggest moderation.[1] For example, they wanted the king to avoid both excessive indulgence and complete austerity in pleasures. He (p 145) wrote, 'There is no need for such a king to deprive himself of all sensual pleasures and lead a life of total austerity so long as he does not infringe his *dharma* or harms his own material well-being (1.7).'

King's Enlightened Self-interest: Kautilya reminded the king that his hold on power depended on public support, which had to be earned through good deeds and administration of justice.

- **Public Support to a King was Tied to His Being Just:** Kautilya (p 573) observed, 'When a strong but unjust king is attacked, his subjects will not come to his help but will either topple him or go over to the attacker. On the other hand, when a weak but just king is attacked, his subjects will not only come to his help but also follow him until death (7.5).'
- **Public Support to a King Linked to Economic Development:** Kautilya (p 159) argued, 'When a people are impoverished, they become greedy; when they are greedy, they become disaffected; when disaffected, they either go to the enemy or kill their ruler themselves (7.5).' He suggested, 'Therefore, the king shall not act in such a manner as would cause impoverishment, greed or disaffection among the people; if however, they do appear, he shall immediately take remedial measures (7.5).' It may be noted that a little vague but a definite distinction between positive and normative economic analysis is discernible in the above statements.

Case II: $M \cap S \cap P^C$ = Morally Right, in Public Interest but Against King's Own Interest. According to Kangle (2000, part III, p 92), E H Johnston believed that Kautilya paid only lip service to a king's moral duty and relentlessly advanced a king's self-interest. Kangle (2000, part III, p 92) quotes E H Johnston: 'According to the *Dharamshastra*, the institution of kingship exists for the maintenance of order and the preservation of the structure of society, the *Arthashastra*, no doubt, pays lip service to this ideal, but the essential doctrine underlying the entire work is that a king's sole pre-occupation is his own self-aggrandizement and that in its pursuit, he should be restricted by no considerations except those of enlightened self-interest. The originality of the *Arthashastra* lies, in my view, not in the conception of this principle which was probably already in the air, but in the relentless logic with which all its implications are worked out.'

Kangle (part III, pp 92-94) refutes Johnston's assertion that Kautilya ignored a king's moral duty (as specified by the *Dharmashastras*, ie. scriptures) of protecting his subjects. It is claimed here that both of these views are incomplete representations of Kautilya's ideas. Since Johnston's claim that the king pursues only his own interest, excludes case II, which urges the king to make sacrifices because that is his moral duty and Kangle's refutation ignores case V, which is in public interest (as well as the king's interest) but goes against established moral norms.

Recommendations Regarding Welfare Programmes: According to Kautilya, it was the moral duty of a king to commit himself fully to the upliftment of his public. He (p 377) explained, 'A king who observes his duty of protecting his people justly and according to law will go to heaven, whereas one who does not protect them or inflicts unjust punishment will not (3.1.42).' He suggested a comprehensive package of welfare programmes. (i) According to him, a king should take care of his subjects like a guardian (see Chapter 8). (ii) He recommended the provision of a safety net to the poor (discussed in Chapter 12). (iii) According to Kautilya, the king must help the people during calamities, like a famine (Chapter 13 contains a detailed discussion on preventive and remedial measures). Kautilya (p 128) believed, 'It is the duty of the king to protect the people from all calamities (4.3).' (iv) He suggested helping the helpless in legal matters (see Chapter 15).

Case III: $M \cap S^c \cap P$ = Morally Right, in King's Interest but Against Public Interest. This is an interesting case since the king was discouraged to undertake such activities, which harmed public interest. For example, Kautilya was against installing a lazy or wicked son on the throne even if the king wanted to, since it was not in public interest. He (p 169) wrote, 'Unless there are dangers in it, succession of the eldest son is praiseworthy. An only son, if he is wicked, shall not [under any circumstances] be installed on the throne. A king with many sons acts in the best interests [of the kingdom] only if he removes a wicked one from succession (1.17).' Clearly Kautilya gave priority to public interest over tradition and king's interest.

Case IV: $M \cap S^C \cap P^C$ = Morally Correct but Against Both Public and Private Interests. Kautilya did not want anyone to become a monk even if that was considered morally right at the time since that was against both public interest and a king's interest. It was against public interest since the family of that person would suffer and would require public assistance and was also against the king's interest, since national security might be affected adversely if many young adults became monks. He (p 405) wrote, 'No one shall renounce his marital life [to become an ascetic] without providing for his wife and sons (2.1).'[2]

Case V: $M^C \cap S \cap P$ = Both in Public and King's Interests but Immoral. Kautilya invented this possibility and has drawn the maximum criticism for it. He would recommend to the king not to hesitate in the use of immoral methods to eliminate criminals, and in dealing with an aggressor, to enhance safety and security of his public. For example, he (p 269) suggested, 'A king, who finds himself in great financial difficulty, may collect [additional] revenue [using the methods described below] (5.2.1).' He (p 272-273) recommended expropriating temple property, exploiting the gullibility of the people and by hook or crook confiscating the properties of traitors and wicked people. Kautilya (p 540) added, 'Deceptive occult practices shall be used to frighten the enemy. It is also said that these can be used [against one's own people] in case of a revolt in order to protect the kingdom (14.2.45).'

Numerous writers have incorrectly compared Kautilya's *Arthashastra* to Machiavelli's *Prince*. However, Ray puts Kautilya's recommendations in the proper perspective. He (1999, p 81) remarks, 'The *Prince* was written with the intention of advising the king how to maintain his rule. The aims of the *Arthashastra* are *yogakshema* and *raksana* of the subjects.' (*Yogakshema*=Sanskrit expression signifying welfare—material and spiritual; *Rakshana*=Sanskrit word for protection and maintenance.)

Case VI: $M^C \cap S \cap P^C$ = Morally Wrong, in Public Interest but Against King's Interest. Kautilya (1.18) considered the possibility that a prince, who was worthy to be a future king, but was treated unjustly and faced the possibility of even getting killed by his own father, might consider killing his father and declare himself the king. Clearly, public interest was more important to Kautilya than the continuation of a king, who was unjust and acted against public interest.[3] Sen's (1997) statements regarding the ethical content in the *Arthashastra* are unwarranted.

Case VII: $M^C \cap S^C \cap P$ = Morally Wrong, Against Public Interest but in Private Interest. According to Kautilya (p 133), 'A decadent king, on the other hand, oppresses the people by demanding gifts, seizing what he wants and grabbing for himself and his favourites the produce of the country [ie. the king and his coterie consume more than their due share thus considerably impoverishing the treasury and the people] (8.4).' He added that such a king 'fails to give what ought to be given and exacts what he cannot rightly take'; 'indulges in wasteful expenditure and destroys profitable undertakings'; 'fails to protect the people from thieves and robs them himself'; 'does not recompense service done to him'; 'does not carry out his part of what had been agreed upon'; and 'by his indolence and negligence destroys the welfare of his people' (7.5). Kautilya did warn such kings that the public would remove them at the first opportunity to do so.

Case VIII: $M^C \cap S^C \cap P^C$ = Morally Wrong and Against both Public and Private Interests. According to Kautilya, Case VIII was the worst possible and must be avoided with every possible means. He (p 144) wrote, 'A king who has no self-control and gives himself to excessive indulgence in pleasures will soon perish, even if he is the ruler of all four corners of the earth (1.6.4).' According to Kautilya (p 137), 'Excessive greed and lust bring about humiliation, loss of wealth and association with undesirable persons like thieves, gamblers, hunters, singers and musicians (8.3).' He (p 140) explained, 'Excessive desire leads to the cultivation of evil things while anger causes abandonment of good things (8.3.65).' He (p 141) added, 'A king who flouts the teachings of the *Dharamshastras* and the *Arthashastra*, ruins the kingdom by his own injustice (8.2.12).'

7.2 CHARACTER-BUILDING OF THE FUTURE KING

Ethical Education: Kautilya advocated teaching *Vedas* and philosophy for learning ethical values and self-discipline and economics and political science for acquiring practical skills to lead a good, productive and moral life. He (p 155-156) wrote, 'There can be no greater crime or sin says Kautilya than making wicked impressions on an innocent mind. Just as a clean object is stained with whatever is smeared on it, so a prince with a fresh mind, understands as the truth whatever is taught to him. Therefore, a prince should be taught what is *dharma* and *artha*, not what is unrighteous and materially harmful (1.17).'

Education as a Method for Becoming Wise: Kautilya discussed four functions of education: learning some relevant historical facts (ie. imbibing information), mastering useful skills (knowledge), increasing cognitive abilities, and improving self-control over destructive emotions such as 'anger, lust, greed, conceit, arrogance and foolhardiness' (ie. wisdom). That is, he included not only the three roles of schooling discussed by Conlisk (1996) but also added a fourth one that helped in developing the ability to control emotions, ie. he emphasized that schooling developed the ability to draw inferences and promoted self-discipline.[4] He (p 144) observed, 'The sole aim of all branches of knowledge is to inculcate restraint over senses (1.6)'.

Kautilya also described the process of learning. He (p 142) stated, 'Learning imparts discipline only to those who have the following mental faculties—obedience to a teacher, desire and ability to learn, capacity to retain what is learnt, understanding what is learnt, reflecting on it, and [finally] ability to make inferences by deliberating on the knowledge acquired. Those who are devoid of such mental faculties are not benefited [by any amount of training] (1.5).' He (p 143) added, 'For, [trained] intellect is the result of learning [by hearing]; from intellect ensues yoga [successful application]; from yoga comes self-possession. This is what is meant by efficiency in acquiring knowledge (1.5).' It may be noted that Kautilya believed that a person's innate abilities and his desire to learn were complementary, implying that education could serve as a 'signal' too.

Education, Superstition and Emotions: Kautilya assigned negative roles both to superstition and emotions. He (p 637) observed, 'Wealth will slip away from that childish man who constantly consults the stars (9.4).' It is obvious that he strongly believed that there was a negative relationship or a trade-off between wealth and superstition (irrationality). He (p 636) labelled some emotions as 'obstacles' to achieving the gains from campaigns. He provided a comprehensive list of such emotions. These included: 'Passion, anger, timidity, compassion leading to aversion to fighting, recoiling from awarding deserved punishment, baseness, haughtiness, a forgiving nature, thinking of the next world, being too pious, meanness, abjectness, jealousy, contempt for what one has, wickedness, distrust, fear, negligence, inability to withstand harsh climate and faith in the auspiciousness of stars and days (9.4).'

Kautilya believed that education made a person rational by developing self-control over emotions, that is, in today's terminology an educated person's indifference curves became almost vertical. Caplan (2000) provides a common framework to analyze the controversy between the neoclassical and behavioral approaches. Figure (3) in Caplan's analysis may be used to represent Kautilya's views on the role of education and the trade-off between wealth and irrationality caused by emotions and superstition.

Obviously, one does not need to have vertical indifference curves for a corner solution like point B in the Figure 7.1. But more fundamentally, it implies that preferences are endogenous, that is, the slope of the indifference curve of a child may be influenced by his/her education. It also means that according to Kautilya, rationality, to some extent, is an acquired trait. He stated, 'Discipline is of two kinds—inborn and acquired (1.5).' He believed that one could

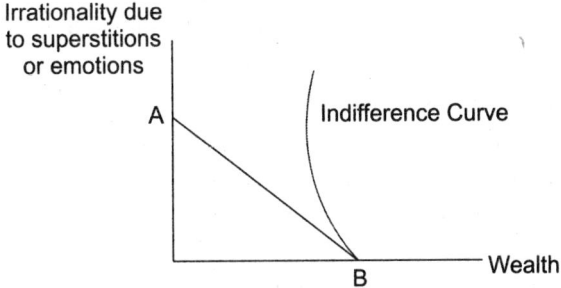

Figure 7.1: Line AB indicates a negative relationship between irrationality and acquisition of wealth. Education reduces irrationality and changes the slope of the indifference curve.

acquire wisdom by imitating wise people. Keeping that in view, he instructed a prince thus: 'With a view to improving his self-discipline, he should always associate with learned elders, for in them alone has discipline its firm roots (1.5).' According to Kautilya, education (along with its other roles) helped in developing discipline, which removed irrationality. However, Elster (1998) concludes his survey, observing: 'The more urgent task is to understand how emotions interact with other motivations to produce behavior.'

SUMMARY

Kautilya believed that an individual's well-being depended on good governance and one's own efforts. He understood the importance of freedom from foreign rule, internal chaos, hunger, disease and ignorance so that individuals had the freedom to pursue their own spiritual and material interests. Although he was unaware of any such distinctions, he did not see welfarism, contractarianism and building of capabilities of individuals (see Sugden (1993)) as mutually exclusive approaches and would have considered them as complementary in promoting the well-being of individuals.

8

Ethics and Economic Growth

> One should not stay where the five do not exist: means of livelihood, security, sense of shame, courtesy, and philanthropy.
>
> —*Kautilya's Sutras*

In recent years, a considerable amount of intellectual effort has been devoted to studying the influence of institutions and good governance on economic growth. In fact, the very origin of economics as a separate discipline during the 4th century BCE may be attributed to the imperative of economic growth and to the studying of its relationship to institutions, good governance and ethics. Kautilya believed that quality of institutions and good governance depended on ethical environment and ethical conduct of the decision-makers.

Kautilya emphasized establishment of quality institutions, such as, a rule of law, protection of private property rights and the provision of good governance. He offered a comprehensive definition of good governance, which included efficient and effective economic policies and caring and clean administration. He recommended removal of 'obstructions to economic growth' and suggested tax incentives to promote economic growth through encouraging capital formation. Section 8.1 contains this discussion.

The discussion in Section 8.2 is focused on considering Kautilya's ideas related to the identification of land, labour, and both human and physical capital as sources of economic growth. According to him, anyone who consulted his stars or depended on gods for a favourable outcome was courting disaster. Kautilya's *Arthashastra* may be considered as the best expression of Indian thought on economic progress and its relationship to social order. He argued that economic growth improved the standard of living and made a nation stronger and more secure. He believed power and prosperity were interdependent (see also Chapters 13 and 18).[1] Kautilya believed that the establishment of rule of law and private property rights were essential to the achievement of prosperity since they created conditions conducive to the full exploitation of opportunities. But good governance was required to create the opportunities. He argued that good institutions reduced the risk and good governance increased the rate of return on private investment. This unique insight is presented in Section 8.3. It has been argued that the decisions to invest and work are dependent on the existence of good institutions and these have been termed as the 'deep determinants' of economic growth. However, according to Kautilya, *dharma* was the 'deep determinant' since the quality of both institutions and governance was dependent on it. Two types of models of growth are discernible from the *Arthashastra*: one guided by enlightened self-interest and the other based on ethical conduct. These are presented in Section 8.4.

8.1 CREATION OF GOOD INSTITUTIONS AND PROVISION OF GOOD GOVERNANCE

According to North (1990), institutions include formal rules and regulations and social norms, which constrain the behavior of individuals. However, Kautilya made a distinction between internal restraints which were due to self-discipline and internalizing of ethical values and external constraints imposed by the society. He considered them qualitatively different, since internal restraints were more reliable than the external constraints in creating trust and preventing systemic risk. Accuracy of prediction is a desirable disciplinary value to have and the behavior of an ethical individual could be predicted more accurately than that of a 'rational fool'. The challenge is: how to make people ethical in a godless world.

Law and Order and Economic Development: Kautilya emphasized the importance of rule of law and protection of private property rights. He (p 108) observed, 'By maintaining order, the king can preserve what he already has, acquire new possessions, augment his wealth and power, and share the benefits of improvement with those worthy of such gifts. The progress of this world depends on the maintenance of order and the [proper functioning of] government (1.4).'

Protection of Private Property Rights: Kautilya (p 121) wrote, 'The wealth of the state shall be one acquired lawfully either by inheritance or by the king's efforts (6.10).' He (p 231) added, 'Water works such as reservoirs, embankments and tanks can be privately owned and the owner shall be free to sell or mortgage them (3.9).' He condemned an immoral and shortsighted king, who did not protect private property rights. According to him (p 133), 'A decadent king, on the other hand, fails to protect the people from thieves and robs them himself; does not recompense service done to him.'

Kautilya used moral incentive to motivate the king to be fair in protecting his subjects. He (p 377) wrote, 'A king who observes his duty of protecting his people justly and according to law will go to heaven, whereas one who does not protect them or inflicts unjust punishment will not. It is the power of punishment alone, when exercised impartially in proportion to the guilt, and irrespective of whether the person punished is the king's son or an enemy, that protects this world and the next. (3.1).' Administration of justice is discussed in Chapter 15.

Good Governance: Kautilya believed that prosperity, national security, good governance, and knowledge were interdependent. According to him, good governance consisted of three basic elements: (i) provision of national security and public infrastructure, such as roads, to facilitate and promote commerce, (ii) formulation of efficient (farsighted and well thought-out) policies and their effective implementation, removal of all obstructions to economic growth and tax incentives to encourage capital formation, and (iii) ensuring a caring and clean administration. These are presented in turn.

Provision of Infrastructure: Kautilya (p 181) suggested, 'Not only shall the king keep in good repair productive forests, elephant forests, reservoirs and mines created in the past, but also set up new mines, factories, forests [for timber and other produce], elephant forests and cattle herds [shall promote trade and commerce by setting up] market towns, ports and trade routes, both by land and water. He shall build storage reservoirs, [filling them] either from natural springs or water brought from elsewhere; or, he may provide help to those who build reservoirs by giving them land, building roads and channels or giving grants of timber and implements (2.1).' He (p 553) added, 'A king makes progress by building forts, irrigation works or trade routes, creating new settlements, elephant forests or productive forests, or opening new mines (7.1).'

Efficient Formulation and Effective Implementation of Policies: Kautilya recommended that the king promote capital formation, remove all impediments to economic activities, and pursue productive activities. He suggested considering all aspects of a policy: its proper formulation and effective implementation. He (p 116) wrote, 'In the interests of the prosperity of the country, a king should be diligent in foreseeing the possibility of calamities, try to avert them before they arise, overcome those which happen, remove all obstructions to economic activity and prevent loss of revenue to the state (8.4).'

Incentives to Encourage Capital Formation: He suggested many measures to encourage capital formation. He (p 231) recommended

- **Tax Holidays**: 'Anyone who brings new land under cultivation shall be granted exemption from payment of agricultural taxes for a period of two years. Similarly, 'for building or improving irrigation facilities' exemption from water rates shall be granted (3.9).'
- **Concessionary Loans** (p 179): '[On new settlements] the cultivators shall be granted grains, cattle and money which they can repay at their convenience (2.1).'
- **Duty Free Imports** (p 238): 'Any items that, at his discretion, the Chief Controller of Customs, may consider to be highly beneficial to the country [such as rare seeds]' (2.21) are to be exempt from import duties. He was against putting any excessive tax burden on the people (see Chapter 12).

Effective Implementation of Policies: Kautilya assigned the role of executing the king's orders to the ministers. He (p 200) stated, 'The ministers shall [constantly] think of all that concerns the king as well as those of the enemy. They shall start doing all that has not [yet] been done, continue implementing that which has been started, improve on works completed and, in general, ensure strict compliance with orders. The king shall personally supervise the work of those ministers near him. With those farther away, he shall communicate by sending letters (1.15).' He (p 123) listed the responsibilities of a minister as follows: 'All state activities have their origin in the minister, whether these be the successful execution of works for [the benefit of] the territory and the population, maintenance of law and order, protection from enemies, tackling [natural] calamities, settlement of virgin lands, recruiting the army, revenue collection or rewarding the worthy (8.1).'

Recommended an Ethical, Clean and Caring Administration
Clean Administration: Drekmeier (p 256) points out, 'Restraints on the king were not formal; they were restrictions imposed by the obligation to uphold custom and sacred law and to fulfill the requirements of *rajadharma*.'
Caring: Kautilya believed that a king should take care of his subjects like a father takes care of his children. He (p 128) wrote, 'Whenever danger threatens, the king shall protect all those afflicted like a father

[protects his children] (4.3).' He (p 180) added, 'He shall, however, treat leniently, like a father [would treat his son], those whose exemptions have ceased to be effective (2.1).'

Accountability: Interestingly, Kautilya was concerned, at least to some extent with accountability of the king's own family members and officials of his administration. For example, he (p 275-276) recommended specifically the listing of revenue collected from 'fines paid by government servants' and 'gifts'. He (p 276) also wrote, 'Expenditure will be classified according to the major Heads, as given below: The Palace [expenditure of the King, Queens, Princes etc.] (2.6).' He (p 284) added, 'Every official who is authorized to execute a task or is appointed as a Head of Department shall communicate [to the king] the true facts about the nature of the work, the income and the expenditure, both in detail and the total (2.9).'

Kaufmann *et al* (2003) have developed six indicators to measure the quality of governance: (i) voice and accountability (ii) political stability (iii) government effectiveness (iv) regulatory quality (v) rule of law and (vi) control of corruption. The first two synthetic indices capture how a government is elected, replaced and monitored. The next two indicate the quality of the formulation and implementation of government policies and the final two capture the level of corruption and the rule of law. It may be noted that their definition of governance is incomplete since it concentrates only on efficiency and ignores equity considerations.

8.2 CAPITAL, LABOUR AND LAND AS SOURCES OF ECONOMIC GROWTH

Kautilya encouraged the use of 'rare seeds' but there was no account of explicitly stated exogenous or endogenous technological progress in his growth analysis, and increases in the factors of production were the primary sources of economic growth.[2] Interestingly, he emphasized the contributions of both physical and human capital to economic growth.

Identification of Factors of Production as Sources of Growth: Land, labour and capital as distinct factors of production had been identified even before Kautilya. However, it was he, who recognized them (particularly capital) as sources of economic growth.

Importance of Capital: Kautilya (p 637) argued, 'Man, without wealth, does not get it even after a hundred attempts. Just as elephants are needed to catch elephants, so does wealth capture more wealth. Wealth will slip away from that childish man who constantly consults the stars. The only [guiding] star of wealth is itself; what can the stars of the sky do? (9.4)'. He (p 621) added, 'A king who trusts in fate and does not believe in human effort will fail because such a king never begins a work and never achieves anything (7.11)'. The above observations by Kautilya completely refute Mokyr's claim that Hindu civilization makes people fatalistic.[3] Also, according to Kautilya, availability of capital improved labour productivity a hundred fold.[4]

Distinction between Consumption and Investment Goods: Kautilya (p 149) suggested, 'Hence the king shall be ever active in the management of the economy. The root of wealth is economic activity and lack of it brings material distress. In the absence of fruitful economic activity, both current prosperity and future growth are in danger of destruction. A king can achieve the desired objectives and abundance of riches by undertaking productive economic activity (1.19)'.

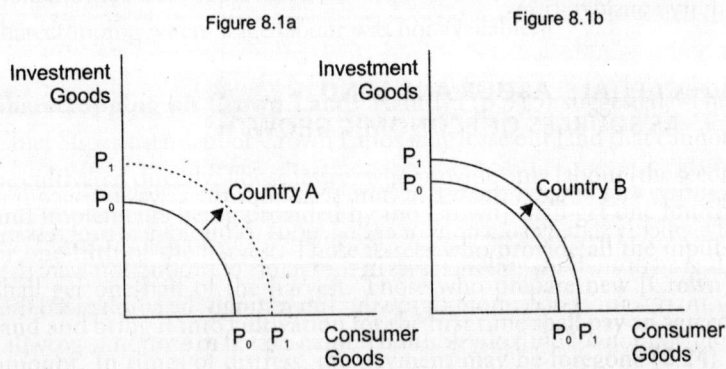

Figures 8.1a and 8.1b: $P_0 P_1$ is the initial production possibility frontier between investments goods and consumption goods and its shift is larger in country A than that of country B.

Kautilya put very heavy emphasis on capital formation. His argument for a maximum possible investment may be illuminated by the familiar production possibility frontiers. Figure 8.1a indicates a larger shift in PPF due to a larger amount of investment goods and in Figure 8.1b the shift in the PPF is smaller due to the smaller investment.

Importance of Labour: He (p 619) stated, 'The value of land is what man makes of it (7.11).' He assigned due weights to the size and to the other characteristics of a land tract, but ranked human effort the highest since without human effort, the piece of land would be worthless.

Distinction between Man-hours and Effort: He (p 572) observed, '[When shares are specified before the start of the campaign] it is normal to base them on the proportion of troops contributed; however, fixing the shares on the basis of the efforts made by each one during the campaign is the best type (7.4).'

Human Capital: Kautilya used the phrase *'elephants are needed to catch elephants'* to emphasize the importance of capital. Similarly, he used the phrase *'like the hunter outwitting the elephant'* to emphasize the importance of intelligence and knowledge. The power of good analysis and judgment helped both directly by devising sound economic policies to promote '*artha* [material well-being]' and indirectly as discussed below, by enhancing national security and conquering new territories since it was considered superior to physical power.

Importance of Land: Kautilya (p 617) stated, 'Among the signatories to a treaty for a joint campaign, he who acquires land [whether settled land or virgin land] with [the maximum number of] ideal qualities and with many developed productive facilities outmanoeuvres the others (7.10).' Particularly, the conquest of settled territory, which brought with it labour and capital was preferred.[5]

8.3 INSTITUTIONS, GOVERNANCE AND RISK-RETURN TRADE-OFF

Since the mid '90s, a considerable amount of intellectual effort has been devoted to study the nature of relationship between institutions, good governance and economic growth. One group of economists argues that institutions are the most important determinant of economic growth. In fact, these economists call institutions as the 'deep determinants' of growth. For example, Rodrik *et al* (2004) claim, 'This exercise yields some sharp and striking results. Most importantly, we find that the quality of institutions trumps everything else.' The other group of economists gives only secondary importance to institutions. Glaeser *et al* (2004, p 298) conclude: 'But institutional outcomes also get better as the society grows richer, because institutional opportunities improve. Importantly, in that framework, institutions have only a second-order effect on economic performance. The first order effect comes from human and social capital, which shape both institutional and productive capacities of a society.'

Impact of Good Institutions and Good Governance on Risk-return Trade-off: Kautilya settled this debate more than two thousand years ago. He argued that an improvement in law and order situation reduced the investment risk and good governance increased the return on investment. That is, both are essential to prosperity.

Establishment of Law and Order Lowered Investment Risk: Kautilya understood the concept of risk premium. He suggested different interest rates for different types of loans depending on the level of risk. For example, he suggested a rate of 15% on normal transactions, a rate of 60% on normal commercial transactions, a rate of 120% if risky travel through forests was involved and a rate of 240%, if the travel was by sea. He (p 426) added, 'No one shall charge or cause to be charged a rate higher than the above, except in regions where the king is unable to guarantee security; in such a case, the judges shall take into account the customary practices among debtors and creditors (3.11).' The suggestion that the interest rate could be higher 'where the King is unable to guarantee security' is quite significant implying the importance of law and order in reducing risk on private investment and promoting commerce.

Good Governance Improves Rate of Return: According to Kautilya, the provision of good governance contributed in two ways to the raising of the rate of return on private investment: (i) by reducing expropriation by government officials, such that individuals could retain more of what they had earned and (ii) by raising the rate of return through sound economic policies, by removing 'all obstructions to economic activity' and productive investment.[6] Only recently, these insights have been fully appreciated.[7] He was way ahead of his time since he was concerned about these factors more than two millennia ago.

Kautilya's ideas if expressed in today's language, imply that the risk-return feasibility (Markowitz-Sharpe efficiency) frontier shifts upwards as well as becomes more concave. This may be captured by Figure 8.2.

Based on Kautilya's analysis, provision of good governance raises the rate of return and good institutions lower the risk on private investment. Kautilya's insights may be expressed not only as a shift in the possibility frontier but also as a change in its curvature. As discussed in Chapter 12, he preferred an income tax to raise revenue to provide for public goods. A lump-sum tax might appear unfair, generate resentment and create political instability and thus might deny the benefits of a reduction in risk.

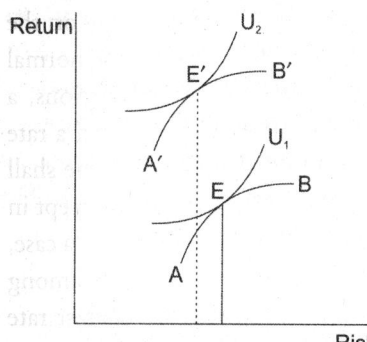

Figure 8.2: AB and A'B' are the risk-return possibility frontiers. U_1 and U_2 are investor's indifference curves. The risk-return possibility frontier, AB shifts to A'B' and also becomes more concave. That makes it possible for an investor to move from point E to point E'.

8.4 INTERDEPENDENCE OF KNOWLEDGE, GOVERNANCE, NATIONAL SECURITY AND ECONOMIC GROWTH

Dharma as the Real Deep Determinant of Growth: Ancient sages had emphasized the role of ethics for attaining salvation from the birth-death-rebirth cycle. As mentioned earlier Kautilya also supported this role of ethics. He (p 106) wrote, '[The observance of] one's own *dharma* leads to heaven and eternal bliss. When *dharma* is transgressed, the resulting chaos leads to the extermination of this world.' He further expanded the role of ethics. He argued that ethics was the most effective catalyst in attaining salvation from poverty. He (p 107-108) asserted, 'For the world, when maintained in accordance with the Vedas, will ever prosper and not perish. Therefore, the king shall never allow the people to swerve from their *dharma*.' He believed that laws, rules, regulations and government policies guided by ethics would enrich all segments of society. He (p 177) summarized his advice to a king as: 'Ever victorious and never conquered shall be that *Kshatriya*, who is nurtured by *Brahmins*, made prosperous by the counsels of able ministers and has, as his weapons, the precepts of the *shastras* (1.9.11).' In contrast, the Greek philosophers did not identify a link between ethical values and prosperity.

Kautilya believed that both good institutions and good governance depended on the ethical environment and ethical conduct of the decision-makers. According to him, the king must be ethical and then he should make sure that his administration was not corrupt, since corrupt government servants would promote corrupt people and themselves would participate in corrupt practices. He (p 493-494) asserted, 'Thus, the king shall first reform the administration, by punishing appropriately those officers who deal in wealth; they, duly corrected, shall use the right punishments to ensure the good conduct of the people of the towns and the countryside (4.9).' The following table presents Kautilya's conceptual framework on the link between *dharma* and prosperity.

Table 8.1: **Conceptual Framework on *Dharma* and Prosperity**

Objective	Human Security	Freedom from Wants (enrichment of the people)
		Freedom from Fear (Safety and Security)
Sources of Economic Growth	Increases in inputs	Man-power and Work-intensity
		Capital Accumulation
		Increases in Land under Cultivation
	Good Governance	Provision of Infrastructure
		Formulation of Efficient Economic Policies and Their Effective Implementation
		Clean, Caring and Fair Administration
	Quality of Institutions	Rules of Game, Regulations, Constitution
Foundation	Dharmic Values (The real Deep Determinants)	Non-violence, Compassion, Tolerance, Honesty, Truthfulness and Cleanliness

Ethical Conduct and Prosperity: Kautilya argued that a king, whether he fulfilled his moral duty or followed his enlightened self-interest, had to enrich his subjects. However, he understood the major differences between them: according to the moral duty, the king wanted to enrich the public whereas according to the enlightened self-interest, the king had to enrich the public. He preferred an ethical king rather than a king motivated by his enlightened self-interest. The following Figure 8.3 may be used to express his ideas on comparing the relative consequences of following moral duty to those of enlightened self-interest.

136 Ethical Foundation to Freedom from Wants

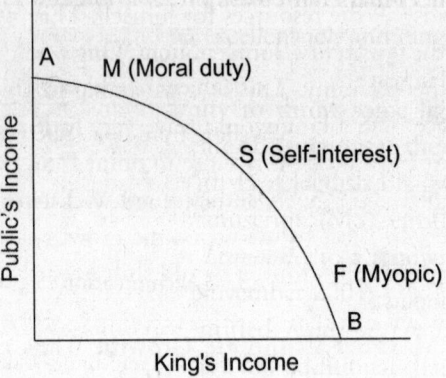

Figure 8.3: AB is the income possibility frontier. Point M denotes the combination (high public income, low king's income) if the king follows his moral duty. Point F denotes the combination (very low income for the public, very high income for the income) when the king is immoral. Point S denotes the combination (somewhere in between points M and F) when the king is amoral, that is, follows his enlightened self-interest

Kautilya Specified Three Possibilities

- His argument based on moral duty implied that a *rajarshi* (king, wise like a sage) would take a very modest amount for his own consumption, that is, point M would not be too far away from point A on the vertical axis.[8] Such a king would promote ethical behavior, use almost all the tax revenue on the provision of public goods and welfare programmes and follow judicious polices to encourage economic growth. As a consequence there would be both spiritual and economic (ie. over time the income possibility frontier would shift outwards) enrichment of his subjects.
- A king, motivated by his enlightened self-interest, would promote public interest to the extent that it promoted his own interest, that is, promotion of public interest was merely a means to the promotion of his own interest (whereas in the above-mentioned case (i) promotion of public interest was an end in itself). Kautilya's argument based on enlightened self-interest implied that the king might choose a point like, S.[9]
- According to Kautilya, a myopic and unethical king would try

to grab almost all the resources for himself. This is indicated by point F on the possibility frontier. Such a king would ruin himself as well as the economy. This is comparable to Olson's 'roving bandit'. Since such a king would leave very little for the public, that is, point F would be very close to point B on the horizontal axis (in Figure 8.3). Such extortionary and myopic behavior would adversely affect future economic growth (ie. most likely, the income possibility frontier would shift inwards).

Minimal and Maximal Economic Growth: Thus two types of growth models are discernible from the *Arthashastra*: one based on moral duty and the other based on enlightened self-interest. Kautilya preferred the one based on moral duty since that would lead to the highest possible growth in income of the people. Whereas the growth rate based on enlightened self interest was the minimum required of a king to stay in power. That is, so long as the king managed to keep income above the poverty line, $y > y_{pl}$, (the poverty level of income) and judicial fairness, $J > J_R$ at a reasonable level of fairness (that is, punishment somewhat proportionate to the crime and low probability of judicial errors), there would be law and order and the king could stay in power. However, the king had to provide some infrastructure and have pro-growth policies to promote economic growth. Thus, even in this model, both institutions and governance were needed for generating economic growth and institutions alone could not be labelled as the 'deep determinant' of growth.

Good and Stable Government Essential to Growth in Knowledge and Income: As mentioned earlier, according to Kautilya, economic progress depended on maintenance of law and order and good governance. Kautilya (p 108) wrote, 'The progress of this world depends on the maintenance of order and the [proper functioning of] government (1.4).' He believed that no acquisition of human capital would take place unless a fair rule of law had been firmly established. He (p 142) asserted, 'The three sciences [philosophy, the three Vedas and economics] are dependent [for their development] on the science of government. [For, without a just administration, no pursuit of learning or avocation would be possible.]' However, according to him, establishment of the rule of law alone did not initiate economic growth. Instead, the formulation and effective implementation of sound policies were needed to encourage human and physical capital formation, which contributed to economic growth. That is, rules were needed to play a game in an orderly and fair manner but these did not determine the quality or intensity of the game, which depended, along with other factors, on the training, discipline, material and intrinsic motivation of the players, and the quality of coaching.

Knowledge as Determinant of Governance, National Security and Income: According to Kautilya, knowledge helped the king develop self-discipline, which was critical in preserving independence. Kautilya (p 144) believed, 'The sole aim of all branches of knowledge is to inculcate restraint over senses. A king who has no self-control and gives himself up to excessive indulgence in pleasures will soon perish, even if he is the ruler of all four corners of the earth.'

Kautilya considered knowledge and intelligence as the most important factors in maintaining (and expanding) the kingdom and enhancing economic growth. He (p 628) argued, 'The power of good counsel, [good analysis and good judgment] is superior to [sheer military strength]. Intelligence and knowledge of the science of politics are the two eyes [of a king]. Using these, a king can, with a little effort, arrive at the best judgment on the means, [the four methods of conciliation, sowing dissention etc.] as well as the various tricks, stratagems, clandestine practices and occult means [described in this treatise] to overwhelm even kings who are mighty and energetic.'

Income as Determinant of Governance, Knowledge and National Security: As also mentioned earlier, Kautilya (p 252) stated, 'All state activities depend first on the Treasury. Therefore, a king shall devote his best attention to it. A king with a depleted Treasury eats into the very vitality of the citizens and the country.' Thus, paying efficiency wages to qualified advisers, provision of infrastructure and national security, subsidizing the intellectuals and welfare programmes, etc. depended on the tax revenue and that directly depended on income.

Ethical Values an Input to Political Stability and Economic Growth: Ethical conduct was considered essential for the stability of government and achievement of economic prosperity. Kautilya considered ethical conduct as a means to prosperity in this world and to paving the way to heaven after death. Kautilya (Shamasastry, 1915, p 394) wrote, 'As virtue is the basis of wealth and as enjoyment is the end of wealth, success in achieving that kind of wealth which promotes virtue, wealth and enjoyment is termed success in all.'

It is clear from the above statements that Kautilya believed that establishment of law and order was essential to growth in knowledge, and knowledge in turn, was essential (by restraining the king) in maintaining political stability and enhancing economic growth by helping in the formulation of sound policies. Similarly, political stability and independence were essential to economic growth, which in turn helped to strengthen national security. Thus, according to Kautilya, knowledge, governance, national security and prosperity were determined endogenously. But he was not aware of any such distinction between exogenous and endogenous variables. A sustained growth required a government to be stable, efficient, and ethical (honest and fair).

Specification of Kautilya's Model: Kautilya could not and did not have even the faintest idea about model specification, identification or proper estimation since there was no calculus, probability theory or econometrics available to him. However, based on his statements, a formal model may be specified as:

Max $U(C, S)$
Subject to:

$$Y = A F (K_p, L_f, T) \quad (8.1)$$
$$A = G (GG, M, KN, K_G) \quad (8.2)$$
$$GG = GG (M, Y, KN) \quad (8.3)$$
$$M = M (EED, EE) \quad (8.4)$$
$$dKN/dt = Z (GG, Y, KN, L_{KN}) \quad (8.5)$$
$$dK_p/dt = (1-t) Y - C \quad (8.6)$$
$$dK_G/dt = \beta (0.75) t.Y \quad (8.7)$$
$$WB = (1-\delta-\beta) (0.75) t.Y \quad (8.8)$$

$$DE = \delta (0.75) t Y \tag{8.9}$$
$$t (0.75) Y = DE + WB + d K_G / dt \tag{8.10}$$
$$P = X (J, H) K^\lambda (E L_m)^{(1-\lambda)} \tag{8.11}$$
$$S = S (P_1/P_2) \tag{8.12}$$
$$E = e (W, MM) \tag{8.13}$$
$$L = L_f + L_{KN} + L_m \tag{8.14}$$

Where C =consumption, S = national security, Y= income, K_p = capital in the private sector, K_G= public infrastructure, T = land, t Y =tax revenue, WB= expenditure on welfare programmes, DE (defense expenditure) = K (horses, elephants, chariots, armament, etc.) + Salary for soldiers, P =power, P_1 and P_2 = powers of king one and king two respectively, RP_1= relative power of a king (king one) to his potential enemy (king two). KN= knowledge, L_f= labor devoted to food production, L_m =labour joining the military, private investment, d K_p / dt = (1–t) Y–C, A= efficiency parameter, H = experience and analytical skills of the advisers and availability of information through intelligence, E = enthusiasm and training, EED= ethical education, EE= ethical environment, J = level of public support for a just and kind-hearted king, d KN /dt =increase in knowledge of all four disciplines (KN), L_{KN} = knowledge creating workers (Brahmins), GG=good governance, M=ethical conduct and F (K_p, L_p, T) is the production function and MM=moral motivation.

Sections 8.2 and 8.3 presented Kautilya's ideas on sources of economic growth and importance of institutions and governance. Equations (8.1) and (8.2) capture these ideas. It indicates that a country that had better governance, ethical conduct, infrastructure and knowledge base would have a higher standard of living than another, even though they both might have the same levels of land, labour and capital. The level of productivity, A depended on good governance, ethical conduct, income and knowledge as captured by equation (8.2). According to Kautilya, good governance depended on income, ethical conduct, and knowledge. Equation (8.3) is used to explain this relationship.

Private investment is captured by equation (8.4). Equation (8.5) indicates that growth in knowledge depended on knowledge-creating workers, income and existing knowledge. Kautilya did not explicitly mention income as a relevant factor to the creation of knowledge but the very existence of an intellectual class depended on the level of income. Drekmeier notes that the emergence of an economic surplus made it possible to support a rich culture and help in the rise of an empire in ancient India. He (1962, p 105) says, 'With the coming of an agricultural economy, there came also the promise of economic surplus—the production of goods and services in excess of what was needed for survival. This is the condition of civilization: the possibility of supporting a culture-creating class of professionals.'

Twenty-five per cent of the tax revenue was earmarked for administration and the remaining was allocated among public infrastructure (equation 8.7), welfare benefits (equation 8.8) and defense (equation 8.9). Equations (8.11), (8.12) and (8.13) reflect Kautilya's ideas on national security. According to him, power of a nation, P, depended on the army, armament, army's enthusiasm, experience and intelligence of advisers and public support. Equation (8.11) represents this relationship. According to equation (8.12), national security S depended on the relative power of King One compared to that of King Two. According to him, enthusiasm (E) depended on both material incentives (Wage) and moral motivation (MM). The total available labour was allocated among agriculture L_f, military L_m and knowledge producing workers L_{KN}, as indicated by equation (8.14). As mentioned in Chapter 2, there was a shortage of labour and Kautilya did everything possible to increase its growth rate.

According to him, government could create good institutions and could provide good governance but it could not create desire among people to exploit the existing opportunities. He extolled the public about the virtues of getting rich. He (Subramanian, p 50, 52, 54, 61, 79) believed, 'Poverty is death, while living. There is no enemy equal to hunger. A poor man's word, even if apt, is not heard. It is not difficult for the rich to do good deeds. Death is preferable to poverty.' The presence of capital, land and labour in equation (8.1) captures the intensity of desire in the attainment of prosperity.

SUMMARY

Kautilya argued that ethical conduct was the 'deep determinant' and not the institutions as claimed by some economists. He was the first economist who identified labour, capital and land as sources of economic growth. He believed that good policies were needed to create opportunities and fair institutions were needed to exploit those opportunities. That is, good institutions and good governance are complements and not substitutes and both were essential to economic prosperity. Recent contributions have not properly tested the virtuous cycle hypothesis and instead their tests are specified to validate their own brands of hypotheses.[10]

It is truly remarkable that Kautilya's ideas are as relevant today as they were in his times. Drekmeier (1962, p 300) puts it very aptly, 'Today the Indian state is as new as it was in Kautilya's time. And it is as old as all states must be in an age when sovereignty has proven an inadequate answer to the organizational requirements of security and peace. A solution as creative as that put forth in *Arthashastra* is needed if the amoral tribalism of our century is not to end.'

Kautilya recommended codification[s] of the rules and emphasized compliance. The public and the government servants were to be constrained by rules and regulations, and also by making appeal to the moral values while the enforcer (the king) was to be restrained by reminding him of his moral duty, and self-interest, ie. identity of his interest with that of the people.

9

Preventing Market and Government Failures

Theologians, moral philosophers, sociologists, political scientists and economists have been debating, surmising, evaluating and commenting for over two thousand years on the performance of market as a harbinger of miracles or menaces. A considerable amount of intellectual energy has been devoted to finding answers to many fundamental questions, such as, is the market moral?[1] and has it been a civilizing force or a destructive influence on the moral foundations of a society?[2] Each discipline offers its unique perspective and the scholars are spread all over the spectrum from pro-market ones to anti-market ones. Theologians and moral philosophers usually discuss the fairness aspect of the market. Pro-market scholars argue that the market allows freedom of choice and encourages creativity and entrepreneurship. On the other hand, the anti-market scholars deplore the fact that those who do not have any purchasing power are excluded from the market. However, they often ignore the Paretian efficiency considerations.[3]

Generally speaking, economists concentrate on the Paretian efficiency conditions for evaluating the performance of markets. The traditional view in the West, at least since Adam Smith, has been that unless monopolies, public goods and externalities, and other contributors to market failures, were present, markets would remain efficient. Again, since the Sherman Act of 1890, the traditional response to these market failures has been government regulation. Jonathan Baker (2003) discusses the 'necessity and successes' of Anti-Trust enforcement. However, the beneficiary effects of Anti-trust laws have been challenged, particularly since the last quarter of the last century. Clifford Winston (2006) collects and synthesizes many empirical studies on market and government failures and concludes that often the cure for market failure has been worse than the disease. He lists shortsightedness, inflexibility and contradictory policies as the causes of government failure to cure the market failure. The underlying assumption for such an analysis has been that the political stability was unaffected even if the system became blatantly unfair over time.

Kautilya believed that market failure was bad, government failure was worse but moral failure was the worst of all. According to him, a nation grew at a faster rate if its people were anchored to Vedic values since he believed that Vedic values created trust, harmony and peace, which promoted economic prosperity, which, in turn helped in the preservation of those core values. He argued that often, moral failure and poor organizational design were the root causes for both market and government failures. He believed that prevention was always better than cure and proposed an ethics-intensive education for building sound moral character and well thought out organizational design, with an intended goal of preventing both market and government failures and to have legal measures at hand to correct them if they occurred.

Kautilya followed a very pragmatic approach and recommended a mixed economy in which both the private sector and the public sector played complementary roles. He proposed establishment of law and order, provision of public infrastructure and tax incentives to encourage investment by the private sector. Additionally, government played an active role in providing national security, stabilizing the economy, regulating monopoly and pollution, banning child labour and sexual harassment, and protecting the consumers against fraud. According to him, the state (king) had three basic responsibilities: *rakshana* (protection), *palana* (nurturing, administration) and *yogakshema* (welfare—material and spiritual) of its citizens. He recommended that the government should not only help the old, the sick, children and the helpless but also should provide insurance against natural disasters to everyone. Thus, the usual distinction between a residual and a universal welfare state may not be a very useful one in visualizing the functioning of Kautilyan state.[4]

Kautilya recognized the potential of the human tendency of self-centeredness, and believed that while it could be a positive force in bringing prosperity, if unchecked, it could become a negative one by indulging in rent-seeking activities, shirking from duties or pursuing corrupt practices (due to excessive greed). Various possibilities under which *moral, market and government failures* could occur are discernible from his observations. Section 9.1 presents his implied taxonomy of these failures explicitly. Kautilya was quite concerned about the disastrous consequences resulting from possible occurrence of both market and government failures. He identified the traditional market failures and surprisingly, some post-modern information-based market failures also. He believed that if a country did not have sovereignty, it would have nothing but misery and squalor. He emphasized national security and assigned its provision to the government (as discussed in Part Five). According to him, the second important role of government, as discussed in the previous chapter, was to maintain law and order, which he considered as a prerequisite to prosperity.

He believed that monopolies and monopsonies were a serious threat not only to the functioning of the market but also to political stability. Consequently, the disruption costs to the economy might be much larger than the distortionary costs. Additionally, he essentially equated monopoly rents to theft and considered their existence not only a market failure but also a moral failure. He proposed regulation of monopolies and other externalities for correcting the market failure. He suggested measures for combating the 'moral hazard' problem also. These ideas are contained in Section 9.2. This section also includes laws to protect consumers. He was equally concerned about the government failure resulting from corruption, inefficiency and indifference. These ideas are contained in Section 9.3. He advocated writing the laws clearly to reduce the scope for multiple interpretations. Secondly, he proposed an organizational structure that reduced the scope for conflicts of interest. Section 9.4 presents Kautilya's ideas on organizational design and rules and regulations for reducing fraud.

9.1 IDENTIFICATION OF MORAL, MARKET AND GOVERNMENT FAILURES

Kautilya's goal was to establish a prosperous and secure nation. The prevailing conditions at the time were not conducive to the attainment of prosperity or national security. He was aware of the powerful force of self-interest in bringing riches, but was concerned about its potential for pursuing socially unproductive or harmful activities. He classified individuals into three categories: moral, amoral (utility maximizing agent) and immoral. According to him, there would not be any government failure if the king and the bureaucrats were ethical and similarly there would be no market failure if the private sector were ethical. On the other hand, if the government administration and the private sector were immoral, the whole system would collapse. Kautilya was aware of various combinations of these and, therefore, many scenarios are implicit in his statements. However, the presentation here is confined to the amoral case only, since it has drawn a lot of attention and also is more relevant to describing today's situation in most countries. The following table presents his general understanding of the various failures for the amoral case.

Table 9.1 **Taxonomy of Various Failures**

King (President, Congress or any Public Official)			
Personal Interest		Not in Personal Interest	
Public Interest	Not in Public Interest	Public Interest	Not in Public Interest

Contd...

	King (President, Congress or any Public Official)			
	Personal Interest		Not in Personal Interest	
Private Interest	Best Case I	Conflict of Interest (rent-seeking activities) Case III	Conflict of Interest (classic red tape or undermining) Case V	Case VII
Not in Private Interest	Inducing the private sector to be benevolent Case II	Overzealous public official Case IV	Case VI	Rejected by everyone Case VIII

Case I: This is the ideal situation since there is no moral dilemma. Activities, such as building of public infrastructure, that would enhance the productivity of the private investment, are in everyone's interest. In this case there is no moral, market or government failure.

Case II: Kautilya emphasized compassion. The private sector was unlikely to care for the public interest, such as, making charitable donations for helping the needy unless it was induced by moral and material incentives. In a broader sense, reduction of inequality was in public interest. According to theologians, market fails to reduce it. They label it a moral failure. Kautilya recommended many programmes to help the poor and the sick.

Case III: Moral, Market and Government Failures. Kautilya was particularly concerned about Case III, Case IV and Case V. Incidentally, these are relevant even today. Case III is a real case of conflict of interest. It has drawn a lot of attention. In fact, the debate concerning market failure versus government failure is centered on this possibility. Many rent-seeking activities, such as lobbying, financial manipulation and monopoly etc. exist due to moral, market and government failures. It appears that unethical public officials and the private sector are like conjoined twins with a common stomach. A public official and a private party could join together to impoverish the public. For example, exercise of monopoly power would indicate market failure and government failure both of which were due to moral failure, that is both the private sector and the king and his administration were unethical.

Case IV: Tax collectors were rewarded with promotions etc. if they brought in larger amounts of revenue. However, according to Kautilya, overzealous tax collectors could work against both, the public and private interests (see Chapter 12 for details).

Case V: Kautilya specifically mentioned this possibility. A policy that served both, the public and private interests, should not be discussed with an adviser, who was likely to be adversely affected by that policy. He (p 200) recommended, 'No one who belongs to the side likely to be adversely affected by the project shall be consulted (1.15).'

9.2 CONSEQUENCES OF MARKET FAILURE

> Merchants are all thieves, in effect, if not in name; they
> shall be prevented from oppressing the people (4.1)
> — *Kautilya (p 236)*

According to Kautilya, the very origin of government indicated market failure since the private sector could neither maintain law and order, nor provide protection against foreign aggression. He (p 820) wrote, 'When there was no order in society and only the law of the jungle prevailed, people [were unhappy and being desirous of order] made Manu, the son of Vivasvat, their king; and they assigned to the king one-sixth part of the grains grown by them, one-tenth of other commodities and money. The king then used these to safeguard the welfare of his subjects (1.13).'

Traditional Market Failures: We know it today that unfettered private markets do not work efficiently in the presence of monopolies, public goods and externalities. Just like the classicists, Kautilya did not label them as market failures. However, he recognized these problems and recommended the provision of public goods and the regulation

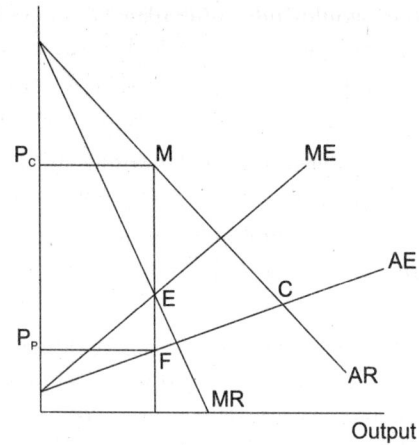

Figure 9.1: AE=average expenditure, ME=marginal expenditure, AR=average revenue, MR=marginal revenue, P_p=price paid to the producers and P_c=price charged from the consumers. Posner's Monopoly-Monopsony rents=rectangle FMP_cP_p and Harberger's deadweight loss=triangle FCM.

of monopoly, monopsony, and externalities by the government.

Regulation of Monopoly and Monopsony: Both monopoly and monopsony were perhaps serious problems during the ancient times.[5] Kautilya (p 236) stated, 'Merchants are all thieves, in effect, if not in name; they shall be prevented from oppressing the people (4.1).' He (p 134) added, 'It is the frontier officer who promotes trade, whereas traders form cartels in order to raise prices [for the goods they sell] or lower them [for the goods they buy]; they are profiteers making one hundred *panas* on one *pana* or one hundred measures on one measure of [grain].' The Figure 9.1 presents his ideas.

According to Kautilya, traders behaved like a monopsonist in buying goods particularly foodgrains from farmers and selling them like a monopolist to the consumers. That is, paying producers (farmers) a significantly lower price P_p while charging consumers a much higher price P_c. Although Kautilya was aware of the monopoly-monopsony rents (Posner's rectangle FMP_cP_p,1975) since he explicitly mentioned profits, He did not mention the use of any resources for capturing those monopoly rents. Similarly, he was not concerned with Harberger's (1971) triangle FCM, although it might have been quite large. He was primarily concerned with political unrest arising from producers, who were paid a very low price and from consumers, who were charged a very high price. It may be noted that it was not a case of bilateral monopoly since it was the same cartel of traders behaving both as a monopsonist and a monopolist.

It is from time immemorial that both ordinary consumers and kings have expected fair and honest dealings from suppliers of products and services. Kautilya discussed consumer protection at length.[6] He (p 250) recommended, 'cartelisation by artisans and craftsmen with the aim of lowering quality, increasing the profits or obstructing the sale or purchase and by merchants conspiring to hoard with the aim of selling at a higher price (4.2).' would be dealt with stiff punishments of 1000 *panas* for such offenses. Such a high penalty indicates the perceived seriousness of the offense. He (p 249-250) recommended punishment for 'adulteration', 'fraud', 'false description in selling', 'showing one product and selling another', and 'stealing precious metal in making new objects' etc. (4.2). According to him, all such practices were unethical; he equated charging high prices through the formation of cartels to theft.

In the absence of fully developed competitive markets and product warranties, all that the consumers could depend on was the protection accorded by the government. Two points are worth noting. First, Kautilya's recommendations were almost as specific as the Clayton Act (USA, 1913) in defining the illegal behavior of the monopolies. Secondly, Adam Smith (p 232) had similar concerns when he wrote, 'People of the same trade seldom meet together, even for merriment and diversion, but the conversation ends in a conspiracy against the public or in some contrivance to raise price.'

Externalities: An externality obtains when the actions of a decision-maker have a positive or negative effect on the availability of possible consumption or production choices to others. Kautilya's suggestion to regulate an externality was not based on the Pigovian distinction between social marginal cost (or benefit), and private marginal cost (or benefit), and imposition of corrective taxes (or subsidies). But he did correctly identify an externality and suggested a fine to prevent it. At that time, one of the major sources of pollution was cow dung or dirt. He (p 373) suggested a fine of 1/8th of a *pana* for 'throwing dirt on the road' 1/4th of a *pana* for 'blocking it with mud or water' (2.36). And he (p 375) recommended a fine for 'Having a dung hill, a sewage channel or a well too near a neighbour's house as to cause nuisance' and also for 'Causing obstruction and preventing the enjoyment of others' (3.8).

Nowadays, businesses and governments are concerned with the harmful effects of smoking on health and worker productivity. Kautilya too showed concern about consumption of liquor. He (p 349) recommended, 'Liquor shall only be drunk in the drinking house, and no one shall move about while drunk. Liquor shall not be stored in large quantities nor taken out of a village. The dangers in allowing large stocks or unrestricted movement are that workers may spoil the work allotted to them, even a dignified person may behave immodestly and assassins may be encouraged to behave rashly (2.25).'

Modern Market Failures: Problem of shirking (called 'moral hazard' problem) and the sellers not providing full information to the buyer (trying to sell a lemon) are labeled as information-based market failures. Although Kautilya could not imagine that today, such things would be called information-based market failures and certainly did not develop any theoretical models but he went much farther than the classicists.[7] He not only understood many of them but also applied them appropriately to specific situations. Similarly, he did not make any formal distinction between 'hidden actions' and 'hidden information' but showed awareness of such a distinction and suggested post-modern solutions to deal with them.

Hidden Actions: Kautilya recognized the problem of 'shirking'. He (p 283) remarked, 'The king shall have the work of Heads of Departments inspected daily, for men are, by nature, fickle and, like horses, change after being put to work.' He suggested 'efficiency wages' to mitigate this problem (see Chapter 11 for an in-depth analysis). Similarly he (p 317) recommended, 'They (a herdsman, milker, a churner and a hunter-guard) shall be paid in cash, because if they are paid in milk or butter oil, they will starve the calves to death [by milking the cows dry, leaving nothing for the calves] (2.29).'

Hidden Information: Kautilya showed awareness of the concept of what is nowadays called 'asymmetric information' and how to benefit from possession of such private information. For example, according to him, a king knew the quality of his land, which was poor but the buyer of the land did not know anything about its quality. He (p 621) stated, 'If a settlement of a tract is likely to entail heavy losses or expenditure, a king shall first sell the land, with the intention of re-acquiring it, to one who will fail in the attempt at settlement. Such agreements shall remain verbal (7.11).' Current Lemon Laws are based on this type of market failure.

Handling Missing Markets: At that time, no system of market insurance existed against losses from fire, floods, diseases, epidemics, and famines. Benefits were provided out of general revenue. Kautilya (p 128) prescribed, 'It is the duty of the king to protect the people from all calamities (4.3).'

Solving Another Problem of Moral Hazard: In order to guard against any possible 'moral hazard' problem, Kautilya (p 373) recommended a fine for 'not providing fire-fighting equipment' such as, water pots, a big jar, a trough, a ladder, an axe, a hook, a hooked rake, a skin bag etc. and for 'not hastening to save his own house on fire (2.36).'

9.3 CONSEQUENCES OF GOVERNMENT FAILURE

According to Kautilya, in the beginning government had a very limited role to play as it was confined exclusively to the maintenance of law and order and protection against foreign aggression. However, he greatly expanded its role to meet the challenge created by the new realities of his time. Drekmeier (p 260) writes, 'By the fifth and fourth centuries BC the ancient tribal institutions had lost their ability to regulate society effectively. New modes of production, new types of social relationships, new salvation theologies were changing the old ways. Kautilya was the theorist who most clearly saw the need for expanded state authority to fill the ever-widening gaps left by the declining authority of tradition. The king needed greater freedom of movement if he was to provide security and the conditions of prosperity.'

Avoiding Failure at the Bureaucratic Level: According to Kautilya, good governance also meant not to allow corruption at the bureaucratic level. He was quite aware of the possibility and the difficulty of detection of corruption at the bureaucratic level. He (p 281) stated, 'Just as it is impossible to know when a fish moving in water is drinking it, so it is impossible to find out when government servants in charge of undertakings misappropriate money (2.9).' He (p 283) continued, 'It is possible to know even the path of birds flying in the sky but not the ways of government servants who hide their (dishonest) income.'

He (p 221) pointed out, 'There are thirteen types of undesirable persons who amass wealth secretly by causing injury to the population. [These are: corrupt judges and magistrates, heads of villages or departments who extort money from the public, perjurers and procurers of perjury, those who practice witchcraft, black magic or sorcery, poisoners, narcotic dealers, counterfeiters and adulterators of precious metals.] When they are exposed by secret agents, they shall either be exiled or made to pay adequate compensation proportionate to the gravity of the offense (4.4).' He (p 493-494) asserted, 'Thus, the king shall first reform the administration, by punishing appropriately those officers who deal in wealth; they, duly corrected, shall use the right punishments to ensure the good conduct of the people of the towns and the countryside (4.9).'

Poor Governance or Government Failure at the Highest Level: According to Kautilya, government failure could occur at the highest level as well as at the bureaucratic level. His statement that a decadent king 'fails to protect the people from thieves and robs them himself' indicates that government failure could occur both due to inaction and inappropriate action, that is, due to poor governance. Additionally,

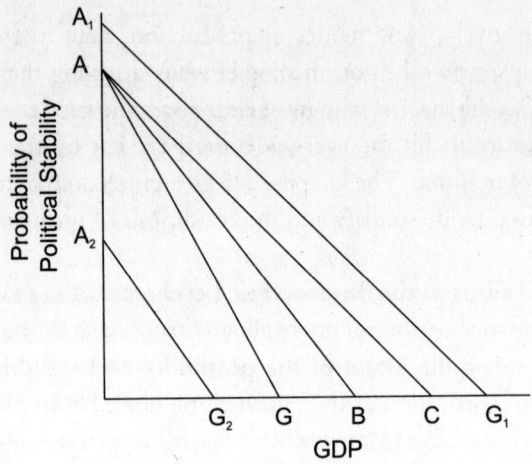

Figure 9.2: AB= the possibility frontier between GDP and the probability of political stability under monopoly, A_1G_1=possibility frontier under good governance, A_2G_2=possibility frontier under poor governance. AC=Possibility frontier if perfect competition is restored through antitrust laws and AG=possibility frontier under government failure in trying to correct market failure.

[according to Kautilya,] if the king were corrupt, the bureaucracy would also be corrupt. Figure 9.2 may be used to express Kautilya's ideas.

Kautilya believed that good governance (which included regulation of monopoly) improved political stability as well as brought prosperity implying that the possibility frontier, AB, under monopoly shifted to possibility frontier $A_1 G_1$. On the other hand, according to Kautilya, government failure (due to corruption, indifference, and inefficiency) was a lot more serious.[8] Since he believed that the AB possibility frontier most likely would shift to the left, to $A_2 G_2$, implying political unrest and a much lower income.

The current debate on market versus government failure is one-dimensional and is limited to the distortionary effects only (ie. to marginal changes in GDP). Presumably, the anti-trust laws were passed with the intended goal of rotating the possibility frontier from AB to AC, the possibility frontier under competition.[9] However, those who oppose government regulation of monopolies argue that instead of rotating the AB curve to AC, it most likely has been rotated to the possibility frontier AG, which they label as a government failure. Both the proponents and opponents of government regulation, for example, of monopolies, take it for granted that the political stability would not be affected.

9.4 RULES, REGULATIONS AND ORGANIZATIONAL DESIGN TO REDUCE FRAUD

> The ruler should avoid appointing persons who are fraudulent, dishonest, cruel, without enthusiasm, incompetent and cowardly
> —*Kautilya's Sutras*

Kautilya believed that prosperity required creation of wealth, both in the private and public sectors. He suggested many economic policies to encourage the creation of wealth in the private sector. Similarly, he advocated minimizing government spending on administration in order to generate the maximum surplus for building the necessary public infrastructure. Additionally, in his scheme, some enterprises, eg. liquor sales and gambling, were to be managed by the government. Each public enterprise was required to generate a maximum amount of profit without crossing the ethical bounds. Therefore, accurate measurement of the economic performance of a public enterprise and elimination of opportunities for misappropriation of public funds by government employees became absolutely critical.

For these reasons, adoption of an appropriate format for bookkeeping and codification and compliance of financial rules could not be left to the discretion of individual enterprises. He attempted to develop solutions to mitigate such problems through uniform bookkeeping rules, for recording data systematically by advocating frequent periodic reporting, and adopting independent audits to reduce the probability of system failure. He suggested incentive-based compensation mechanisms to reduce 'moral hazard' problems. As noted below, the Comptroller-Auditor (one official), who was ultimately responsible for all financial matters, must be knowledgeable, efficient and incorruptible.

He realized that the fiscal health of the Treasury depended not only on developing an economically sound fiscal policy that increased the taxable capacity of the economy through economic development, but that depended also on honest and efficient financial management. He was quite concerned about the possibility of fraudulent accounting by government servants. Kautilya listed forty possible ways in which corrupt employees could cheat and believed that it was not easy to detect cheating. His primary goal was to minimize the scope of such possibilities.

Kautilya provided insights into possible inadvertent as well as deliberate accounting errors or irregularities, which decrease revenue in public enterprises. He believed that revenue losses might be caused both by system failure and moral failure. Accordingly, he identified the potential sources of such losses as: (i) inadvertent recording errors, (ii) deliberate deceptive accounting, (iii) collusion among employees to misappropriate revenue, and (iv) loss in productivity due to in-fighting among employees.

According to him, the major underlying factor for resorting to aggressive and creative accounting (which he called 'false accounting') practices, was excessive greed, and he tried to contain it through moral persuasion and legal means. He proposed three kinds of measures to deal with the situation. (a) He believed that employees must be informed of the laws. With that in mind, he modified, extended, and above all codified the existing rules and regulations. Often, accounting rules are vague and thus open to varying interpretations, presenting opportunities to test or extend the limits of acceptable practice. Some enterprises might resort to massaging the numbers to paint a rosy picture of an otherwise barren situation. According to Kautilya, the laws must be very clear, without any ambiguities or loopholes, and should be as comprehensive as possible. (b) He proposed an organizational structure, which reduced the scope for conflict of interests. (c) He suggested long lists of rewards for commendable service and punishments for cheating the government.

Laws Must Have Clarity, Consistency, and Completeness and be in Written Form: Kautilya (p 212) wrote, 'The rule of kings depends primarily on (written) orders; even peace and war have their roots in them (2.10).' He believed that effective enforcement (to reduce scope for 'creative accounting') of rules and regulations required clarity, absence of loopholes, completeness, and consistency and must be in a written form. He (p 213) envisaged that the Royal Scribe, 'Has a [thorough] knowledge of all conventions, be quick in composition and have good handwriting. He shall also be able to read [clearly] documents and edicts (2.10.3).' He recommended that the Royal Scribe be one of the highest paid (48000 *panas*) employees, to emphasize and ensure that the Royal Edicts had desired characteristics. He (p 215) went so far as to suggest, 'Cutting off both feet and a hand or 900 *panas*' for a 'Royal Scribe deliberately writing down wrongly a Royal Edict, omission or commission (4.10.14).'

Designing an Organizational Structure to Minimize the Scope for Conflict of Interest: Kautilya was an organizational man.[10] He understood the concept of bounded rationality (see Chapter 10 for an in-depth analysis). He realized the necessity of creating a bureaucratic structure to ensure implementation of projects and to provide continuity of operations over the long run. He believed in cognitive division of labour and suggested creation of 28 departments for providing services related to industry and mining (7 departments), agriculture, forestry and livestock (4), trade and transport (7), treasury (2), gambling and entertainment (3), accounting (1), miscellaneous (4) and additional six departments were related to defense services. Interestingly, at least two departments were created to protect the consumers (Chief Superintendent of Precious Metals and Jewellery and the Chief Controller of Private Trading) and one department was created for animal welfare and prevention of cruelty to them.

Kautilya proposed the establishment of two very important offices to monitor and manage the financial health of the state: the positions of a Treasurer and a Chief Comptroller-Auditor. They were very well paid and, in turn, they must be incorruptible and efficient. It is very interesting to note that he divided financial responsibility between the

Treasurer and the Comptroller-Auditor. Both were supposed to report directly to the king. The Chief Comptroller-Auditor was responsible for auditing the revenue and expenses of each enterprise and delivering the net balance for each unit to the Treasurer. He was then envisaged to report to the king on how much was delivered. The Treasurer reported to the king how much was received. This cross-checking would, it was believed, reduce, to some extent, the scope for corruption.

But more importantly, creation of two independent positions reduced scope for corruption in another way. Suppose the Auditor was subordinate to the Treasurer and the Treasurer was corrupt and stole from the Treasury. The Auditor might be too afraid to report to the king. Also the Treasurer might ask the Auditor not to audit certain units.

The Treasurer was responsible for managing the assets and the Comptroller-Auditor handled: (i) the construction and maintenance of the Records Office, (ii) maintenance of Records, (iii) compilation of rules, (iv) inspection, (v) audit, and (vi) preparing and presenting financial reports to the king. Thus, Kautilya attempted to encourage specialization, accountability and to limit the scope for conflict of interests.

According to Kautilya (p 225), 'The Comptroller shall be responsible for the compilation of all fixed rules as well as the conventions used (2.7.3).' It appears, even at that time there were some conventions, which today would be called GAAP (generally accepted accounting principles) and the Comptroller-Auditor would have the combined powers of FASB (Financial Accounting Standards Board) and the SEC (Securities and Exchange Commission).

Labour Management Policy: Finally, according to Kautilya, the role of labour management policies could not be ignored in reducing fraud. Book-keeping is not restricted to compiling data, but also to correcting inadvertent errors and to discouraging and reducing manipulation or fraud. Similarly, audits test data and cannot ensure that all transactions are recorded accurately. Even in Kautilya's time, he was concerned about the possibilities of overstating expenditures and understating revenues by employees and siphoning off state resources.

Kautilya was aware of the possibility that some employees might shirk work and also become corrupt. He suggested both preventive and remedial measures to overcome such problems. As mentioned in Chapter 6, he stressed ethical anchoring for preventing moral hazard problems and corruption. He suggested several other measures. He emphasized accountability. He devoted Book two, which is about one fourth of the Arthashastra to specifying in detail the responsibilities of each employee to ensure accountability. He tried to reduce the scope for conflict of interest situations. He recommended an appropriate mix of salary, strings and supervision to elicit effort (see Chapter 11 for details).

SUMMARY

Kautilya believed that market failure and government failure were like conjoined twins with a common stomach. Market failure could not occur without government failure and government failure could not happen unless there were moral failure and poor organizational design. According to Kautilya, the government should protect, nurture and enrich the people. He suggested helping children, the sick and the old but did not want to create their dependency on the government. He believed that government must be proactive and progressive and remove all obstacles to economic growth. It must be vigilant and, if possible, should try to prevent natural disasters and, if they occurred, should provide maximum possible relief to the affected. He believed that the creation of a prosperous and fair economy required not only the removal of all obstructions to economic growth but also the building of infrastructure, establishing of law and order, and private property rights, prevention of monopoly and fraud and providing the services in which private markets did not exist. Thus Kautilya expanded the role of government to regulation of monopoly and externality and mitigation of the problem of 'moral hazard' and, thus, correct market failure. In this context, he also demonstrated sufficient awareness of the problems of inefficiency, indifference and corruption among public servants and suggested effective ways to deal with their sins of omission and commission.

Kautilya did not want the suppliers of goods and services and traders to subsidize their customers. However, he expected that they deliver the best possible quality products and services, and do not cheat or charged monopoly prices Thus he expected suppliers to be efficient and ethical. He believed that encouragement of ethical behavior and designing of a sound organizational structure provided best insurance against corruption and consequently lowering the probabilities of various failures. He proposed a very comprehensive approach for effectively dealing with various kinds of failures. Parmar (1987, p 14) aptly quotes Beni Prasad as observing: 'The *Arthashastra* is unsurpassed in the Hindu literature. It is complete in its perspective, detailed in its regulations, thorough in its treatment. It makes provisions for all contingencies and for all imaginable possibilities. As a statement of Hindu administrative theory, it hardly leaves anything to be desired.'

10
Information, Knowledge, Wisdom and Management

Since the seventies there has been an information revolution. Just like the Inada conditions, specification of the information matrix has become a regular fixture in economic analysis. The theoretical models based on free and full information are no longer acceptable since information is both costly and imperfect. Kautilya explicitly discussed the importance of information gathering and insisted on having maximum possible information for making informed choices. His list included the collection of detailed information on both economic and non-economic variables. After experimenting with some other expressions, Simon (1957) coined the word 'bounded rationality'. However, Kautilya did not use today's jargons like bounded rationality, irrationality and asymmetric information, etc. but he was the first writer, who applied these concepts appropriately and extensively. Kautilya's recognition of bounded rationality and his emphasis on (i) king's own education and (ii) hiring of advisers and benefiting from their good counsel and judgment for relaxing the cognitive constraint could provide guidelines for twenty-first century CEOs.

In recent years, knowledge management (KM) has acquired a pivotal place in business strategies for survival and growth. Current research rightly considers data management as a subset of information management and that, in turn, a subset of knowledge management. It appears though as if knowledge management is a new tool to acquire a competitive edge. However, Kautilya understood the importance of knowledge management to economic prosperity more than two thousand years ago but considered it as a subset of wisdom-based management. His analysis offers at least three insights, which may be relevant to today's enterprises. First, he believed that wisdom was the most valuable asset and advocated a wisdom-based management. According to him, information, knowledge, and intelligence were the critical inputs to management by wisdom. A wise person, depending on the situation, understood how to reconcile, negotiate or coordinate, sometimes, the conflicting forces arising from ideas, institutions, and interests. Secondly, he indicated how one became wise and included acquisition of ethical values as an important component of knowledge. Thirdly, according to him, a wise CEO (king) was ethical, self-disciplined, farsighted, foresighted, humble, preferred moderation, open-minded and appreciative of the wisdom of others, that is, in essence was both efficient and ethical. Such a CEO understood the inherent trade-off between maintaining confidentiality and sharing information and knowledge.

According to Kautilya, reflection on knowledge squeezed the nectar (insight, wisdom) out of it. He suggested the study of *Vedas* and philosophy for learning the ethical values, such as honesty, non-violence, compassion, tolerance and truthfulness. Similarly, he recommended the study of economics and political science for acquiring information and knowledge for survival and material enrichment. A wise person was not only knowledgeable of ethical values and practical skills, but also reflected on them and practiced them.

Kautilya's recognition of bounded rationality is presented in Section 10.1. This section also includes collection of information on economic variables. The current research on KM concentrates on acquisition, codification, transfer, sharing, and using knowledge and puts heavy emphasis on knowledge workers and knowledge-intensity. Kautilya believed that wisdom, and not knowledge as such, was the most valuable asset and a king (CEO) needed wisdom to manage or harness the full potential of knowledge workers. He emphasized the learning of wisdom. He offered insights as to how one could become wise. Particularly the role of education in the learning of wisdom is presented in Section 10.2. Almost all studies on KM focus on the benefits of sharing information and knowledge and some discuss the risks associated with sharing knowledge. Kautilya discussed how much information needed to be shared with the subordinates and the trade-off between pooling knowledge and confidentiality. This insight is presented in Section 10.3.

10.1 ON BOUNDED RATIONALITY

Relevance of Bounded Rationality: Conlisk (1996) offers four arguments for incorporating 'bounded rationality' into modeling economic behavior. He asserts, 'First, there is abundant empirical evidence that it is important. Second, models of bounded rationality have proved themselves in a wide range of impressive work. Third, the standard justifications for assuming unbounded rationality are unconvincing; their logic cuts both ways. Fourth, deliberation about an economic decision is a costly activity, and good economics requires that we entertain all costs'. Finally, he resorts to the usual 'as if' argument to advance his case. He expresses it as: 'To gain perspective, it is entertaining to imagine an accidentally different history for economic theory. Imagine that modern decision theory began, not with perfect rationality and imperfect information, but with the opposite.' Kautilya did begin decision theory this way and Conlisk has to find some other avenue to entertain himself.

However, for quite some time, some researchers even avoided using the expression 'bounded rationality'. For example, Haltiwanger and Waldman (1985, fn.1) remark, 'Note, this limited ability to process information is sometimes referred to as bounded rationality.

However, because of its frequent association with the related concept termed "satisficing", we will refrain from using the term bounded rationality in this paper.' They prefer to call it 'limits of rationality'. Similarly, Palma, Myers, and Papageorgiou (1994) call it 'imperfect ability to choose' or 'competence-difficulty'.

Definition of Bounded Rationality: It is not claimed that Kautilya called it 'bounded rationality', although his discussions contain the concept.[1] He (p 177) observed, 'A king can reign only with the help of others; one wheel alone does not move a chariot. Therefore, a king should appoint advisers as councilors and ministers and listen to their advice (1.7).' Clearly, the phrase 'one wheel alone does not move a chariot' indicates a complementary nature of relationship between the king's own abilities and the advice from the advisers, which may be critical in ensuring survival and progress of the kingdom. He (p 196) added, 'Because the work of the government is diversified and is carried on simultaneously in many different places, the king cannot do it all himself; he, therefore, has to appoint ministers who will implement it at the right time and place (1.9).' That is, according to him, there were two kinds of limitations: (i) the ability to process information and draw inferences and (ii) the impossibility of being physically present at various locations simultaneously implying that the king could not run the country alone. He recommended that the king himself must be well educated, and also have advisers to relax the bounded rationality constraint. For relaxing the second limitation, the king should appoint ministers and delegate responsibility to them for providing various services to the public. Vishalaksha (a pre-Kautilyan thinker) also appears to have emphasized limitations on rationality.

Collection of Information on Economic Variables: Kautilya believed that availability of information was critical in arriving at an informed decision and, therefore, was obsessed with the collection of information on economic as well as non-economic variables. He recommended the appointment of a Record Keeper for every five to ten villages, who kept detailed records on almost everything in the villages. He (p 220) suggested, 'The villages shall be classified as best, average or lowest. They shall also be classified according to whether [they are tax paying or] tax exempt, whether they supply soldiers [in lieu of tax], and whether they supplied [fixed amounts of] grain, cattle, gold, forest produce, labour or other commodities. [Within each village,] every plot of land shall be numbered and its use recorded according to the classification: cultivated or fallow, dry or wet cultivation, park, vegetable garden and orchard, enclosed area, forest, sanctuary, temple, water works, cremation ground, rest-house, public drinking-water facility, holy place, pasture and roads. These records shall be used for determining the location of fields, forests and roads [in case of boundary disputes] and to record transactions such as gifts, sales, charitable endowments and tax exemptions. [Likewise,] each house shall be numbered and classified as whether taxpaying or tax-exempt. Records of the inhabitants shall also be kept under the following headings: (i) the varna; (ii) occupation (such as farmer, cowherd, trader, craftsman, labourer or slave); (iii) the number of males and females as well as the number of children and old people, their [family] history, occupation, income and expenditure; (iv) livestock and poultry owned; (v) the amount of tax payable in cash or in free labour; and (vi) tolls and fines that may be due (2.35).'

10.2 WISDOM-BASED MANAGEMENT AND ECONOMIC PERFORMANCE

Although Kautilya did not formally define information or knowledge but such definitions are discernible from his applications. According to him, information may be defined as organized data (he designed a format), knowledge as skills, strategies, tactics, approaches or methods and wisdom as an extracted *manna* (nectar, insight) from knowledge and experience aided by intelligence.[2] That is, wisdom was like separating the grain from the husk and offered vision and insights. A wise person understood that it was shortsighted to be unethical. He looked at all aspects of management for achieving the highest possible economic performance. According to him, a wise person knew how to use information and knowledge for removing gaps between vision and reality and understood the challenges and opportunities presented by ideas, information, institutions and interests.

Importance of Wisdom: Kautilya argued that the power of sound analysis and judgment enhanced economic performance directly, as well as indirectly, by enhancing national security that was a prerequisite for economic development, which, in turn, enhanced the power of the army through increases in tax revenue and also by winning public support. Accordingly, as also earlier mentioned in the context of discussion on the concept of 'opportunity cost' in Chapter 4, he (p 600) suggested, 'When there is choice between a wise son and a brave son, it is better to give the brave son, who though valorous, lacks wisdom. For, a wise son, though timid, uses his intelligence in his endeavors; like the hunter outwitting the elephant, the intelligent outwit the brave (7.17).' If a king was forced to give up a son, he should give a brave son as a hostage. Since the opportunity cost in terms of loss in national security and economic growth of giving up a wise son, who 'uses his intelligence in his endeavors' was much higher than that of a brave son. Accordingly, he advised the king for transferring power only to the wise son, who was both ethical and efficient. He emphasized wisdom in almost every context and indicated that both knowledge and intelligence were the critical inputs to sound judgment (see Chapter 18).

Wisdom-based Management and Economic Performance: According to Kautilya, economic performance depended on wisdom, which was acquired through learning and imitation (emulation).[3] He believed that aptitude for learning and intelligence were prerequisites to benefiting from education. Table 10.1 may be used to summarize Kautilya's ideas on the link between wisdom and economic performance:

Table 10.1: Kautilya on Wisdom and Economic Performance

Economic Performance
Management by Wisdom
Sources of Wisdom

Contd...

Imitation	Education			
Watching and interacting with the elders	Information (Historical)	Ability to think (reflection, evaluation, synthesis, creating new knowledge)	Knowledge	
			Vedas and Philosophy for character-building (self-discipline and ethical conduct)	Economics and Political Science for learning skills, methods, strategy and tactics

He summarized, 'Only a king who is wise, disciplined, devoted to governing of the subjects and [ever] conscious of the welfare of all beings will enjoy the earth unopposed (1.5).'

10.3 TRADE-OFF BETWEEN POOLING KNOWLEDGE AND CONFIDENTIALITY

> A king can reign only with the help of others; one wheel alone does not move a chariot. Therefore, a king should appoint advisers (as councilors and ministers) and listen to their advice.
>
> — *Kautilya (p177)*

Kautilya understood the importance of pooling information and knowledge but was also concerned about maintaining confidentiality. He visualized the conflict between sharing and creating knowledge, on the one hand, and the danger of leaking that knowledge to potential rivals, on the other.[4] He believed that the probability of a successful campaign critically depended on power, particularly the intellectual power, and protection of its confidentiality.

Good Counsel and Imperfections in Rationality: Kautilya considered knowledge and intelligence as the most important factors in maintaining (and expanding) the kingdom and enhancing economic growth. He understood the limits of human cognitive ability. He suggested the appointment of advisers to relax this constraint. He provided an in-depth analysis of (i) the need to have advisers for arriving at a superior decision, (ii) how many advisers to have to achieve an optimum probability of success of a project, and (iii) who should be hired as an adviser? As noted above, according to him, the over-all survival of a kingdom as well as the success of undertaking a project depended on good counsel. Along with it, he emphasized the importance of secrecy. He (p 562) asserted, 'He who cannot maintain secrecy will undoubtedly find his efforts destroyed like a broken boat in the sea even if temporarily there are some appearances of success (7.13).'

The Optimum Number of Advisers: The answers to some of the important questions as to how many advisers to have, and how much and with whom to share information were tied to how 'both objectives of sound advice and maintaining secrecy will be achieved'. The level of sophistication achieved on this topic was unparalleled for his time. Elementary calculus (such as, the optimum number of advisers is determined by the condition where the net additional gain of an additional adviser is zero) and graphs are used to bring it out.

Kautilya (p 198-199) critically examined the various ideas expressed by four of his predecessors (Bharadvaja, Vishalaksha, Parasara, and Pisuna) before reaching his own conclusions regarding the number of advisers. According to Kautilya, 'Bharadvaja says: "a secret [prematurely] divulged is fatal to the well-being of the king and the officials entrusted with the task. Every adviser has his own adviser, and latter, in turn, his adviser [and so on]. Thus [the series become too long and] the secret is divulged [somewhere along the line]. Therefore, a king shall deliberate by himself [without advisers]." [As the saying goes:] "None shall know what a king sets out to do. Only those who have to implement it should know when the work is begun or when it has been completed (1.15)". Thus, according to Bharadvaja, a king should not have any advisers because that might compromise secrecy.'

However, Vishalaksha criticized Bharadvaja's conclusion. Kautilya stated, 'Vishalaksha says "never can a single person arrive at the right decision". The work of government is dependent on [complete] knowledge—that which the king personally knows, that which is reported to him and that which he has to infer.[5] To find out what is not known, to clarify doubts when there are alternatives, to obtain more information when only a part is known—all these can be done only with the help of advisers. Hence a king shall conduct his deliberations with advisers of mature intelligence. [As the saying goes:] "Despise no one, [but] listen to all views; for, wise man pays heed to all sensible advice, even those of a child' (1.15)." It may be added that certainly, the information revolution has been an important improvement over the earlier paradigm of full and free information. However, knowledge is much more important than information, which is passive.

Precursor of Muth Expectations: The above statement, 'the work of government is dependent on [complete] knowledge—that which the king personally knows, that which is reported to him and that which he has to infer' implies using all the available information in making decisions. Thus, the rational expectations hypothesis, at least in some rudimentary form, seems quite old. The role of information is emphasized throughout the *Arthashastra* and Kautilya insisted on having maximum possible information. He placed a high premium on information and did not apply economic analysis to (cost of) information collection. He anticipated Muth expectations.[6]

Yet a third thinker, Parasara, pointed out that the advice offered by Vishalaksha emphasized the importance of good counsel only and did not address the need to keep secrecy. He suggested that a king could pose hypothetical questions and thus, might get answers without compromising secrecy. A fourth thinker, Pisuna, criticized Parasara's solution, asserting that the advisers might not take this hypothetical case seriously and might, therefore, provide 'ill-conceived' answer or may 'talk about it openly'. Kautilya wrote that according to Pisuna, 'Therefore, the king should consult [only] those who will be involved in the task to be accomplished. Both objectives—getting sound advice and maintaining secrecy—will be achieved (1.15).'

Kautilya provided a synthesis of the above differing views. He found Pisuna's answer to be unsatisfactory. He (p 199) argued, 'This method is inherently unstable. [To involve everyone concerned with the work would impose no limit on the numbers. To change advisers for every task would mean a different set for each one.] A king shall confine his deliberations to [at the most] three or four advisers. If he consults only one, he may find it difficult to reach a decision on complicated questions; for a single adviser can behave as he pleases without restraint. If there are only two advisers, they may either combine together and overwhelm him or fight and neutralize each other (1.15).'

He concluded, '[There should be no more than four advisers] because, with more than four, secrecy is rarely maintained. [While, normally, the king should consult three or four advisers,] he may, depending on the nature of the work and the special circumstances of each case, take a decision by himself, consult just one adviser, or even two. The opinions of the advisers shall be sought individually as well as together [as a group]. The reason why each one holds a particular opinion shall also be ascertained (1.15).'

Kautilya (p, 200) also recommended, 'No one who belongs to the side likely to be adversely affected by the project shall be consulted (1.15).'

Thus, according to Kautilya, as the number of advisers increased, the king received better council which increased the probability of success of a task but the problem of secrecy might become serious and hurt its chances of success. Ignoring the cost of educating the prince (the future king) and compensation to the advisers, Kautilya's views may be expressed as follows:

$S = E(K) + \theta N^{\alpha} - \varphi N^{\lambda}$ (10.1)

By differentiating with respect to N we get

$\pi' = dS/dN = \alpha \theta N^{\alpha-1} - \lambda \varphi N^{\lambda-1}$ (10.2)

Solving for N, we get

$N^* = (\varphi \lambda / \theta \alpha)^{1/(\alpha-\lambda)}$ (10.3)

Where S = the probability of success of a project, E (K) = king's education level and N = the number of advisers, θN^{α} = the functional specification for good council, φN^{λ} = the functional specification for secrecy and π' = the marginal probability of success. The above discussion may be captured by Figure 10.1.

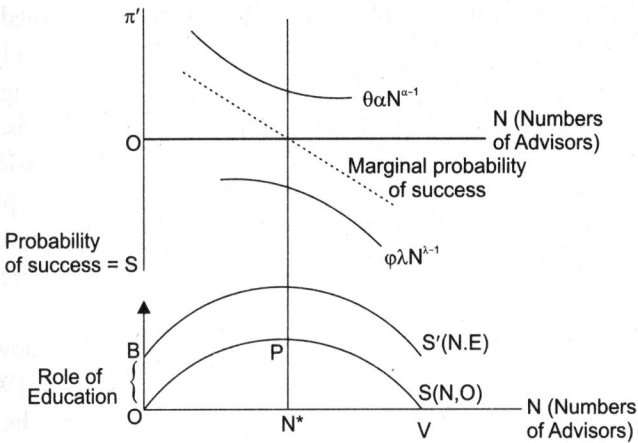

Figure 10.1: The broken line in the upper figure represents the marginal probability of success curve. S (N, O) and S' (N, E) in the lower figure represent the probability of success curves. Point B represents Bharadvaja's views, point V represents Vishalaksha's suggestion and point P represents Parasara's suggestion.

According to Kautilya, a king's own education shifted the probability of success function, S (N, O) upwards to S' (N, E) by enhancing his ability to process information and draw inferences and also by reducing his irrationality by developing controls over emotions such as anger (ie. it reduces imperfection in rationality).

He provided a very rich analysis: for example, the comparison with the chariot implies that the inputs (i.e., the king's cognitive ability and advisers' counsel) were considered complementary and a Cobb-Douglas type multiplicative functional form specification would be more appropriate. On the other hand, the suggestion that for certain projects, the king could decide without any help from any adviser implies an additive functional form, ie. the functional form depended on the type of project.

However, as an illustration only the additive case is discussed here, which is the simplest one. For example, in equation (10.1), if $N = 0$, $S = E(K)$ and similarly, if $N = 1$, $S = E(K) + \theta - \varphi$. Under the additive functional form, the optimum number of advisers is unaffected by the cognitive abilities of the king.

According to Vishalaksha, Bharadvaja was so concerned with secrecy that he did not recommend any adviser. In this case, the probability of success is given by point B, which is sub-optimal. According to Parasara, Vishalaksha ignored the negative impact of too many advisers on maintaining secrecy and his solution leads to point V, which was also sub-optimal. Pisuna pointed out that Parasara's solution amounted to compromising both on secrecy and efficiency and thus selecting a point like P, which was not efficient either.

According to Kautilya, Pisuna made two points: (i) consult everyone who was going to be involved with the project and (ii) there should be a different group of advisers for different projects. Kautilya believed that Pisuna's first suggestion amounted to selecting an inefficient point just like V, since there was no limit on the number of advisers. He believed that Pisuna's second suggestion to constitute a new group of advisers for each new project would create instability and involve too many advisers. He instead recommended that the maximum number of advisers should not be more than four and depending on the task, a sub-group of one, two or three out of the four may be consulted. Interestingly, he was aware of the conflict of interest problem and did not want to seek a biased advice from an adviser who was likely to be adversely affected by the project.

Who Should be Hired as an Adviser? After a careful review of the prevailing views on this topic, Kautilya (p 197) concluded, 'A king may appoint a childhood friend, so long as he is not allowed to overreach himself; or an associate in secret activities so long as he is not allowed to blackmail the king; or one of proven loyalty; provided he has also proved himself efficient in government; or one from a hereditary family so long as he does not become all-powerful; or bringing new blood, if he has both theoretical ability and practical experience. In any case, anyone who is appointed as a councilor must have the highest personal qualities.' According to Kautilya, a king (CEO) should have an open mind and must carefully weigh the pros and cons of each candidate for hiring him as an adviser (also see next Chapter for additional information).

SUMMARY

According to Kautilya, information, knowledge, intelligence and deliberations were critical inputs to the making of sound decisions. He was acutely aware of the limitations on human rationality and emphasized the roles of education and advisers in overcoming the imperfections in rationality. According to him, wisdom was the most valuable asset and a source of guiding principles and insights. He recommended knowing everything worth knowing about his own economy and the economies of adversaries. Of course, one wonders as to what techniques were used in drawing inferences. However, as discussed in Chapter 5, Kautilya emphasized the critical role of explanation and prediction in the evaluation of a policy. He would not have recommended pleasure-seeking perks like membership to exclusive golf clubs and turning the office into an art museum. He put stakeholders' interest ahead of his own interest, that is, he was satisfied with 'leftovers' and would never conceive of back-dating stock options or creative accounting.

11

Labour Policy: Moral and Material Incentives, Effort

> The ruler's duties are stated to be five: punishment of the wicked, rewarding the righteous, development of state revenues by just means, impartiality in granting favours and protection of the state.
>
> — *Kautilya (Subramanian, p 88)*

The words incentives and economics have become almost synonymous. Canice Prendergast (1999) aptly describes the current scope of economics as: 'Incentives are the essence of economics.'[1] Innumerable books and articles have appeared during the last three decades, suggesting incentive-compatible contracts for alleviating the problem of 'moral hazard' created by asymmetric information and lack of precise links between effort and efficiency in situations related to principal-agent relationships and insurance contracts.[2] The 'design and enforceability' of contracts have occupied center stage in industrial organization literature. Ruth Grant (2002) explores in-depth the history of incentives during the last couple of centuries in the Western world and deplores their excessive and indiscriminate use in economic matters, without paying adequate attention to their ethics. Grant places incentives at par with coercion and persuasion as instruments of power and control, and suggests evaluating incentives with a broader perspective of philosophy and political science, rather than with that of economics. Both factual and substantive arguments are advanced to enrich her observations regarding the true origin, scope and ethics of well thought-out incentives.

Grant points out that the classical economists (with the exception of J S Mill and David Ricardo) did not even use the word incentive. However, at least two ancient thinkers assigned an important role to economic incentives, provided those were based on fairness. It should come as no surprise that Nobel Laureate Herbert Simon had to search the writings of ancient thinkers for any reference to incentives. He (1957, p 165) specifically acknowledges the contributions of Xenophon (430-354 BCE), a contemporary of Plato, by opening part III of his seminal work with a quote from Anabasis.[3] The ideas of the other ancient writer, Vishnugupta Chanakya Kautilya, who wrote the *Arthashastra* (the science of economics) during the last half of the fourth century BCE are presented in this chapter.

It may be noted that Kautilya was the first economist who recognized the principal-agent problem and suggested various mechanisms to induce the agents to supply optimum effort, and also not to collude, quarrel, steal or desert the king.[4] He implicitly proposed a conceptual framework, which was comprehensive and consisted of three components.

Matching Incentive-type to Agent-type: He introduced material incentives and disincentives to alleviate the problem of moral hazard and considered them as complementary to persuasion as well as to existing moral incentives and never as a substitute for them.[5] Incidentally, modern economists also fully understand that even incentive compatible contracts serve much better in an ethical environment since contracts are usually incomplete and implicit.[6]

Kautilya understood that different individuals possessed different propensities and therefore to ensure effectiveness, he recommended a matching of an incentive-type to an agent-type. According to Kautilya's conceptual framework, material incentives were intended to strengthen the practice of ethics and not to undermine it. His implicit conceptual framework on incentives and their relationship to persuasion are made explicit in Section 11.2.[7]

Matching Material Incentive-type to a Worker's Needs and Position: Kautilya offered an analysis, which was much broader than the usual trade-off between incentives and insurance against risk or just a combination of rewards and punishments.[8] He attempted to find the right kind of mix of security (job tenure), servings (efficiency wages), strings (limit distractions) and sanctions (ie. disincentives, such as investigation or auditing, fine and dismissal) to address the problem of 'moral hazard' and promote economic efficiency. He also realized, if the agent was opportunistic, even a blend of moral and material incentives was not likely to work and needed to be combined with auditing or supervision. His understanding and suggestions on introducing combinations of appropriate incentives and disincentives to elicit optimum effort and loyalty are contained in Section 11.3. His other incentive programmes, such as, payments of bonuses to appreciate better quality and extra output, and recommendation for promotions, and job tenure for honesty are also assembled in this section.

The 'Design and Enforceability' of Payment Systems: Kautilya implicitly proposed incentive compatible labour contracts to alleviate the problem of moral hazard, that is, designing of a contract such that people choose to behave honestly. For example, customarily wages were paid as a share of the produce. But he made two exceptions, which come very close to what nowadays are called multi-tasking. Similarly, he proposed a wage payment system where supervision was possible and desirable but otherwise sharecropping was to be adopted. These are presented in Section 11.4. Section 11.1 offers a brief introduction to his ideas linking a worker's pay to his abilities, expertise and experience, and his conceptual framework on incentives, which links the presentations in Sections 11.2 and 11.3.

11.1 CONCEPTUAL FRAMEWORK ON INCENTIVES

Stylized Facts: According to Kautilya, the King could not run the country alone and, therefore, needed to establish a bureaucratic set-up to assist him. Also, he recommended many enterprises to be run by the public sector. These included: cultivation of Crown agricultural lands; mining and metallurgy; animal husbandry; manufacturing (textile, salt, and liquor), leisure and entertainment (betting and gambling, courtesans, prostitutes and entertainers) activities.[9] Interestingly, the state had a monopoly over the manufacturing and sale of liquor and also controlled betting and gambling. All the public enterprises were run primarily for profit (but without compromising ethical values), deriving a major portion of revenue to the state. Therefore, ethical and efficient management was heavily emphasized.

Kautilya believed that some employees might be opportunistic. He (p 283) suggested, 'The king shall have the work of Heads of Departments inspected daily, for men are, by nature, fickle and, like horses, change after being put to work.' According to him, some bureaucrats might become corrupt and lazy. However, perhaps, due to the methods of recruitment, training or rewards, the secret service agents were believed to be honest and were deployed to check on the honesty and loyalty of the routine officials and also of the taxpayers.

He believed that it might not be easy to detect the corrupt practices of the bureaucrats. He did not have the tools to develop a formal model of the trade-off between market failure and government failure (corruption etc.) but he clearly understood the issue.[10]

Description of Job-Qualifications: Kautilya presented not only a complete system of salary structure according to qualifications but also developed comprehensive procedures to verify the credentials of potential candidates. He (p 120) described, 'A councilor or minister of the highest rank should be a native of the state, born in a high family and controllable [by the king]. He should have been trained in all the arts and have logical ability to foresee things. He should be intelligent, persevering, dexterous, eloquent, energetic, bold, brave, able to endure adversities and firm in loyalty. He should neither be haughty nor fickle. He should be amicable and not excite hatred or enmity in others (1.9).'

Linked Salary to Qualifications: Kautilya (p 120) stated, 'Those who have all the qualities are to be appointed to the highest grade (as Councilors), those who lack a quarter to the middle grades and those who lack a half to the lowest grades (1.9).' He (p 289-292) specified the salaries of the highest grade between 4,000 to 48,000 *panas*, of the middle grade between 250 to 3,000 *panas* and of the lowest grade between 60 to 120 *panas*. Interestingly, a salary of 48,000 *panas* for the Chief of the Defense equaled the combined salaries of all other senior management officials (the four Chief Commanders 8,000 *panas* each and four Divisional Commanders 4,000 *panas* each).

Verification before Appointment: Kautilya recommended complete verification and evaluation of an applicant's abilities and capabilities. He (p 201) specified, 'Of these qualities, nationality, family background and amenability to discipline shall be verified from reliable people [who know the candidate well]. The candidate's knowledge of the various arts shall be tested by experts in their respective fields. Intelligence, perseverance and dexterity shall be evaluated by examining his past performance while eloquence, boldness and presence of mind shall be ascertained by interviewing him personally. Watching how he deals with others will show his energy, endurance, ability to suffer adversities, integrity, loyalty and friendliness. From his intimate friends, the king shall find out about his strength, health, and character (whether lazy or energetic, fickle or steady). The candidate's amiability and love of mankind [absence of a tendency to hate] shall be ascertained by personal observation (1.9).' It is obvious that he followed contemporary hiring practices, including requiring (i) reference letters (ii) character references, and (iii) inviting the candidate for a personal interview.

He (p 201-202) stated, 'The ancient teachers have laid down that the king shall allot duties to the ministers appropriate to their integrity as determined by the four tests. For example, he shall appoint those proved pure by the test of *dharma* to judicial and law and order posts. Those proved pure by the *artha* test shall be appointed as the Chancellor or the Treasurer, those proved pure by the test of *kama* as controllers of recreation inside and outside the palace and those proved by the test of fear to duties near the [person of the] king. Those who succeed in every test shall be appointed to the highest office of councilor. Those who fail every test shall be sent off to [difficult] posts such as mines, forests, elephant forests or factories (1.10).' According to Kautilya (and other ancient thinkers), a person should be appointed as a judge only if he had unbending moral values (*dharma* test) and a person should be appointed as a Treasurer or Chancellor only if he was incorruptible (*artha* test).

Discarded Coercion as an Instrument of Control: Kautilya was against the indiscriminate use of coercion. He was aware of the unethical use of power and he wanted to accomplish with incentives what was accomplished earlier by coercion. Moreover, he believed in the rule of law and the protection of private property, which were considered essential for providing security and incentives to save and invest, and also implied the exclusion of coercion as an instrument to accomplish any economic ends. He was concerned about the prevalence of shirking and corruption, despite heavy emphasis on moral education. He realized that moral persuasion or reasoning alone was insufficient in making people behave honestly, if they were lazy or opportunistic. He introduced the concept of material incentives to complement the moral incentives. Figure 11.1 may be used to explain his three insights.

Each isocost curve indicates the various combinations of efficiency wages (W) and payment for supervision (S), monitoring or auditing required for achieving a certain level of output.[11] For example, a cost function for a Cobb-Douglas technology may be written as: $C(W, S, y) = B W^{\alpha} S^{(1-\alpha)} y / A$. Where B is a constant, W=wage to the worker, S=payment to the supervisor, y=level of output and A= an efficiency parameter, which may depend, among other things (such as infrastructure, technology), on the ethics of both the worker and

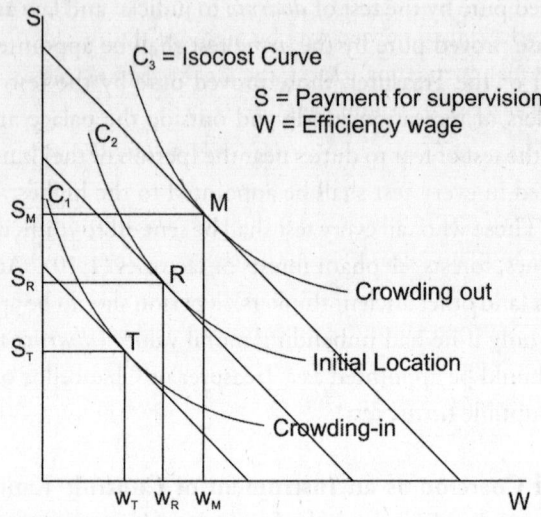

Figure 11.1: C_1, C_2 and C_3 are the isocost curves. Ethical work environment leads to crowding-in effect, the iscost curve C_2, shifts downwards to C_1. Unethical work environment leads to crowding-out, isocost curve C_2, shifts upward to C_3.

the supervisor. If the supervisor does not respect a worker's privacy, engages in sexual harassment, is controlling or adopts confrontational style, parameter A would be adversely affected and thus shift the cost curve upwards.

Section 11.2 presents his first insight that material incentives should be used to complement the moral incentives such that the isocost curve does not shift upwards. The middle isocost curve may be used to explain Kautilya's other two insights. (i) Both efficiency wages and supervision are required to elicit effort. (ii) According to him, upper management might respond better to higher efficiency wages and less supervision, that is, points to the right of point R whereas, for lower management, emphasis is on more supervision, that is, points to the left of R. Section 11.3 presents Kautilya's these two insights.

11.2 MATCHING INCENTIVE-TYPE TO AGENT-TYPE

> The miser should be won over by means of wealth, the proud man by offering respect, the fool by flattery, and the learned one by truthfulness.
>
> — *Kautilya (Subramanian, 116)*

Kautilya knew that incentives were a blunt instrument unless tailored to each person individually, that is, a matching of incentive-type to agent-type was critical for their effectiveness. He identified three types of agents: Upright (moral), opportunistic (amoral) and wicked (immoral). For example, he (p, 168) stated, 'Sons are of three kinds. A wise son is one who understands *dharma* and *artha* when taught and also practices these.[12] A lazy son is one who understands what is taught but does not practice them. A wicked son is he who hates *dharma* and *artha* and [therefore] is full of evil (1.17.44-47).' He continued, 'An only son, if he is wicked, shall not [under any circumstances] be installed on the throne.' Clearly, according to Kautilya, reasoning or understanding of moral values alone is not enough in motivating an amoral or an immoral person to undertake any initiative. He (Subramanian, 129) suggested, 'A fool should be avoided, he is a two-footed animal. He hurts with sharp words like an unseen thorn.' He would avoid such individuals and also the evil ones if he could. Table 11.1 captures Kautilya's insights.

Several remarks are in order. First, Kautilya tried to move an amoral agent from case IX to case XII with the help of both moral and material incentives without ignoring persuasion. That is, he was concerned with both types of 'moral hazard' problems: dishonesty and shirking. However, most of contemporary economists practice value-neutral economics and try to move an agent from case IX only to case XI.[13] It means that modern economists also have the right perspective, which may be incomplete but not wrong. The agents are believed to be rational and 'thinking machines', implying that they have to be convinced of the fairness and benefits of the incentives (and worthiness of the project). In fact, economists' assumption of 'supra-rationality' of agents has come under severe criticism. Grant believes

Table 11.1: Kautilya on the Role of Persuasion and Incentives

Incentive-Type	Agent-Type					
	Upright (Moral)		Opportunistic (Amoral)		Wicked (Immoral)	
	Persuasion	No Persuasion	Persuasion	No Persuasion	Persuasion	No Persuasion
None	Effort level (Optimum) Case I	Effort level (Less than optimum) Case V	Effort level (Low) Case IX	Effort level (Minimal) Case XIII	Effort level (Minimal) Case XVII	Effort level (Minimal) Case XXI
Moral	Effort level (Optimum) Case II	Effort level (Less than optimum) Case VI	Effort level (Less than optimum) Case X	Effort level (Low) Case XIV	Effort level (Minimal) Case XVIII	Effort level (Minimal) Case XXII
Material	Effort level (Optimum) Case III	Effort level (Less than optimum) Case VII	Effort level (Less than optimum) Case XI	Effort level (Low) Case XV	Effort level (Low) Case XIX	Effort level (Low) Case XXIII
Both Moral and Material	Effort level (Optimum) Case VI	Effort level (Less than optimum) Case VIII	Effort level (optimum) Case XII	Effort level (Less than optimum) Case XVI	Effort level (Low) Case XX	Effort level (Low) Case XXIV

that in practice, material incentives alone are used to motivate the agent. This observation regarding the practicing of incentives is not disputed. But its labeling as the 'perspective of economics' is disputed. Since economics is much more than materialism. Moreover, businesses, politicians or parents do not follow economists' suggestions regarding the proper use of incentives (or other concepts) and instead do what seems to them simple or expedient.[14]

Second, only the wicked one, who did not care for the persuasion, might respond to incentives and supervision. Kautilya (Subramanian, p 44, and p 126) believed, 'The evil one harms, even if treated well. Between a serpent and an evil man, the serpent is preferable. The serpent bites occasionally, but the evil man at every step'. Third, a moral agent needed only persuasion to motivate him. Grant is correct in saying that an offer only of material incentives without any persuasion (Cases V to VIII) to a moral person might infuriate him. Fourth, Kautilya believed that material incentives alone without any regard to moral motivation might do more harm than good. His ideas may be expressed algebraically as follows. The principal offers a package (w) (of wage, and supervision etc.) and ensures fairness and participation in the designing of the package and consults frequently during the execution of the task. Kautilya's ideas related to a worker's effort might be written as:[15]

E (w, F (w), M, EE)

Where E denotes the agent's effort, which depends on the wage package but also on its fairness F [w], moral incentives (M) and ethics of the employer (EE). Given all other things equal, as the incentive increases, the worker is expected to supply more effort (ie. $[\partial E^*/\partial w] > 0$).

Emphasized Fairness of Incentives: Kautilya believed that any unfair material incentive might do more harm than good. On the other hand, if the agent considered the wage package to be fair, he would work harder $((\partial E/\partial F)(\partial F/\partial W) > 0)$. According to him (p 519), 'The types of people who are likely to be angry with the king are: someone to whom a promised reward has not been given' and 'of two people equally skilled or efficient, the one who is humiliated (1.14).' He believed that violation of horizontal equity and reneging on a promised reward would result in a crowding-out effect.

Fairness demands that it is acknowledged that the other ancient writer, Xenophon was also concerned with fairness. For example, S Todd Lowry (1987, p 67) observes, 'According to Xenophon, a certain Chrysantas addressed the assembled nobles who were participating in an expedition, pointing out that "some have come out with us who are of superior merit, others who are less deserving than we. Now, if we meet with success, these will all expect to have and share alike. And yet I do not believe that anything in the world is more unfair than for the bad and good to be awarded equal shares" (II.2.18).' He (p 68) concludes, 'The most important aspect of the exposition is the clear presentation of the use of an incentive system, rationalized in terms of the potential for and necessity of initiative and participation by the common soldiery to assure success.'

Moral Motivation: According to Indian moral philosophy, an ideal person seeks: *dharma* (spiritual health), *artha* (material health), *kama* (sensuous pleasures) and *moksha* (salvation). That is, the moral incentive to go to heaven (salvation) and an economic incentive to achieve material health have been considered very powerful and as complementary to each other. According to Kautilya, a decline in moral motivation would shift the isocost curve (see the Figure in Section 11.1) upwards requiring payment of higher wages, and also incurring extra expenditure on monitoring for achieving the same level of output. Nowadays this is called crowding-out.[16] However, if material incentives are designed properly they strengthen moral motivation, implying that the isocost curve shifts to the left, which currently is called a crowding-in effect. According to Kautilya (p 712), the king should say to his troops, I am as much a servant [of the State] as you are; we shall share the wealth of this state.' He continued, 'Bards and praise-singers shall describe the heaven that awaits the brave and the hell that shall be the lot of cowards. They shall extol the clan, group, family, deeds and conduct of the warriors (10.3).' He emphasized three things, common objective 'service to the state', an economic incentive ('share the wealth') and a moral incentive ('the heaven that awaits').

Believed Worker's Effort Affected by Employer's Ethics: According to Kautilya, an employer's ethical behavior had a positive effect on a worker's effort.[17] He wanted the king to be a role model and worthy of emulation. He (p 123) wrote, 'Whatever character the king has, the other elements also come to have the same (8.1).' Thus, according to Kautilya, a king should be impartial, benevolent, far-sighted, disciplined and energetic and set an example to his employees and subjects.

Importance of Feedback and Consultations: Kautilya (Kangle, p 34) suggested (to the king), 'He should look into the affairs with those who are present. With those who are not present, he should hold consultations by sending out letters (1.15).'

Kautilya preferred Cases I to IV (Table 11.1) since a moral agent always worked hard, whether material incentives were provided to him or not. However, according to him, it would be more effective if both the moral and material incentives were provided to an amoral agent rather than just material or just moral ones. It is not claimed that economic incentives transform a person from being amoral to a moral one. In fact, Kautilya (Subramanian, p 58) believed, 'It is difficult to change intrinsic nature'. Rather the claim is a very modest one that carefully designed incentives are likely to make him behave like a moral one. Moreover, economics does not claim to have the necessary tools for accomplishing such a conversion.[18]

11.3 TAILORED TYPES OF MATERIAL INCENTIVES TO AGENT'S HIERARCHICAL POSITION

> The ruler should avoid appointing persons who are fraudulent, dishonest, cruel, without enthusiasm, incompetent and cowardly.
> — *Kautilya (Subramanain, p 128)*

Kautilya realized that the same type of material incentive might not work for the Chief of Defence and for an ordinary soldier. Accordingly, he considered many kinds of material incentives, such as efficiency wages, promotion and job tenure to match the specific needs and position of an individual employee. He was, perhaps, the first economist who suggested payment of efficiency wages. The credit for initiating the current literature on efficiency wages probably goes to Robert Solow (1979). According to this theory, the employer pays a wage, which is higher than the market wage so that the worker does not want to take the chance of losing his job by engaging in shirking. As Prendergast (1999) notes, some of the payment mechanisms are designed to eliminate or reduce rent whereas an efficiency wage is offered to create rent to induce effort.

Material Incentives, Inspection (Auditing) and Punishments (Fines): Kautilya suggested that material incentives be matched to the specific rank of the employee to elicit maximum possible effort. He suggested that the king should rely more on payment of efficiency wages to upper grade employees, such as Chief of Defence, Councilors, Chancellor, Treasurer, Auditor and Ministers. On the other hand, the king should rely more on granting promotion and job tenure to the middle and lower grades employees, awarding prizes to soldiers and giving gifts to piece-rate workers.

Four possibilities for eliciting optimum effort from a worker: by using a combination of (i) paying efficiency wages and monitoring, (ii) monitoring and investigation[19], (iii) paying efficiency wages and investigation and (iv) a judicious mix of efficiency wages, monitoring and investigation since monitoring competes both with the paying of efficiency wages and investigation in eliciting effort. Interestingly, Kautilya dealt with the possibility (iii), which is discussed below and surprisingly so far has not been explored by any modern economist.

Combining Efficiency Wages and Auditing (Investigation) for Upper Grade Employees: Kautilya advised the king to treat the councillors and ministers (about eighteen officials) with respect and dignity and compensate them handsomely since their wisdom and intelligence were the most important resource for the survival and economic growth of the country. Particularly the councillors were the most prized employees and every effort was made including the payment of a salary of 48,000 *panas* to retain them.[20]

Kautilya was also aware of the fact that sometimes, an instrument might not be available or might be unnecessary. For example, he realized that it was physically not possible to supervise the Chancellor and recommended efficiency wages and auditing to reduce cheating. The Chancellor and the Treasurer were the most important civil servants in charge of collecting and handling the revenue of the state. According to him (p 217-218), the Chancellor was responsible for collecting revenue from the countryside and the Treasurer, in addition to his other duties, was responsible to 'appoint trustworthy men to assist him in receiving and storing the revenue of the state'. He (p 289) suggested that the Chancellor and the Treasurer be paid 24,000 *panas* annually, 'enough to make them efficient in their work (5.3).'

Similarly, Kautilya recommended a handsome salary of 12,000 *panas* for a Minister. It was 200 times the suggested minimum wage of 60 *panas*. As mentioned above, most capable individuals were appointed as Councillors, whose role was to advise the king. But Ministers were the actual executors of whatever had been decided by the king. He (p 123) assigned a very important role to the Ministers, 'All state activities have their origin in the Minister, whether these be the successful execution of works for the territory and the population, maintenance of law and order, protection from enemies, tackling calamities, settlement of virgin lands, recruiting the army, revenue collection or rewarding the worthy (8.1).' He (p 200) continued, 'The ministers shall think of all that concerns the king as well as those of the enemy. They shall start doing all that has not been done, continue implementing that which has been started, improve on works completed and, in general, ensure strict compliance with orders (1.15).' He added, 'In an emergency, the king shall call together both the group of councillors and the council of ministers and seek their advice. He shall follow whatever the majority advise or whatever is conducive to the success of the task in hand (1.15).'

Auditing (Investigation): Kautilya (p 226) stated, 'High officials shall render accounts in full for their respective activities, without contradicting themselves (2.7).' According to him (p 226), the Chief

Comptroller-Auditor (one person) reported directly to the king. He was responsible for auditing all the officials, including the Chancellor. It was physically impossible for the king to monitor the activities of various officials, the Chancellor being one of them. In this situation, the king had only the instruments of efficiency wages and inspection (auditing) at his disposal. Thus, Kautilya suggested payment of efficiency wages and auditing (investigation) to ensure efficiency and honesty of the Chancellor. However, the emphasis was on paying efficiency wages.

Combining Job Tenure, Promotion and Inspection for Middle and Lower Grade Employees: Kautilya was aware of human tendencies of risk-aversion and shirking (leisure-seeking). Therefore, middle and lower grades employees, who might be highly risk-averse, would appreciate job tenure. He recommended that this group of employees, who were honest, efficient and loyal, be made permanent. But he also advised inspection so that these employees did not slack after getting tenure. Such a policy-mix is discussed below.

Job Tenure: He recommended rewards for good management and stiff punishment for mismanagement. He (p 281) stated, 'Those officials who do not eat up the king's wealth but increase it in just ways and are loyally devoted to him shall be made permanent in service (2.9).'

Promotion: Kautilya (p 284) suggested, 'An officer who accomplishes a task as ordered or better shall be honored with promotion and rewards (2.9).'

Inspection: It seems that Kautilya considered both (i) direct inspection of the work of the officials and (ii) an indirect one through consumers' complaints to ensure the quality of work. He (p 283) suggested, 'The king shall have the work of Heads of Departments inspected daily, for men are, by nature, fickle and, like horses, change after being put to work. Therefore, the king shall acquaint himself with all the details of each Department or undertaking, such as – the officer responsible, the nature of the work, the place of work, the time taken to do it, the exact work to be done, the outlay and the profit (2.9)'. He (p 221) added, 'The Chancellor, working through the magistrates, shall be responsible for inspecting Heads of Departments, judicial officers and their subordinates (4.9).' He (p 516) again suggested, 'The agents of the Chancellor shall report on the honesty or otherwise of village officials and heads of departments (4.4).'

He also recommended an indirect method of investigation. He (p 742) wrote, 'Any official who incurs the displeasure of the people shall either be removed from his post or transferred to a dangerous region (13.5).'[21] He believed, employees, if not inspected, might shirk work. He was aware of the need for inspections and payment of efficiency wages to elicit effort. However, it is not claimed that Kautilya could trace the efficiency frontier between efficiency wages and the probability of inspection. The *Arthashastra* does not contain any theoretical models (as we know them) to determine their optimum levels. Usually, too much emphasis is put on variability in an employee's pay but, according to Kautilya, a safe working environment was equally important.

Reward for Extra and Better Work by the Piece-rate Workers: Kautilya was aware of the fact that piece-rate workers paid less attention to quality. He recommended extra payments as an incentive to these workers so that they made products of better quality and also worked on holidays. He (p 233) suggested, 'For better work [or greater productivity], women who spin shall be given oil and myrobalan cakes as a special favor. They shall be induced to work on festive days [and holidays] by giving them gifts. Weavers, specializing in weaving any fabrics of flax, dukula, silk yarn, deer wool and [fine] cotton shall be given gifts of perfumes, flowers and similar presents of encouragement (2.23).'

Tournaments: Nowadays, the vice presidents in a corporation are supposed to compete hard to reach to the top of the ladder and enjoy the status, salary, leisure and perks accompanying the promotion. The idea of a tournament and the winner being awarded a prize as an incentive to extract maximum effort was very much alive during Kautilya's time (Olympics started around 776 BCE) too. He (p 714) suggested, 'The Chief of Defense shall make the troops happy with wealth and honors and announce the following rewards—a hundred thousand *panas* for killing the enemy king, fifty thousand for a prince or the Army Chief, ten thousand for a division chief, five thousand for an elephant or chariot warrior, thousand for a horse, one hundred for an infantry section leader, twenty for a soldier, as well as double normal wages and whatever booty they seize (10.3).' It may again be noted that both profit sharing and the winner receiving a prize were common practices to induce effort. Clearly, the concept of tournament originated in a different context but the objective was the same: to make participants compete hard for the prize. However, as noted above, not only were material incentives offered but also an equal attention [was] paid to moral incentives to maintain and strengthen motivation.

Reducing Distractions: There were enough distractions in Kautilya's times to warrant his attention to modes of reducing them.[22] He (p 180) wrote, 'There shall be no grounds or buildings intended for recreation [in the new settlements]. Actors, dancers, singers, musicians, professional story-tellers and minstrels shall not obstruct the work [of the people], because in villages which provide no shelter [to outsiders], the people will be [fully] involved in the work of the fields. [Consequently] there will be an increase in the supply of labour, money, commodities, grains and liquid products (2.1).'

Punishments: Kautilya recommended severe and certain statutory punishments (normally monetary) for mismanagement and corruption. According to him, the magnitude of punishment should vary with the nature and severity of [the] mismanagement, that is, whether it was due to ignorance, laziness, timidity, corruption, short temper, arrogance or greed of the official. He (p 283) observed, 'Those officials who have amassed money [wrongfully] shall be made to pay it back; they shall [then] be transferred to other jobs where they will not be tempted to misappropriate and be made to disgorge again what they had eaten (2.9)'. He (p 284) continued, 'An officer negligent or remiss in his work shall be fined double his wages and the expenses incurred (2.9).'

11.4 PAYMENT-SYSTEM DESIGN TO ALLEVIATE MORAL HAZARD

Kautilya understood the importance of contract designs, which could eliminate the 'moral hazard' problem in certain situations. Even in an agrarian economy, at least some moderately complex situations could arise. He observed at least two such situations and provided some insights, which may be relevant even for modern corporations.[23] He emphasized the sanctity of contracts. He (p 450) recommended, 'The agreement between a labourer and the one hiring him shall be made in public. Labourers shall be paid wages as agreed upon. If there is no prior agreement, the labourer shall be paid in accordance with the nature of the work and the time spent on it at customary rates (3.13).' He believed that contracts made in public were verifiable and, therefore, enforceable. He indicated that the customary rate was one-tenth of the produce but [he] modified this customary practice in two cases.

Case (a): He (p 317) recommended, 'they (a herdsman, milker, a churner and a hunter-guard) shall be paid in cash, because if they are paid in milk or butter oil, they will starve the calves to death [by milking the cows dry, leaving nothing for the calves] (2.29).' This may be made explicit as follows. Let X be the total milk output, which a cow produced and θX, be the calf's share. If the agent (a herdsman, milker, churner or a hunter-guard) was paid in kind as a share, α of the output, $(1-\theta) X$ left after providing for the calf [ie. his share would be $\alpha (1-\theta) X$]. The agent would try to maximize his utility V. Clearly, θ, the calf's share was under his control. He would maximize the following:

Max V $[\alpha (1-\theta) X]$

Maximizing with respect to θ

$dV/d\theta = -V'\alpha X < 0$. That means the agent would set $\theta = 0$. That is, he would not leave anything for the calf and essentially his wage would be αX. The principal would not know how much milk the calf was getting. Certainly, he could look at the health of the calf and fire the agent if it did not look healthy. But the next agent would do the same thing because there was a built-in incentive to starve the calf. It implies that the agent had to be paid a cash wage equal to or higher than αX. The principal (the king) was interested in maximizing the total output, X and also its efficient allocation between current consumption, (1−θ) X, and investment, θX (which was calf's share) and Kautilya recommended θ to be decided by the principal and the agent should have no stake in it.

Two observations are in order. First, in terms of a modern corporation, a determination of θ essentially amounts to the allocation of profit between retained earnings and dividends. At present, this decision is made by the management (the agent) and not by the shareholders (principal). Accordingly the shareholders have to search for the stocks, which match their preferences related to growth and income. According to Kautilya, the shareholders themselves should be allowed to decide θ. Particularly, the institutional investors perhaps wouldn't mind making this decision. Anyhow, its feasibility and efficiency deserve exploration.

Secondly, it is a very simple example but carries a profound idea— [the need] to recognize and resolve the 'moral hazard' problem. The milkman had an incentive to squeeze the calf and thus could hurt the growth of livestock and subvert the objective of the principal. Similarly, the CEO of a modern corporation may resort to squeezing both the workers, and the stockholders (with or without the provision of stock options) to advance his own interest. For example, the stock options have made super magicians out of the CEOS and CFOs, who have been producing eggs out of thin air and getting rich by hatching them. The point is that stock options alone, even if they are included in the expenses, cannot be the solution to the principal-agent problem.

Case (b): Kautilya (p 288) stated, 'If the [amount of actual cash in the] treasury is inadequate, salaries may be paid [partly] in forest produce, cattle or land, supplemented by a little money. However, in the case of settlement of virgin lands, all salaries shall be paid in cash; no land shall be allotted [as part of the salary] until the affairs of the [new] village are fully stabilized (5.3).' Obviously, supervising the settlement of virgin lands was a full time job. If the officers were allowed to work on the land, they might spend very little time on the official duties and disproportionately more time working on the land, that is, ignore their primary responsibilities. This observation also has a direct implication for modern corporations. The part-time Directors of corporations are really no matches to the sophistication of the full-time CEOs and CFOs, some of whom have been busy cooking the books (see Chapter 9), or to the complexities of the modern businesses. It is obvious that the current system of corporate governance cannot guarantee either accountability or transparency.

Wage Payment System versus Sharecropping: Recently, Robert Gibbons (1998) notes that the trade-off between insurance and incentives may be captured by the work of Lee Alston and Robert Higgs (1982) on sharecropping. According to them, there were three kinds of contracts. If the output, y, depends on effort of the agent and there is some uncertainty, ε, $y = a + \varepsilon$, and the agent is paid a wage w such that $w = s + b y$. If (i) $b=0$, then the worker is paid a cash wage, (ii) if $0 < b < 1$, the worker shares the risk and (iii) if $b=1$, the worker assumes all the risk and pays rent to the land owner. Kautilya emphasized that land should belong to the tiller and thus the case (iii) in general had no place in his scheme, that is, absentee landlords contracting out their pieces of land for a rent was not recommended.

Irrigation and Sharecropping: Sharecropping implies sharing both the return and the risk. But the presence of risk creates a disincentive to a risk-averse agent.[24] However, if there is an input, which reduces risk and also increases expected return, a risk-averse agent is likely to be encouraged to use such an input even under a sharing arrangement (ie. sharecropping or profit sharing system). For example, irrigation leads to a higher yield and a reduction in its variability and, therefore, sharecropping may be an efficient arrangement for both the supplier and the user of such an input. Kautilya recommended sharecropping, if a farmer supplied water from his private water-works to the neighbouring farmers. He (p 231) stated, 'Owners may give water to others by dredging channels or building suitable structures, in return for a share of the produce grown in the fields, parks or gardens (3.9).' Such an arrangement offered incentives for both of them, and additionally, being neighbours, the cost of ascertaining the level of output would have been minimal.

Supervision and Wage Payment System on Crown Land: Crown land was to be managed by the Chief Superintendent of Crown Lands. According to Kautilya (p 313), the Chief Superintendent 'Shall be conversant with the science of cultivation, water management and the proper care of plants (2.24)' and he (p 314), 'Shall employ such experts as are necessary in order to cultivate profitably Crown lands and supervise the following operations: seed collection, land preparation, seed preparation and sowing, manuring and protection, harvesting and threshing (2.24).' Kautilya (p 315) added, 'On Crown lands, he shall employ slaves, labourers and persons working off their fines (2.24).' These workers would be provided food according to their family sizes and a cash wage of one and a quarter *panas* per month.

It is obvious from the above statement that Kautilya recommended supervision where management had a better knowledge of the production techniques than those of the workers. That is, he recommended a wage system where close supervision was required on efficiency grounds and sharecropping where wage labour was not available.[25]

Sharecropping on Crown Land: Kautilya (p 315) suggested, 'The Chief Superintendent of Crown Lands may lease out land that cannot be cultivated directly. Those lessees who provide only labour [the seeds and implements being provided by the Crown] shall get one fourth or one-fifth of the harvest. Those lessees who provide all the inputs shall get one-half of the harvest. Those who prepare new [Crown] land and bring it into cultivation for the first time shall pay an agreed amount. In times of distress, the payment may be foregone (2.24).' Apparently, sharecropping was recommended when the state did not have the manpower to cultivate it.

SUMMARY

Kautilya was definitely aware of the principal-agent problem, which arises whenever institutional structures are created. He explored many types of incentives to mitigate the harmful effects of the agency problem. He recommended moral motivation along with a judicious mix of efficiency wages, and investigation to elicit optimum effort, honesty and loyalty. Kautilya's analysis provides several valuable insights, such as (i) if possible, an attempt should be made to match an incentive-type to an agent-type. (ii) Material incentives should be tailored to an employee's hierarchical position and under certain special circumstances, imposition of some restrictions on him may be desirable. (iii) Most important of all, material incentives be designed in such a way that they are perceived as fair, so that moral motivation is not undermined. Kautilya's insights are as relevant today as they were two thousand years ago.

12

Taxation: Principles and Policies

> If there is competition among buyers and a higher price is realized, the difference between the call price and the sale price along with the duty thereon shall go to the Treasury
> —*Kautilya (p 239)*

Kautilya proposed several principles of taxation, such as fairness, which included a safety net; stability of tax structure; collecting taxes only when they were due, that is, only after the harvest; maximization of the difference between revenue and expenditure, and fiscal federalism. He provided some unique insights into the possible origin of income tax and the institution of kingship. He formulated a whole set of economic policies to give a concrete shape to his vision of creating a prosperous economy. His approach was very methodical and complete. He suggested building up of taxable capacity through providing infrastructure, rather than heavy tax to raise revenue as such.

Significantly, he recommended a linear income tax and tax compliance as an integral part of his tax system. Additionally, he showed awareness with several modern theoretical concepts, such as, the producer surplus, the Dupuit-Laffer Curve and the non-cooperative nature of the relationship between the taxpayer and the government.

He emphasized the financial health of the state and understood that a sound treasury was a prerequisite to accomplishing other goals. He (p 252) stated, 'All state activities depend first on the Treasury. Therefore, a king shall devote his best attention to it. A king with a depleted Treasury eats into the very vitality of the citizens and the country.' He (p 147) attached great significance to this aspect and envisaged that a king should start his day by receiving 'reports on defense, revenue and expenditure.' He added, 'If receipts and expenditure are properly looked after, the king will not find himself in financial difficulties.' Therefore, he emphasized that a king must carefully manage the financial affairs of the state.

Kautilya's views on the origin of income taxation are provided in Section 12.1. His principles of taxation, such as fairness, stability, compliance and fiscal federalism are discussed in Section 12.2. He recommended the provision of a safety net for the poor, the old and the sick and thus supplemented the customary benefit principle by adding the ability to pay principle to it. He understood the limits to the government's power to tax and this insight is discussed in Section 12.3. His ideas on a few related concepts, such as producer surplus, a functional classification of the government budget into the current account and capital account are discussed in Section 12.4.

12.1 ORIGIN OF THE INCOME TAX AND THE INSTITUTION OF KINGSHIP

On the Origin of the Maxim 'Taxation with Representation': Kautilya mentioned the existence of a proportional income tax during his time.[1] He also noted that the income tax and the institution of kingship originated together. According to Weller (1978, Vol 18, p 134) the war between the Pandavas and Kauravas took place around 3102 BCE and, even at that time, the institution of kingship was well established. Thus, in India, the income tax probably came into being more than five thousand years ago.

On the Origin of the Benefit Rule of Taxation: Kautilya (p 820) discussed the origin of income tax. He described it as: 'When there was no order in society and only the law of the jungle prevailed, people [were unhappy and being desirous of order] made Manu, the son of Vivasvat, their king; and they assigned to the king one-sixth part of the grains grown by them, one-tenth of other commodities and money. The king then used these to safeguard the welfare of his subjects. Those who do not pay fines and taxes take on themselves the sins of kings, while kings who do not look after the welfare of the people take on themselves the sins of their subjects (1.13).'

Attention may be drawn to some significant features of this approach. First, income tax was found more natural than a lump-sum tax. Secondly, the income tax rate itself was decided directly by the individuals. The rationale for income tax was based on the protection principle, that is, the benefit approach. It is also significant to point out that at that time too, compliance could not be taken for granted.

New Institutionalists' Claim Validated: Hodgson (1998) argues, 'Attempts to explain the origin and sustenance of institutions on the basis of the assumption of given individuals have internal flaws and inconsistencies. Accordingly, attemps to explain institutions in this way may have to be abandoned.' He continues, 'The central "new" institutionalist project of explaining institutions from individuals alone is thus misconceived.' The [above] statement by Kautilya cited in the previous paragraph not only sheds some light on the origin of income tax but also supports the new institutionalist's approach in explaining the origin of, at least, one institution, the kingship. It seems that at least Manu (more than 5000 years ago) was the first and perhaps the last king elected by the people.

12.2 PRINCIPLES OF TAXATION

Using an Imaginary Lump-sum Tax as a Standard: There are two questions regarding any direct tax: is it feasible and what is the magnitude of deadweight loss created by it? A lump-sum tax does not produce any substitution effect, that is, it does not affect economic behavior and, therefore, does not create any deadweight loss. Although a poll tax was imposed in ancient Greece, Rome and some European colonies, women, paupers, handicapped and war veterans were exempted from it, implying that it could not be called a true lump-sum tax. Since income and service in the army were the underlying factors, which determined who would pay the tax, it implied that the tax could have affected economic behavior. Similarly, Seligman (1927-28, p 159-160) notes, 'In some countries they have developed this poll tax according to classes, as the head of a workman is worth more than the head of a beggar and the head of a duke worth more than that of a workman, etc.' The hard fact remains that no society has ever implemented a true lump-sum tax. Clearly, if deadweight loss were the only consideration, a lump-sum tax would have been preferred. Surprisingly, this historical fact is ignored and an income tax, which creates a deadweight loss because of the distortions caused by the substitution effect, is invariably compared to an imaginary lump-sum tax. Kautilya has been the only thinker, who made an attempt to explore the possibility that there might be some other types of costs associated with a lump-sum tax. According to him, political stability was a prerequisite for economic development and fairness was essential for political stability. He believed that a lump-sum tax might be considered unfair by the public and therefore, was likely to create resentment, political unrest and impose heavy cost on the economy. He, as discussed below, suggested measures such as an income tax and administration of justice to ensure fairness in all walks of life.

Apparently, humanity has been concerned with fairness since antiquity. For example, Kautilya recommended an income tax when a lump-sum tax might have been feasible. He (p 820) linked the origin of income tax to the benefit principle. Kautilya accepted the customary income tax on agricultural income. The non-agricultural income, other than those of prostitutes, was taxed only during emergencies.

He believed that merchants dealing with gold and silver must be making more money than those dealing with wood and accordingly recommended a graduated tax. He (p 271) suggested taxing merchants and professionals as follows (in terms of *pana* that was the unit of account and medium of exchange at that time):

Gold, silver and gems	50 panas
Copper, brass, perfumes etc.	40 panas
Grain, liquids etc.	30 panas
Workers in glass and other highly skilled craftsmen	20 panas
Other craftsmen	10 panas
Wood, bamboo, stoneware and earthenware	5 panas

Similarly, he suggested a graduated tax (during an emergency in addition to the regular income tax of 1/6th) on land holdings according to the yield from them. He (Kangle, part II, p 296) suggested to the king, 'He should demand a third or a fourth part of the grains from a region, whether big or small in size, that is not dependent on rains and yields abundant crops; from a middling or inferior one, according to yield (5.2).'

Kautilya accepted an income tax partly because of the fact that he was unaware of the concept of deadweight loss but primarily, perhaps due to concern regarding the possible disruptive effects of a lump-sum tax. Although he did not say it explicitly, but his awareness may fall into the category of what Waterman calls 'read into'—that a lump-sum tax was unfair and could create resentment and lead to political instability and disruptions. That is, given his views on the absolute need to be fair in all aspects of human activity, it seems quite plausible that he understood the cost of disruptions of a lump-sum tax. That means that the current approach ignores the possible disruptive effects of a lump-sum tax. Kautilya's ideas essentially amount to comparing the impact of a lump-sum tax to that of an income tax on earnings and risk. He considered a situation where, suppose more revenue could be collected by a lump-sum tax (it does not have a deadweight loss), which permitted a higher level of public infrastructure and helped in raising the earnings of an individual more than under an income tax. However, according to Kautilya, the probability of retaining those

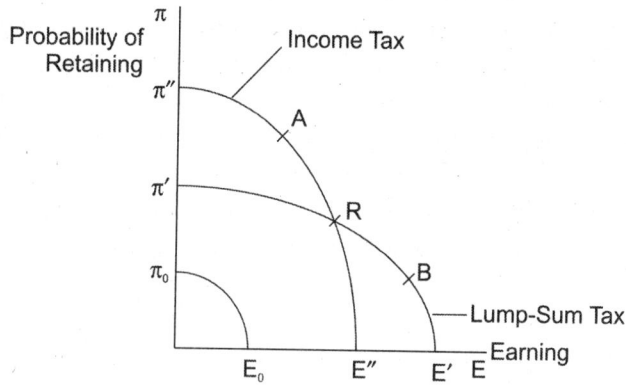

Figure 12.1: $\pi_0 E_0$ the initial possibility frontier. Lump-sum tax shifts it to π' E' and an income tax shifts it to π'' E".

higher earnings rose more under an income tax than under a lump-sum tax. Figure 12.1 may be used to capture his ideas.

E_0 and π_0 represent an individual's earnings and the probability of retaining his earnings, respectively. That is, an individual allocates his time between working to earn money and taking protective measures to retain it. Suppose taxes are imposed to provide protection of private property rights and establishing law and order. A lump-sum tax is likely to shift the possibility frontier to π' E' and an income tax to π'' E", and it would be difficult to say a priori whether a society prefers any point to the left of R or to the right of R, that is, whether it prefers an income tax or a lump-sum tax. However, as noted above, the choice has been definitely in favour of an income tax.

The current approach compares point E" to point E' since it assumes that the law and order situation is unaffected by the type of tax. Unsurprisingly, a lump-sum tax is declared better than an income tax and the equity-efficiency trade-off is confined essentially to the segment E"E', whose length depended on the specifications of the income tax. However, Kautilya wanted to exclude any possibility of disruptive effects caused by a lump-sum tax, since maintenance of law and order was considered critical for survival and economic progress.

It is obvious that Kautilya's ideas complement the current approach, which focuses only on the deadweight loss of an income tax and ignores the possibility of negative consequences of a lump-sum tax.

Kautilya had two additional reasons for adopting an income tax. By definition a lump-sum tax has to be uniform. He was concerned about the well-being of the poor, who couldn't pay any tax and needed help. He (p 182) suggested, 'King shall maintain, at state expense, children, the old, the destitute, those suffering from adversity, childless women and the children of the destitute women (2.1).'

His *Arthashastra* may be described as a treatise on the imperative of economic growth. As mentioned above, tax revenue was necessary in providing infrastructure, army and armament. As also mentioned earlier, he (p 252) stated, 'All state activities depend first on the Treasury. Therefore, a king shall devote his best attention to it. A king with a depleted Treasury eats into the very vitality of the citizens and the country.' He linked tax revenue to economic prosperity. He (p 116) suggested, 'In the interests of the prosperity of the country, a king should be diligent in foreseeing the possibility of calamities, try to avert them before they arise, overcome those which happen, remove all obstructions to economic activity and prevent loss of revenue to the state (8.4).' A lump-sum tax could not raise the desired level of revenue since its magnitude would be constrained by the paying capacity of the poorest in the society. There is some evidence on this. For example, Seligman (1927-28, p 159-160) mentions that some Southern states in USA imposed a poll tax with the clear intent to deny the poor Black people from exercising their right to vote since they, it was thought, would not be able to pay the tax.

It may be noted that there would be no shift in the possibility frontier if the revenue is siphoned-off by corrupt public men (that would include both politicians and bureaucrats in present times). That is why Kautilya was much concerned about corruption. For example, as was mentioned earlier too (see Chapter 9, Section 9.3), he (p 281) stated, 'Just as it is impossible to know when a fish moving in water is drinking it, so it is impossible to find out when government servants in charge of undertakings misappropriate money (2.9).' He devised various ways to reduce it.

Combined the Ability to Pay and the Benefit Principle: According to him, a tax rate lower than 1/6th would reduce tax revenue and consequently reduce the provision of infrastructure and public goods—national defence, and law and order. He (p 125) added, 'It is the army which is dependent on finance. If not paid, [the soldiers] either go over to the enemy or even kill the king. Finance is necessary to undertake any state endeavor and is the chief means for both *dharma* [righteous duty] and *kama* [enjoyment] (8.1).' Similarly, he argued that a tax rate higher than 1/6th would anger the taxpayers and might result in a reduction in tax revenue (see more below in Section 12.3). One may wonder why he accepted the existing income tax when the imposition of a lump-sum tax seemed feasible. There may be several reasons for that: (i) the most important seems to be that income tax was sanctioned by a majority of taxpayers. (ii) He realized that fairness was not merely an end in itself but also a means to ensuring political stability. A lump-sum tax could generate political instability by creating a perception of inequity and thus, might lower the overall economic efficiency. Models, which compare an income tax to a lump sum tax by assuming a representative taxpayer, assume away the possible disruptions caused by political instability. (iii) A per head tax might have encouraged migration of people to other regions, thus compromising national security.

Safety Net: There was a very clear demarcation of responsibilities between the individual and the state. According to Kautilya (p 182), 'Every man has an obligation to maintain his wife, children, parents, minor brothers and dependent (unmarried or widowed) sisters. No man shall renounce the life of a householder in order to become an ascetic without providing for the maintenance of his wife and children (2.1).' The head of the household was primarily responsible for the family and there was a punishment of 12 *panas* (p 194) for the failure (2.1). However, he (p 182) suggested, 'King shall maintain, at state expense, children, the old, the destitute, those suffering from adversity, childless women and the children of the destitute women (2.1).' He (p 293) added, 'If a government servant dies while on duty, his sons and wives shall be entitled to his salary and food allowance. Minor children and old or sick relatives shall be suitably assisted. On occasions such as funerals, births or illnesses, the families of the deceased government servants shall be given presents of money and shown honor as a mark of gratitude to one who died in the king's service (5.3).'

The above statements indicate a comprehensive package of benefits: disability payments to those suffering from adversity, social security to the old, supplemental security income to the children and welfare payments to the poor.

Anticipation of a Linear Income Tax System: The true appreciation of Kautilya's insight on income tax may be gleaned by comparing it to the recent developments in the theory of income tax.[2] It is apparent from the above discussion that he implicitly recommended a linear income tax with the marginal tax rate, being 1/6th (if T=tax revenue, Y=income, T= —a +b Y, T= —a if Y=0 and T=b Y for Y>0). Moreover, no exemptions, other than a very few for promoting new investment, were allowed, and, therefore, it comes very close to the comprehensive definition of Haig-Simons (see Atkinson and Stiglitz, 1980, p 260 for details) for the income tax. Surprisingly, the magnitude of the flat income tax rate mentioned in political debates in the USA is not much different from 1/6th, the rate recommended in the *Arthashastra*.[3]

It appears that Kautilya implicitly combined both, the benefit principle and the ability to pay principle. According to both, the benefit principle and the ability to pay principle, rich people should pay more.[4] However, the benefit principle does not allow any subsidy to the poor. But he suggested the payment of a subsidy to the poor, implying the use of the ability to pay principle.

Collecting Taxes only when they are due: According to him, it made no sense in collecting taxes before the crops were harvested. Since (i) taxes were due only after the harvest, (ii) it was useless to collect raw grains and (iii) also annoyed the farmers. He (p 253) observed, 'Just as one plucks fruits from a garden as they ripen, so shall a king have the revenue collected as it becomes due. Just as one does not collect unripe fruits, he shall avoid taking wealth that is not due because that will make the people angry and spoil the very sources of revenue (5.2).'

Maximization of the Net Tax Revenue: Kautilya (p 218-220) envisaged a Chancellor, who was to be responsible for: '(i) the collection of revenue from the fortified towns, the country-side, the mines, the irrigation works, forests and trade routes, and (ii) the preparation of the budget and maintenance of detailed accounts of revenue and expenditure as prescribed (2.6).' As discussed in Chapter 5, Kautilya introduced accounting methods and every official had to follow the format. Also, the officer had to constantly manage the revenue as well as expenditure such that the net did not fall. He (p 220) added, 'A wise Chancellor is one who collects revenue so as to increase income and reduce expenditure. He shall take remedial measures if income diminishes and expenditure increases (2.6).' He would reward those officers who were honest and collected tax only what was due. Kautilya (p 281) recommended, 'Those officials who do not eat up the king's wealth but increase it in just ways and are loyally devoted to him shall be made permanent in service.'

Stability of the Tax Structure: As mentioned above, during normal times, he accepted the customary income tax rate of 1/6th on agricultural production on private farms and on income of private prostitutes. There was no income tax on the salaries of state employees. Merchants paid some sort of professional taxes only during emergencies. Undoubtedly, the tax rates were different for normal and emergency times but were known in advance. Thus, he preferred a stable tax structure and similarly, the existence of a few exemptions on investment created only a little uncertainty regarding the tax base.[5]

Fiscal Federalism: Kautilya specified the sources of revenue for the central government and for the villages separately.[6] Villages collected their revenue mainly from charges for grazing and fines levied on the villagers for not participating in community works. He (p 366) mentioned separately the charges for grazing only, grazing and resting and grazing and staying overnight.

Village Governance: According to him, the Village Headman and the Village Elders were responsible for managing the village. He (p 182) recommended, The village elders shall act as trustees of temple property and the inheritance of minors (till they come of age) (2.1).' He (p 432) suggested, 'Boundary disputes between two villages shall be decided by a group from the neighbouring five or ten villages, using natural or man-made boundary marks (3.9).' He (p 427) added, 'When a debtor is unable to redeem a pledge because of the absence of the creditor, he may deposit the amount due with village elders and take away his pledge (3.12).'

He (p 365) listed the responsibilities of the Village Headman as follows: '(i) The Village Headman shall have a fence with pillars erected all the way around the village at a distance of 600 feet from it. (ii) He shall ensure that cattle do not graze or stray into cultivated private fields or gardens or eat the grains in storage sheds and thrashing fields and shall be responsible for protecting them from injuries or harsh treatment. (iii) He shall collect the revenue for the village from the charges levied on grazing in common land, from the prescribed fines and the fines levied by the state. (iv) He shall not eject any settler from a village except for reasons of theft or adultery (3.10).' It may be noted that it appears that the enclosure movement in India took place almost two thousand years earlier than in England (see Ashton, 1972, p 38-48 for details). But more important: 'Local matters were in local hands.' Apparently, fiscal federalism was possible even under monarchy.

Kautilya tried to develop 'civic virtues' of cooperation among the villagers.[7] He (p 365) stated, 'All the people in a village shall contribute their share of the community work and costs of festivals and entertainments (3.10).' He added, The people of a village shall obey the orders of anyone who proposes any activity beneficial to all. They shall not conspire against such a person to attack or harm him. When the Headman has to travel on village business, he shall be accompanied by some of the residents of the village, who shall take the duty in turns (3.10).'

Compliance: First of all, it appears that Kautilya believed that tax compliance depended on the tax system. He recommended an income tax on agricultural income and a form of occupational tax on non-agricultural income to plug loopholes for income-shifting. He (p 271) stated, 'The tax shall be recovered, in cash, from those skilled in their work. Their offences shall not be forgiven, for they are apt to [evade the tax and] pretend that the sales made by them were on behalf of someone else (5.2).' Apparently, he was aware of the difficulty of collection of an income tax on the non-agricultural income, due to the scope for tax evasion. On the other hand, a tax collector could go to the agricultural fields at the time of harvesting and have a pretty accurate estimate of the output and the resultant tax liability. This is not a far-fetched possibility. For example, Bennett (1999, p 25) states, 'Others, however, have pointed out that there exist in modern India professional appraisers, called *kaniya*, who estimate the crop yield for land-owners with uncanny accuracy. Because their reliability has been established from year to year, their results are rarely questioned.'

Slemrod (1990) notes, 'If optimal tax theory is to be a reliable guide to action, it must consider the issues that arise in operating the tax system.' Enforcement was an integral part of Kautilya's tax system. There was a Record Keeper for every five to ten villages, who kept detailed records on almost everything in the villages. The Record Keepers were responsible for collecting the taxes and there were magistrates to 'inspect their work and to ensure proper collection of taxes' (2.35). Additionally, he (p 510) recommended, 'Spies in the guise of ascetics shall be [directly] responsible to the Chancellor for reporting on the honesty or dishonesty of farmers, cowherds, merchants and Heads of Departments (2.35).' Thus, Kautilya's discussion on taxation may fall in spirit under what Slemrod calls 'the realm of optimal tax systems rather than optimal taxation.'

Tax evasion in the *Arthashastra* was treated as a criminal offence and the penalty was related to the magnitude of tax evasion rather than the magnitude of income concealed. Interestingly, this is more like the American penal tax code than the British penal tax code (which is the currently prevailing one in India). Relating the penalty to the magnitude of tax evasion is desirable, as Yitzhaski (1974), shows, only then does its effect become predictable.

Non-cooperative Game: According to Kautilya, a trader was supposed to declare the price of his product at the city gate so that the tariff could be assessed correctly and collected before he was allowed to sell his product. He was concerned about the possibility of the government being cheated of taxes by the traders in certain circumstances, by understatement and in others by overstatement of the prices.

Tax Evasion by Understatement of Price: He seemed to refer to three prices: p_G was the price declared by the merchant at the city gate, pw, the price the merchant was willing to accept (cost plus some reasonable profit), and p_S the price at which sale was materialized. He (p 341) recommended a fine 'Eight times the difference between actual and declared price' for 'declaring a lower price in order to pay less duty' [ie. if $p_G < p_W$, penalty = $8(p_W - p_G)$ per unit].

Tax Evasion by Over-stating the price: According to Kautilya, the producer surplus should go the government. But he anticipated the possibility that a merchant might try to appropriate part of the potential producer surplus by overstating the price at the city gate. He (p 342) recommended that the penalty for 'Calling out too high a price at the gate [anticipating competitive bidding] will be equal to the difference between actual sale price and the price originally called or double the duty (2.21).' Thus, according to Kautilya, if the call price at the gate, $p_G > p_w$ (and $p_s \geq p_G$), there would be a penalty equal to the difference between p_s and p_w. As an illustration, let me discuss this case. Suppose in anticipation of a strong demand for his product, a trader overstated the price, let t be the tax rate, λ, the penalty rate and Q, the quantity to be sold, then if not caught, he gained, $Y = Q(1-t)(p_G - p_w)$. If caught he lost, $X = Q\lambda(p_G - p_w)$. Suppose c is the cost of auditing, ϕ the probability of auditing and π the probability of cheating. The following payoff matrix may be used to express Kautilya's ideas.

Matrix 12.1: Pay-offs (tax authority, merchant)

	Probability of cheating (π)	Probability of not cheating ($1-\pi$)
Probability of detecting (ϕ)	(X–c), (–X)	(–c), (0)
Probability of not detecting ($1-\phi$)	(–Y), (Y)	(0), (0)

By solving this, the probability of cheating, $\pi = c/(X+Y) = c/[Q(\lambda+1-t)(p_G-p_w)]$, implying that it depends positively on the cost of detection and negatively on the penalty rate. The probability of detection, $\phi = Y/(X+Y) = (1-t)/(\lambda+1-t)$. It depends inversely on the penalty rate, implying that the tax authorities could save resources on detection by raising the penalty rate. For example, Kautilya specified $\lambda = 2$, the tax rate, $t = 0.2$ and thus $\phi = 0.286$. The expected revenue of the government $= \pi (X-c) + (1-\pi)(-c) = -c\phi$ and the expected gain to the merchant $= \phi (-X) + (1-\phi) Y = 0$.

It is not claimed that Kautilya could calculate the values of ϕ and π. The only claim made is that he understood the non-cooperative nature of the relationship between the taxpayer and the tax authorities. The above analysis could be extended further.[8]

12.3 ANTICIPATION OF DUPUIT-LAFFER CURVE BY KAUTILYA

Kautilya Curve: He believed that any tax rate lower than 1/6th would be insufficient in providing an adequate level of infrastructure which, in turn, meant a lower level of income, Y. According to him, initially, as tax rate increased, tax revenue increased, which allowed increases in the provision of public goods and, as a result productivity of factors of production increased. Infrastructure (building roads) opened up new markets for the existing products, created potential for division of labour and specialization and integrated segmented markets and broke up local monopolies, ie. the production possibility frontier shifted outwards. So, initially, as the tax rate increased the tax base also increased, consequently there would be a steep rise in revenue. That is, as the tax rate was increased, the tax revenue, R (t Y) increased more than proportionately to the increases in the tax rate. He (p 284) asserted, 'He who causes loss of revenue swallows the king's wealth (2.7).'

Similarly, Kautilya believed that any income tax rate higher than 1/6th would hurt private production. He (p 284) asserted (regarding the behavior of the tax collectors), He who produces double the [anticipated] revenue, eats up the *janapada* [the district; countryside and its people], by leaving them inadequate resources for survival and future production] (2.9).' He (p 181) suggested for the king, 'He shall protect agriculture from being harassed by (onerous) fines, taxes and demands of labour (2.1).'

The above statements imply that the revenue would start declining rapidly as the tax rate rose beyond the optimum rate due to: (i) a reduction in the growth rate of productive capacity of the private sector as the farmers would be left with very little to maintain productive capacity. (ii) Some individuals might migrate from the state. Nowadays too, individuals 'vote with their feet' and move to states with lower or no income taxes, and many corporations move to other countries with lower or no taxes (so called tax havens). (iii) Others might work less or revolt against the king or evade taxes (presumably, under a flat tax with no deductions and exemptions, there was perhaps, not much scope for tax avoidance through professional help!) Nowadays individuals may replace a government with their voting power. Not only was Kautilya against excessive taxation but also, as noted earlier, against collection before the due date (ie. before harvesting). The broken curve may be labeled as the Kautilya-Curve.[9] According to him, the optimum tax rate should be 1/6th as was also traditionally held.

Spengler (1971, p 72) also remarks, 'Kautilya's discussion of taxation and expenditure, apparently in keeping with traditional doctrine, gave expression to three Indian principles: taxation power is limited; taxation should not be felt to be heavy or excessive; tax increases should be graduated. One of his main concerns seems to have been the collection and expenditure of revenue in such ways as to build up the permanent revenue-yielding capacity of the economy.'[10]

Spengler continues, 'While he manifested little knowledge of tax shifting and incidence, he emphasized the long run, cautioned against too heavy taxation in the short run, and noted that a ruler could not tax at his pleasure, particularly in frontier regions whence disgruntled taxpayers could flee to neighbouring countries.'

Apparently, Kautilya did consider the distortionary effect of heavy taxation, although in a very limited sense that some taxpayers might move out of the state. However, his arguments were primarily directed towards the investment side: at initial stages of economic development,

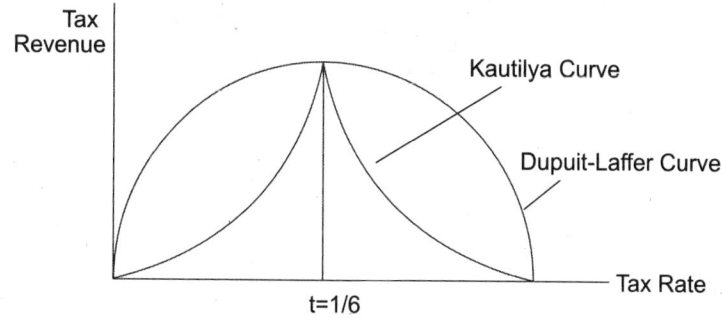

Figure 12.2: The broken curve indicates Kautilya Curve whereas the solid curve is the Dupuit-Laffer Curve, t=1/6 is the optimal tax rate.

provision of infrastructure increased the productivity of private inputs and consequently, level of output, but heavy taxation might starve private investment and adversely affect output.

12.4 VIEWS ON OTHER RELATED CONCEPTS

Anticipation of the Concept of Producer Surplus by Kautilya: Initially, Marshall (p 811, fig. 39) was credited for originating the concepts of the consumer surplus and the producer surplus. However, later on when Dupuit's work was discovered, along with Marshall, he was also given the credit for consumer surplus. Now Marshall may have to share the credit for producer surplus also – this time with Kautilya.

Capture of the Producer Surplus by the State: Kautilya (p 239) stated, 'After the duty is paid, the merchant shall place himself near the customs house and declare the type, quantity and price of his goods. He shall call out for bids three times and sell to anyone who is willing to buy at the price demanded. If there is competition among buyers and a higher price is realized, the difference between the call price and the sale price along with the duty thereon shall go to the Treasury (2.21).' Figure 12.3 may be used to capture his ideas.

As defined above, P_s = sales price and P_w = the price the seller is

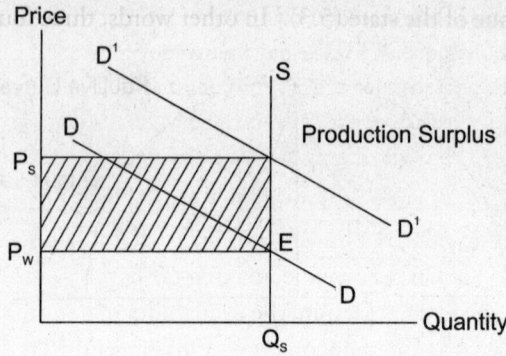

Figure 12.3: DD and D'D' are the demand curves, the shaded area represents the producer surplus, P_s = sales price and P_w = the price the seller is willing to accept and $P_w ES$ indicates the supply curve such that Supply, $Q = 0$ if $P_s < P_w$ and $Q = Q_s$ if $P_s \geq P_w$

willing to accept (in this case $P_w = P_G$). The supplier does not supply any amount of his product if he does not get his call price, P_w, that is, supply is not a given constant. According to Kautilya, the difference between the sale price and the price the seller is willing to accept [ie. the producer surplus = the shaded area = $(p_s - p_w)Q_s$] should go to the treasury.

Distinction between Current Account and Capital Account: He expanded the role of government from simple national defense and law and order to building infrastructure, providing relief to the public against natural disasters, fire and theft and taking care of the poor, sick and the old. He introduced other taxes and user fees to finance the additional functions. For example, he (p 177) asserted, The root of wealth is economic activity and lack of it brings material distress. In the absence of fruitful economic activity, both current prosperity and future growth are in danger of destruction (1.19).'

Accordingly, a significant portion of the revenue was directed towards productive activities. He (p 288) stated, 'The [total] salary [bill] of the state shall be determined in accordance with the capacity [to pay] of the city and the countryside and shall be [about] one quarter of the revenue of the state (5.3).' In other words, three fourths of the revenue was earmarked for capital formation.

SUMMARY

Kautilya's *Arthashastra* contains many essential ingredients of a sound fiscal structure, such as a linear income tax, stability of tax structure, maximization of net tax revenue, making tax payable at the right time and fiscal federalism.[11] Despite the availability of a lump sum tax, he preferred levy of a linear income tax. Only recently, tax compliance has been incorporated into the discussion on optimal taxation but Kautilya proposed tax compliance as an integral part of a tax system. The concepts, at least in embryonic forms, of the Dupuit-Laffer Curve, and the Marshallian producer surplus were present in his analysis. He also provided a rare insight into the origin of an income tax and the institution of kingship. His observations are congruent with the new institutionalists' approach. It is truly an independent piece of evidence since he could not have anticipated the debate between the new and the old institutionalists regarding the origin of institutions.

13

Kautilya on Famine and Freedom

> In the interests of the prosperity of the country, a king should be diligent in foreseeing the possibility of calamities, try to avert them before they arise, overcome those which happen, remove all obstructions to economic activity and prevent loss of revenue to the state (8.4).
> —*Kautilya (4th Century BCE, p 116)*

World food security became a major concern during 1972-1974. The World Food Conference of November 1974 was organized to handle the prevailing food crisis and to devise preventive and remedial measures to eliminate such threats forever. Unfortunately, no consensus was reached on undertaking any effective measures, perhaps due to divergence of national interests and lack of adequate understanding of the basic issues. Since then, apparently the world community has learnt a lot about the causes and consequences of famines and also has added some new terms, such as 'entitlement' and 'FAD' to its list of jargons. Despite such an understanding, so far only a weather-index-based insurance programme has been introduced and that too on a pilot basis and still there is no comprehensive plan in place. Consequently, world food security remains a major concern. There is a possibility that in the absence of adequate measures, more than a billion people might face starvation.

Actually, an adequate learning related to the causes and consequences of famines and devising of both preventive and remedial measures to deal with them had occurred more than two thousand years earlier. Book 8 of Kautilya's *Arthashastra* contains five chapters, which specifically deal with managing systemic risk related to various natural and man-made calamities, adversities and vices. Building infrastructure, and provision of irrigation facilities for ensuring growth and stabilization of food production, and creation of buffer stock of food grains and its fair distribution were recommended for reducing the probability of a famine.

Kautilya wanted to create a prosperous and secure nation. He (p 121) described his ideal nation as: 'It should be beautiful, being endowed with arable land, mines, timber forests, elephant forests, and good pastures rich in cattle. It should not depend [only on] rain for water. It should have good roads and waterways. It should have a productive economy, with a wide variety of commodities and the capacity to sustain a high level of taxation as well as a [large] army (6.1.8).' Several salient features are worth mentioning. First, the statement 'It should not depend [only on] rain for water' emphasized the need for irrigation projects for reducing variability in agricultural output. Secondly, the statement 'capacity to sustain a high level of taxation as well as a [large] army' indicates that the economy must have the potential for generating an agricultural surplus for building infrastructure and maintaining strong defense. Thirdly, the statement 'It should be beautiful, being endowed with arable land, mines, timber forests, elephant forests, and good pastures rich in cattle' implies a diversified economy. Finally, 'It should have good roads and waterways' for facilitating commerce and fulfilling defense-related needs. Kautilya devised various policies to realize his vision of a strong and prosperous nation.

He approached each potential threat to the envisioned ideal nation very methodically and comprehensively. He tried to identify all possible sources of risk and rank them according to their seriousness. Section 13.1 contains his identification of natural disasters as potential risks and a comparative risk assessment analysis. According to him, in an agricultural economy, a drought had a devastating impact on the availability of work (ie. the livelihood of the people). His conceptual framework for handling risk arising from a drought is also presented in the same Section. His insights regarding the impact of famines on economic growth and freedom are presented in Section 13.2. Final section contains a few concluding observations.

13.1 KAUTILYA'S CONCEPTUAL FRAMEWORK FOR PREVENTION OF FAMINES

Ranking of Natural Disasters according to their Impact: Kautilya ranked the seriousness of the various natural disasters. He first compared the relative seriousness of a drought to that of too much rain and concluded that drought was more serious. He (p 129) asserted, 'a drought is worse than too much rain, because drought destroys livelihood (8.2)'. Then he compared the seriousness of floods to that of fire. He (p 131-132) added, '[Which of the divine calamities are more serious than others?] Some teachers say that fire is more serious than floods because destruction by fire is irremediable, consuming all; one can escape from floods and its damage can be alleviated. Kautilya, however, considers floods to be more dangerous because it destroys hundreds of villages while fire destroys [only] one village, or a part of it.' He concluded floods to be more serious.

Then he proceeded to compare the seriousness of a famine to that of disease and epidemics. He argued, 'Some teachers say that disease and epidemics are worse than famine, because pestilence brings all state activities to a stop with men falling ill and dying but during famine all work does not stop and it is still possible to collect revenue in gold or commodities or cattle. Kautilya disagrees. Pestilence usually devastates only a region of the country and remedies can be found for the disease. Famine, on the other hand, affects the whole country and deprives the people of their livelihood (8.4).'[1] Kautilya argued that threat of a drought created a systemic risk since it affected the whole economy, whereas, fires, epidemics and floods did not create any systemic risk.

Foresightedness as a Critical Requirement for Risk Management: According to Kautilya, the king as well as his advisers should have the 'ability to foresee things'. He described some desirable attributes of a king. He (p 119-120) wrote, 'He should be just in rewarding and punishing. He should have the foresight to avail himself of the opportunities (by choosing) the right time, place and type of action (6.1).' Similarly, he (p 120) described, 'A councilor or minister of the highest rank should be a native of the state, born in a high family and controllable [by the king]. He should have been trained in all the arts and have logical ability to foresee things (1.9).'

He provided a very broad definition of a calamity. He (p 122) wrote, 'That which deprives (*vyasyati*) a person of his strength and goodness is a *vyasana* (a vice, adversity or calamity) (8.1.4).' According to him, a king should take preventive and remedial measures to reduce the impact of a calamity. He (p 116) stated, 'In the interests of the prosperity of the country, a king should be diligent in foreseeing the possibility of calamities, try to avert them before they arise, overcome those which happen, remove all obstructions to economic activity and prevent loss of revenue to the state (8.4).'

Preventive Measures: He emphasized investment on expansion of irrigation facilities and infrastructure. He (p 181) suggested, 'Not only shall the king keep in good repair productive forests, elephant forests, reservoirs and mines created in the past, but also set up new mines, factories, forests [for timber and other produce], elephant forests and cattle herds [shall promote trade and commerce by setting up] market towns, ports and trade routes, both by land and water. He shall build storage reservoirs, [filling them] either from natural springs or water brought from elsewhere; or, he may provide help to those who build reservoirs by giving them land, building roads and channels or giving grants of timber and implements (2.1).' He (p 552) stated, 'A king makes progress by building forts, irrigation works or trade routes, creating new settlements, elephant forests or productive forests, or opening new mines (7.1).'

Importance of Irrigation in Reducing Variability in Output: He (p 619) stated, 'As between land dependent on rain and land with flowing water [ie. a river], a smaller tract with flowing water is preferable to a larger drier one because with flowing water, which is always available, the production of crops is assured (7.11).'

Price Support and Buffer Stocks: There were constant threats of wars and crop-failure at that time. Kautilya (p 336) proposed, 'When there is an excess supply of a commodity, a buffer stock shall be built up by paying a price higher than the prevailing market price (2.16).' Clearly, there was no coercion used to build the buffer stocks rather the farmers, who were mostly Shudras, were paid a price higher than the prevailing market price. He (p 312) added, 'The Chief Superintendent of Warehouses shall, at all times, keep half of the commodities in store as reserve stock for use in times of calamities and use [only] the other half for [current needs]; he shall [constantly] replace old stock with new (2.15).' He (p 181) suggested to the king, 'He shall protect agriculture from being harassed by [onerous] fines, taxes and demands of labor (2.1.37).'

In the light of the above statements by Kautilya, the following remark by Jeremy Swift clearly shows his ignorance. Swift (1993) remarks, 'A very different type of redistributive system is not normally thought of as reciprocity at all, although it shares some important features with it: this is the vertical redistribution which takes place usually within hierarchic economic and political systems, where elites or rulers extract resources from dependants or low status or junior people in the system through taxes, levies or other forms of contribution including labour service, and in certain circumstances redistribute these resources to dependants or low status people in need. An early statement of such a system is contained in the classic India book of statecraft, the *Arthashastra*, written between 300 BC and 150 AD (Kautilya 1992: 130).'

Kautilya's Disaster Relief Act: He suggested an exhaustive list of measures to provide relief against every natural disaster. As an illustration, let us consider his list of the steps proposed to deal with a famine (that would also show the thoroughness with which he addressed every topic he covered). This may appropriately be called as the Kautilya Disaster Relief Action Plan in the context of the predominantly agricultural economy prevailing in his time. He (p 130) recommended the following measures to provide relief against famine: '(i) distribute to the public, on concessional terms, seeds and food from the royal stores; (ii) undertake food-for-work programmes, such as building forts or irrigation works; (iii) share out the royal food stocks; commandeer for public distribution private stocks of food; (iv) seek the help of friendly kings; (v) shift the affected population to a different region; (vi) encourage [temporary] migration to another country; (vii) move the entire population [with the king and the court] to a region or country with abundant harvest or near the sea, lakes or rivers; and (viii) supplement the harvest with additional cultivation of grain, vegetables, roots and fruits, by fishing and by hunting deer, cattle, birds and animals (4.3).'

Several remarks are in order. First, he essentially recommended measures, like commandeering the private stocks of food, to avoid market failure and several other measures, such as distribution of food grains to the people from royal stocks to avoid government failure. Several measures were recommended by Kautilya to prevent natural disasters by promoting economic development and reduction of variability in income. He suggested (i) 'removing all obstructions to economic activity', (ii) building infrastructure, and (iii) reducing dependence on rain by developing irrigation sources. Similarly, he suggested devising remedial measures, such as creation of buffer stocks of food grains, setting up distribution outlets, the introduction of food for work programmes during periods of crop-failure, etc. and keeping them in a state of readiness well before the occurrence of a calamity. It is remarkable that Kautilya provided a very comprehensive and insightful economic analysis of the famine and recommended the post-modern measures to deal with it.[2]

Secondly, Ehrlich and Becker (1972) have coined the term 'self-protection' for Kautilya's phrase *'try to avert them before they arise'* and 'self-insurance' for his phrase, *'overcome those which happen'*. Thirdly, according to Kautilya, the most critical role of foresightedness was to foresee and devise preventive and remedial measures well in advance of the possible occurrence of calamities or adversities.[3] That is, a multi-period analysis is discernible in his recommendations. He recommended that the king should be tireless in his efforts to prevent the occurrence of a disaster. Note, foresightedness and forecasting may be complements since foresightedness helps in finding long-term and reliable solutions whereas forecasting helps in devising immediate remedial measures. Unfortunately, the methods of forecasting the business cycles, floods or droughts are still not very precise.[4]

Fourthly, Kautilya advised the king that it was absolutely essential to identify all possible risks related to various calamities, such as a crop-failure due to lack of rain or flood, foreign aggression and civil unrest. Finally, it is obvious that according to Kautilya, both the preventive and remedial measures were directed towards enhancing the productive potential of the economy, $H(F_1, F_2)$, and providing utility, $U^3[Y_0 + H(F_1, F_2)]$ beyond the short run (that is, beyond the next period). The following formulation makes his implicit analysis explicit.

Max
$$EU = U^0[Y_0 - F_1 - F_2] + P(F_1) U^1[Y_0 + G(F_1) - L(F_2)] + [1 - P(F_1)] U^2[Y_0 + G(F_1)] + U_3[Y_0 + H(F_1, F_2)] \quad (13.1)$$

Let $X = [Y_0 - F_1 - F_2]$, $Z = [Y_0 + G(F_1) - L(F_2)]$

Y_0 = Income in current period

$U_0[X]$ = utility during the current period

F_1 = Investment during the current period on expanding irrigation facilities for reducing the probability of a crop-failure during the next period and beyond that.

F_2 = Creation of buffer stocks of food grains during the current period for reducing the loss caused by a drought during the next period or beyond that.

There are two possibilities
Possibility 1: probability, $P(F_1)$ of an occurrence of a drought

$G(F_1)$ = impact of irrigation on output, during the next period.

$U^1[Z]$ = utility during the next period

Possibility 2: Probability, $[1-P(F_1)]$ of no drought during the next period

$U^2[Y_0 + G(F_1)]$ = utility during the next period

$H(F_1, F_2)$ = future output due to increased irrigation facilities, F_1 and use of food grains, F_2 for building public infrastructure.

$U^3[Y_0 + H(F_1, F_2)]$ = utility beyond the next period

Differentiating (1) with respect to F_1, and F_2 we get the following FOC:

$$U^0_1 = P_1(F_1)\{U^1[Z] - U^2[Y_0 + G(F_1)]\} + \{P(F_1)U^1_1 G_1 + [1 - P(F_1)]U^2_1 G_1\} + U^3_1 H_1 \quad (13.2)$$

$$U^0_1 = -P(F_1) U^1_1 L_1 + U^3_1 H_2 \quad (13.3)$$

From equations (13.2) and (13.3)

$$P_1(F_1)\{U^1[Z] - U^2[Y_0 + G(F_1)]\} + \{P(F_1)U^1_1 G_1 + (1-P(F_1))U^2_1 G_1\} + U^3_1 H_1 = -P(F_1) U^1_1 L_1 + U^3_1 H_2 \quad (13.4)$$

$U^0_1 = \partial U^0/\partial X > 0$, $U^1_1 = \partial U^1/\partial Z > 0$, $G_1 = \partial G/\partial F_1 > 0$, $H_1 = \partial H/\partial F_1 > 0$, $H_2 = \partial H/\partial F_2 > 0$, $L_1 = \partial L/\partial F_2 < 0$, $U^2_1 = \partial U^2/\partial[Y_0 + G(F_1)] > 0$, $U^3_1 = \partial U^3/\partial[Y_0 + H(F_1, F_2)] > 0$.

Where $P(F_1)$ = probability of an occurrence of a calamity (for example a significant decline in the output of grains due to lack of rain), F_1 = measures undertaken for a reduction in the probability of a crop-failure (such as, an increase in irrigation facilities), that is, $P_1(F_1) = \partial P/\partial F_1 < 0$. L = loss of income in the absence of any remedial measures resulting from the occurrence of a drought, F_2 = remedial measures (such as, the creation of buffer stocks of food grains to be used during a drought period).

Equations (13.2) and (13.3) are the usual first order conditions which equate marginal cost to expected marginal benefits. The left hand side term U^0_1 indicates the marginal cost of sacrificing current consumption and the right hand side terms indicate the marginal benefits. Equation (13.4) indicates that the marginal benefits of self-protection should be equal to the marginal benefits of self-insurance. However, a few points are noteworthy. First, Kautilya recommended expanding irrigation facilities for reducing the probability of a loss from drought (self-protection) as well as increasing the growth potential, thus handling stabilization and economic growth together. In equation (13.2), the terms within the first bracket $[P_1(F_1) \{U^1[Z] - U^2[Y_0 + G$

$(F_1)]\}]$ capture the benefits due to a decline in the probability of a loss caused by a drought and the terms in the second bracket $\{P(F_1)U^1_1 G_1 + (1-P(F_1))U^2_1 G_1\}$ provide the benefits of irrigation on growth of output. Secondly, Kautilya considered more than two periods since the benefits accrued over several periods. For example, the terms $U^3_1 H_1$ and $U^3_1 H_2$ indicate the long-term (that is, beyond the next period) marginal benefits of preventive and remedial measures respectively. Thirdly, buffer stocks of food grains, created to stabilize agricultural prices, were to be used for preventing a drought from becoming a famine and to enhance the productive capacity of the economy by implementing food for work programmes during a drought.

13.2 IMPACT OF FAMINES ON INCOME AND FREEDOM

Kautilya believed that economic prosperity and national security were jointly determined and an occurrence of any calamity, adversity or vice posed a serious threat to sustained economic growth and sovereignty. He (p 149) suggested, 'Hence the king shall be ever active in the management of the economy. The root of wealth is economic activity and lack of it brings material distress. In the absence of fruitful economic activity, both current prosperity and future growth are in danger of destruction. A king can achieve the desired objectives and abundance of riches by undertaking productive economic activity (1.19).'

Kautilya understood the decline in food production and lack of its fair distribution as the causes of famines and their dire consequences for freedom and prosperity. He believed that it was a king's moral duty as well as in king's own interest to bring prosperity to his citizens and protect them against foreign aggression, and natural and man-made calamities, adversities and vices. At that time agriculture was the main economic activity. Most of the production was carried out for self-consumption, financial intermediation was very limited and there was no Keynesian type gap between saving and investment. So, there were business cycles not due to the fluctuations in investment or technological innovations, instead there were real business cycles caused by by flood, droughts and other natural disasters. That is, there were only supply shocks.

Dynamic Feedback: He argued that a drought affected an economy in two ways. First, according to him, a supply shock created unemployment of the production workers, a decrease in current output and consequently a decline in tax revenue. Secondly, due to lower tax revenue, investment in public infrastructure would be negligible if any and thus, adversely affecting the growth in future income. More formally:

$$Y = A (H, G, K_G) K_p^\alpha L^\beta T^\gamma + u \qquad (13.5)$$
$$\Delta KG = \theta (1-t) Y \qquad (13.6)$$

A = the efficiency parameter, which depended on knowledge (H), good governance (G), K_G = stock of public infrastructure, K_p = stock of capital in the private sector, L=labour, T=land, t= the tax rate, θ = proportion of tax revenue allocated to building of infrastructure, such as roads and u= additive error term.

According to Kautilya, a crop-failure would lower the tax revenue and consequently, and most likely, no addition to public infrastructure could occur. He (p 253) stated, 'All state activities depend first on the Treasury. Therefore, a king shall devote his best attention to it. A king with a depleted Treasury eats into the very vitality of the citizens and the country [2.8.1-2].' The figure (13.1) may capture Kautilya's ideas.

If income declined from Y_0 in period T_0 to Y_1 in period T_1, tax revenue declined and that reduced investment in public infrastructure. In period T_2, income returned only to Y_0 (or a little higher) instead of to Y_3 since there was no (or little) investment in period T_1.

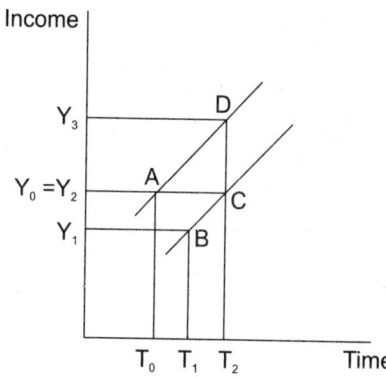

Figure 13.1: Y_0 initial income, Y_1=income in period one if there was a drought and Y_2 if no drought in period two. Y_3 Income in period one if no drought and may still be higher if no drought in period two.

Suppose two countries at time T_0 had equal GDP and were growing at the same rate. If country one was faced with a crop-failure and as a result its income fell to Y_1 in period T_1, whereas the other country was not affected by a drought and kept growing along the path AD. Even if the weaker country recovers from a drought in period T_2, it would grow only along the path BC. Consequently, the other country got stronger and could attack the weaker country. Kautilya believed that freedom was the most precious good. According to him, if a country lost independence, income would be lowered to a bare minimum. For example, per capita income in India stagnated from 1757-1947 while she was under the British rule.

SUMMARY

Basham (1959, p 217) remarks, 'It is striking that ancient Indian political theorists anticipated by over 2,000 years the plans put forward by the Food and Agriculture Organization of the United Nations for maintaining a stable level of prices of staple commodities on a world-wide scale.' Similarly, Sen (1997) notes, 'Thus, the *Arthashastra* presents ideas and suggestions on such practical subjects as famine prevention and administrative effectiveness that remain relevant even today—more than 2,000 years later.'

In the light of the above analysis and Sen's own statement, the following assertion by Sen's publisher on the 1981 book seems to be somewhat misplaced: 'The main focus of this book is on the causation of starvation in general and of famines in particular. The traditional analysis of famines concentrates on food supply. This is shown to be fundamentally defective—it is theoretically unsound, empirically inept, and dangerously misleading for policy. The author develops an alternative method of analysis—the 'entitlement approach', which concentrates on ownership and exchange.'

14

International Trade Policies

Kautilya suggested promotion of imports rather than exports. During ancient times, efforts were made to remove almost insurmountable hurdles rather than create them to impede the flow of imports. The challenge for the world leaders is to bring back Kautilya's internationalism in the post-modern, post-industrialized, and interconnected world and exploit the full potential. Everyone understands that globalization without a feeling of internationalism limits potential gains from trade. Thanks to the advances in modes of communication and transportation, the physical integration of the world has been progressing at a brisk pace but unfortunately, our thinking essentially has been stuck at the national boundaries and refuses to embrace openness. Decades have been wasted in useless negotiations as if the nations were really on the Pareto efficient contract curve.

For obtaining a fuller understanding of Kautilya's theory of the gains from trade, his ideas related to international trade are presented here. Moreover, this may also serve as a commentary on the status of our understanding of that era. Section 14.1 contains his policies related to the promotion of imports. Section 14.2 offers his views on the nature of trade during the ancient times. Kautilya's theory of the gains from trade is presented in Section 14.3.

14.1 POLICIES ON PROMOTION OF IMPORTS

Kautilya's primary goal was, by facilitating imports, to increase the availability of a maximum number of consumer goods to a maximum number of individuals. It may be noted that before the introduction of modern technology for mass production, every product, whether it was a pair of shoes or a shirt was catered to individual tastes and requirements. Moreover, during the ancient times, the choice between having a larger variety at a higher cost and fewer varieties at a lower cost (by mass production) was not available. Also at a low level of income, a preference for two different goods rather than two varieties of one good perhaps would be much stronger.

Guidelines for Fair Trading: Kautilya listed guidelines for ensuring fair trading. For example, he (p 336) stated, 'Both locally produced and imported goods shall be sold for the benefit of the public. Even a large profit shall be foregone if it is likely to cause harm to the public. No artificial scarcity be created by accumulation of commodities in demand; these shall not be subjected to restrictions on when they be sold (2.16).'

Specific Policies of Import Promotion: The idea of devising any import substituting or export promoting policies had not germinated yet. Not surprisingly, Kautilya, instead, proposed import-promoting policies. He (p 236-237) recommended:
- 'Imports shall be sold in as many places as possible [in order

to make them readily available to people in the towns and the countryside]';
- '[local] merchants who bring in foreign goods by caravans or by water routes shall enjoy exemption from taxes' and a 10% profit margin shall be allowed on imports as compared to a 5% profit margin on locally produced goods and
- 'foreign merchants shall not be sued in money disputes unless they are legal persons in the country (2.16)'.

Kautilya believed that a policy of allowing a higher profit margin on imports than that on domestic trade (there is no evidence of any lobbying by the importers) was necessary to compensate the importers for undertaking the extra risk, otherwise they might not import at all. He recommended a 20% *ad valorem* tariffs on imports. Similarly, he recommended export duties ranging from 4% to 16%. Tariffs were recommended to raise revenue and not to restrict trade. Thus, on the whole, he was a strong proponent of free trade.

It is noteworthy that he suggested the waiver of the import duty in the case of an import of a 'rare seed'. There were practically no restrictions on imports (other than on those which were considered harmful or worthless), but he suggested some controls on the export of arms and any other product that might help the enemy. He (p 239) suggested prohibition of exports of certain products, such as: 'Weapons and armour of all kinds including coats of mail; metals; chariots; jewels and precious stones; grains and cattle (2.21).' According to him, jewels and precious stones were used to win friends or making pay-offs to avert certain adverse circumstances. Any excess of grains was used to build buffer stocks to protect against poor harvests, rather than export one year and import the next year. Apparently, the concern for national security has existed since antiquity. For example, nowadays, due to a concern for national security, the exports of certain items (like super computers) are banned to some countries. It appears that Kautilya's position on international trade was much more liberal than Adam Smith's, which, in turn, was undoubtedly much more liberal than that of the mercantilists.[1]

14.2 NATURE OF INTERNATIONAL TRADE IN ANCIENT TIMES

Cooper (1977, Vol 26, p 910-916) indicates that during ancient times, trade was risky, consisted of light and high-valued products due to the presence of risk and poor means of transportation, and was based on natural advantages implying its pattern to be self-evident.[2] Kautilya's *Arthashastra* is the only known book, which has survived and describes issues related to international trade during the 4th Century BCE. There are, at least, four points worth noting in his formulation. First, Kautilya considered both high value and low value products as tradable. He (p 239) suggested, 'The frontier officer shall inspect the caravans carrying foreign goods and classify as those of high value or of low value (2.21).' He added, 'All dutiable goods shall be weighed, measured or counted and the duty payable on goods of low value shall be determined carefully [not ignoring them as insignificant] (2.21).' Clearly, goods of both high value and low value were considered importable.

Secondly, according to Kautilya, precious goods attracted bandits much sooner than the inexpensive ones, implying that the risk varied directly with the value of the product. It may appear reasonable to believe that transportation of goods of light and high-value should be cheaper and easier, but Kautilya pointed out that it could be more than neutralized by the increased cost of extra protection needed for high value products. He (p 238) stated, 'If the Chief Controller of State Trading sends a caravan by a land route, he shall choose a safe route. One quarter of the goods shall be of high value. Jungle chieftains, frontier officers and governors in the city and the countryside shall be contacted beforehand for assuring security. Steps shall be taken to ensure the protection of the members of the caravan and goods of high value (2.16).'

It is obvious that the existence of high risk for high value products, to some extent, worked against them. Additionally, Kautilya noted that the market in precious goods was very thin. He (p 623) stated, 'Buyers of high-valued products are rare and found only after a long search; there are many buyers and a steady demand for products of small value (7.12).' Apparently, trade in high-valued products was not that attractive during ancient times. Interestingly, instead of the buyer undertaking the search it was the seller, who had to do it.

Risk Minimization through Diversification: Kautilya emphasized the principle of diversification by requiring a combination of high value and low value goods. Since extra spending on protection would reduce both expected return and risk, implying that he considered risk, to some extent, as endogenous. An awareness of the trade-off between expected return and risk is clearly discernible in his analysis.[3]

Handling Missing Markets: At the time there were no markets to insure against theft. Kautilya (p 235) stated, 'Frontier officers shall be responsible for the safety of the merchandise passing on the roads and shall make good what is lost (2.21). Traders may stay inside villages after letting the village officers know of the value of their merchandise. If any of these is lost or driven away, the village headman shall recompense the trader (4.13).' The security of trade was thus ensured through making the local officers accountable in terms of compensation for any loss.

Thirdly, Kautilya was aware of the transportation constraint and tried to relax it. He (p 235) recommended, 'The king shall promote trade and commerce by land and by water and market towns/ports. Trade routes shall be kept free of harassment by courtiers, state officials, thieves and frontier guards and from being damaged by herds of cattle (2.1).' He made here two additional points: (i) integration of markets and (ii) economies of scale.

Integration of Markets: He (p 623) stated, 'Many inferior routes are preferable to a few important ones (7.12).' His goals were to open new markets in the process and facilitate a fuller integration of the existing ones.

Economies of Scale: He (p 623) explained, 'A route usable by carts is preferable to a foot path for men and animals only because of the larger quantities that can be transported on carts (7.12).' This statement implies that he has at least some idea of the concept of the economies of scale.

Fourthly, even during ancient times, some choices had to be made regarding trade–some of which appear quite sophisticated. The conclusions by Caves, Frankel and Jones (2002) in this respect are based on the assumptions of the existence of inexpensive modern transportation and communications facilities, low insurance premium, credit extensions from financial institutions, foreign exchange markets, and of already identified markets.[4] However, it was not so evident two thousand years ago when there were potentially too many risk factors.

14.3 THEORY OF GAINS FROM TRADE

Kautilya (p 237) stated, 'The Chief Controller of State Trading shall ascertain the profitability of a trading operation with a foreign country using the following method. The price of the goods to be sold in the foreign country and the price likely to be realized on the goods imported in exchange shall be estimated. From the gross margin, all expenses, as described below, shall be deducted:

For caravans: customs duty, road cess, escort charges, tax payable at military stations, ferry charges, daily allowances paid to merchants and their assistants and the share payable to the foreign king.

For trade using ships: all the above plus the following additional charges: ie. the cost of hiring ships and boats, provisions for the journey.

He shall, in general, trade with such foreign countries as will generate a profit; he shall avoid unprofitable areas (2.16).'

Although there is no theory of comparative advantage here, in the sense of predicting the pattern of trade, the rule proposed for gainful trade is the one that correctly implies that gains from trade will ensue if the rule is followed by the ruler of a country where market prices reflect social costs.

A few further points are worth noting. First, Kautilya explicitly incorporated the cost of transportation and other expenses into his gains from trade argument. During his time, not only travel between two countries was hazardous but also the costs of transportation associated with international trade were significant. Secondly, Kautilya, unlike mercantilists, did not argue for generating trade surplus. Kautilya did not have any systematic theory on what determined the trade pattern, however, the *Arthashastra* contains several intriguing and pertinent observations.[5] He listed sources of imports depending upon climate or presence of mines, implying that he was aware of the influence of natural factors on production patterns. He mentioned that pearls could be imported from Ceylon (Sri Lanka), Barbara and Arachosia, aloe from Burma (Myanmar), woolen cloth from Nepal, furs and horses from Gandhara (Afghanistan), Vanayu (Arabia or Persia) and Bahilika (Bactria) and wine from Afghanistan and Scythia. As for exports, he mentioned (p 803-4) live animals, food, fresh produce, preserved food, liquor, medicines, spices and perfumery, raw materials, manufactured goods (garments, carpets, leather goods, earthenware) and gems and jewellery. Aside from natural resources as a factor that conferred production and trade advantage, Kautilya also referred to the role of exogenous productivity differences and also of capital—both physical and human.

SUMMARY

Kautilya would not have realized that his condition for generating a profit was an alternative way to approach the theory of the gains from trade. He understood the contribution of both physical and human capital on labour productivity two thousand earlier than the classical economists. Pirenne (1937) points out the existence of internationalism before the emergence of mercantilism. Kautilya understood that a country did not need a trade surplus to enjoy the gains from trade and he, in fact, specified the condition to engage in trade. Trade was not considered an engine of growth. Rather, the objective was to expand the availability of a maximum number of products at a maximum number of places. It is obvious that there was no need for a WTO at that time and its existence now serves only as a reminder of nationalism. It is also obvious that our understanding of the nature or level of trade during the ancient times is painfully inadequate. Although, for sure, international trade was not an engine of growth but it was not insignificant either.[6] The point emphasized is that the history of economic thought in this respect is still incomplete.[7]

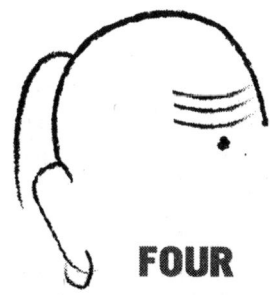

FOUR

Ethics and Freedom from Fear of Crime

Kautilya envisioned a society free from crimes. He called criminals 'social thorns' and suggested legal measures to remove them. Part Four has the following three chapters that present Kautilya's ideas on providing safety against crimes.

Chapter 15: Administration of justice. It sets out the general principles and the judicial process for administration of justice.

Chapter 16: Contract and Property Rules. It contains Kautilya's ideas on the sanctity of contracts and labour theory of property.

Chapter 17: Penance, Penalty and Prevention. It presents Kautilya's proposal of a mix of penance and penalty for effective and ethical tort laws.

15

Administration of Justice

> It is the power of punishment alone, when exercised impartially in proportion to the guilt, and irrespective of whether the person punished is the king's son or an enemy, that protects this world and the next.
>
> — *(Kautilya, p 377)*

Book Three and Book Four of Kautilya's *Arthashastra*, which have 20 Chapters and 13 Chapters, respectively, are devoted to the administration of justice. Kautilya's Judicial System is called '*Dandaniti*', 'the science of law enforcement' and constitutes an important aspect of its overall policy framework. Kautilya codified, modified and created new laws related to loans; deposits; pledges; mortgages; sale and purchase of property; inheritance and partition of ancestral property; labour contracts; partnership[1]; defamation and assault; theft and violent robbery, and sexual offenses. He thus dealt with law and justice issues relating to both the civil law and the criminal law. He offered a truly comprehensive system of justice, which not only incorporated all the salient elements of the present-day system but also provided invaluable additional insights.

Kautilya's *Arthashastra* discusses many issues, which are currently under intense research.[2] His contributions relating to law and order issues may be classified under three headings:

Importance of the Rule of Law: According to Kautilya, existence of law and order was a pre-requisite for economic growth.[3] He (p 108) observed, 'The progress of this world depends on the maintenance of order and the [proper functioning of] government (1.4).' He continued, 'Unprotected, the small fish will be swallowed up by the big fish. In the presence of a king maintaining just law, the weak can resist the powerful (1.4).' Kautilya argued that corruption retarded economic growth by siphoning-off resources and by adversely affecting law and order. He (p 286) listed corruption and greed among the causes of loss in tax revenue, implying a lower provision of public infrastructure, which was essential to economic growth.

Laws must be clear, consistent and in a written form: Kautilya (p 213) stated, 'The rule of kings depends primarily on [written] orders; even peace and war have their roots in them [2.10].' There are at least two reasons as to why he codified the laws.[4] First, many of the traditional laws were outdated or were insufficient to deal with the new situation. As Charles Drekmeier (1962, p 260) explains, 'By the fifth and fourth centuries BC the ancient tribal institutions had lost their ability to regulate society effectively. New modes of production, new types of social relationships, new salvation theologies were changing the old ways. Kautilya was the theorist who most clearly saw the need for expanded state authority to fill the ever-widening gaps left by the declining authority of tradition.'

Secondly, Kautilya was quite concerned about the possibility of 'green justice', that is, judges accepting bribes in exchange for rendering favourable verdicts. He codified the laws and introduced material incentives, such as efficiency wages to complement the existing moral incentives to resolve the principal-agent problem. Recently, Edward L Glaeser and Andrei Shleifer (2002) assert, 'Codification emerges in our model as an efficient attempt by the sovereign to control judges as his knowledge of individual disputes deteriorates (as it did when the states and the economies developed). The simplicity of bright line rules, and the possibility of verifying their violation, enables the king to use them to structure incentives contracts for judges.' It is difficult, however to put any specific label to Kautilya's views since he combined elements of historical, metaphysical, imperative and sociological schools of jurisprudence.

Effective Administration of Justice: His insights into the administration of justice are the focus of the current study. According to Kautilya, effective law enforcement depended on (i) *Honesty of the Law Enforcers*: He emphasized that the law enforcers themselves including the king must be honest and law-abiding.[5] This is presented in Section 15.1. (ii) *Importance of Judicial Fairness*: Similarly, he emphasized the standard of proof, prompt trials, minimization of Type I error, and implicitly the minimization of type II error (since the king was required to compensate the victim if the crime was not solved). These issues, which come under the rubric of judicial fairness, are presented in Section 15.2. (iii) *Impartiality, proportionality and certainty of punishment:* Kautilya's emphasis on impartiality, certainty and proportionality of punishment and discretion in sentencing are provided in Section 15.3. Kautilya preferred monetary fines to non-monetary punishment and making sure that fines were paid-off. This and some other related issues are collected in Section 15.4.

15.1 ON CORRUPTION OF ENFORCERS AND CRIME DETERRENCE

Insistence on Honest Enforcers as a Pre-requisite for Effective Law Enforcement: Kautilya was acutely aware of the possibility that some law enforcers might resort to extortion. He believed that honesty on the part of law enforcers was a prerequisite for effective law enforcement (government failure is discussed in Chapter 9). Similarly, he was concerned about the dishonesty of judges.

Guidelines on Judicial Conduct: Kangle (part III, p 215) notes, 'The judges are called *dharmasthas*, a name which apparently refers to the *dharma* or law, by which they are to be guided in their work.' This could also mean that they epitomize and swear by *dharma* while performing their function. Kautilya provided a detailed set of guidelines to ensure the judicial process to be fair and impartial. According to him (p 381), 'A judge shall not: threaten, intimidate, drive away or unjustly silence any litigant; abuse any person coming before the court; fail to put relevant and necessary questions or ask unnecessary or irrelevant questions; leave out of considerations answers relevant to his own questions; give instructions on how to answer a question; remind one of a fact; draw attention to an earlier statement; fail to call for relevant evidence; call for irrelevant evidence; decide on a case without calling any evidence; dismiss a case under some pretext; make someone abandon a case by making them tired of undue delays; misrepresent a statement made in a particular context; coach witnesses; or rehear a case which had been completed and judgment pronounced. All these are punishable offenses; in case the offense is repeated, the judge shall be fined double and removed from office (4.9).'

Kautilya offered a comprehensive list of ways in which a judge could affect the outcome of a case. He believed that a judge must be competent and must not compromise with the judicial process to ensure impartiality. It is obvious that the judges themselves were not above the law. Kangle (part III, p 221-222) observes, 'Such treatment expected to be meted out to members of the judiciary strikes us today as being very strange. If judges are themselves to be fined, the dignity that is expected to be attached to their office is bound to disappear. The judges, in the scheme of this context, occupy a position subordinate to the executive and are far from being independent of it.' However, there was no other practical way to remove them since there did not exist any legislative body to have hearings for the removal of corrupt judges.

In fact, there were guidelines even for the judge's clerk. Kautilya (p 382) wrote, 'The clerks who record statements made before the court shall: record the evidence correctly; not add to the record statements not made; hide the ambiguity or confusion in evidence badly given; make unambiguous statements appear confused; or change, in any way, the sense of the evidence as presented. All these are punishable offenses (4.9).'

He advised the king to compensate the victims and punish the corrupt officials. He (p 297) recommended, 'A proclamation shall then be issued calling on all those who had suffered at the hands of the dishonest official to inform the investigating officer. All those who respond to the proclamation shall be compensated according to their loss (2.8).'

15.2 ON JUDICIAL FAIRNESS AND MINIMIZATION OF LEGAL ERRORS

Current discussion on issues related to judicial fairness is focused primarily on the standard of proof and minimization of legal errors.[6] Kautilya's judicial system incorporated all the essential ingredients of fairness in resolving disputes. These are explained below.

Expedient Trials: The judicial trials were initiated very promptly, perhaps not to adhere to the dictum that 'justice delayed is justice denied' but due to the belief of an increasing unreliability of evidence as time passed. Kautilya (p 462) argued, 'Because interrogation after some days is inadmissible [unreliable?], no one shall be arrested on suspicion of having committed theft or burglary if three nights have elapsed since the crime, unless he is caught with the tools of the crime (4.8).' However, he (p 472) did state, 'An offender shall not go scot-free [just because of passage of time] (3.19).' He (p 386) suggested, 'The maximum time allowed for a defendant to file his defense shall be three fortnights (3.1).'

Standard of Proof: According to Kautilya (p 386), '[In any case before the judges] admission [by the defendant of the claim against him] is the best. If the claim is not admitted, then the judgment shall be based on the evidence of trustworthy witnesses, who shall be persons known for their honesty or those approved by the Court. [Normally,] there shall be at least three witnesses (3.11).' He (p 388) added, 'In determining a suit in favor of one or the other party, the following shall be taken as strengthening a party's case: statements of eyewitnesses, voluntary admissions, straightforwardness in answering questions and evidence tendered on oath. The following shall go against a party: contradiction between earlier or later statements, unreliable witnesses or being brought to court by secret agents after absconding (3.1).'

A few remarks are in order. First, Kautilya's goal was to prevent the incidence of crimes and to ensure judicial fairness if a crime occurred. His conceptual framework offers a reference point. For example, there was no jury, a team of prosecutors or of defence lawyers at that time. The simple question is: has this institutional change improved upon the delivery of justice? According to Kautilya, judicial fairness depended on the amount of evidence and its reliability. Obviously, non-availability of statistical methods at that time was not a big handicap in measuring the reliability of the evidence. Since objective measures of probabilities regarding the accuracy of evidence were neither available during the 4th century BCE nor are they available now—most likely the judge formed some subjective measure of reliability. Even today every judge or juror has to form some subjective measure of reliability of evidence. That is why, a concerted effort is made both by defence and prosecution to appeal to the juror's emotions to influence his/her subjective measure of reliability. Secondly, Kautilya considered the 'number of witnesses', that is, the amount of evidence also in deciding a case. Usually, nowadays the prosecutor stresses the 'mountain' of evidence whereas the defense questions its reliability, that is, tries to create a reasonable doubt. According to Kautilya, witnesses must be independent and known for their honesty, implying that the current practice of allowing testimonies of biased and paid expert witnesses or of convicted jailhouse inmates may be helpful in convicting the innocent or setting the guilty free (ie. in committing legal errors) but not necessarily in the delivery of justice.

Kautilya (p 462) recommended, 'Anyone arrested shall be interrogated in the presence of the accuser as well as witnesses from inside and outside the house of the accuser (4.8).' He (p 463) asserted, 'A suspect may admit to being a thief, as Ani-Mandavya did, for fear of the pain of torture. Therefore, conclusive proof is essential before a person is sentenced (4.8).' Kautilya insisted on solid evidence for conviction (although the above story is told a little differently in the Epic *Mahabharata*—that a sage did not want to break his vow of silence to declare his innocence but the implication is the same). Kautilya (p 464-65) offered a detailed discussion on forensic evidence for establishing the cause of death. However, he (p 466-467) did recommend torture to elicit confession but only in those cases (excluding the sick, the minors, the aged, the debilitated, the insane, those suffering from hunger, thirst or fatigue after a long journey and a pregnant woman) where there was a strong suspicion of guilt. He (p 467) cautioned, 'A person can be tortured only on alternative days and only once on the permitted days. Torture shall not result in death; if it does so, the person responsible shall be punished (4.8).' It may be noted that the accused was to be questioned in front of the accuser, implying that Kautilya would not have approved the current practice of giving a choice to the accused, whether to take the witness stand or not.

Punishment for Perjury: Perjury was a punishable offence. Kautilya (p 388) stated, 'Witnesses are obliged to tell the truth. For not doing so, the fine shall be 24 *panas* and half for refusal to testify (3.11).'

Futility of Witness Tempering: Kautilya (p 389) added that if a party to a suit 'conspires with witnesses by talking to them in secret when such conversation is prohibited (3.1),' this would be an adequate ground against the party.

Cost of Type I Error: Kautilya (p 493) wrote, 'An innocent man who does not deserve to be penalized shall not be punished, for the sin of inflicting unjust punishment is visited on the king. He shall be freed of the sin only if he offers thirty times the unjust fine (4.13).' According to Kautilya, convicting an innocent person was a 'sin', that is, an ethical lapse and also a huge monetary loss ('thirty times') for the state.

Cost of Type II Error: Kautilya (p 437) suggested, 'If a king is unable to apprehend a thief or recover stolen property, the victim of the theft shall be reimbursed from the Treasury (ie. the king's own resources). Property [unjustly] appropriated shall be recovered and returned to the owner; otherwise, the victim shall be paid its value (3.16).' Two remarks are in order. First, a much broader and more relevant definition of Type II error is discernible from Kautilya's statement since he did not make a distinction between the guilty who were arrested but not convicted and those guilty defendants who had evaded arrest (this is explained below). Whereas the commonly advanced definition of type II error is confined only to the guilty defendants who are arrested but not convicted due to lack of sufficient evidence against them. Secondly, at that time, no private insurance policies (a case of missing markets) were available against the possibility of loss caused by theft and burglary and the king was asked to fulfill this role. Consequently, there was a built-in incentive to prevent crimes from happening and solving them if they happened otherwise the king had to compensate for the loss. Certainly a market for insuring such losses has been created, which is a good thing but in the process the built-in incentive to prevent and solve such crimes has been lost. The following numerical table may be used to make Kautilya's definitions of Type I and Type II errors explicit.[7]

A Numerical Example to Calculate Type I and Type II Errors

		Guilty	Not Guilty	Total
Arrested		100	10	110
	Convicted	80	5	
	Not Convicted	20	5	
Not Arrested		900	98990	99890
Total		1000	99000	100,000

Kautilya's definitions: Probability of Type I error (notations are explained in end notes 7 and 8) = $(1-\delta) P_i (A/ G_c)$ =5/99000. It may be noted that given other things constant, the probability of Type I error increases as the number of arrests increases. In actuality as the number of arrests increase, the police may get over-burdened and courts get crowded and consequently both δ and P_i are adversely affected. The probability of arresting and convicting the criminal $=\pi = \delta P_g$ A/G = 80/1000 and this is relevant if the goal is the prevention of crimes. That is precisely the definition, Gary Becker considers for preventing crimes. As mentioned above, Kautilya did not make a distinction between those defendants who were arrested but not convicted and those guilty defendants who were not even arrested. Since the king was asked to compensate for all the unresolved cases—therefore, according to Kautilya, the Type II error probability = $1-\pi$ =920/1000. It may be noted that given other things equal, the probability of Type II error decreases as the arrests increase.[8]

Of course, Kautilya's goal was to avoid the arrest of an innocent person and if arrested not to convict him, that is, if possible to achieve, $\delta =1$, or $P_i = 0$. However, if $\delta = 1- \delta$ or $P_g = P_i$, that is, if the probabilities of arrest or conviction were the same for the guilty and the innocent, there would be a chaos. He was quite concerned about the possibility of such a situation.

Reduction of Errors through Additional Evidence: In this context, Kautilya (p 389) explained, 'If there is a conflict in the evidence given by different witnesses, the judgment shall take into account the number of witnesses, their reliability and the [opinion of the court on their] disinterestedness (3.11).' It is significant to note that according to Kautilya, additional evidence, such as, 'the number of witnesses', was assumed to reduce the magnitudes of both the Type I and Type II errors (see Thomas H Wonnacott and Ronald J Wonnacott, 1977, 2nd ed., p 259-260). Figure 15.1 may be used to explain Kautilya's insight:

The probability distribution of evidence against an innocent person is indicated by (f^I) and that against a guilty person by (f^G). Kautilya's analysis implied that the probability distributions shrank as the amount of evidence increased. The probability distribution for the innocent shrank from f^I to f^I_i and the probability distribution for the guilty shrank from f^G to f^G_i. Consequently the Type I error was reduced[9] from α to α^1 and the Type II error was reduced from β to β^1.

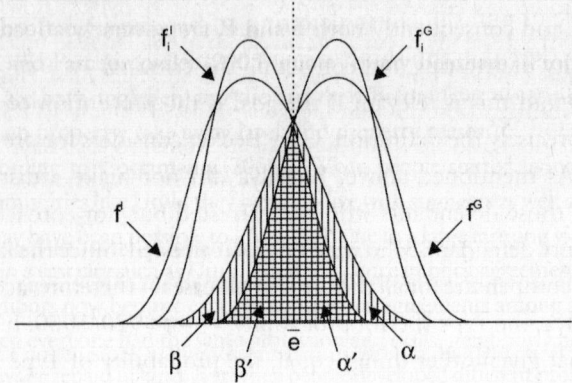

Figure 15.1: (f^I) = probability distribution of evidence against an innocent person, (f^G) = probability distribution of evidence against a guilty person. As evidence increased, the probability distribution for the innocent shrank from f^I to f^I_i and the probability distribution for the guilty shrank from f^G to f^G_i and Type I and Type II errors decreased.

15.3 ON THE OPTIMUM LEVEL OF PUNISHMENT

Role of the Judge: In the absence of a jury, a defense lawyer and a prosecutor, there was a very heavy burden on the judges and magistrates to keep legal errors to the minimum. Kautilya (p 377) expected, Judges shall discharge their duties objectively and impartially so that they may earn the trust and affection of the people (3.2).' And in return, as mentioned above, Kautilya recommended a decent salary of 8,000 *panas* for a judge (magistrate).

Guidelines on Sentencing: Kautilya laid down a set of guidelines relating to sentencing. It is obvious that fairness is not a modern notion since mankind has been concerned with it for a long time.[10] It constitutes the very justification for the creation of state. Kautilya (p 377) wrote, 'A king who observes his duty of protecting his people justly and according to law will go to heaven, whereas one who does not protect them or inflicts unjust punishment will not. It is the power of punishment alone, when exercised impartially in proportion to the guilt, and irrespective of whether the person punished is the King's son or an enemy, that protects this world and the next. (3.1).'

The above statement indicates that Kautilya emphasized the critical role of punishment in deterring crimes and understood that to be effective, the punishment must be certain, impartial and in proportion to the severity of the crimes. Kautilya (p 108) elaborated on this theme, 'Some teachers say: "Those who seek to maintain order shall always hold ready the threat of punishment. For, there is no better instrument of control than coercion." Kautilya disagrees [for the following reasons]. A severe king [meting out unjust punishment] is hated by the people he terrorizes while one who is too lenient is held in contempt by his own people. Whoever imposes just and deserved punishment is respected and honored. A well-considered and just punishment makes the people devoted to *dharma, artha* and *kama* [righteousness, wealth and enjoyment]. Unjust punishment, whether awarded in greed, anger or ignorance, excites the fury of even [those who have renounced all worldly attachments like] forest recluses and ascetics, not to speak of householders. When, no punishment is awarded through misplaced leniency and no law prevails, then there is only the law of fish [ie. the law of the jungle] (1.4).'

According to Kautilya, punishment up to a point helped law and order situation but beyond a certain level it was likely to hurt it. He believed that judicial fairness was absolutely essential to the survival of a state. It means that the implication of Becker's model that 'catch a few and hang them' may not reduce crime. Almost all the studies on crime and punishment assume that social and political stability are unaffected by the level of punishment. Kautilya questioned that assumption. However, as discussed in Chapter 6, he believed that ethical environment was a pre-requisite to administration of justice.

Balance between Rules and Discretion: Kautilya provided a detailed list of sanctions matching the severity of different types of crimes. However, lest the system should become too rigid, the judges were permitted some discretion. He (p 493) laid down, 'The special circumstances of the person convicted and of the particular offense shall be taken into account in determining the actual penalty to be imposed (3.2). Fines shall be fixed taking into account the customs (of the region and the community) and the nature of the offense (2.22).

Leniency shall be shown in imposing punishments on the following: a pilgrim, an ascetic, anyone suffering from illness, hunger, thirst, poverty, fatigue from a journey, suffering from an earlier punishment, a foreigner or one from the countryside (3.20).' According to Kautilya, a judge should take into consideration both the mitigating and the aggravating (egregious) circumstances and the characteristics of the defendants in the determination of the punishment.

The current debate on rules versus discretion is mostly about the polar cases, that is, whether to have rules or to have discretion. In Kautilya's scheme of things, rules were like focal points (or guide posts) around which discretion had to be exercised. Too many rules and strict adherence to them might deny gains from changed circumstances or other unexpected opportunities and similarly, too much discretion might lead to substantial abuses[11] and opportune behavior which, might result in erosion of credibility.

15.4 ON OTHER RELATED ISSUES

Preference for a Monetary Punishment: Kautilya recommended monetary punishment over non-monetary ones and also the 'penal slavery'. In fact, at that time imprisonment as a punishment did not exist. Prisons were used simply to hold the defendants temporarily for the duration of the trial. Kautilya proposed long lists of different kinds of physical punishments or monetary fines. However, if the convicted person wished, physical punishments prescribed for non-serious crimes could be substituted with monetary fines. For example, according to Kautilya (p 495), a convicted person could pay 54 *panas* to spare the mutilation of his thumb and forefinger or the tip of his nose. He (p 490) suggested that convicted persons were released from prison only 'if they had paid off, by their work[12], the amount owed by them' or 'after receiving a payment for redemption' or redeemed by charitable persons (2.36).

Crime Deterrence through Parading the Thieves: Kautilya (p 221) recommended, 'When thieves and robbers are arrested, the Chancellor shall parade them before people of the city or the countryside [as the case may be] and proclaim that the criminals were caught under the instructions of the king, an expert in detecting thieves. The people shall be warned to keep under control any relative with criminal tendencies, because all thieves were bound to be caught [like the ones paraded before them]. Likewise, the Chancellor shall parade before the people forest bandits and [criminal] tribes caught with stolen goods as proof of the king's omniscience (4.5).' Clearly, the policy of parading the thieves was intended by Kautilya to increase the perceived probability of catching them.[13] It also carried a preventive aspect.

It is interesting to note that in the case of government officials, who stole property of others, other than that of the king, Kautilya (pp 302-3) recommended 'shaming' in lieu of monetary fines as punishments. He suggested 'smearing with cow dung in public', 'smearing with cow dung and ashes in public', 'parading with a belt of broken pots and exile' or 'shaving off the head' as the amounts of thefts increased in lieu of monetary fines of 3 *panas*, 6 *panas*, 12 *panas* and 24 *panas* respectively. One wonders how he calculated the equivalence between the magnitude of a fine and a particular method of shaming. In any case, Kautilya was clearly aware of the deterrent role of shaming (*Gandhigiri*) as a punishment.

The Four Strikes and You Are Out Rule: Kautilya (p 493) recommended, 'In all cases, the punishment prescribed shall be imposed for the first offense; it shall be doubled for the second and trebled for the third. If the offense is repeated a fourth time, any punishment, as the king pleases, may be awarded (2.27).' He thus emphasized the deterrent aspect of punishment.

Protection of Whistle Blowers: Kautilya (p 298) suggested, 'Any informant, to whom an assurance against punishment has been given [even if he had participated in the fraud], shall, if the case is proved, receive [as reward] one-sixth of the amount involved; if the informant is a state servant, one-twelfth. If the case is proved, the informant [shall be permitted to escape the wrath of the guilty and] may either remain in hiding or attribute the information to someone else (2.8).'

State Representation of the Helpless: Kautilya did show compassion for the helpless. He (p 385) stated, 'The judges themselves shall take charge of the affairs of gods, Brahmins, ascetics, women, minors, old people, the sick and those that are helpless [eg. orphans], [even] when they do not approach the court. No suit of theirs shall be dismissed for want of jurisdiction, passage of time or adverse possession (3.2).' This pro-active and *suo motu* responsibility of the judges, which also justifiably involves a measure of administrative empowerment, coupled with some discretion in awarding punishment, made them fully accountable for the proper execution of punishment in Kautilya's scheme of justice. He, thus, laid down a very comprehensive and balanced approach to handle crime and punishment. Kangle (part III, p 230) concludes it quite aptly, 'This very brief review of the law found in Kautilya will, it is hoped, show how it has been treated by him in the most systematic manner. The treatment is also as full as possible.'

SUMMARY

There are several salient features of Kautilya's judicial system Kautilya's goal was to attain a crime-free society but 'the removal of thorns' was to be achieved only by resorting to legal means. Secondly, government must make sure that everyone could have access to justice. Thirdly, the emphasis was on prevention of crimes through ethical anchoring. Fourthly, he proposed a judicial system, which had built-in fairness. If a crime was not solved, the king had to compensate the victim. So there was an incentive to solve it. Similarly, there was an incentive not to commit a Type I error in solving the crime since the king had to pay thirty times the amount of fine imposed on the innocent. Thus there was a built-in incentive to minimize the costly errors of omission and commission. Fifthly, according to Kautilya, monetary punishments imposed in lieu of physical punishments must be collected.

Finally, he emphasized the cardinal principles of justice that punishment must be certain, proportionate to the crime and imposed impartially. He pointed out that excessive punishment due to 'anger, greed or ignorance' was counterproductive since people lost respect for the law. Kautilya believed that fairness was essential for political stability, which was a prerequisite for prosperity. Recently, A Mitchell Polinsky, and Steven Shavell (2000) assert, 'The earliest economically oriented writing on the subject of law enforcement dates from the eighteenth century contributions of Montesquieu (1748), Cesare Becceria (1767) and especially, Jeremy Bentham (1789), whose analysis of deterrence was sophisticated and expansive.' In the light of the above presentation of Kautilya's ideas on crime and punishment, their conclusion needs modification, as described above, Kautilya's judicial system was quite advanced and comprehensive and evolved two thousand years earlier.

16

Contract and Property Laws

> A king who flouts the teachings of The Dharmashastras and *The Arthashastra*, ruins the kingdom by his own injustice.
>
> — *Kautilya (p 141)*

As we know, property rules, tort laws and contracts are some of the important distinguishing features of a market economy. It is not surprising that the emerging capitalism and increasing urbanization during the fourth century BCE would have necessitated the assignment of firm property rights and effective enforcement of those rights. Similarly, contracts would be essential for promoting trade and commerce. As mentioned earlier, Kautilya argued that moralistic and legalistic approaches to ethics were complementary.[1] The moralist approach helped in character building and the legalist approach helped in developing rules, regulations and appropriate sanctions for dealing with non-compliance. He suggested the creation of laws, which promoted both economic efficiency and ethical behavior, that is, there was no crowding out.[2]

The Arthashastra contains discussion on both criminal and civil laws, which consist of contracts, property laws and tort laws regarding negligence, defamation and privacy. He presented a story (see Chapter 12) about the possible origin of a salaried king based on social consent. Individuals agreed to pay 1/6th of their produce as taxes and the king, in return, promised to protect them. Kautilya's story implies that Lockean first occupancy theory might be a necessary condition for property rights but social consent was needed as the sufficient condition. Kautilya's ideas on contracts between the government and individuals and among individuals themselves are presented in Section 16.1. He showed respect for the existing private property rights, but on the new settlements private ownership of property was conditional on its productive use. He proposed a labour theory of property. Section 16.2 presents his ideas on the labour theory of property and protection of private property rights.

In fact, during the last half century, the economic analysis of law has been approached from many perspectives, such as, the positive analysis, the normative analysis, the institutional analysis, and the functional analysis. Each perspective adds realism and depth to the analysis and in that sense they are complementary rather than alternatives. Kautilya combined all of them.

16.1 CONTRACT LAWS BETWEEN INDIVIDUALS & GOVERNMENT AND INDIVIDUALS

Kautilya on the Origin of the Contract between the Ruled and the Ruler: As mentioned in Chapter 12, Kautilya referred to a factual or hypothetical original contract for the establishment of secure private property rights and the institution of kingship. Many scholars of Kautilya have commented on that. Basham (1959, p 82) puts it as: 'Thus, in ancient Indian thought on the question of the origin of monarchy two strands are evident, the mystical and the contractual, often rather incongruously combined.' As explained by Basham himself, the mystical and the contractual origin of kingship was deliberately combined by Kautilya. Drekmeier (1962, fn. b, p 245), believes, 'Kautilya, however, occupies a position intermediate between Greek and Hindu theories.'

Kautilya would remind the king that it was his moral duty and also in his interest to provide protection to his public. Similarly, he would use every argument to convince the people to maintain law and order since it was in their interest to do so. Basham (p 83) explains, 'The author of *The Arthashastra* had no illusions about the king's human nature, and seems to have had little time for mysticism, but he recognized that legends about the origin of kingship had propaganda value. In one place he advises that the king's agents should spread the story that, when anarchy prevailed at the dawn of the aeon, men elected the mythical first king Manu Vaivasvata to kingship. He thus encourages a contractual theory.'

Anyhow, all the commentators have confined their analysis to the exploration of the origin and nature of the institution of kingship only from the perspective of political science. A few additional points are noteworthy. According to Kautilya, the origin of the institutions of property and kingship were utilitarian in nature. Both property and law were created together, thus anticipating Bentham.[3] However, unlike Bentham, Kautilya never separated law from ethics. For example, Basham (1959, p 153) observes, 'The humane regulations of the *Arthashastra*, probably unique in the records of any ancient civilization, are perhaps survivals of Mauryan laws, and it is therefore not surprising that Megasthenes declared that there was no slavery in India.' The origin of these institutions was based on individuals' explicit (not tacit) consent, that is, it was individualistic, human invention and not God's creation although 'endorsed by God'. Manu, the first (and the last) elected ruler was the son of Vivasvat, the Sun god implied divine endorsement. However, there was no mention that Manu had any supernatural powers. It is also obvious that everyone at that time was almost similarly situated and, therefore, John Rawls' 'veil of ignorance' was not needed for any moral justification of the contract theory. Incidentally, Kautilya was also aware of the possibility of free riding. Once the law and order and protection of property rights were established, a non-payer of taxes also benefited.

Hampton (1993/2005) distinguishes between the approaches of Hobbes and Locke, the two leading philosophers of the seventeenth century, to the determination of the terms of a social contract. She (p 380) states, 'When the people agree to obey the ruler, do they surrender their own power to him, as the philosopher Thomas Hobbes (1651/1990) tried to argue? Or do they merely lend him that power, reserving the right to take it from him if and when 'they see fit, as John Locke (1690/1991) maintained?' In this debate, where does Kautilya's description of the terms of the social contract fall? According to Stuart Gray (2009), neither of these theories applies to Kautilya's approach to social contract. He argues that the underlying assumption regarding the 'state of nature' in the Indian situation was very different from that of Hobbes or that of Locke. Also Kautilya's king must be ethical, efficient, energetic, and of noble-birth but not necessarily from a warrior class (*Kshatriya*) as assumed by Gray; whereas neither Hobbes nor Locke would put such requirements to the ruler chosen by his peers. However, one thing is common with that of Locke that the individual did not surrender his sovereignty to the king and could withdraw his support to him if he did not keep his part of the contract.

Requirements for a Valid Contract: Since due to the increasing urbanization and commercialization, explicit contracts were becoming perhaps necessary and more common.[4] Therefore, Kautilya emphasized the sanctity of contracts to promote commerce. However, according to Kautilya (p 442), 'Contracts entered into by dependants or unauthorized persons are invalid, unless the person was specifically authorized to do so. Contracts entered into when one of the parties was angry, intoxicated, mad or under duress shall be invalid (3.1).'.

General Principles of Contracts on Loans and Deposits: Kautilya provided an exhaustive list of rules relating to loans and similar transactions.

Suing for Recovery: Kautilya specified as to who could be sued for breach of a contract. According to Kautilya, loans between son and father and between husband and wife were not recoverable in law. He (p 423) suggested, 'A wife shall not be sued for a debt incurred by her husband if she had not agreed to the borrowing, though this rule does not apply to herdsmen's families or to farmers leasing land jointly. A husband shall be responsible for the debts incurred by his wife if he has gone away without providing for her. Farmers and servants of the Crown shall not be arrested for non-payment when they are at work (3.11).'

A few important aspects of the above-mentioned rules are obvious. According to Kautilya, law should be reasonable, manageable (there could be countless cases if couples are allowed to sue each other) and family friendly. The sentence 'Farmers and servants of the Crown shall not be arrested for non-payment when they are at work' implies that law should be least disruptive to productive operations.

Obligations of debtors and creditors: Kautilya (p 423) wrote, 'The obligation of a debtor [eg. interest on loan] shall not increase if he is: engaged in performing rites, which take a long time; ill, under tutelage in a teacher's house; a minor; or insolvent (3.11).' He believed that rules should be formulated in such a way that the weak in the society, such as the sick, a minor and an insolvent were protected (there was some bankruptcy protection even at that time).

- *Sureties:* According to him, minors could not be sureties and also any surety was limited to the particular transaction.
- *Limitation:* He suggested that a loan was not recoverable if a creditor ignored it for ten years (did not apply to minors and those away on long journeys).
- *Obligations of heirs and Successors:* He recommended that those, who were to inherit property of the deceased, should be responsible of payment of the debt.
- *Many Creditors:* He suggested that 'the debts owed to the King or Brahmins learned in the *Vedas* shall have priority'. He was always concerned about the welfare of the intellectuals.
- *Exemptions for unforeseen circumstances:* According to him, if a person was affected by calamities (such as plundering of village, caravan or herds, breakdown of law and order, destruction by fire or floods), he was not obliged to return the entrusted property to him.

Contract and Property Laws   255

- *Use of deposits:* He (p 425) suggested, 'Anyone who uses a deposit for his own benefit shall pay compensation to the depositor. A person to whom a property is entrusted shall not misappropriate, substitute, sell, mortgage or lose it nor allow live property to escape.'

Contracts on Loans: Pre-Kautilyan thinkers had already identified wages, interest, rent and profits as separate factor payments indicating [the] existence of urbanization. According to Kautilya, the first six rules noted above applied to loans also. He (p 425) added, 'No one shall recover interest without agreeing on the rate with the debtor at the time of making the loan. Once agreed upon an interest rate shall not be changed during the course of the loan (3.11).' He (p 426) suggested, 'The lawful rates of interest (on money lent) for different purposes shall be on: normal transactions 15% per annum; commercial transactions: normal 60%; risky travel: through forests 120%; by sea 240%. No one shall charge or cause to be charged a rate higher than the above, except in regions where the king is unable to guarantee security; in such a case, the judges shall take into account the customary practices among debtors and creditors (3.11).'

Kautilya on Risk Premium: Three remarks are in order. (i) It is obvious that he recommended a higher risk premium for undertaking the extra risk. In today's notations: $r = r_n + \pi$, where r= rate of interest on risky transactions, r_n = normal (prime) rate (which was suggested to be 60% on commercial loans), π =risk premium. Clearly the risk of default was quite high. It seems that most of the risk was borne by the financier of the loans and not by the merchant. Since the rate of profit allowed was only ten per cent. It is a mystery as to how Kautilya calculated the risk premium. (ii) He believed that an improvement in law and order situation lowered the risk premium (see Chapter 8 for more details). (iii) At that time there were no Usury laws prohibiting the payment of interest on loans. Kautilya proposed appropriate, in fact quite liberal, risk premia on risky loans but at the same time put upper limits on the interest rates to be charged by lenders to protect the borrowers. He was aware of market imperfections. For example, as was cited earlier also, he (p 236) stated, 'Merchants are all thieves, in effect, if not in name; they shall be prevented from oppressing the people (4.1).' Books three and four of the *Arthashastra* deal with legal issues, such as regulation of monopoly and that is why, the policy related to interest rates appears in the legal context so that the lenders could not exercise their monopoly power. Thus, Kautilya not only considered risk premium in formulating economic policies but also provided at least a rough measurement of it.

Sternbach (1965, Vol I, p 512) comments, 'Therefore, in such enterprises where the capital appeared to be endangered, it was not possible to advance loans with a fixed rate of interests which amounted to one and a quarter per cent per month because the lender realized that in such a contract he was running too great a risk. Therefore, the law harmonized with the requirements of economic conditions permitted in such cases to receive or to agree to higher rates of interests.'[5] According to Sternbach, Kautilya created laws to promote commerce by accommodating lender's economic interests.

There was no known system of financial intermediation in the fourth century BCE and the transaction of a loan occurred directly between the borrower and the lender (out of his own savings). But the fact that Kautilya devoted Chapter 11 entitled: Non-payment of Debts, and Chapter 12 entitled: 'Concerning Deposits of Book Three', indicates prevalence of at least a modest level of borrowing and lending activity. The capital markets were highly imperfect. Kautilya specified some rules and regulations governing transactions related to loans and deposits.

Salient Features of Labour Contracts: The very fact that Kautilya discussed explicit labour contracts is significant in itself. In fact, he devoted a whole chapter to labour laws. He (p 450) recommended, 'The agreement between a labourer and the one hiring him shall be made in public. Labourers shall be paid wages as agreed upon. If there is no prior agreement, the labourer shall be paid in accordance with the nature of the work and the time spent on it at customary rates'. He continued, 'The customary rate can be modified by prior agreement (3.13).' He (p 451) recommended, 'An employee shall have the right, if he is ill, in distress, incapable of doing the work or if the work is vile: to have his contract annulled or to have it done by someone else. An employee shall not be obliged, against his will, to continue working for his previous employer if he had completed the task allotted to him and already accepted employment under another. An employee shall have the right to additional compensation if he does more work than agreed upon (3.14).'

Collective Labour: There was no restriction on forming labour groups. Kautilya (p 452) explained, 'The rules about rights and obligations of individual labour also apply to groups of workmen who contract collectively to do a specified task. Workmen belonging to collective groups shall divide the earnings among themselves either equally or according to shares agreed upon earlier (3.14).'

Marriage Contracts: Kautilya listed eight types of marriages and depending on parents' approval and performance of sacred duties four of them were considered both sacred and lawful and the other four only lawful. Divorce was permitted based on incompatibility and misconduct.

Maintenance of Wife after Separation: Although Kautilya was not against divorces but did not recommend no-fault divorces. However, according to him, it was not only the husband's moral duty to support his former wife but also his legal responsibility to do so. He suggested, 'If the maintenance payments to a wife are to be made periodically, the husband shall calculate and pay the required amounts in [suitable] installments. If no regularity of payment has been decided upon, the husband shall provide the necessary food and clothing, or more than necessary, according to the income of the husband. Such maintenance shall also be paid in cases where the wife had not received the dowry, her property and her compensation for supersession. The husband shall not be sued for maintenance if the wife is supported by the family of her father-in-law or if she is [financially] independent (3.3).'

16.2 COMMON PROPERTY AND PROTECTION OF PRIVATE PROPERTY RIGHTS

According to Kautilya, as noted above, institutions of property and kingship originated together, that is, there were no property rights until the king enforced them. According to him, there was no link between property rights and natural rights. The original assignment of property rights was based on social consent. The owners had the rights to use, exclude others and transfer their properties. Private property rights were almost unconditional on the existing settlements since according to the original contract, the king was not supposed to modify them. However, according to Kautilya, the property rights on the new settlements were to be made conditional on putting the properties to productive use. Remember the original contract involved only protection and not prosperity, provision of public infrastructure or other welfare benefits. Thus the extension of the king's responsibilities required some modifications to the original contract. The original contract and the modifications suggested by Kautilya to deal with the changed objectives and circumstances are presented in turn.

Abstention from Expropriating Private Property: The king should refrain from himself expropriating private property. Kautilya (p 121) wrote, 'The wealth of the state shall be one acquired lawfully either by inheritance or by the king's efforts (6.10).' As cited earlier also, he (p 133) maintained, 'A decadent king on the other hand, oppresses the people by demanding gifts, seizing what he wants and grabbing for himself and his favourites the produce of the country [ie. the king and his coterie consume more than their due share thus considerably impoverishing the treasury and the people.] (8.4).' And continued that such a king 'fails to give what ought to be given and exacts what he cannot rightly take'; 'fails to protect the people from thieves and robs them himself'; 'does not recompense service done to him' (7.5). Kautilya did warn such kings that the public would remove them at the first opportunity to do so.

Unconditional Private Property Rights on the Existing settlements: The owners could use their properties in any way they saw fit, could rent, sell or transfer them. Kautilya (p 231) suggested, 'Water works such as reservoirs, embankments and tanks can be privately owned and the owner shall be free to sell or mortgage them (3.9).'

Special Importance to Self-acquired Property and Skills: According to him (p 414), 'Partition of inherited property shall be made in accordance with the customs prevalent in the region, caste, guild or village [of the family]. The laws of inheritance do not apply to self-acquired property (3.5).' He (p 421) added, 'The sons who are proficient in the craft shall inherit everything and maintain the others. If no son is a skilled craftsman, all sons shall share equally (3.6).' He suggested the waiving of customary inheritance rules related to bequeathing self-acquired property. He also made an exception in the case of a business requiring special skills such that economic efficiency and equity were preserved. This could be described as an evolutionary stage between physical capital and intellectual property rights.

Kautilya Implicitly Defined Surplus Created by Transfer of Property: Kautilya suggested that an owner, who wanted to sell his house, should announce in the presence of his neighbors its price, which he was willing to accept. If due to bidding among buyers the price of the house turned out to be higher than the asking price (reserve price), the excess would go to the government. He (p 434) wrote, 'The owner shall name his price and ask three times: "Who is willing to buy at this price?" If, during this time, no one has challenged [the owner's right to sell] prospective buyers may make their bids. Bids by proxy are not allowed. If there is a competition among buyers and a higher price is realized, the difference between the call price and the sale price along with any tax payable shall go to the Treasury. The tax [due on the transaction] shall be paid by the successful bidder (3.9).' Not only, all the necessary steps, such as title verification, responsibility of payment of taxes were specified but also the concept of a surplus 'the difference between the call price and the sale price' is discernible.

Assignment of Private Property Rights on New Settlements: Kautilya's three insights are highlighted here. These are related to:

- the importance of clearly defined property rights,
- granting the village headman the right to levy a user fee to mitigate 'the tragedy of commons' and avoid the 'tragedy of anti-commons', and
- Kautilya saw the need to modify property rights, but without violating the original contract. With that constraint in view, he suggested modification of the property rights only on the new settlements (and also with self-acquired property on the existing ones). He suggested rewarding hard work by granting ownership rights and thus proposed a pure labour theory of property, that is, without mixing it with the labour theory of value.

Clearly Defined Property Rights: Kautilya understood the importance of good governance and good institutions: unambiguous private property rights, and maintenance of law and order.[6] He (p 371) wrote, 'The boundaries of every residential property shall be clearly demarcated by pillars at the corners with wires strung between them (3.8).' Similarly, he (p 179) stated, 'Each boundary of a village shall be one or two *krosas* and be [clearly identifiable using] a river, a mountain, a forest, a dry-bed, a cave, an embankment, or trees like the silk cotton, acacia and milktree (2.11).'

Kautilya considered three types of property rights: *collective property*, common property and private property. Collective Property: Residents rather than local authorities were involved in deciding, building and maintaining some facilities. According to him (p 370), 'Every one shall contribute his share to the building of common facilities. No one shall obstruct or prevent the lawful use of such facilities by others in the neighbourhood. Such facilities shall not be destroyed (3.8).' He (p 371) added, 'It is preferable that sheds, courtyards, latrines, fire places, places for pounding grain and all open spaces are used as common property (3.8).' He believed that sharing these facilities was likely to promote cooperation and harmony among people and therefore, it was undesirable to put any restriction on their use. For example, he (p 365) wrote, 'All the people in a village shall contribute their share of the [community] work and the costs of festivals and entertainments (3.10).' He (p 366) added, 'The people of a village shall obey the orders of anyone who proposes any activity beneficial to all. They shall not conspire against such a person to [attack or] harm him (3.10).'

Common Property: Kautilya considered pasture as a common property but treated it differently than collective property. According to him, anyone could use the pasture subject to a user fee and the revenue collected from the user fee was designed to finance the local administration. He (p 366) suggested grazing charges as follows: 'Small animals 1/16 *pana*, cattle, horses and donkeys 1/8 *pana* and buffaloes and camels ¼ *pana* (3.10).' There were additional charges for additional uses, such as resting or staying overnight. However, he added, 'Bulls belonging to village temples, stud bulls and cows up to ten days after calving are exempt from payment of grazing charges.'

A few points are worth noting. First, it is not claimed that Kautilya was aware of the distinction between social marginal cost (SMC) and private marginal cost (PMC), or he could calculate the optimum level of user fee (ie. user fee = SMC—PMC). But his

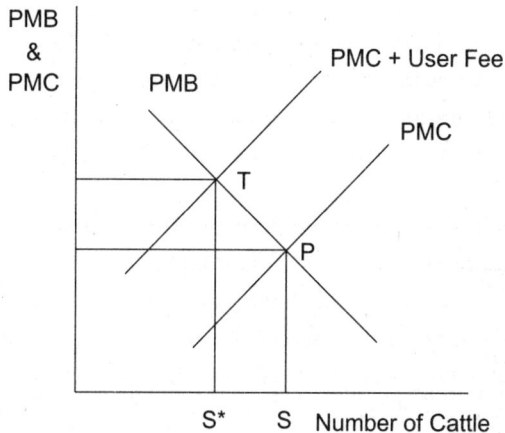

Figure 16.1: PMB is the private marginal benefit curve and PMC is the private marginal cost curve. In the absence of a user fee, a farmer would keep S number of cattle heads on the common grazing land and the number would be S* if a user fee is imposed.

suggestion to levy the user fee not only raised the needed revenue for the local administration but also reduced the overuse of the common grazing land. That is, his suggestion avoided Aristotle's major concern that 'common to the greatest number has the least care bestowed upon it'. Similarly, a grazing field if divided among the residents would face 'the tragedy of anti-commons' since each piece of land would become too small to be useful for grazing and also would require expensive fencing. Secondly, it is significant to note that even though grazing field was a common property but the village headman had the clearly defined right to exclude non-payers and thus the Coasian insight is also discernible. Thirdly, Kautilya's suggestion indicates that individual authority for management and not necessarily ownership is the necessary condition for economic efficiency. For example, Posner (2003, p33) remarks, 'The creation of individual (as distinct from collective) ownership rights is a necessary rather than a sufficient condition for the efficient use of resources. The rights also must be transferable.' Fourthly, Kautilya advanced the benefit principle of taxation. Since the user fee was lower for smaller animals than that on larger ones, presumably the smaller animals consumed less grass than the larger ones. Finally, his recommendation that 'cows up to ten days after calving are exempt from payment of grazing charges' is a true case of law protecting both the ethical values and economic efficiency. According to him, cattle rearing was the second most important economic activity and allowing the cow and calf to stay free of charge ensured their good health and consequently to a higher growth in their population.

Ownership of property on the new settlements was conditional on its being put to productive use. Vaughn (1978) remarks, 'Grotius and Pufendorf had both argued that private property was established in the state of nature by the consent of all mankind who once shared in the original communistic ownership of these resources. Such a theory of property, implied, however, that since property only existed at the consent of society, this consent could be withdrawn or modified by the society which sanctioned it originally, a conclusion which Locke sought to avoid. Instead, he argued that private property was established in the state of nature not by the consent of mankind, but by natural law.'

However, according to Kautilya, a king should be allowed to modify property laws (and other laws too) if that promoted public interest. In any case, he never advocated linking property rights to natural rights.

Kautilya Proposed New Settlements on Virgin Land: Kautilya emphasized the building of irrigation facilities for increasing output and particularly reducing its variability (he displayed high risk-averse behavior) but in the absence of modern inputs, bringing new land was the primary source of growth in agricultural output. Kautilya based the decisions regarding (i) the selection of site for a new settlement, (ii) characteristics of its settlers and (iii) the type of property rights to be granted to them, on the cost-benefit analysis.

Selection of a Site for Settlement: Kautilya (p 179) stated, 'The king shall avoid [settling] any part of the country which is liable to attack by enemies or jungle tribes and which is likely to be afflicted by disease and famine. He shall avoid excessive expenditure (2.1).' Clearly, settlement of virgin land was treated like a business investment and the selection of its site was based on analyzing the risk-return trade-off.

Selection of the Settlers: According to Kautilya (Kangle, part II, p 55), 'He should cause villages to be settled consisting of mostly of *shudra* agriculturists, with a minimum of one hundred families and a maximum of five hundred families, with boundaries extending over one *krosa* or two *krosas*, (and) affording mutual protection (2.1).' It is significant to note that Kautilya trusted the *shudra* agriculturists, who were the lowest in the four-fold social stratification, but were known to be hard working and most experienced for achieving the stated objective of maximization of agricultural output. On the other hand, Aristotle justified private property in that it promoted prudence and responsibility and only the aristocracy should own a larger share of the property. For Kautilya, 'prudence and responsibility' were requirements to own private property on new settlements. Cooter and Ulen (2004, p 116) remark, 'In Aristotle's conception, it is just that aristocrats receive an unequal share of wealth because they use it for more worthy ends than do others.'

Assignment of Property Rights: Kautilya (p 179) suggested to the king, 'He shall grant land to Brahmins [of different categories] teachers, *purohitas*, experts in the *Vedas* and those who officiate at ritual sacrifices. Such land shall be exempt from fines and taxes and be transferable to heirs. He shall [also] grant land [after the village is fully established] to heads of departments, accountants, record keepers (*gopas*), divisional officers (*sthanikas*), doctors, couriers and horse trainers. Such land shall not be sold or mortgaged by the possessor [being a perquisite associated with the job] (2.1).' Apparently, Kautilya's goal was to promote a well-balanced community consisting of intellectuals, the merchants, the moneylenders and the government officials. It is also obvious that Kautilya had a lot of respect for the intellectuals, who were 'experts in *Vedas*.'

Kautilya Implicitly Proposed the Labour Theory of Property: According to Kautilya (pp 179-180), 'Arable land shall be allocated to tax-payers for their lifetime [only]. Unarable land, prepared for cultivation by any one [by their own efforts] shall not be taken away from them. Land allotted to those who do not cultivate it shall be confiscated and given to others. Alternatively, employees of the village, whether salaried or not, or [village] merchants may cultivate them. The loss suffered by the state due to non-cultivation shall be made good by the offending holder. [On new settlements] the cultivators shall be granted grains, cattle and money which they can repay at their convenience. Favours and exemptions shall be granted either at the time a settlement is organized or as when people move in. Grants can also be made later [to people in existing settlements] provided that such grants result in increased revenue and/or avoid losses to the Treasury; for, a King with depleted Treasury eats into the very vitality of the country. He shall, however, treat leniently, like a father [treat his son], those whose exemptions have ceased to be effective (2.1).'

A few points are noteworthy. Both, the labour theory of property and the labour theory of value, have received a sustained interest for more than two centuries. Ellerman (1992) provides their comprehensive intellectual history. He believes that John Locke's second treatise on government could be credited with the origination of these theories. However, Kautilya's statement 'unarable land, prepared for cultivation shall not be taken away' indicates that he not only anticipated Lockean justification for private property but also was more specific as to its requirements. For example, Locke did not make any distinction between arable land and unarable land. Additionally, as Ellerman (1992, Chapter 4) points out that Locke did not distinguish between labour performed and labour owned (wage labour). The following paragraph has drawn a lot of criticism from the leftists that Locke treats the horse and the worker alike.

'Thus the Grass my Horse has bit; the Turfs my Servant has cut; and the Ore I have digg'd in any place where I have a right to them in common with others, become my Property, without the assignation or consent of any body. The labour that was mine, removing them out of that common state they were in, hath fixed my Property in them. [Locke, Second Treatise, Section 28].'

This type of criticism has no merit and can easily be ignored. However, this paragraph shows logical inconsistency. First, existence of wage labour in the natural state of nature appears unnatural. Second, the existence of wage labour indicates the existence of markets. But that implies the existence of property rights because markets cannot exist in their absence. Thus, the existence of wage labour essentially invalidates Locke's justification for the labour theory of property. Also the use of the phrase, 'the loss suffered by the state due to non-cultivation shall be made good' by Kautilya indicates that he was aware of the concept of opportunity cost.

Kautilya on the Labour Theory of Value: Ellerman remarks, 'The labour theory of property has throughout its history been entwined with and often totally confused with the labour theory of value. The admixture of the two labour theories was present even in Locke who had a somewhat rudimentary form of the labour theory of value.' Waldauer et al (1996) conclude, 'Kautilya was far ahead of his time in developing a labour theory of value in trying to determine what was a "just" wage for workers.' According to Vaughn, labour theory of value has three possible meanings. However, none of these meanings of the labour theory of value can be attached to Kautilya's ideas. First,

Kautilya did stress the importance of labour. For example, he (p 619) stated, 'The value of land is what man makes of it (7.11).' But, as was also pointed out earlier, he (p 637) argued, 'Man, without wealth, does not get it even after a hundred attempts. Just as elephants are needed to catch elephants, so does wealth capture more wealth (9.4).' He stressed the importance of both capital and labour as sources of value. In fact, Kautilya attributed only one third of agricultural output to labour and the remaining two-thirds to land, seeds and other inputs. Secondly, as mentioned above, the price of a good depended on demand factors (competitive bidding) also and not just on cost. That is, labour content alone was not used to determine relative prices. Thirdly, Kautilya on normative grounds also did not suggest that two goods with identical labour content should have identical prices. Therefore, it may appear at first glance that he was implicitly proposing a labour theory of value. But he had a much broader perspective than considering labour as the only source of value or the only measure of value.

SUMMARY

Kautilya understood the importance of ethical conduct and compliance with laws for economic prosperity. He proposed a true labour theory of property but social consent was needed to sustain it. Despite the fact that Kautilya advocated a contract theory between the ruler and the ruled, that a king was a salaried public employee and that it was utilitarian in nature, unlike Bentham, he still appealed to the moral motivation. For example, he (p 377) stated, 'A king who observes his duty of protecting his people justly and according to law will go to heaven, whereas one who does not protect them or inflicts unjust punishment will not (3.1.42).' Most importantly, Kautilya never separated economics from ethics.

17

Penance, Penalty and Prevention of Torts

Kautilya's *Arthashastra* and Manu's *Code of Law* also known as *Manava-Dharmashastra* have been considered as the most important treatises on the civil and criminal laws in ancient India. Kautilya's objective was to complement the existing expiation methods with a comprehensive secular law.[1] In his conceptual framework, the Brahmin took responsibility for performing ceremonies for freeing the defendant from his sins through penance/expiation and the judge was in charge of the judicial process and the imposition of the punishment on the defendant. Recently, Donald Davis (2010), Timothy Lubin, (2007) and Patrick Olivelle (2011) have explored in-depth the elements of spiritual law (ecclesiastical) and the secular law (based on judicial proceedings) in the *Dharmashastras*. Eminent Sanskrit scholars Kangle (1972) and Olivelle (2005) argue that the *Arthashastra* was one of the primary sources of Manu's *Code of Law*.[2] Also it seems that Manu's primary objective in writing the codes was to undermine the secular law and reestablish the social hierarchy.³

Kautilya's *Arthashastra* is a treatise on wealth and welfare of the citizens. According to Kautilya, survival of a kingdom depended on economic prosperity, which among other things depended on wealth creating and preserving laws and fair judicial process. He developed a set of comprehensive secular laws related to property, contracts and torts. He considered both ethical and economic perspectives on creating laws. His proposal on tort law contained many noteworthy elements. First, he considered both deterrence and corrective justice as important social objectives but treated them separately. Secondly, he recommended monetary fines to complement the existing expiation measures used for freeing the wrong-doers from their sins. Thirdly, liabilities were based on negligence since that was considered as preserving and promoting ethical values. Fourth, punitive damages were large and all the receipts went to the Treasury. Finally, in addition to the punitive damages, the injurer was required to compensate the victim for serious physical injuries and for all financial losses.

There existed some tort laws but pre-Kautilyan writers had primarily elaborated on expiation methods, which were intended to free the defendant from his sins and to enhance deterrence by modifying his behaviour. These are presented in Section 17.1. Kautilya's objective was to complement the expiation methods with the introduction of a comprehensive set of secular laws. The implications of his conceptual framework are brought out in Section 17.2. It is indicated that a monetary penalty alone or penance alone is less effective as a deterrent than a penalty-penance mix. Interestingly, the defendant may also prefer a mix of penalty and penance than either one of them alone. It means that a specific penalty-penance mix can be designed to tailor to the specific circumstances of a defendant. Kautilya's conceptual framework offers some insights into the working of the prevailing tort law systems, which are heavily focused on monetary penalties. He proposed a set of negligence-based tort laws such that the social objective of deterrence without weakening the ethical norms was accomplished. Surprisingly, he discussed tort liabilities related to some modern problems, such as consumer fraud, tress pass, malpractice, privacy and defamation. These are discussed in Section 17.3.

17.1 TORT LAWS BEFORE KAUTILYA

Patrick Olivelle (1999) deserves credit for translating the pre-Kautilyan *Dharamsutras* of Apastamba, Gautama, Baudhayana and Vasishtha. No one really knows for sure when these *dharmasutras* were written but one could say with a high degree of confidence that these were written before Kautilya. All of these writers emphasized various kinds of penances for emancipating the defendant from minor and major sins. However, they did introduce some tort laws. Apastamba (Olivelle, 1999, p 34) wrote, 'If someone kills a Kshatriya, he should give a thousand cows to erase the enmity, a hundred if he kills a Vaishya, and ten if he kills a Sudra. In addition a bull is to be given in each case as an expiation. The same applies for killing women of these classes'. This sounds like the 21st century law. Since a murder was considered a crime against society, as well as a tort (private wrong). This indicates that he understood tort liabilities.

It is interesting to note that the economic value of a *Kshatriya's* life was considered equal to the economic values of 1000 cows *plus* a bull. It appears that the economic value of a person's life was dependent both on social and economic factors. According to these thinkers, everyone was born as a *Sudra* (uneducated—a characteristic of those belonging to lowest of the fourfold social strata) and only by acquiring skills and knowledge, a person lifted himself upwards, implying that the economic value of a *Kshatriya's* life would be higher than that of a *Sudra's*. Clearly, they understood the importance of human capital. Unfortunately, none of these writers recommended universal education and some individuals remained as *Sudras*.

Apastamba (Olivelle, 1999, p 71) also wrote, 'If someone sees cattle that have been carelessly allowed to wander into the wilderness, he should bring them to the village and return them to their owners. If such negligence happens again, he should return them after impounding them, and thereafter he should ignore them'. One may conclude from this paragraph that he did not establish tort law as a distinct branch of law.

However, Gautama proposed a genuine negligence-based tort law although limited only to an agricultural economy. He understood the four elements of tortuous liabilities: 'each individual owed duty of care to others; it should not be breached; no harm would have occurred without the breach of duty of care and the breach was the cause of harm.' Gautama (Olivelle, 1999, p 98-99) recommended, 'The owner is at fault when his animals cause damage; but if a herdsman was looking after them at the time, then it is the herdsman's fault. If the damage is done to an unfenced field by the side of a road, then the fault lies with both the herdsman and the owner of the field. For damage done by a cow, the fine is five *Mashas*; by a camel or a donkey, six; by a horse or a buffalo, ten; by sheep or goats, two for each. If the whole field is destroyed, the fine is the value of the crop.' Apparently, by Gautama's time, some monetization had taken place and imposition of fines in terms of cows was getting replaced by cash (*Masha* was the unit of account and medium of exchange).

Darmasutras (religious scriptures before Kautilya) on Penance as a Deterrent: The Brahmin (priest) took responsibility for performing ceremonies or rituals required for removing the guilt incurred from the sins. Patrick Olivelle (2005) lists four means of expiation. He (p 227) states, 'A sinner is freed from his sin by declaring it publicly, by being contrite, by performing acetic toil, and by reciting the Vedas; during a time of adversity, also by giving gifts.' In fact, penance not only served as a deterrent by publicly acknowledging guilt but also reduced victim's intensity of vengefulness. Robert Lingat (1967/2004, p 64) notes, 'Penance inflicted on the wrongdoer often provides a kind of public reparation for the victim sufficient to assuage his desire for vengeance. Occasionally, too, the penance devised takes into account reparation to the victim.'[7] Clearly, besides monetary compensation, non-market methods could be effective in reducing vengeful tendencies.

Robert Lingat (1967/2004, p 68) points out, 'The religious law and the secular law thus interpenetrate each other. The two domains are never clearly distinguished. However, the rules of penal law occupy little space in the *Dharmasutras*. They are not arranged systematically, as are sins and penances. The topic was plainly secondary and accessory so far as our authors are concerned.'

However, as mentioned earlier, all these ancient writers put heavy emphasis on ethical conduct. For example, Apastamba (Olivelle, 1999, p 34) wrote, 'Refraining from anger, excitement, rage, greed, perplexity, hypocrisy, and malice, speaking the truth; refraining from overeating, calumny, and envy; sharing, liberality, rectitude, gentleness, self-control, amity with all creatures…benevolence and contentment.'

Kautilya also believed that an ethical person would avoid causing any financial or physical harm to others. He wanted to create secular laws that did not conflict with or weaken the moral codes or social norms and cause any crowding-out.[4] He considered secular laws as complementary to the prevailing penance/expiation measures. In fact, he designated the judge as a '*dharmastha*'—upholder of *dharma*. He provided incentives to the Brahmins to move to the new settlements so that they were available for performing the rituals. He (p 179) suggested to the king that, He shall grant land to Brahmins [of different categories]: teachers, purohitas, experts in the Vedas and those who officiate at ritual sacrifices. Such land shall be exempt from fines and taxes and be transferable to heirs (2.1).' He strongly believed that the *Arthashastra* contained useful advice for achieving all the worthy goals.

According to Charles Drekmeier (1962, p 194), 'There is, in Indian philosophy, a hedonistic current that ridicules religion and ethics, but Kautilya is always aware of the instrumental value of religious rites and ethical norms in preserving the social structure.' He adds, 'Yet statute law must be compatible with the Vedas and the social order defined therein.' According to Kautilya, ethical anchoring was both an end (a source of joy) and a means (to preventing wrong).

17.2 KAUTILYA PROPOSED PENANCE-PENALTY MIX FOR AN EFFECTIVE DETERRENCE

Kautilya was a pragmatist and today's labels like conservative, liberal or libertarian do not apply to him. He considered prosperity as essential to internal stability and security against foreign aggression.

According to him, preservation and creation of wealth maximization, but subject to maintaining the moral fabric of the society, was essential to prosperity. He devised tort laws keeping in view the twin objectives of preservation of wealth and moral fabric of the society. Moreover, there were some inequalities but were not that serious like today's, implying that initial distribution of wealth was not that objectionable to the goal of wealth maximization.

Minimization of the Probability of Accidents: Kautilya, just like Jeremy Bentham, Adam Smith or David Ricardo, was not hostage to Pareto's static efficiency optimization conditions. He still suggested wealth maximization tort laws.[5] He put heavy emphasis on prevention. He suggested complementing the existing expiation measures with: (a) traffic codes to reduce the probability of an accident, license to practice medicine to reduce the probability of wrong treatment, building codes to protect privacy and industrial zones to reduce the probability of a fire; and (b) imposition of monetary fines. The emphasis was on developing a comprehensive approach.

Traffic Code and other Measures to Reduce Probability of an Accident: Kautilya suggested curtailing human activities where the probability of an accident was high. He (p 369) envisaged, 'A cart shall not [be allowed to] move with no driver in it; only an adult can be in charge of a cart; a minor driver shall be accompanied by an adult (4.13).' The penalty for not obeying this rule was the confiscation of his cart. It is significant to note that he understood the distinction between tort liability and regulatory liability.[6] a (ii) Medical License Requirement: L Sternbach (1965, part I, p 301) states, in ancient India, it was necessary for a physician to obtain permission of the king for starting medical practice. Non-licensed and ignorant physicians were called companions of diseases.'

Building Codes: Kautilya recommended building codes to protect privacy. He (p 371) wrote, 'The doors and windows shall be so made as not to cause annoyance by facing directly a door or a window of a neighbouring house. Any window made for lighting shall be high up [so that it does not overlook a room of another house] (3.8).'

Setting up Industrial zones: He suggested setting up industrial zones to minimize fire hazards by limiting the craftsmen to the specified industrial areas. He (p 193) wrote, 'The Governor-General of the City shall make all those who work with fire [e.g., blacksmiths] live in one locality (2.36).' He (p 349) suggested, 'Liquor shall only be drunk in the drinking house, and no one shall move about while drunk (2.25).' He suggested making provision for sleeping beds. Interestingly, he cited many externalities of drunkenness, such as workers spoiling the work, behaving immodestly or even committing murders.

Note, prevention (or deterrence) is forward-looking whereas remedial measures, like corrective justice are backward-looking, that is, after the fact. Although Kautilya separated the social objective of deterrence from the corrective justice objective, he understood their interaction. He understood that administration of justice was critical to prevention (discussed in Chapter 15).

Kautilya proposed complementing the prevailing penance measures at the time by monetary penalties to reduce the harmful activities. He tried to fill this vacuum by providing a systematic, comprehensive, secular body of laws. In his conceptual framework, the Brahmin took responsibility for performing ceremonies for freeing the defendant of his sins through penance/expiation and the judge was in charge of the judicial process and the imposition of the monetary penalty on the defendant. Both monetary penalty and penance are bads (less the better), implying concave indifference curves.[7] A defendant could prefer a mix of penance and penalty to penance only or only monetary penalty, as a punishment. Since both are bads, a lower indifference curve is preferable to a higher one. We can get a sense of the implications of Kautilya's ideas here through the indifference curve apparatus.

Figure 17.1 is used to express his ideas on a defendant's choice between penance and penalty. For example, he might prefer point E on a lower indifference curve A_0B_0 to point A_1 or B_1 on a higher indifference curve A_1B_1. Since penance involved some labour-intensive

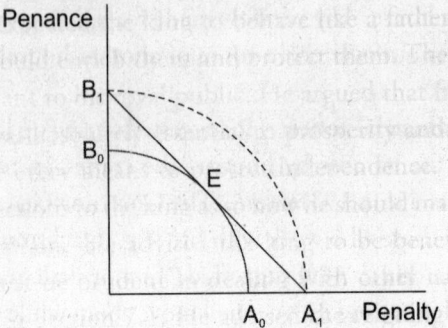

Figure 17.1: $A_0 B_0$ and $A_1 B_1$ are the defendant's indifference curves for penalty and penance (the two bads, less the better). The defendant prefers point E to point A_1 or to point B_1 since it is on a lower indifference curve $A_0 B_0$.

rituals, a rich defendant might have preferred a higher monetary penalty and less penance than a poor defendant, who might have preferred more penance and less monetary fine. That is, punishment could be tailored to each defendant.

Kautilya made a few noteworthy suggestions related to tort law. First, he considered both system-building and corrective justice as desirable goals of tort law. But punitive component of the penalty went to the treasury and not to the plaintiff. He, as mentioned above, suggested formulating traffic rules, such as specifying the minimum age and training requirement of a bullock cart driver for reducing the probability of an accident. Nowadays we have stop signs, red lights, require driving licenses, minimum age to get a license, marked lanes, road dividers, which side of the road to drive rules, inspection stickers for cars to reduce breakdowns, animal and railroad crossing signs, speed limits and their enforcement to reduce the probability of an accident. Since tax payers finance expenditure on these preventive measures, so the punitive damages should go to the treasury, he suggested. Second, he considered penance and penalty as complements, that is, monetary fines were proposed to complement the existing penance measures and not replace them. Figure 17.2 is used to capture his ideas.

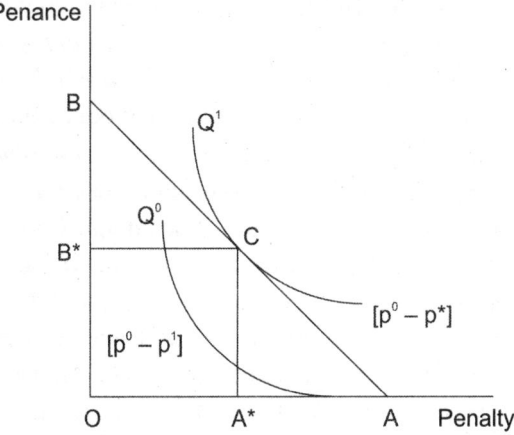

Figure 17.2: Isoquant Q^0 represents a deterrence level of $[p^0-p^1]$ and isoquant Q^1 represents a higher deterrence level of $[p^0-p^*]$.

A penalty at the level of OA, but without any penance, achieves a deterrence level of $[p^0-p^1]$ as indicated by the isoquant Q^0. However, if accompanied with penance, a higher level of deterrence $[p^0-p^*]$ as shown by isoquant Q^1 may be achieved, indicating that a proper-mix of penalty and penance, such as OA* of penalty and OB* of penance may achieve a higher level of deterrence. Similarly, it can also be shown that penance alone would be a less effective tool in deterring accidents. As a general rule, two instruments are better than one, implying that both the judge and the Brahmin (priest) may help in ensuring of an effective deterrence. In today's society, along with other avenues, community service may constitute a large component of penance.

The monetary penalty OA* in Figure (2) consists of two components: the punitive damages and the compensation to the victim for his loss. According to Kautilya, as discussed below in Section III, punitive damages went to the Treasury. That is, according to him, there was no need to split the punitive damages with the plaintiff. He implicitly indicated that the social objective of deterrence through monetary fines should be delinked from the corrective justice goal of compensating the victim for the loss, since there were other ways a plaintiff could be compensated by the society.[8]

A numerical example may help in clarifying Kautilya's ideas. Let P be the initial probability of an accident and P^0 be the reduced probability due to traffic codes, that is, traffic codes help in reducing the probability by $[P–P^0]$ and, larger the difference between them, higher the deterrence. If P^0 is the probability of an accident before any precautions were taken by an individual and P^1 is the reduced probability of an accident if precautions are undertaken in response to a monetary penalty, the difference between P^0 and P^1, that is, $[P^0–P^1]$ will measure the deterrent effect of a penalty only and $[P^0–P^*]$ indicates the impact of a combination of penalty and penance. Let us say $P=0.50$, $P^0=0.15$, $P^1=0.08$, $P^*=0.03$, then traffic codes reduce the probability of an accident by 0.35 $(=[P–P^0])$, monetary fine reduces it by 0.07 $(=[P^0–P^1])$ and a combination of monetary fine and penance by 0.12 $(=[P^0–P^*])$

According to Isaac Marcushamer (2005), plaintiff's indifference curves have changed from almost flat to almost vertical in the vengefulness-monetary compensation space (indicating a shift away from vengefulness). That is, two-three hundred years ago, even a large amount of monetary compensation was, more or less,

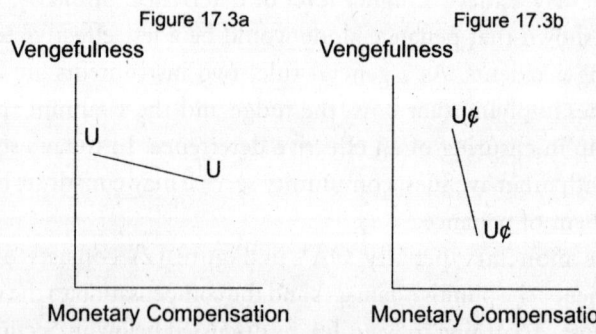

Figure 17.3a   Figure 17.3b

Figure 17.3a: is used to depict the relatively flat indifference curve, U U between vengefulness and monetary compensation, implying ineffectiveness of monetary compensation. Similarly, **Figure 17.3b** is used to indicate the transformed, almost vertical indifference curve, U' U' between vengefulness and monetary compensation and implying effectiveness of monetary compensation.

ineffective in reducing victim's feelings of vengefulness (implying flat indifference curves),whereas, now-a-days, smaller amounts of monetary compensation are needed in pacifying a victim's feelings of vengefulness. This development is captured by Figure 17.3.

Marcushamer cites two explanations for moving away from vengefulness and towards monetary compensation: (i) attaining of 'psychological maturity' by Ehrenzweig and (ii) 'shifting of moral standards into objective standards' by Holmes. Moving away from vengefulness has been a positive development but in this transformation, the positive role for moral sense got eliminated. Guido Calabresi (2007, p 6) points out that this transformation has led to an entitlement mentality to seek maximum possible monetary compensation from the defendant, implying a harmful development. It may also be noted that this type of development has undermined the role of expiation measures. For example, incorporation of an explicit role for expiation into current tort laws would shift the indifference curves in both Figure 17.3a and Figure 17.3b towards the origin. That is, a victim would have the same level of utility, but with a lower monetary compensation and also would have reduced feelings of revenge.

This development most likely has changed the slope of the plaintiff's indifference curves to almost vertical in the penance-penalty (=monetary compensation) space. This development is captured by Figure 17.4.

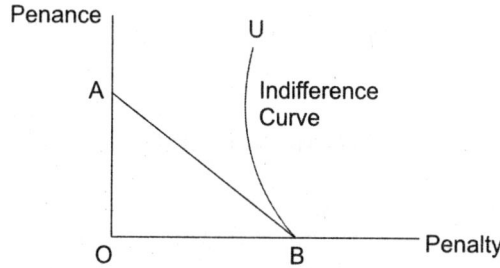

Figure 17.4: Victim's indifference curve UB is almost vertical, implying a preference only for monetary compensation.

Some victims do prefer receiving a monetary compensation, along with an expression of remorse from the defendant. But it appears that a majority of the victims not only expect, but also leave no stone unturned to extract as much monetary compensation as possible, that is, they prefer the corner point A in Figure 17.4. On the other hand, often the defendant may want to say sorry but is afraid to do so, since that is an open invitation to a lawsuit and a larger judgment against him. In any case, after paying a huge penalty (including the punitive damages etc.), the defendant does not want to express any remorse. It means that going through the court ordered rehabs and driving courses etc. by the defendants are just rituals without any feeling of remorse on their part. Thus, the exclusive emphasis on monetary compensation might have not only increased the level of litigation by manifolds but also has eliminated the need to experience guilt or shame on the part of the injurer, that is, it might be contributing to the phenomenon aptly termed as 'dead man walking'– a human skeleton without a soul. This implies that the society may have already lost or may be close to losing the instrument of penance as a deterrent and a pacifier.[9]

There are two additional points worth making. First, on balance, are we better off or worse off from moving towards monetary compensation and away from moral sense and vengefulness? That is a very fundamental question but Pareto static efficiency criterion cannot help in answering it. Secondly, it is a hopeful sign that preferences could be changed by appropriate, particularly, moral incentives. According to Kautilya, as mentioned above, ethical anchoring was not only a source of joy but also an instrument for preventing wrongs and, therefore, should be favoured.

17.3 KAUTILYA ON NEGLIGENCE-BASED TORT LAW

Kautilya described the prevailing laws at the time as inflexible, illogical and inadequate to the needs of increasing urbanization and industrialization. He (p 286) pointed out that all the previous thinkers had suggested fixed rates of penalty, without any consideration of the circumstances and some of the rates were quite high—up to twenty times the loss. He also pointed out that some suggestions by his predecessors on tort laws were illogical, such as, in a dispute between gamblers (p 355), the loser was to be fined 200-500 *panas* whereas the winner was to be fined only 48-96 *panas* or to levy (p 494) a surcharge on the basic penalty. Kautilya's goal was to recommend a set of logical, comprehensive set of tort laws, which reduced the probability of predictable and avoidable injuries and losses caused due to negligence. He believed that tort law based on negligence, combined with the existing arrangements for penance, encouraged responsibility and reciprocity.

Obviously, the application of negligence-based tort laws required some understanding of the relationship between liability and predictability, since under negligence-based tort law, failure to prevent only a predictable wrong was subject to liability. Kautilya did understand the link between liability and predictability. He argued 'if the cause is knowable and hence foreseeable', that is, prediction was possible if the cause could be identified. And it was possible to identify the cause if 'its origin is human', thus implying that outcome of human action could be predicted (discussed in Chapter 5). This methodology made it possible to link liability to the outcome of human action. He classified tort laws into two broad categories: (a) those related to physical injuries and (b) those related to financial losses. These are discussed in turn.

Tort Laws Related to Physical Injuries: Increasing urbanization led to increased inflow of agricultural products into the towns by carts and other draft animals. Also, foreign traders were attracted to the town markets. Kautilya suggested building of roads to promote commerce and, particularly, imports. He understood that in addition to the pain and suffering caused to the victim, the economy would needlessly be impacted adversely due to physical injuries, resulting from preventable accidents due to negligence since he indicated in several contexts that both labour and capital were limited whereas these inputs were crucial for economic growth. He (p 369) wrote, 'No one shall cause injury to others by: [the collapse of] a rickety dwelling or cart; an unsupported pillar [or beam]; an unsheathed weapon; an uncovered or concealed pit or well; or allowing his horned or tusked animal to hurt someone, particularly by failing to come to the rescue when entreated to do so. A person shall not be held guilty of assault by causing injury, if he gives suitable warning (such as 'get out of the way!') when: felling a tree; leading by the rope an animal being trained; driving or riding an untrained animal (4.13).'

Kautilya always tried to be as thorough as possible. He listed the various possibilities, which could have arisen in the countryside, added the precautionary warning; and just like today, the injurer was not to leave the scene of accident and was expected to help the victim. He recommended neither a fine nor any compensation to the victim if the injurer took all the necessary precautions to reduce the occurrence of an accident. Apparently, Kautilya expected the pedestrian also to take precautionary measures to avoid an accident. That is, an injurer was not liable if sufficient warning, such as 'get out of the way!', was provided.[10]

Kautilya seemed confident in predicting the outcome of human actions but did not claim to predict those of animals. He recommended a heavy monetary fine if a person caused injury due to his negligence. However, a defendant was not liable for unforeseen or unpreventable injuries. He (p 369) wrote, 'One who injures another by driving his cart [recklessly] shall be punished except [in cases of unforeseen accidents as] when: the nose string of a bullock or the yoke of the cart breaks [accidentally]; the draught animals move [suddenly] backwards or sideways; or there is a large throng of animals and men (4.13).' He (p 475) recommended a fine of 200-500 *panas plus* the cost of treatment for 'injuring the thigh, neck or eye; any injury affecting speech, movement or eating'. He recommended full compensation to the victim for all financial losses and only for serious physical injuries resulting from defendant's negligence. He recommended a fine of 48-96 *panas* for causing less-serious physical injury due to negligence.

Kautilya (p 475) did recommend compensating the victims for the cost of treatment of serious physical injuries. Given the state of medical science and practices at the time, one may assume that the principle of *'restitutio in integrum'* did not make any sense. However, a physician's skills and services were considered valuable. Kautilya (p 715) suggested that 'physicians with surgical instruments, equipment, medicines, oils and bandages' should accompany the army in the battlefield. He recommended a handsome salary of 2000 *panas* for the king's physician (note 60 *panas* could support an average family for a whole year). There is no mention if the king's personal physician was allowed to see other patients.

Malpractice: Health care was a private affair. He prescribed punishment if the physicians caused any harm to the patients. He (p 246) stated, 'Physicians shall inform the authorities before undertaking any treatment which may involve danger to the life of the patient. If, as a result of the treatment, the patient dies or is physically deformed, the doctor shall be punished (4.1).' Only information and not prior authorization was required, indicating that the authorities (unlike the insurance companies) did not claim to know more than the physician. He listed different levels of punishments, depending on the severity of the offense.

- If a physician caused 'physical deformity or damage to vital organ', he recommended a middle standard punishment, which was between 200-500 *panas plus* the cost of treatment. He described punishment for minor physical injuries in Chapter 19 of Book III and it varied from 24 to 96 *panas*.
- If the physician operated on a patient without informing the authorities prior to the treatment, he recommended a fine of 48-96 *panas* if the patient died. The patient died despite correct treatment. It is not clear if the punishment was for not taking permission prior to the treatment or it was unwittingly the beginning of strict liability.
- If the death was due to wrong treatment, the fine was 200-500 panas. In the absence of liability insurance, such a high penalty might have reduced the supply of physicians but perhaps forced them to be more careful. The following equation (5.1) (see Chapter 5) may be used to determine the liability in this case.

$$Y = XB + \epsilon \qquad (5.1)$$

Y= 1 if the patient got well

$Y = 0$ if the patient did not get well

Y may be defined as the outcome of a medical procedure/ treatment and X the standard medical procedure/ treatment (human action). According to Kautilya, if a physician, instead of adopting the correct procedure, X, adopted a wrong procedure/ treatment say Z, and the patient did not get well that would be a case of malpractice.

L. Sternbach (1965, part I, p 320) comments, 'The rules relating to the responsibility of physicians for their improper medical treatment were not introduced primarily to safeguard the patient, but rather to safeguard the good administration of the State. There is no specific mention in the *Dharmashastra's* and *Arthashastra's*, therefore, of the right of the patient to an indemnity; the penalty was imposed by the State and paid to the State (king).'

A few remarks are in order. First, as mentioned above, the plaintiff was compensated for serious injuries. Secondly, according to Kautilya, the victim should not care how he was compensated by society, that is, from the treasury or directly by the defendant. Thirdly, Kautilya wanted to delink the social objective of deterrence from the compensation to the victim by the defendant. Finally, the government could use the punitive damages to spend on preventive measures and take care of the family, if the breadwinner died or was disabled (p 182).

At that time, cutting the tip of the nose was perhaps used like wearing a 'scarlet letter', a sign of social disapprobation. However, a new class of private entrepreneurs, in this case surgeons, came into existence to remove that stigma by fixing the nose. Kautilya provided the defendant a choice between paying the fine and going through the pain of mutilation and incurring the cost of repairing the nose. For example, he suggested a monetary fine of 54 *panas* in lieu of cutting the tip of the nose as a punishment. The defendant could compare the cost of physical pain from mutilation of the nose *plus* medical cost and pain of getting it fixed *plus* opportunity cost of lost wages to paying 54 *panas*. Similarly, he suggested monetary equivalents to cutting one hand, both hands, one leg, both legs, one eye, both eyes or death. Fines being just transfers, this suggestion might have reduced demand for those who were hired to cut the limbs and the surgeons who cared for after such mutilations, and thus diverting resources away from unproductive activities probably to productive ones (see Chapter 8).

Physicians were not Subjected to Physical Punishment: Kautilya did not recommend any physical punishment to a physician for negligence in providing medical care. It was perhaps due to the long training and admirable character of the physician. Robert Lingat (p 303) observes (about the kind of penalties), 'They were not similar to the penalty fixed in other ancient codes, eg the Hammurabi's Code, because the Ancient Indian sources of law did not foresee in this case *lex tallionis* but imposed on the physician a fine, the extent of which varied according to circumstances.' Lingat (p 303, fn. 6) elaborates, 'Probably, the oldest code in which we can find the rule concerning the medical responsibility of physicians for their carelessness is the Hammurabi's *Code of Law*. According to this code, any physician who operated on a man or an animal and caused death was liable, in case of a man, to the penalty of his fingers cut off (*lex tallionis*).' Similarly, M Stuart Madden (2005, p 840) observes, 'In the Asian context, numerous Indian groups, in contrast, demonstrate, without exceptions, "a general disapproval of retaliation as a means of obtaining justice."' (Also, see Kautilya on the Silver Rule in Chapter 6.)

Tort Laws Related to Financial Losses: Kautilya saw the relevance of tort law to the agricultural economy also. He (p 438) recommended 'twice the value of the damage for causing extensive damage to another while irrigating his own field (3.9.28)' and (p 366) recommended compensation double the amount of damage to the person whose crops had been eaten by the owner's animal. As discussed in Chapter 5, Kautilya fully understood the concept of value-added. Therefore, he (p 232) suggested compensation according to damage caused to 'another's ploughed or sown field by letting water overflow from a reservoir, channel or field.'

Charging a fee for animal grazing on common pastures was a primary source of revenue to the village administration. Kautilya (p 367) suggested a fine of 24 *panas* for 'animals grazing on village pastures due to owner's negligence' and for animals straying into gardens and 48 *panas* for 'breaking down fences or eating grains in stores and threshing floors'. He recommended a fine of 48-96 *panas plus* payment of compensation if the animal died in the accident. According to him (p 320), 'When a sick animal's condition becomes worse due to wrong treatment or carelessness' the veterinary doctor had to compensate for the loss of the animal. Essentially, the objective of tort laws was to prevent avoidable loss of goods and animals.

As the agriculturists started having marketed surplus, they were likely to buy textiles, pottery and jewellery from the semi-urban areas. Also brewing liquor and tertiary industries such as laundry services, trading, entertainment, gambling and betting were responding to the increasing demand from urban dwellers. Kautilya was quite concerned about the defrauding of consumers by the suppliers, particularly by the goldsmiths and silversmiths. He (Book IV, chapter 1) proposed almost a mini consumer protection act.

Kautilya covered all the services which were getting established at the time. He suggested a very high penalty for wrongs, which offered high pay-offs and could be committed with ease. Washer-men were fined for not washing clothes on smooth wooden boards, wearing and tearing them, renting out or losing customer's clothes. For example, He suggested 'compensation of value of garment *plus* twice the value as fine for 'losing or substituting customer's garments.' Weavers were fined for measuring less, weighing less or substituting another cloth. Merchants were fined for wrong committed by their employees towards the customer. He suggested relatively higher penalties on the merchants, goldsmiths and silversmiths. For example, he suggested a penalty of '8 times the actual value' for describing an article of lower quality as one of 'higher quality' by a merchant. His list of wrongs committed by goldsmiths and silversmiths was very long but just as an illustration, he suggested a penalty of 500 *panas* for substituting gold by a cheaper metal or alloy by a goldsmith.

He considered availability of insurance as a pre-requisite to having any commercial activity since travel was very risky and market insurance was not available at that time. He suggested a government-based provision of insurance to handle this 'missing market' problem and, as pointed out earlier also, (p 235) prescribed, 'Frontier officers shall be responsible for the safety of the merchandise passing on the roads and shall make good what is lost (2.21). Traders may stay inside villages after letting the village officers know of the value of their merchandise. If any of these is lost or driven away, the village headman shall recompense the trader (4.13).'

Tort Laws Related to Defamation: Perhaps, due to stable neighbourhoods, the loss of one's reputation was considered, at least as, important as a loss of property. For example, Kautilya (p 493) suggested that students, forest recluse and hermits, who had no money, might be required to perform penance, such as keeping fast in lieu of paying the monetary fines. However, he made an exception in case of defamation. He (p 493) wrote, 'This rule does not apply to [serious crimes such as] defamation, theft, assault and abduction; in such cases, the prescribed punishment shall be implemented (3.16.38-41).' This indicates that he considered defamation as a serious breach of social norms meriting relevant penances and penalties.

At that time there were no printing presses, newspapers or tabloids to slander anyone's reputation. So, use of verbal expression for defamation was sufficient for tort liability. Interestingly, even a true statement about another person's defects was not allowed as a defense. Kautilya (p 471) suggested, 'The punishment shall be highest for a sarcastic defamation and lowest for a true one (3.18.3).' However, entertainers were given some latitude in this respect. He (p 247) wrote, 'In their performances, they may, if they wish, make fun of the customs of regions, castes or families and the practices or love affairs [of individual] (4.1.59).'

The detailed classification of defamation cases also indicates its seriousness. According to Kautilya (p 470), 'A verbal attack is of three kinds—simple defamation, aggravated defamation and intimidation. The offense is categorized as simple defamation when a person is disparaged about any of his qualities, such as, his body, his nature or character, learning and attainments, profession or place of origin (3.18)'. He (p 471) defined aggravated defamation as, 'Taunting a person with being leprous, mad or impotent or of low birth.' He suggested penalties according to the gravity of defamation but no compensation to the victim. Similarly, he attached a high value to privacy since he (p 376) suggested a fine of 100 *panas* for 'interfering in a neighbour's affairs without reason.'

No Sovereign Immunity: Kautilya's king was more like a steward and was not above the law. According to him, there should be no sovereign immunity from wrongs and that was very rare at that time. He (p 490) recommended a fine of 48-96 *panas* for 'holding anyone acquitted in custody'. He (p 491) recommended a fine of three *panas* on a jailer for 'hindering the daily activities like eating, sleeping etc'. Similarly, the jailer was fined for torturing, withholding food or drinks or killing a prisoner. Clearly, water boarding would have been a punishable offence. As also mentioned earlier, he (p 493) wrote, 'An innocent man who does not deserve to be penalized shall not be punished, for the sin of inflicting unjust punishment is visited on the king. He shall be freed of the sin only if he offers thirty times the unjust fine (4.13).' He (p 383) suggested fining a judge for imposing a fine on an innocent person. He (p 228) suggested imposition of a fine on city guards for 'stopping authorized movement and failing to stop unauthorized movement'. He (p 367) suggested a fine of 24 *panas* on the village headman for 'ejecting a legitimate settler' from the village. As noted in Chapter 15, even the king (system) was not spared of penalty if he fell short of his obligation to protect the property of the citizen.

Trespass (malfeasance): Kautilya (p 439) recommended a fine of 48-96 *panas* for trespass into another's house during the day time and a fine of 200-500 *panas* during the night time. In this case, there was no need to prove malice or negligence. However, he (p 435) made some exceptions. For example, entry by 'beggars, tradesmen, drunks or madmen' and under certain circumstances by neighbours would not be considered trespass.

Culpable Inaction (nonfeasance): He (p 372) suggested a fine of 48-96 *panas* 'for not coming to the rescue of someone being hurt by his horned or tusked animal' and a fine of 200-500 *panas* for 'failing to respond to cries for help'. Similarly, he (p 373) recommended a fine of 12 *panas* for 'not hastening to save his own house on fire' and a fine of 100 *panas* (p 376) for 'not running to help a neighbour in distress.' Again, it is obvious that Kautilya suggested tort laws to preserve property and save human lives.

SUMMARY

Tort law has ancient origins. As presented above, Kautilya proposed tort laws based on simple negligence during the 4th century BCE. Similarly, Aquilius had introduced Lex during the Roman Empire in 286 BCE. M Stuart Madden (2005) offers a fascinating and encyclopedic survey of the cultural evolution of tort laws for all major civilizations since the time of Hammurabi (1796-1750 BCE). Based on Kautilya's ideas, the choice is not necessarily between 'eye for an eye' and the market-based system of monetary compensation to the victim for the loss since non-market methods, such as penance (expiation) by the injurer, could be as effective as the monetary compensation to the victim in reducing his vengeful tendencies. Historically, penance has been accepted as an expression of remorse, and it has, although imperfectly, worked in modifying an injurer's behavior and also pacifying the victim. Therefore, penance need not be abandoned altogether.[11] Secular and spiritual measures may be considered as complements and not substitutes for each other.

According to the ancient wisdom, the expiation measures hit the head by generating a genuine feeling of guilt and the excruciating pain resulting from the pricks of conscience, whereas monetary sanctions hit only the stomach. Kautilya initiated the discussion on the role of secular law only as a complement to the existing expiation measures. He believed that positive or secular law without ethical anchoring was unlikely to have positive outcomes. He suggested compensating the victim for all financial losses but only for serious physical injuries caused due to negligence. He suggested breaking the link between compensation to the plaintiff and imposition of penalty on the defendant, for preventing accidents by lowering the probability of their occurrences. This approach was intended to achieve other objectives also, such as, the victim receiving compensation just sufficient to cover his loss, the defendant not getting hostile to the victim as the punishment was apparently imposed by society and the punitive damages supplemented the general revenue of the government. Thus, ancient insights might help in devising ways to achieve corrective justice without compromising with efficiency.[12]

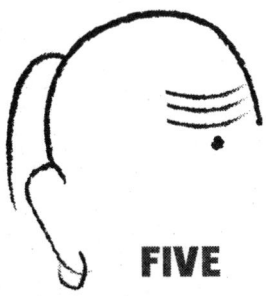

FIVE

National Security

Kautilya believed that freedom from wants was not enough to enjoy life if not accompanied by freedom from fear. At that time there was no such thing as live and let live. A country always faced a threat of an aggression. Kautilya considered both defensive and offensive measures to maintain freedom from foreign rule. The following three Chapters present Kautilya's ideas on National Security.

Reducing the Threat of an Aggression. (Chapter 18)

How to balance the Risk-Return Trade-off from Joint Campaigns. (Chapter 19)

Minimizing Losses if Attacked by a Stronger Aggressor. (Chapter 20)

He developed and applied several important concepts, such as, public goods, asymmetric information, risk-return trade-off, and time inconsistency problem in dealing with these issues.

18
Defending Freedom by Every Means and at Any Cost

> In times of trouble, the fort provides a haven to the people and the king himself.
>
> — *Kautilya (p 658)*

Kautilya advanced a people-centric approach to human security. He believed that every individual desired freedom from fear of an attack by a foreign army or an attack by an intruder and freedom from wants. His objective was to ensure freedom from all sources of fear. According to him, protection and prosperity were both necessary and sufficient for enjoying life to the fullest and other requirements, such as dignity, empowerment, etc. were redundant. He considered national security as a subset of the freedom from fear component of human security. He suggested an exhaustive list of measures to reduce the probability of an attack by an enemy.

Kautilya shows some understanding of the distinction between public and private goods. He invariably applied cost-benefit framework to every undertaking, including waging of a war (discussed in the next Chapter). But he did not apply the usual cost-benefit approach to the provision of national security, which he argued was too fundamental to be decided by such calculations. Section 18.1 contains an explicit presentation of these ideas implied in the *Arthashastra*. According to him, a nation had to match or exceed the power of her potential adversary since national security depended only on the relative power. Section 18.2 develops his relative power equation. He argued that the protection and prosperity components of human security reinforced each other. Section 18.3 presents Kautilya's ideas on national security and the relative asset hypothesis which is implicit in Kautilya's arguments and throws some light on the scope of loss-aversion hypothesis. Kautilya's observations challenge Markowitz's invariance hypothesis. Section 18.4 contains this discussion. Kautilya argued that power bred more power. This is presented in Section 18.5.

18.1 KAUTILYA'S IDEAS ON THE PROVISION OF PUBLIC GOODS

Kautilya understood that national security was essential to economic development, which in turn promoted national security. He (p 175) argued, 'A foreign king, on the other hand, is one who has seized the kingdom from a legitimate king still alive; because it does not belong to him, he impoverishes it by extravagance, carries off its wealth or sells it. If the country becomes too difficult for him to handle, he abandons it and goes away (8.2).' He (p 132) also maintained, 'Harassment by the enemy's army not only affects the whole country but also ruins it by plunder, slaughter, burning and destruction (8.4).'[1] It is thus clear [from the above statements] that Kautilya had a strong belief that both economic prosperity and dignity were incompatible with [a] foreign rule. He (p 541) asserted, 'An enemy's destruction shall be brought about even at the cost of great losses in men, material and wealth (7.13).'

Measures to Reduce the Probability of Foreign Aggression: He suggested an exhaustive list of measures to reduce the probability of an attack by an enemy. He recommended: (a) building of forts, (b) building a large army and armour, (c) setting up an intelligence gathering and analysis unit and (d) diplomatic initiatives. These are in turn discussed below. The other measures, such as winning public support and hiring qualified advisers are discussed in the next Section.

Building of Forts: Kautilya (p 179) envisages for the king, 'On the frontiers, he shall construct fortresses under the command of frontier chiefs to guard the entrances to the kingdom. The area between the frontier forts and the settled villages shall be guarded by trappers, archers, hunters, Candalas and forest tribes (2.1).' Although Kautilya did not have a complete or formal definition of public goods, but his insights relating to their role are quite modern. He (p, 658) recommended to the king, 'If he lacks [physical] protection, he shall build an impregnable fort. For, he who is defended by forts and allies is respected by his own people and by others (7.14.14).' He argued, 'In times of trouble, the fort provides a haven to the people and the king himself (7.14.20).' It is obvious from the above statements that at the time, forts were a major part of national security and the phrase 'haven to the people and the king himself' and 'respected by his own people and by others' truly describe the 'non-rivalry' nature of national security, a pure public good.

Maintaining Elephant Forests: Availability of elephants offered a distinct advantage in a battle and therefore, their habitat must be protected. Kautilya (p 620) argued, 'Some teachers say that land with productive forests is preferable to land with elephant forests, because a productive forest is the source of a variety of materials for many undertakings while the elephant forests supply only elephants. Kautilya disagrees. One can create productive forests on many types of land but not elephant forests. For one depends on elephants for the destruction of an enemy's forces (7.11).'

Establishment of Intelligence Administration: He understood the importance of information in deriving sound inference. He (p 506) recommended, 'A king shall have his own set of spies, all quick in their work, in the courts of the enemy, the ally, the Middle, and the Neutral kings to spy on the kings as well as their eighteen types of high officials (1.12.20).' He (p 562) added, 'He shall always station envoys and clandestine agents in all states of the circle. These shall cultivate those acting against the interests of the conqueror and, while maintaining their own secrecy, destroy repeatedly such inimical persons (7.13).'

Work Assignment: Intelligence agents would perform the following tasks: '(i) neutralize the principal officers who, though living by service under the king, work for the enemy; (ii) keep under surveillance people of the country who are likely to fall prey to the incitement of the enemy; (iii) wage psychological warfare against the enemy; and (iv) weaken the enemy (5.1.3).'

Similarly, about the functioning of an envoy, he (p 576-577) suggested, 'On the way to the place of his mission, the envoy shall: (i) establish good contacts with jungle chiefs, frontier officers, chief officers of the cities and countryside; (ii) observe, both the territory of his own king and that of the other king, the places suitable for stationing troops, fighting, support facilities and fall-back positions; and (iii) find out the size and extent of the other king's territory and forts, the strength of the economy, and the strong and weak points in its defenses (1.16).'

He (p 710) also cautioned, 'The enemy can ascertain the strength of the conqueror's army by counting it when they march in single file or from the quantity of fodder, food and bedding, or from the number of cooking fires, banners and weapons the army carries. Therefore, all of these shall be kept well hidden (10.2).'

Diplomatic Initiatives: He (p 568) recommended, 'When the benefit accruing to kings under a treaty, irrespective of their status as the weaker, equal or stronger king, is fair to each one, peace by the agreement shall be preferred course of action; if the benefits are to be unfairly distributed, war is preferable (7.8).' It is also clear from another statement. Kautilya (p 635) asserted, 'That which entails small losses is a gain by diplomacy rather than by war (9.4).'

18.2 KAUTILYA ON RELATIVE POWER EQUATION

Kautilya understood the complexity of the provision of national security. He believed that national security (and its resultant—independence) depended on the relative power of a king to that of his potential adversary. He considered public support and military strength as the sources of power. He argued that public support depended on economic prosperity and fairness. According to him, military power consisted of three components: power of good counsel (good analysis and good judgment), power of mighty army and rich treasury and the power of enthusiasm and energy. He believed that good counsel was the supreme power.

He offered a very strong justification as to why good counsel was the most important power. He proceeded to justify that in two stages. He first compared the relative power of enthusiasm to that of might and concluded that might was more important than enthusiasm. He (p 627-28) explained, 'Some teachers hold enthusiasm to be more important than might. [They argue:] so long as a king is himself brave, strong, healthy and expert in the use of weapons, he can defeat, with only the army to help him, even a mightier king. Kautilya disagrees. A mighty king, by his very might, can overpower an energetic one; for, a mighty army, richly endowed with horses, elephants, chariots and instruments of war, can move unhindered anywhere. Further, a mighty king can get the help of another energetic one or he can hire or buy heroic fighters. [It is known that] even women, children, the lame and the blind have conquered the world after winning over or buying heroic fighters with their might.'

Then he proceeded to justify why the power of good counsel and judgment was more important than the power of might. He argued, 'Some teachers hold might to be more important than the power of good counsel and judgment. [They argue:] howsoever good a king's analysis and judgment, he thinks but empty thoughts if he has no power. Just as a drought dries out the planted seeds, good judgment without power produces no fruit. Kautilya disagrees. He explained his disagreement as: "The power of good counsel [good analysis and good judgment] is superior [to sheer military strength]. Intelligence and [knowledge of] the science of politics are the two eyes [of a king].

Using these, a king can, with a little effort, arrive at the best judgment on the means, [the four methods of conciliation, sowing dissention, etc.] as well as the various tricks, stratagems, clandestine practices and occult means [described in this treatise] to overwhelm even kings who are mighty and energetic."'

He concluded, 'Thus, the three components of power,—enthusiasm, military might and the power of counsel—are in ascending order of importance. Hence, a king who is superior, as compared to his enemy, in an item later in the list, outmanoeuvres his adversary (9.1).'

It is obvious that he believed that the relative weight for good counsel, w_c, was much higher than the relative weight for might, w_m and which was higher than the relative weight for enthusiasm w_e. It might seem very tempting to construct a power index such as $P = \Sigma w_i x_i$, where w_i is the relative weight and x_i is the magnitude of the various kinds of powers. However, despite our knowledge of as to how to construct indices, neither Kautilya nor we could construct such an index. We still do not know how to measure, 'good counsel, good analysis and good judgment'. The fact is that we cannot measure accurately even the contribution of knowledge-based industries to GDP.

Kautilya adopted an alternative intuitive approach to compare the relative powers of two kings. Most likely, he compared the relative strengths of their armies and their enthusiasm levels, the number of advisers and their qualifications and public support. For example, he (p 609) stated, 'When, among a group of allies, many give equal help in terms of manpower, it is specially advantageous to get the troops from one whose troops are valorous, able to tolerate hardship, loyal and versatile (7.9).' He understood that these three powers were complementary.

Public Support to a King Linked to Economic Development: He strongly believed that a king could win public support only by raising their standard of living. He (p 159) argued, 'When a people are impoverished, they become greedy; when they are greedy, they become disaffected; when disaffected, they either go to the enemy or kill their ruler themselves (7.5).' He suggested, 'Therefore, the king shall not act in such a manner as would cause impoverishment, greed or disaffection among the people; if however, they do appear, he shall immediately take remedial measures (7.5).' Formally, Kautilya's ideas on relative power may be expressed as follows:

$$P = A (J, H) (K)^{\lambda} (E L_m)^{(1-\lambda)} \quad (18.1)$$
$$RP_1 = P_1/P_2 \quad (18.2)$$

Where P_1 and P_2 = powers of king one and king two respectively, A= efficiency parameter, H = experience and analytical skills of the advisers in utilizing the information made available through intelligence, K = horses, elephants, chariots and armaments, E = enthusiasm and training, L_m = military strength, J = level of public support for a just and kind-hearted king and RP_1 = relative power of nation one. Kautilya believed that H was the most important factor in enhancing national security.[2]

According to Kautilya, no country became prosperous under foreign rule, implying national security was essential to prosperity. Similarly, a poor country could not afford to provide for adequate national security, implying prosperity was essential to national security. Kautilya reasoned that the recruitment of soldiers and their enthusiasm and the manufacturing of arms, hiring of qualified advisers were dependent on the tax revenue, which was directly dependent on the level of income. Clearly, he understood the interdependence of national security and prosperity on each other.

18.3 NATIONAL SECURITY AND KAUTILYA'S RELATIVE ASSET HYPOTHESIS

He was always comparing the relative economic strength of a state to that of another state (hostile one) and under no circumstances he wanted a state to slide into a weaker position because that could tempt its enemy to attack it. He wanted to make sure that the investment was directed to the most productive projects and capital accumulation was taking place. For example, he (p 554) stated, 'It is a decline for the conqueror if the enemy's undertakings flourish; conversely, the decline of an enemy's undertakings is progress for the conqueror. Parity between the two is maintained when both make equal progress. A small gain for a large outlay is decline; the converse is progress. A gain equal to the expenditure on an undertaking means that the conqueror has neither progressed nor declined. Hence a conqueror shall seek to obtain a special advantage by undertaking such works [as building forts] which would produce a large profit for a small expenditure (7.12).'

As discussed earlier in Chapter 8, growth in capital was considered as a leading source of growth in income. Kautilya (p 637) argued, 'Man, without wealth, does not get it even after a hundred attempts. Just as elephants are needed to catch elephants, so does wealth capture more wealth. Wealth will slip away from that childish man who constantly consults the stars. The only [guiding] star of wealth is itself; what can the stars of the sky do? (9.4).' Keeping that in view, Kautilya paid special attention to capital formation in the native country to that of a potential adversary.

Thus, according to Kautilya, a king's utility depended on his wealth relative to that of his enemy. That is, $U = U(R)$ Where $R = W_1/W_2$, W_1 = a king's own wealth and W_2 = enemy's wealth.

According to Kautilya's hypothesis, only the relative standing was relevant and not the marginal changes in one's own wealth.[3] The utility function may be highly concave in the relative assets and could have a kink if the value of R was less than one.[4] Since in that case, any adverse change in R could affect the survival of a king, therefore, such a reference point is justified. But in general, one has to explain how an individual determines a reference point, how it shifts and how much time he takes to assign it the status of a reference point.[5] The current assets are unlikely to be a reference point unless linked to something intrinsic. The loss-aversion hypothesis, at best, in its current form, seems to be incomplete since it does not answer such questions satisfactorily.

18.4 KAUTILYA ON INVARIANCE HYPOTHESIS

Prosperity and Shift in the Utility Function: Machina (1982) discusses the Markowitz's 'invariance hypothesis' at length. Markowitz observed that both poor and rich individuals play lotteries and buy insurance policies. A fixed utility function cannot explain this invariance. Therefore, according to Markowitz, as the wealth of a person increases, his utility function shifts horizontally. Kautilya (p 624) stated, 'The king may face dangers even from a trusted king of equal power, when the latter has achieved his objective. Even an equally powerful king tends to become stronger after the task is accomplished and, when his power has increased, becomes untrustworthy. Prosperity changes peoples' minds (7.5).' According to Kautilya, a king might become less risk-averse, implying that the utility function was concave for $R \leq 1$ but became almost linear for $R > 1$. That is, utility function's shape might change significantly. Thus, according to Kautilya, the invariance hypothesis was not valid. It seems that the invariance hypothesis is incompatible with loss-aversion hypothesis.

It may be emphasized that Kautilya was very critical of gambling, and considered it as a zero-sum game and gamblers as irrational, implying that a rational investor would not have any convexity in his utility function. According to him (p 138-139), 'Of the two parties [in gambling], one has to lose as we know from the stories of Nala and Yudhishtira. The same wager won by one is, to the loser, a fish-hook which becomes a source of enmity. A gambler never knows how much wealth he has got, tries to enjoy wealth which he has not got and loses it before he can enjoy it. Being irregular in his habits, he contracts stomach, urinary and bowel disorders'. He (p 140) continued, 'Gambling is the most evil among vices, because it destroys the ruling class by depriving them their ability to govern (8.3)'. However, he considered some limited but highly controlled gambling to raise revenue for the state. He recommended a five per cent tax on winnings. He (p 355) suggested, 'The Chief Controller shall be responsible for ensuring that gambling is carried out [only] in designated places under the supervision of honest gambling masters, in order to detect men who follow secret activities [like spying] (3.20).'

18.5 KAUTILYA'S HYPOTHESIS: POWER BREEDS MORE POWER

Kautilya believed as the relative asset ratio R increased, the probability distribution of returns changed. He listed three sources of such a change.

- **Acquisition of Additional Wealth with Every Conquest:** He (p 259) stated, 'With increased wealth and a powerful army, more territory can be acquired, thereby further increasing the wealth of the state (2.12).'
- **A Stronger King Secured a Favourable Treaty:** He (p 587) observed, 'An equal treaty is one in which the stronger king gets a larger share, an equally powerful king an equal share and a weaker king a smaller share. An unequal treaty is one in which a strong, equal or weak king does not get a share according to his power (7.8).'
- **Strength Won Support:** He mentioned that 'a mighty king can get the help of another energetic one or he can hire or buy heroic fighters' (9.1). That is, it was easier for a powerful king to win the support of other kings.

Now-a-days, rich clients are treated differently by brokerage firms (they are designated as premium accounts) and face a more favourable efficiency frontier. A small investor cannot participate in the hedge funds or buy even one share of Berkshire Hathaway. Big investors also have informational advantage and sometimes benefit from after hour trading, implying that financial markets may be segmented. That implies that the separation theorem may not hold.

SUMMARY

It is not claimed that Kautilya understood the vertical summation of individual demands curves or the concept of deadweight loss or developed demand revealing mechanisms. However, he appears to understand the non-rivalry nature of public goods. A foreign ruler deprives the country of its culture and prosperity. Kautilya advised the king to protect national freedom by every available means and at every cost.

The *Arthashastra* contains a detailed discussion on the organizational structure of the defence services and the responsibilities and salaries of the key officials. Kautilya also stressed the war-readiness of both mammals and equipment. For example, he (p 693) wrote, 'The horses shall be bathed twice a day and decorated with garlands and perfumes (2.30).' Roger Boesche (2002, p 105) comments, 'In this, Kautilya makes us pause in surprise. Do we want a state this intrusive? Does the state really need to command us to bathe horses twice a day, to wash clothes only on smooth stones, to prescribe penalties for tossing dirt in the road or for harming bushes, and to tell us at what time we must cover our windows at night?' Boesche is not paying attention. Kautilya was not giving any command to private individuals as to how they took care of their horses. Kautilya was talking about horses in the king's stable, which were going to be used in a battle. Keeping them clean was critical to protect them against diseases. This instruction was for a state employee who was responsible for their readiness for a battle.[6] We might take it illustratively–as a small example–signifying his concern for all time defence preparedness.

19
Risk-return Analysis of Campaigns

Markowitz has been rightfully acknowledged as the founder of the modern portfolio theory. His (1952) seminal contribution showed how to construct a diversified portfolio.[1] He (1999) provides a historical review of the contributions of several writers, including Shakespeare, from 1600 onwards to the portfolio theory. Rubinstein (2002) adds a few more contributions, including Bernoulli's (1738), on the desirability of diversification, which was left out of Markowitz's list of contributions. Varian (1993) describes the pre-Markowitz state of portfolio theory, 'The fact that investors should care about both, the risk and the return of their investments is so commonplace today that it is hard to believe that this view was not appreciated in 1952.'[2]

All these historical reviews regarding the developments in the portfolio theory have been limited to Europe and only to the last four hundred years. It is remarkable that Kautilya, two thousand years earlier than Bernoulli (or Shakespeare), considered risk-return trade-offs in making choices involving risky situations. Although he was not aware of the terms, such as portfolio balancing, diversification, mean-variance approach, the relative risk-aversion, absolute risk-aversion, risk premium, and expected or non-expected utility theory, he did use some of these concepts in making various choices.

Kautilya's goal was to bring the whole Indian sub-continent under one rule but he pursued it very cautiously. He is the first known economist, who explicitly used the risk-return trade-offs in making alliances for joint campaigns. This is discussed in Section 19.1. Similarly, Kautilya used the risk-return trade-off in the acquisition of land and its location. This analysis is presented in Section 19.2. He suggested diversification to reduce risk and a few applications of the principle of diversification are discussed in Section 19.3. Section 19.4 presents his unique insight in analyzing the complementary nature of variables, which were considered relevant in the determination of success of a campaign.

19.1 RISK-RETURN TRADE-OFF IN MAKING ALLIANCES

Machina (1987) remarks, 'During the development of modern probability theory in the 17th century, mathematicians such as Blaise Pascal and Pierre de Fermant assumed that the attractiveness of a gamble offering the payoffs $(x_1...x_n)$ with probabilities $(p_1...p_n)$ was given by its expected value $\overline{x} = \Sigma x_i p_i$'. Pascal-Fermant correspondence was concerned with making sure that there was equity in sharing the winnings from gambling. Nicholas Bernoulli (1713) produced the St Petersburg paradox to show the inadequacy of the expected value in ensuring equity, and also challenged something very fundamental: a belief prevailing at the time that there was no tension between reasonableness and prudence.[3] Daniel Bernoulli (1731/1738) proposed the replacement of the expected value by expected utility, which he called 'moral expectation'. He proposed a logarithmic utility function to resolve the St Petersburg paradox and used it to justify the desirability of diversification.

Kautilya considered choices involving risky situations as an important part of economics.[4] In fact, Kautilya applied the risk-return trade-off in all kinds of activities, that is, whether it was an acquisition of an asset, the selection of an ally or waging a war. A few applications of such trade-offs are provided below. It is not claimed that Kautilya had a fully developed theory of portfolio balancing. Rather, the claim is that he was aware of the relevance of both risk and return in making choices under situations involving risk.

Kautilya (p 634) asserted, 'A small revolt in the rear outweighs a large gain in the front; for, when the king is not there, a small revolt in the rear may be worsened by the anger of the people or by traitors, enemies and jungle tribes. If this happens, a large gain in front, even if actually obtained, will be eaten up by the subjects, allies, losses and expenses. Therefore, a king shall not undertake a campaign when the gain in front is [less than] a thousand times the likely loss due to a revolt in the rear or, at least, a hundred times the loss. A well-known proverb is: 'Misfortunes are, [in the beginning] not longer than the point of a needle' (9.3).' He continued, 'The king shall undertake a march when the expected gain outweighs the losses and expenses (9.4).'

It is significant that Kautilya explicitly stated that a king should go on a campaign only if the expected gain was larger than the expected loss (of trained men and animals and reduction in wealth and grains). He specified this as a necessary condition for undertaking a project. If the above statement is interpreted in an overall context, it has two salient features: (i) display of a highly risk-averse behavior. That is, the king should not start a campaign unless the expected gain was several times the expected loss. (ii) He wanted to make sure that all the losses were added up so that an appropriate decision could be made.[5]

Kautilya on Risk-return Trade-off: He (p 608) asserted, 'When there is a choice between two possible allies, both in difficulties, of whom one is constant but not amenable to control and the other is temporary but controllable, which one should be preferred? Some teachers say that the constant friend, though not controllable, is to be preferred because, even if he cannot help, he can do no harm. Kautilya disagrees. The one amenable to control, though a temporary ally, is preferable because he remains an ally only as long as he helps. The real characteristic of friendship is giving help (7.9).' He (p 608) continued, 'When there

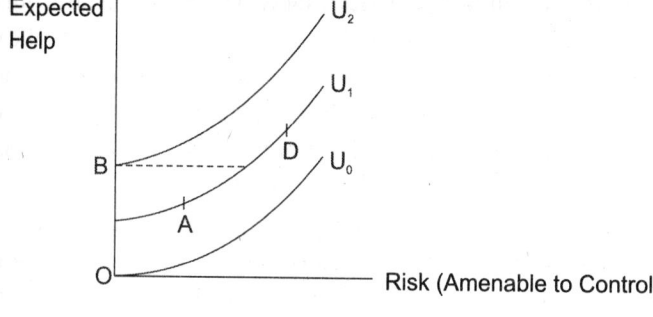

Point O = reliable but no help
Point A = some help but temporary (not reliable)
Point B = only a little help but reliable
Point D = substantial help but temporary (not reliable)

Figure 19.1: U_0, U_1 and U_2 are the indifference curves showing risk-return preferences. Points A, B, D and O represent available choices related to risk and return (help).

is a choice between two possible allies, both amenable to control, of whom one can give substantial but temporary help and the other a constant help but only a little, which one should be preferred? Some teachers say that a temporary friend giving substantial help shall be chosen because such a friend, by giving a lot of help in a short time, helps to meet a large outlay. Kautilya disagrees. The constant ally giving smaller help shall be preferred. The temporary friend giving substantial help is likely to withdraw for fear of having to give more or, even if he actually provides the help, will expect it to be repaid. The constant ally, giving a small help continuously, does, in fact, give great help over a period of time (7.9)'. Figure 19.1 captures his reasoning.

Kautilya considered four types of allies: (i) (reliable, no help) represented by point O; (ii) (not reliable, some help) indicated by point A; (iii) (not reliable, large help) indicated by point D and (iv) (reliable, small help) given by point B (this is like a return on a safe asset). First, he compared point O to point A and according to him, point A should be preferred and then, he compared point D to point B and he preferred point B to point D. Additionally a reliable friend 'giving a small help continuously' would have resulted in a shift of the indifference curve U_2 upward and, therefore, even more desirable.

19.2 RISK-RETURN TRADE-OFF IN ACQUIRING LAND

Type of Land: During the fourth century BCE, there was no stock market, a market for bonds or even paper money and there were no financial institutions or financial derivatives. The only assets available were the different types of land, precious metals like gold and silver, and precious stones like diamonds. Yet, it is remarkable that Kautilya considered the expected return and risk of an asset as critical factors in its acquisition. He (p 619) stated, 'As between land dependent on rain and land with flowing water [ie. a river], a smaller tract with flowing water is preferable to a larger drier one because with flowing water, which is always available, the production of crops is assured. As between two irrigated tracts, one on which cereals can be grown is preferable. [However], if one of them is larger, the larger one unsuitable to the cultivation of cereals is preferable to the smaller one, which is suitable. For, not only can different types of wet crops, dry crops and medicinal plants be grown in [different parts of] a large area but also many forts and defensive works can be built. The value of land is what man makes of it (7.11).'

The above statement by Kautilya contains three comparisons. Let us compare them separately.

The first one involves comparing an irrigated tract of land, which might provide lower but more 'assured' yield to a dry tract of land, which might provide a higher but less certain yield. Figure 19.2 is used to capture this comparison.

The risk-return trade-off for the irrigated tract is represented by point B and that for the dry tract of land is represented by point A. Kautilya preferred Point B to point A, despite the fact that the expected return at point B was lower than that at point A because the risk was also lower at point B. He displayed a risk-averse behavior.

Between two irrigated tracts of land, the one, which was suitable for growing cereals, was preferred, since both the tracts were irrigated implying that risk was the same. However, it seems that the return from cereals was higher than that from non-cereals. Therefore, point B, which represents the cereal production, was preferred to point A.

Between two irrigated tracts of land, the one, which was larger

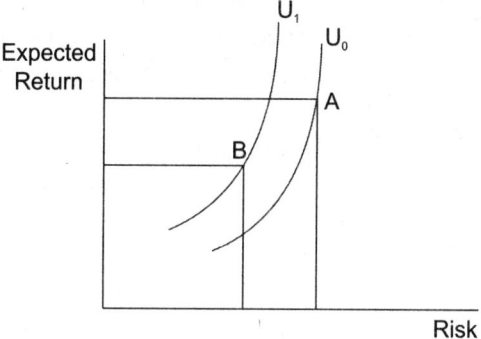

Figure 19.2: U_0 and U_1 are the indifference curves showing risk-return preferences. Points A, and B represent available choices related to risk and expected return.

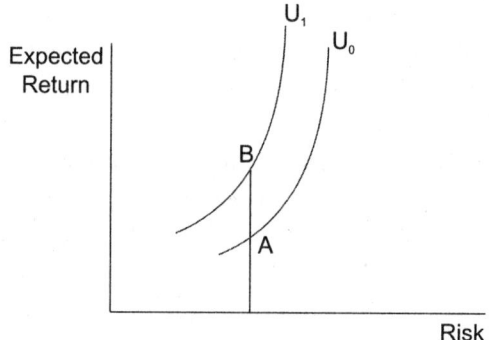

Figure 19.3: U_0 and U_1 are the indifference curves showing risk-return preferences. Points A, and B represent available choices related to risk and expected return.

and unsuitable for growing cereals, was preferred to the one, which was smaller but suitable for growing cereals. He offered several possible explanations for this choice. According to him, a larger tract was likely to offer a larger number of choices. This would be because potentially, a larger variety of crops and plants could be grown to satisfy diverse consumption and medicinal needs. Also, it might have provided suitable sites to build forts and other defense works to enhance national security. Thus, the total expected return from a larger tract might be much higher than that from a smaller tract on which cereals could be grown (both tracts were irrigated implying the same degree of risk). It is apparent that he considered both return and risk in making a selection (figure similar to Figure 19.3 could be used in this case).

Risk-return Trade-off in Deciding on the Location of the Land: Kautilya, in addition to the economic risk, considered a political risk also in acquiring a piece of land. He (p 618) asked, 'Which is better—a rich land with permanent enemies or poor land without permanent enemies?' He answered it as follows: 'Some teachers say that, because a rich land enables one to get wealth and an army with which to destroy the enemies, a rich land with permanent enemies is preferable. Kautilya disagrees. Acquiring land with such enemies, one only adds to one's number of enemies; and an enemy remains an enemy whether he is helped or harmed: on the other hand, a temporary enemy can be made to be quiet through favours or at least by not harming him (7.10).' He was comparing the risk and return from this choice, which may be expressed by Figure 19.4.

Point A indicates a higher expected rate of return and a higher risk as well (rich land with permanent enemies) compared to those indicated by point B (not as fertile but without permanent enemies). Thus he would prefer point B on the higher indifference curve U_1 to Point A on a lower indifference curve U_0.

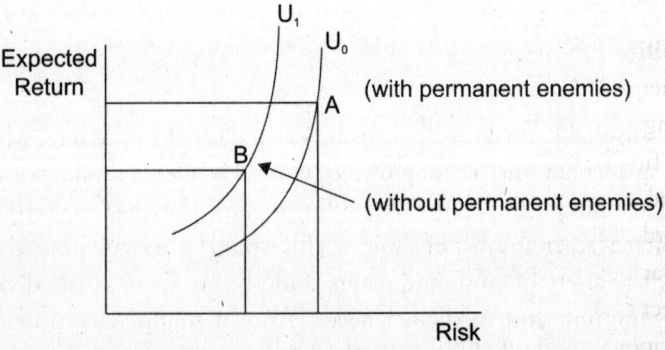

Figure 19.4: U_0 and U_1 are the indifference curves showing risk-return preferences. Points A, and B represent available choices related to risk and expected return.

19.3 RISK REDUCTION THROUGH DIVERSIFICATION

Nobel Laureate James Tobin (1958) provided a formal analysis in justification of the ancient maxim. Not to put all your eggs into one basket. The modern concepts of variances and co-variances were not available to Kautilya, but his insights on risk reduction through diversification are quite modern.[6] He proposed its application in several economic and non-economic situations. A few of them are presented below.

Not to Keep All Soldiers in one Place: According to Kautilya (p 561), if a king 'Perceives [that it will be of advantage to him] he may [in the following situations] wish power and happiness even to his enemy. If a powerful enemy is likely to antagonize his subjects by harming them verbally or physically or destroying their property or if an enemy enjoying his success is to become negligent or weak due to [excessive] indulgence in hunting, gambling, women or drink, it will be easy to overpower him. If an enemy, when attacked, is likely to be found with all his troops in one place other than his fort, he will be easily overpowered, being friendless and unprotected by his fort (6.2).'

Two remarks are in order. First, according to Kautilya, wise kings (individuals) didn't put all their soldiers at one place and also did not indulge in gambling and other vices. Secondly, he showed awareness of a backward bending supply curve ('enjoying his success is to become negligent').

Mobilization of No More Than Three-Fourths of the Army: He further emphasized diversification. He (p 629) stated, 'A conqueror, having assured himself about his superiority in *power, place and time*, shall first leave behind a third or a quarter of his army to protect his capital, the rear, the forest regions and the borders; he shall then march towards the enemy taking with him enough wealth and forces to help him achieve his objective (9.1).' He wanted territorial expansion, subject to the preservation of existing territory. He advanced the basic principle: not to invest hundred percent in a risky venture. Although the context has changed, but the goal of risk reduction through diversification is an invariant one.[7]

19.4 MULTI-VARIABLE APPROACH TO SUCCESS OF A CAMPAIGN

Power, Place and Time: Kautilya (Kangle (Part II, p 407-408)) reviewed the relative importance of various factors as: '"Of power, place and time, however, power is superior", say the teachers. For, one possessed of power is able to counter-act (the difficulties of) marshy or dry region and (those) of time with cold, heat or rain. "Place is superior", say some. For, a dog on land drags a crocodile; a crocodile in water drags a dog. "Time is superior" say some (others). "By day a crow kills an owl, at night an owl kills a crow". "No" says Kautilya. Power, place and time are mutually helpful (9.1).'

Kautilya (p 681) suggested that a king should avoid harsh conditions, such as, 'having to fight in an unsuitable terrain and having to fight in an unsuitable season', which might adversely affect the efficiency of the army. He believed if the goal was to maximize the probability of success of a campaign with a minimum effort, a king should consider their most favourable combination since these variables were complementary to each other. That is, a king could not afford to ignore any one of them and therefore, should not concentrate on judging their relative influences. His ideas may be expressed as:

$$S = \alpha_0 + \alpha_1 RP_1 + \alpha_2 D_1 + \alpha_3 D_2 + \alpha_4 D_1 D_2 + u \qquad (19.1)$$

Where $D_1 = 1$ for an appropriate place
= 0 otherwise

Where $D_2 = 1$ for an appropriate time
= 0 otherwise

Where, S = success, relative power, $RP_1 = P^1/P^2$ = power of king one/power of king two (see Chapter 18 for notations) and u = random error.

According to Kautilya, the coefficient α_4 in Equation 19.1 should be positive since it measures the complementary nature of time and place. Of course, he was not concerned with its specification or estimation, which might be quite challenging. Since according to him, probability of success increased more than proportionately to the increases in relative power.

SUMMARY

Kautilya's predecessors compared only the expected returns of various projects or assets but he explicitly incorporated the risk-return trade-offs into his analyses related to various risky situations. He did not know how to measure variances and co-variances, yet he was aware of the possibility of risk reduction through diversification. It would seem that the ancient thinkers were as concerned about dealing with risk as we are. It is apparent that growth in economic knowledge is as much due to the advancement in probability theory and calculus as it is due to economists' own ingenuity.[8]

20

Time Inconsistency Problem and Asymmetric Information

> No enemy shall know his secrets. He shall, however, know all his enemy's weaknesses. Like a tortoise, he shall draw in any limb of his that is exposed.
>
> —*Kautilya (p 177)*

Although Kautilya did not provide any formal analysis on it, his informal approach contained many insights of a modern game theory. He incorporated foresight and the problem of 'credibility' into his analysis of strategic interactions. In fact, the application of the 'time inconsistency' problem in the case of a monetary policy appears to be 'much ado about nothing' compared to the one considered by Kautilya in which the sovereignty of a state was at stake. He emphasized the benefits of possessing asymmetric information in bargaining.

Kautilya envisaged for a king to incorporate the possibility of re-optimization by an ally into his current decision-making. Section 20.1

discusses his ideas on what nowadays is called the time inconsistency problem. He was aware of the role of asymmetric information and a few examples are presented in Section 20.2. It is shown that Kautilya applied an informal game-theoretic analysis.[1] Section 20.3 elaborates on his emphasis on seeking the advantages of private information in bargaining. Kautilya's analysis is implicit and elementary modern methods are used to make his ideas explicit.

He invariably insisted on applying the cost-benefit analysis before undertaking any project including waging a war. For example, Drekmeier (1962, p 157) observes, 'By the age of empire (and implicit in the Arthashastra of Kautilya), war had ceased to be regarded as an aristocratic pastime having as its main objective military glory, and had come to be conceived as an instrument for strengthening the state and enriching its treasury. War is now a serious business, not to be undertaken lightly and without weighing carefully the probabilities of success and defeat.'

20.1 KAUTILYA ON TIME INCONSISTENCY PROBLEM

At the time of Kautilya there was no central bank to undertake any monetary policy. Still the problem of credibility was perhaps quite serious, since not only the well being of the citizens but their independence also was at stake. It was not the public worrying about the credibility of the king but the king himself worrying about the credibility of other kings. The king needed cooperation of other kings to achieve certain objectives but faced a possible threat of a conflict in the future from the very same kings. Kautilya was acutely aware of the problem now called the problem of time inconsistency or credibility.[2]

Specification of a King's Objectives: According to Kautilya, a king should undertake the cost-benefit analysis of various policies, such as, whether to carry out a campaign alone or to form an alliance and how to choose an ally. A king's projected intermediate objective was to acquire power and ultimately enjoy prosperity and maintain independence. Kautilya (p 616) stated, 'Before undertaking a combined operation [with the forces of other rulers] a king shall carefully consider the reasons for waging war or making peace and join forces with powerful and upright rulers.' Further, 'The objective of a joint campaign is to acquire an ally, wealth or land; gaining one later in the list is preferable to one earlier. A king shall enter into a treaty and undertake a joint campaign, always keeping in mind his own objective, and after analyzing the clear and definite benefit or part benefit that will accrue to him (7.5).' Obviously, at that time, there was no opportunity for undertaking joint research ventures.

Implicit Two Period Analysis: Kautilya essentially considered a two period analysis. The policies to be adopted during the current period and the following period were analyzed right in the beginning itself. He discussed how a king should choose an ally, who helped the king achieve his current objective and did not turn against him in the future, causing loss of wealth and even his kingdom.

Insights into the Credibility Problem: The treaty must specify the contributions of King I and King II (his ally) to undertake a joint campaign and their shares in the acquisitions if there was a success in the campaign. Kautilya (p 572) stated, 'When the shares are specified before the start of the campaign it is normal to base them on the proportion of troops contributed; however, fixing the shares on the basis of the efforts made by each one during the campaign is the best type. Shares can also be based on the money contributed by each one or the plunder seized (7.4).' All the terms and conditions were specified before the start of the campaign. It may be noted that this specification falls under the open-loop control approach, whereas the classical approach (Bellman's approach) is categorized as the 'feedback or the closed-loop' control approach.[3]

In the current debate on the credibility problem, the central bank announces its monetary policies, which maximize its objective function, subject to public's reaction function to them. Once the public has incorporated the central bank's policies in its decisions, the central bank might change its initially announced policies to re-optimize its objective function. That is, the central bank may not keep its initial commitment. Kautilya analyzed the possibility of reneging that the commitments made by a strong king to a weak king might not be kept. The stronger king (King II) maximized his objective function, subject to the reactions of the weaker king (King I) to his commitments. King II was assumed to maximize his objective function, G^2 (r_1, r_2, A_1, A_2), which is assumed additive in the two periods. Kautilya's informal analysis can formally be presented as follows:

Max G^2 (r_1, r_2, A_1, A_2) = G^2_1 (r_1, A_1) + G^2_2 (r_2, A_2) (20.1)

Subject to the reaction functions r_1 and r_2 of King I

$r_1 = R_1$ (A_1, A_2) (20.2)

$r_2 = R_2$ (r_1, A_2) (20.3)

Where G^2_1 (r_1, A_1) = Objective function of King II for period one, which depended on the reaction function of King I for period one and his own policies, A_1 to be adopted for the first period, such as specifying his contributions towards the campaign.

G^2_2 (r_2, A_2) = Objective function of King II for period two, which depended on the reaction function of King I for period two and his own promises, A_2 to be kept for the second period, such as a promise of non-aggression and specification of shares in the seizures for period two.

Equation (20.2) indicates the reaction function, r_1 of King I for period one, which depends on the policy decisions of the King II in both the periods (ie. on A_1 and A_2).

Equation (20.3) indicates that the reaction function, r_2 of King I in period two depends on his decisions taken in period one (ie. r_1) and A_2.

Let A^*_1 and A^*_2 be the optimum values such that King II's objective function was maximized subject to the reaction functions of King I.[4] King II announces these policies (promises) at the beginning of period one. King I undertakes his measures, believing that king two would keep these promises. At the end of the first period (beginning of the second period), the reaction function of King I takes the form:

$r^*_1 = R_1$ (A^*_1, A^*_2).

Possible Re-optimization by King II: Kautilya (p 624) stated, 'The king may face dangers even from a trusted king of equal power, when the latter has achieved his objective. Even an equally powerful king tends to become stronger after the task is accomplished and, when his power has increased, becomes untrustworthy. Prosperity changes peoples' minds (7.5).'

Kautilya was quite concerned that the commitments made by King II (the ally) before the start of the campaign may not be honoured after its completion, since the actions of King II could not be constrained by current commitments in any credible way. According to Kautilya, the relative power of a king was one of the important determinants of success in a war and consequently the non-aggression treaty agreed upon by the second king might be annulled and he might turn against King I. Also, whatever shares were specified before the start of the campaign might not be optimal after a successful campaign. According to Kautilya, King II after a successful campaign, particularly if he was equal or stronger (and not upright), might decide to re-optimize. That is, King II could re-optimize his objective function for period two as follows:

Max $G^2_2 = G^2_2 (r_2, A_2)$ (20.4)
Subject to
$r_2 = R_2 (r^*_1, A_2)$ (20.5)

Let A^C_2 be the revised policy adopted to maximize G^2_2 in equation (20.4) subject to r_2 in equation (20.5). According to Kautilya, it was likely to be different from the initial policy A^*_2 that is, $A^C_2 \neq A^*_2$ and particularly, if the second king was not upright. In other words, according to Kautilya, King II was likely to cheat on his promises, implying he could attack King I or not give his due share out of the loot and land acquired through a successful campaign.

Precautionary Measures in Anticipation of Possible Reneging by King II: Kautilya suggested that King I should take defensive measures to protect his interests against the likely reneging by King II (his ally) on the contractual arrangements. He suggested specific actions to be undertaken by King I, depending on the anticipated circumstances. He (p 596) stated, 'If a king believes that the one to whom troops are lent will, after achieving the objective for which they were hired; appropriate them himself, send them to hostile lands or jungles, or, in some fashion make them useless, the forces shall not be lent, using the pretext that they are needed elsewhere.

'If, however, he is obliged to lend his troops, they shall be lent only for the limited period of that campaign, on condition that they shall stay and fight together and be protected from all dangers till the end of the campaign; as soon as the campaign is over, they shall be withdrawn on some pretext (7.8).' Further (p 624), 'If the stronger ruler is not upright, the king shall quickly withdraw under some pretext, when the work has been done. If the stronger ruler is upright, the king shall wait until he is given permission to leave. The king shall make all efforts to move away from a dangerous situation, after ensuring the safety of the queen. Even if the king receives a small share, or even no share, from a stronger king, he shall go away with a 'seemingly' content look. Later, when the strong king comes under the king's power [for any reason], twice the loss shall be exacted.'

Kautilya (p 609) stated, 'An ally who is likely to grow in power after defeating the enemy and thus become uncontrollable shall be embroiled in a conflict with his own neighbour and his own ally; or, a pretender in his family or an unjustly treated prince shall be encouraged to seize the throne; or such actions shall be taken as would oblige the ally to remain obedient, in return for help received (7.18).'

If King I was the Campaign Leader: Kautilya (p 624) suggested, 'The king, when he himself has led the allies to victory, shall let the others go, after giving them their due shares. He should, if necessary, forgo his own share and not deprive them of theirs. It is thus that a king will win the affection of his Circle of States (7.5).'

Several points are noteworthy. First, Kautilya displayed an insight into the time inconsistency problem. His suggestion to King I comprised, taking defensive measures to protect against a possible reneging and a threat of aggression against him by King II. Kautilya was aware of the irresistible temptation, on the part of the leader of a joint campaign, to cheat his followers and advance his own objectives. Blackburn and Christensen (1989) also point out the possibility of such an outcome. They state, 'A non-cooperative Stackelberg game possesses a definite hierarchical structure in the sense that some players (leaders) have the potential to impose their policies on others (followers).' They add, 'This is because of an incentive for a leader to improve his own payoff by reneging (cheating) on his promised action, an indication that the optimal policy in Stackelberg games is dynamically inconsistent.' It also implies that every king would like to be a leader and as Nicholson (1985, p 458-459) notes, which might have disastrous consequences. Secondly, a 'tit for tat' motivation was also present. If the leader of a campaign (King II) did not fulfill his commitments, he should be given the same treatment whenever he came under the leadership of King I. Thirdly, Kautilya recommended to a king to build his reputation to be trustworthy, which might be an asset in maintaining or forming new coalitions in the future.

Trust as the Primary Criterion in the Selection of an Ally: Selecting a conservative Federal Reserve Bank Chairman (or Governor of a Central Bank) has been recommended to resolve the inconsistency or credibility problem. Similarly, Kautilya recommended that an ally should be upright. He ranked possible allies according to their trustworthiness, and current and future potential gains to the king. He (p 606) explained, 'The best ally is one who has the following six qualities: an ally of the family for a long time, constant, amenable to control, powerful in his support, sharing a common interest, able to mobilize his forces quickly and not a man who betrays his friends (7.9).'

Kautilya (p 606) elaborated on these qualities, 'A true friend is one who shares with the king a common objective, is helpful, never changes and never double crosses even when the king is in trouble (7.9).' Further (p 607), 'That friend, whose friendship has endured since earlier times and who protects and is in turn protected out of love and not for mercenary reasons is called a constant ally (7.9).'

An ally should be trustworthy and capable of helping the king. However, sometimes, the choice may not be that easy. For example, some possible allies who are equal or stronger than the king may be capable of helping but not trustworthy and others may be controllable but weak.

Kautilya (p 573) held, 'Amity with a more powerful monarch carries great danger for kings, except when one is actually at war with an enemy (7.2).' Further (p 616), 'As between joining forces with a ruler who is stronger than the king or with two rulers of strength equal to the king, it is better to join two equal kings. For with one ruler, the stronger ruler will have the upper hand during the campaign, whereas with two equals the king can keep control. If one of them turns treacherous, it will be easy for the other two to suppress him and make him suffer the consequences of the dissent (7.5).'

Kautilya favoured weaker kings for an alliance since they could not dare to renege on their commitments whereas equal or stronger kings might not keep their commitments. Also, if a king did not trust another king, he should try to avoid forming an alliance with him. In the light of above statements, matrix 20.1 may be used to capture his ideas regarding potential allies.[5]

Matrix 20.1: Selection of an Ally

King I	King II	
	Not Revise	Revise
Believe	Weaker or upright	
Not Believe		Equal or Stronger and not upright

The above matrix may be used to express Kautilya's classification of all possible allies. For example, if King II had the six qualities or had the reputation to be upright (who did not revise) or was weak (who could not revise), he recommended the strategy (believe, not revise), that is the upper left cell. On the other hand, if King II was equal, or stronger, King I should adopt the strategy (not believe, revise), that is the lower right cell.

20.2 KAUTILYA ON ASYMMETRIC INFORMATION

Kautilya pointed out that for proper formulation and effective implementation of a plan, a king must collect as much information as possible. However, he did not explicitly dwell on the cost of gathering information about other kingdoms and in protecting one's own privacy and might have considered it a normal function of the state. But he did emphasize that possession of private information provided a definite advantage over rivals. His (p 177) advice to a king was: 'No enemy shall know his secrets. He shall, however, know all his enemy's weaknesses. Like a tortoise, he shall draw in any limb of his that is exposed (1.15).' As discussed above (18.2), Kautilya suggested setting-up an intelligence apparatus to gather information on other kingdoms.

He provided several applications of asymmetric information. This section lists some of those applications and presents a detailed analysis of one of them, in the next section.

Offering a Lemon

- A king knew the quality of his land, which was poor but the buyer of the land did not know anything about its quality. Kautilya (p 621) stated, 'If a settlement of a tract is likely to entail heavy losses or expenditure, a king shall first sell the land, with the intention of reacquiring it, to one who will fail in the attempt at settlement. Such agreements shall remain verbal (7.11).'
- Similarly, Kautilya made recommendations as to what kind of land to give to neutralize an antagonist. He (p 612) suggested to give 'useless land' to 'enemies in the rear, such as jungle chiefs'; 'land not yielding a livelihood' to a 'forest thief' and 'land affording no shelter' to 'one who deserts the army' (7.16). The basic idea is the same that the giver knew the quality of the land but the receiver did not.

Treaty Negotiation: Kautilya displayed the same bargaining skill in using the asymmetrical information in giving a hostage as part of a treaty. He (p 599) stated, 'He who gives a treacherous minister or a treacherous son or daughter as a hostage outmanoeuvres [the receiver]. The receiver is outmanoeuvred because the giver will strike without compunction at the weak point— ie. the trust that the receiver has that the giver will not let the hostage come to harm (7.17).' The giver knew the uselessness of the hostage but the receiver did not have this information and therefore, accepted this as part of the negotiated treaty.

20.3 KAUTILYA ON BARGAINING WITH PRIVATE INFORMATION

Although Kautilya was not aware of the distinction between a strategic game and an extensive game, an example of an extensive game from the Arthashastra is presented below. This case deals with a situation in which a weak king faced an aggression from a strong king. Kautilya laid out five stages of an extensive game and provided an exhaustive list of possibilities at each stage. He developed the strategies and actions to be undertaken by the weak king to minimize his losses. According to him, the main objective of a weak king should be to explore such ways as to minimize his losses. He reviewed the prevailing views on how a weak king should respond to an attack by a stronger king. He (p 664) stated (the views of earlier thinkers), 'Bharadvaja says that a weak king, when attacked by a stronger king, shall bend like a reed and surrender his all. For he who submits to a strong king, bows to Indra. [On the other hand] Vishalaksha says that a weak king shall fight with his resources, for only with valour can one surmount calamities. It is the *dharma* of a *Kshatriya* to fight, whether he wins or loses.'

'Kautilya disagrees with both. He, who surrenders all, lives only a life of despair, like a sheep that has strayed from its herd. On the other hand, one fighting with a tiny army perishes like one trying to cross the ocean without a boat. It is better to seek the protection of a powerful king or an impregnable fort. The weaker king shall offer, by one means or another, that which the other will, in any case, take by force. It is life that is worth preserving not wealth which, being impermanent, can be given up without regrets (12.1).'

Kautilya suggested that the strategies and actions to be undertaken by a weak king should depend on the type of the attacker. He (p 664) listed three types of aggressors with their characteristics: '(i) The righteous aggressor is satisfied with submission. The weak yield to him, particularly when there is a danger from another enemy. (ii) The greedy aggressor is satisfied with seizing land and goods. The weak king shall give up wealth to him. (iii) The monstrous aggressor is satisfied only when he takes the land, goods, wives, sons and even the life of the defeated. A weak king may give up land and goods but shall not let himself be taken (12.1).'

Several Points are Worth Noting

- It is interesting to point out that the solution suggested by Bharadvaja is identical to the one reached through backward induction, which is: the realization on the part of a weak king that he was going to lose ultimately, so why fight, to begin with? It is comparable to the 'nuisance suits' in which backward induction leads the plaintiff to drop the case.
- The earlier thinkers suggest only two extreme choices, which according to Kautilya, were undesirable. Kautilya suggested that the weak king should explore additional options such as seeking protection of a strong king or of a fort. He (p 664) recommended, 'When attacked by a strong king, a weak king shall seek the protection of a king who is stronger than the aggressor and who cannot be swayed by the diplomacy of the aggressor trying to outmanoeuvre the weak king (7.5).' He (p 665) added, 'If a weak king cannot find any other king to protect him, he shall seek shelter in a fort; it shall be such that the aggressor, even with a large force, cannot cut off supplies of food, fodder, fuel and water and shall be so impregnable that the aggressor will suffer heavy losses and expenses if he tries to take it (7.15).'
- Moreover, before surrendering, the weak king should find out the 'type' of the aggressor. Since his life and honour might depend on it.
- Kautilya used every opportunity to emphasize the importance ('like one trying to cross the ocean without a boat') of capital.

It seems that Kautilya dealt extensively only with the third type of aggressor (ie. the monstrous one). He laid out an extensive game plan to minimize a weak king's losses. He (p 668-674) listed five stages of an aggression: (i) the strong king was getting ready to attack, (ii) he started the march, (iii) he put the siege on the fort, (iv) weak king's defeat was imminent and (v) after a weak king got defeated, Kautilya recommended various strategies and actions to be undertaken by a weak king at each stage to minimize his losses.

Aggressor Planning to Attack: Kautilya (p 668) stated, 'When an aggressor is on the point of attacking, the weak king has three choices:

he can make peace with the aggressor, try to avert the attack by diplomacy or wage secret warfare. He shall try to win over the sections favourable to him in the aggressor's camp by means of conciliation and gifts and prevent treachery in his own camp by sowing dissension and use of force. At this stage the weak king may make peace without taking any action to harm the aggressor (12.1).'

The Aggressor Started the March: Kautilya suggested that if the attempt to avert the attack failed and the aggressor [has] started the march, [at this stage], the weaker king should consider: (a) suing for peace again (b) reasoning with the aggressor about the soundness of the attack (c) undermining the aggressor (d) using the circle of kings, and (e) counter attack.

Suing for Peace: It may be mentioned that Kautilya preferred peace to war. He (p 568) recommended, 'When the benefit accruing to kings under a treaty, irrespective of their status as the weaker, equal or stronger king, is fair to each one, peace by the agreement shall be preferred course of action; if the benefits are to be unfairly distributed, war is preferable (7.8).' It is also clear from another statement. Kautilya (p 635) asserted, 'That which entails small losses is a gain by diplomacy rather than by war (9.4).'

Kautilya (p 668-669) suggested, 'In negotiating for peace the weak king shall successively offer a quarter more of money and arms each day until the offer is accepted. If the weak king seeks peace on condition of surrendering a portion of his forces and the offer is accepted, he shall give dull and cowardly elephants and horses; if he has to give active and energetic animals, a long-acting poison shall be administered to them. If peace is sought on condition of paying money, the weak king shall give articles of high value for which there are no buyers, or forest produce that is unfit for use in war. If the condition is surrender of land, weak king shall give land that can be easily recovered, which has permanent enemies, which provides no shelter or which can only be settled with heavy losses and expenses (12.1).'

The importance of asymmetric information may be noted here since the weaker king had full information about his mammals and materials but the aggressor did not. Secondly, the administration of a 'poison pill' is an old idea to combat a hostile take-over. Kautilya always preferred friendly mergers than hostile takeovers. Thirdly, he was aware of the illiquidity of high value items. Essentially, the weaker king wanted to make sure that his own resources were not used against him. Finally, it is significant to note that all the elements of bargaining were present in Kautilya's analysis: the frequency of an offer, the cost of rejecting an offer, the number of offers and the magnitude and the rate of adjustment in the offer. For example, just one offer was made every day. That means, the aggressor had to maintain his forces for another day if he rejected the offer. Also, it gives a signal to the aggressor that the weak king was not unduly frightened of him.

Kautilya's Implicit Model of Bargaining: Suppose the aggressor believed that π was the probability of a victory, the expected gain from the attack would be πY (where Y = value of (land + loot + fort)). Let the cost of the aggression, $C = F + V$ where F was the fixed cost of preparation for the war, and $V = s\,t$, the variable cost which depended on the size of the army, s and the time, t during which it was on the move, that is, $C = F + s\,t$.

Expected initial net gain to the aggressor, $Z_0 = \pi Y - F$

If the weak king wanted the stronger king to accept his initial offer, X_0, then

$$X_0 \geq Z_0 \qquad (20.6)$$

For example, if t=0, π =0.6, Y=1000, F= 20, the aggressor would expect that the initial offer by the weak king should be such that, $X_0 \geq 600 - 20 = 580$. If the weak king made an initial offer, $X_0 = 100$, it was likely to be rejected by the aggressor. Kautilya suggested that 'the weak king should successively offer a quarter more of money and arms each day, that is, $X_t = X_0 (1+\theta)^t$, where X_0 was the initial offer and $\theta = 0.25$. As an illustration, the weak king should increase the offer to 125 (= 100 (1+0.25)) the next day and keep doing this until the offer was accepted. However, the net gain to the aggressor would be, $Z_t = 100 (1+0.25)^t - 20 - 5\,t$, if s =5 per day. Kautilya offered many other suggestions to the weak king to escape from this predicament.

Reasoning with the Aggressor: According to Kautilya, a weak king should try to dissuade the aggressor from attacking by bringing out all the consequences of the aggression to him. He (p 669) suggested, 'If the aggressor declines to conclude a peace treaty, the weak king shall try to persuade him to do so by reasoning with him. The arguments to be used are that the strong king (i) was being misled by friends in name but enemies in reality, (ii) was frightening all his allies, (iii) was promoting the interests of his enemies, and (iv) because of all this, he was risking his wealth and his life (12.2).'

If the bargaining for peace failed, the weak king should consider undermining the aggressor, seeking support of his circle of kings and even contemplating a counter attack.

The following argument is particularly worth noting. Kautilya (p 670) stated, '[The envoy, shall also point out the following]. The weak king, who had many allies, would get many more with the things [forces, men, wealth or land] rejected by the strong king: together they could attack the strong king from all sides. While the weak king still enjoyed the support of his own circle of kings, the Middle king and the Neutral king, all these had abandoned the strong aggressor. For they were just waiting for him to start the war, incur heavy losses and expenses, be cut off from his allies and lose his control over his stronghold; then they would strike and overwhelm him (12.2).'

First, according to Kautilya, the weak king should let the aggressor know that there were alternative uses of the men and materials being offered to him. This is quite significant, since it indicates that Kautilya was aware of the concept of opportunity cost. The weak king should negotiate with other kings also. He could present the rejected offer X_t to them, or some other amount, M, to win their support. So long $M \leq X_t$, he was better off by seeking support of his Circle of Kings.

Secondly, according to Kautilya, the weak king should try to convince the aggressor that his estimate of the probability of winning was too optimistic, a more realistic probability was, $\pi^* < \pi$ (his estimate). Similarly, aggressor's estimate of the cost of war was unrealistically low since he was ignoring the losses of men and material in war, and also the loss resulting from the desertion of his allies. Clearly, the aggressor and the weak king had differences over the magnitudes of the probability of winning, the cost of operation and the duration of the operation.[6] The aggressor might be overestimating his power and the weak king might be underestimating the power of the aggressor. They revealed their private information through various rounds of negotiations. But, in the mean time until their differences got resolved, the aggressor was expending resources on keeping his forces moving.

The Aggressor Put the Siege: According to Kautilya, the weak king under siege should consider the following: (a) take some necessary precautions (such as to burn any grass and wood around the fort to improve visibility and deny the enemy any cover) as the aggressor approaches to lay the siege, (b) use of tunnels (to move away men and materials), (c) leave the fort without surrendering, (d) deprive the besieger of men and material, and (e) keep trying to make peace.

Defeat was Imminent: According to Kautilya (p 673), 'When the besieged king's resources are totally exhausted, he shall abandon the fort and escape, by secret tunnel, by digging a new passage or by breaching a wall of the fort. Alternatively, may mount a surprise night attack (12.5).'

After the Defeat: If the weak king was unable to escape, he should hide inside the fort and wait for an opportunity to strike. Kautilya (p 674) suggested, 'If the fort is taken, the king shall hide himself in a sanctuary where plenty of food has been stored. He shall lie low until the victorious occupier forgets him and becomes careless (12.5).'

SUMMARY

Magill and Quinzii (1996, p 14) observe, 'The classical economists, however, provided no explicit description of the way economic activity over time is organized through contracts and, that self-interested behavior may create difficulties for the functioning of a system based on contractual commitments is of much more recent origin.' The reality is quite the contrary. The problem of time inconsistency has been recognized and incorporated into decision-making, at least, by Kautilya. It is clear that Kautilya inherited very little from his predecessors. Credit for anticipating and dealing with the problem of credibility, and showing understanding that the possession of asymmetric information confers advantages in negotiations, goes solely to Kautilya. Additionally, the concept of coordination failure is also discernible in the *Arthashastra*. Kautilya (p 193) asserts, 'The armed forces—elephants, chariots, cavalry and infantry— shall each be under more than one chief. For, with many chiefs, mutual fear will prevent them from succumbing to the temptations of the enemy.' According to him, the coordination problems become almost insurmountable if the number is more than four.

Epilogue
Kautilya's Place in Economic Thought

> Every age has its myths and calls them higher truths.
> — *Anonymous*

Kautilya's *Arthashastra* is a mine full of jewels and this work has brought out only a handful of them to the surface, and a lot of polishing will be required to bring out their full luster. The Arthashastra, far removed in time from the heat of current controversies provides a clearer picture of universal human tendencies, such as risk-aversion, rent-seeking and greed and suggests that society tirelessly search for ways to reduce risk and contain excessive greed and rent-seeking activities.

So far as the Western world is concerned, Adam Smith has been credited with founding economics during the 18th century AD. However, economic reasoning had achieved a much higher level of sophistication two thousand years earlier in India. The detailed expositions of dozens of concepts have been offered in Chapters 3 to 20 to dispel the three long-standing myths that: (i) economics originated in the eighteenth century; (ii) Adam smith was the founder of economics; and (iii) Hindu civilization chose social stability over economic growth. Section 21.1 contains a brief summary of Kautilya's original contributions and their relevance for today's economies to dispel these myths. Kautilya fully embraced and promoted secular virtues as enshrined in the Vedas. He performed a holistic (Vedic) marriage between *dharma* (ethics) and *artha* (economics) and provided sacred vows (guidelines) for this marriage to last forever. This is presented in Section 21.2. Section 21.3 urges the economic profession to honour the true founder of economics.

21.1 RECAPITULATION OF KAUTILYA'S CONTRIBUTIONS

Kautilya (p 99) describes his work as: This *Arthashastra* is a compendium of almost all similar treatises, composed by ancient teachers, on the acquisition and protection of territory. Easy to grasp and understand, free from verbosity, Kautilya has composed this treatise with precise words, doctrines and sense (1.1).' Kautilya was a humble man and wrote the *Arthashastra* in a third person to avoid any feelings of ego. He considered it as a survey of the existing literature on the subject. But it is actually a different sort of survey full of new analytical methods and concepts. Contemporary surveys hardly offer any synthesis or new concepts.

Formalism in economics is a relatively new phenomenon. Just like the classicists, Kautilya did not provide a formal analysis or any formal definitions of the concepts. However, the *Arthashastra* is consistent, comprehensive, broad in scope and above all original. With the exception of a few concepts, such as bounded rationality and identification of factor payments, credit for the origination of other concepts discussed in the *Arthashastra* goes to Kautilya. It is amazing that anyone before Biblical times, was aware of the most fundamental concepts in economics: opportunity cost, producer surplus, efficiency wage, public goods, the Kautilya Curve (nowadays called the Dupuit-

Laffer Curve), risk-premium, time inconsistency, moral hazard, and many more such concepts.

Origin of Economics: Kautilya identified philosophy, political science, the Vedas and economics as four separate disciplines. It appears that at the time there was some controversy as to whether economics was a separate discipline. He reestablished economics as a separate discipline with a very broad scope. In fact, colonization of other disciplines by economics is discernible in his analysis.

Methodology: Kautilya used an inductive approach to make a point. He implicitly, but frequently, resorted to 'all other things being equal' and invariably specified all the variables being held constant. Kautilya used marginalism (discrete), at least a rudimentary demand and supply analysis, and the distinction between the short-run and the long run. His approach was always one of constrained optimization. He came very close to proposing the axioms of comparison and consistency in making choices. It is also obvious from his analysis that the ordinal approach is more natural than the cardinal one and surely came before it.

Self-interest: First of all, it is clear from Kautilya's analysis that self-interest is part of human DNA (or of the survival kit). All the religions, moral philosophy, and constitutions have been attempting to modify or contain it. But so far, these perhaps have succeeded only in sugar coating it. And the other motivations like reciprocity and fairness may be described merely as enlightened self-interest.

Demand and Supply Analysis: Kautilya offered a rudimentary demand-supply analysis, which has a serious claim to be a forerunner of the neoclassical one. He never created the so-called water-diamond paradox. According to him, it was simply a question of demand and supply of diamond in explaining why its price was so high. He was also aware of the instability of demand for durable goods like diamonds. He understood and applied the concepts of illiquidity and to some extent discounting in decision-making.

Law of Diminishing Returns: Kautilya's understanding of this law is at par with that of Ricardo (and of Adam Smith). He had an extensive discussion on the gradations of land and increasing amounts of inputs needed to develop or cultivate them.

Role of the Government: Kautilya proposed a mixed economy with private property rights, along with a very active role for the government. According to him, the government should work for the prosperity, security, and service of the public. He recommended not only national security but security of income also, that is protecting the public not only against foreign aggression but also against poverty, diseases and famines. He emphasized the creation and administration of a fair judicial system and promotion of economic activity. He proposed the regulation of monopoly, monopsony, and externalities.

Consumer Protection: He suggested several measures to ensure product choice, product quality, fair price and service to the consumers and to protect them against fraud.

Labour Contracts: Kautilya was way ahead of his time. He believed in the explicit specification of employment contracts and recommended their strict upholding. Similarly, he displayed a postmodern mental make-up in an ancient body. He proposed laws against child labour, and sexual harassment.

Income Tax: Kautilya implicitly recommended a linear income tax and considered strict compliance as an integral part of the tax system. He understood the harmful effects of heavy taxation. Despite considerable progress in our understanding, we are not any closer to finding an answer to the basic question: how progressive should the tax rate be?

Economic Growth and Ethical Values: Kautilya identified increases in land, labour and capital as the sources of economic growth and suggested several measures to encourage capital formation. He recommended the elimination of all impediments to growth. He argued that increases in inputs were dependent on good institutions and good governance, which in turn were dependent on ethical conduct. According to him, ethical conduct was the deep determinant, and not institutions, of prosperity. It is a gross misconception to suggest that Hindu civilization chose social stability and order over economic growth. Kautilya considered poverty as a living death, and his analysis makes it clear that Mokyr's assertions are vain and counterfactual. There is nothing in Hinduism that hinders economic growth.

Judicial System: Kautilya believed in the rule of law and a fair judicial system. He discussed the role of just, certain and proportionate punishment on prevention of crimes. He specified the standard of proof and made every possible effort to minimize legal errors. He preferred fines to non-monetary punishments. Most significantly, he was aware of the potential threat to judicial integrity from rent-seeking behavior of the law enforcers.

Principal-agent Problem: Kautilya recognized the agency problems (or the moral hazard problem), and recommended profit sharing, the efficiency wages, tenure and promotions, tournaments, merit pay and bonuses to elicit effort. For certain tasks (milking cows), he suggested cash payments only rather than the customary payment as a share of the current output to alleviate the problem of moral hazard. In addition, he recommended restrictions to reduce potential opportunities for distractions (clearly pornographic-sites on the Internet and Facebook are not the only distractions).

Role of Education: The role of education was described as fourfold: (i) learning of some facts (ii) learning of useful skills (iii) learning to think and to help ease the limitations of bounded rationality and (iv) developing self-discipline in controlling harmful emotions (irrationality), implying endogenous nature of preferences. Kautilya did relate a person's innate abilities to his ease of learning implying education serves as a 'signal' also.

Evaluation of a Policy: According to Kautilya, the formulation and evaluation of a policy required the ability to predict and to separate the total variation into the explained and the unexplained components. It is understandable that in the absence of statistical methods at the time, Kautilya did not know how to undertake the analysis of variance but he fully understood its significance in the evaluation of a policy.

Risk-return Trade-off and Diversification: Kautilya incorporated the risk-aversion behavior into decision-making and implicitly alluded to risk premium. It is remarkable that his analysis touched on the invariance hypothesis and the asset reversion hypothesis. Markowitz proposes the invariance hypothesis by pointing out that the poor and the rich behave in a similar fashion since both buy insurance policies and lotteries, implying a horizontal shift in the utility function. However, Kautilya did not believe in the invariance hypothesis, since according to him, the rich and the poor behaved differently. Similarly, Kautilya's analysis throws some light on the current debate over the relevance of loss aversion versus asset-reversion. According to him, where it was a life and death question, loss-aversion might be relevant.

Time Inconsistency: Kautilya was aware of the time inconsistency or the credibility problem and incorporated it in his recommendations to the king to guard against it. He understood the importance of asymmetric information.

Origination of Accounting Methods: Kautilya's contributions, particularly related to the origin of the theory of accounting, are not discussed here. The reader is referred to Mattessich (2000) for an excellent discussion on this subject. However, one specific point needs to be made regarding accounting. Just like the invention of the time clock facilitated measurement of labour productivity, similarly profit maximization is not possible without the knowledge of accounting methods. It means that the innovation of accounting methods, just like the innovations of writing and printing may be labeled a GPT (General Purpose Technology). In fact, Kautilya was so far ahead of his time that most of his insights are as relevant today as they were then.

21.2 KAUTILYA'S NOTEWORTHY INSIGHTS

Kautilya understood the foundational role of *Dharma*. He extended its role to liberation from poverty and to lowering the systemic risk. He accomplished this new role of ethics by performing a holistic marriage between ethics and economics, with each being an equal partner. He realized that unless the formulation and implementation of laws and policies were guided and informed by *dharma*, the newlywed might part ways, that is, they might weaken the ethical foundations or crowd-out moral motivation. That meant, unless the decision-makers were ethical, both formulation of laws and policies and their implementation would, more likely, be guided by self-interest and would be far less effective than intended. Some of the government employees might become corrupt, promote corrupt people and pollute the ethical environment. Therefore, he put heavy emphasis on ethical anchoring of the decision-makers—the king, his advisers and other employees—to prevent moral failure. Let me briefly restate some of Kautilya's insights that have more relevance today than in his day.

- An ounce of ethics was better than a ton of laws. Ethical anchoring could be more effective in preventing systemic risk than a heap of rules and regulations.
- Principles were only as good as the people who practiced them, and policies were only as good as the people who formulate and implement them.
- Material incentives should complement and not substitute moral incentives so that there is no crowding-out.
- Education should include ethical education also. Secular values, such as non-violence, honesty, truthfulness, compassion and tolerance do not violate the separation between religion and state.
- Market failure is bad, government failure is worse but moral failure is the worst since moral failure is true cause for other failures.
- Ethics and foresightedness could improve governance and bring sustainable prosperity for the whole of humanity.
- Sound organizational design could complement the ethics-based

approach by enhancing specialization and reducing the scope for conflict of interest situations.
- Wisdom is the most valuable asset and knowledge-management is a subset of management by wisdom.

21.3 GIVING KAUTILYA HIS DUE RECOGNITION AS THE FOUNDER OF ECONOMICS

Adam Smith came to be accepted as the founder of economics based on the arguments that (i) he was the first one to write a treatise on economics, and (ii) he synthesized brilliantly the existing ideas. Recently, Samuelson has added another argument that Smith was also a good theorist, who made original contributions.

It is obvious from the above analysis in Chapters 3 to 20 that Kautilya was the first economist who accomplished all these feats two thousand years earlier than Adam Smith. Indeed, Kautilya carved out economics as a separate discipline. Additionally, his *Arthashastra* is much more sophisticated both in method and content than Adam Smith's *Wealth of Nations*. In fact, based on the degree of sophistication of Kautilya's analysis, it could be claimed that he was a neoclassical before the classicists.

Over the years, the number of issues has increased significantly, if not exponentially, due to increased urbanization, industrialization, financial sophistication, population and pollution. Correspondingly, economic analysis too has acquired much sophistication. The deductive approach has been supplanting the inductive approach, the Euclidean space is being replaced by Hilbert Space and simple functions are being replaced by 'functionals', the 'shall' has changed into modest 'may' in economic analysis. But, despite the increased sophistication, which at times appears beyond comprehension, the true 'core' of economic analysis, which, certainly has expanded in scope and depth, and the basic assumptions of rationality and optimization subject to constraints, have not changed a whole lot during the last two thousand years. Similarly, despite changes of epic proportions in circumstances, the validity and usefulness of Kautilya's insights have not diminished.

In the light of Kautilya's monumental and original contributions to economics, he should rightfully be acknowledged as the true founder of economics. In fact, the above formulation finds a very close match between the methods and contents of the *Arthashastra* and those of the modern and post-modern economics.

Endnotes

PROLOGUE

1. Ray (1999, p 119) states, 'Apart from the many authors like Asvaghosa, Kalidas, Bana, Visakhadatta, Dandin and others who were conversant with it, we have references to it and quotations from it right down to the days of Millnatha and Charitravardhana in the 14th and 15th centuries AD. It may have lost much of its validity with the establishment of the Mogul Empire and particularly with the advent of the British rule.'
2. It is a well-established fact that the *Arthashastra* has a strong conceptual and theoretical base. Parmar (1987, p 5) writes, 'Kautilya's *Arthashastra* is different from the rest of the ancient works both in its plan and purpose. Whenever Kautilya refers to the views of his predecessors, his scrutiny and analysis are based on a sound judgment and give an evidence of his superior political insight and practical wisdom. He is not merely a preserver of old political ideas but a creator of new ones. He is impatient with the existing unsystematic and chaotic theories of polity and removes

the cobwebs in political thinking through his incisive logic and firm grasp of the realities of statecraft.'

Similarly, Drekmeier (1962, p 167) observes, 'It is a theoretical work, and any attempt to deduce more than the broad outlines of the Mauryan administrative system from it must bear this in mind.' Kumar (1989, p xxv) also notes: 'Thus he stands out as the foremost theorist of ancient India and the first to prepare a scientific treatise on state-craft with economics as the basic factor.'

CHAPTER - 2

1. Kumar (1989, p xviii) notes, 'With a clear, logical mind, he hardly betrays any confusion of thought. One might agree or not with him on all points but he is seldom vague or inconsistent.' However, see Kangle (part III, p 40-42) for a few insignificant ones.
2. Even renowned writers have been inconsistent. As Barber (1967, p 51) notes, 'Smith's talents as a synthesizer, however, were the source of some analytical imperfections in his writing. At a number of points he offered explanations that were ambiguous or inconsistent.' Similarly, the remarks by Grampp (2000) about Adam Smith that 'to make the ideas of Smith consistent, an honour he was not sure he merited' are quite indicative.

    Sandel (2009, p 201) comments, 'Aristotle's own theory of justice provides ample resources for a critique of his own views on slavery.' That is, if Aristotle had followed his own reasoning, he would have rejected slavery.
3. Drekmeier (1962, p 260) writes: 'By the fifth and fourth centuries BC the ancient tribal institutions had lost their ability to regulate society effectively. New modes of production, new types of social relationships, new salvation theologies were changing the old ways. Kautilya was the theorist who most clearly saw the need for expanded state authority to fill the ever-widening gaps left by the declining authority of tradition. The king needed greater freedom of movement if he was to provide security and the conditions of prosperity. The state was forced to take measures that frequently ran counter to the accepted moral standards of the community. But Kautilya well knew that such policies were all that could save society from collapse. He was led inevitably to a theory approximating the reason of state arguments of sixteenth-century Europe. But he sought to emphasize the fact that such actions were

not irresponsible. Indeed, it is the duty of the ruler to his subjects that compels him to take drastic steps to ensure their welfare. Survival and progress are recognized as bestowing authority.'

4. Drekmeier notes that the emergence of an economic surplus in ancient India made it possible to support a rich culture and help in the rise of an empire. He (1962, p 105) describes, 'With the coming of an agricultural economy, there came also the promise of economic surplus—the production of goods and services in excess of what was needed for survival. This is the condition of civilization: the possibility of supporting a culture-creating class of professionals. It may have seemed to many in the sixth and fifth centuries that instead of yearning for a golden yesterday, men might confidently anticipate a bountiful age yet to come. The Ganges valley in the seventh century was the home of a nascent capitalism as well. These new sources of wealth were to make possible the fulfillment of imperial ambitions. Empire had not been economically feasible until this development.' Similarly, Thapar (1997, p 142) remarks, 'The Mauryan period was the culminating epoch of a few centuries of rational inquiry and cultural advance.'

Law (1925) explores the economic conditions during the 5th century BCE in India. He (p 114) concludes, 'We thus see that the wealth of India was already famous even in the early days of Herodotus. There are also a few other evidences which indicate that India was a rich country.'

Basham (1959, p 216) states, 'A form of industrial organization on a larger scale than the individual craftsman, and probably more common than the entrepreneur, was the workmen's co-operative group, perhaps comparable to the pre-revolutionary Russian cartel.'

5. There is other evidence also of an active trade between Mesopotamia and Mohenjodaro (a fully developed city with modern amenities) from the era of the Harappan culture, which flourished in the Indus valley between 2500-1800 BCE. Majumdar (1980, p 274) notes, 'About two dozen seals, some actual Harappan, others copying Harappa, have been discovered from Susa and Mesopotamian cities. Actual exports from Mohenjodaro to these cities, as revealed by exploration, were carnelian beads, and shell and bone inlays, but it is possible that the volume of trade consisted of such perishable material as cotton or cotton textiles, spices, or timber.' He continues, 'There is another evidence which, though not positive, is now practically accepted by all scholars as indicative of trade between Indus cities and Mesopotamia. Sumerian and Akkadian

documents record that in the time of Sargon of Agade (c. 2350 BC) and during the succeeding centuries merchants of Mesopotamia, particularly of Ur, carried [on] brisk trade with various countries including Dilmun or Tilmun, Magan and Meluhha, which are now usually identified with Bahrain, Oman or Mahran and India respectively, though some scholars are inclined to identify Dilmun itself with India.' Majumdar (p 364) adds, 'In the ancient world, Bactria was an important center where the trade routes from India, China, Central Asia and the Mediterranean world joined.'

CHAPTER - 3

1. Groenewegen (2002, p 67-68) approaches the question related to the origin of economics very methodically. He believes that the answer to this question depends on which definition of economics is used. As an illustration, if Robbins' definition is used then the later half of the 19th century may be declared as the era of the origin of economics. He (p 48-68) lists 'concerted scientific effort', 'the widening scope', 'the analysis of capital and the development of a three factor model' and 'the development of some general, unifying principles' as the four unique characteristics of the third quarter (1748-1776) of the 18th century to declare it as the period of the origin of economics. He (p 87) adds, 'The evidence marshalled by Hutchison reinforces the now widely held belief that economics emerged as a separate science during the period of just over a quarter of a century ending with the publication of the *Wealth of Nations* in 1776.'

2. *Scope of Economics since Adam Smith*: The scope of economics has broadened. According to Spiegel, this trend of broadening the scope of economics started with Wicksteed. He (p 528) states, 'His (Wicksteed's) reference to the 'the purposeful selection between alternative applications of resources' was to resound later in Robbins' definition of economics as the science that treats of the allocation of scarce resources among different uses.' He adds, 'The elevation of the logic of choice to an all-encompassing rule guiding human behavior in all its aspects has encouraged later writers to claim for economics a far wider scope than is conventionally accorded to it.' However, Manski (2000) believes, 'Throughout much of the twentieth century, mainstream economics traded breadth for rigor. The narrowing of economics ended by the

1970s. Since then a new phase has been underway, in which the discipline seeks to broaden while maintaining the rigor that has become emblematic of economic analysis.'

Classical Economists on the Scope of Economics: Dorfman (1991) notes, '*Wealth of Nations* was primarily a treatise on economic development.' Indeed, according to the classical economists, the scope of economics was essentially limited to economic growth. Although they also talked about other topics, like income distribution and value, they offered very little. As Samuelson (1978) notes, 'For all their talk about the importance of the problem of distribution between land rent, labor wages, and profits, the classicists succeeded in saying little definite (and correct) on levels of and changes in relative factor shares.' Similarly, according to Deane (1978), classical economists contributed very little to the theory of value. She (p 107) remarks, 'For the moment what needs to be said is that the mature neo-classical school replaced the fragmented, often vaguely-defined, philosophically-oriented analysis of the classical school with an integrated theory of value-in-use and value-in-exchange in which market price was mathematically determined by the intersection of the schedules of demand and supply.'

Neoclassical Economists on the Scope of Economics: According to Marshall (1920, p 1), 'Political Economy or Economics is a study of mankind in the ordinary business of life; it examines that part of individual and social action which is most closely connected with the attainment and with the use of the material requisites of well-being.' He (p 42) adds, 'Economics is thus taken to mean a study of the economic aspects and conditions of man's political, social and private life; but more especially of his social life.'

Current Scope of Economics: Myerson (1999) remarks, 'A generation before Nash could have accepted a narrower definition of economics, as a specialized social science concerned with the production and allocation of material goods.' He adds, 'But today economists can define their field more broadly, as being about the analysis of incentives in all social institutions.' Samuelson (1968) summarizes aptly, 'Harriet Martineau, who made fairy tales out of economics (unlike modern economists who make economics out of fairy tales).'

3. Stigler (1984) and Lazear (2000) label economics as an imperial science because of its colonization of other disciplines such as: sociology, history, political science, and law. Similarly, Spiegel (1991, p xxiv) asserts, 'In the

twentieth century economics came to be called an "imperial science"; its theoretical patterns of analysis came to be applied in other fields such as political science, law, and sociology.'
4. Certainly our ideas about the significance of past ideas or the methodology to evaluate their significance do change. As Schaffer (p 43) quotes Gooding's (1989, p 70) conclusion that 'The identity of an experiment — its importance and significance— is not fixed: it is plastic.'
5. Viner (1954) reviewed Schumpeter's History of Economic Analysis as: 'The fact remains that in the case of some authors he emphasizes their defects as analysts and admits their merits only grudgingly whereas with others he draws attention only to their strong points and leaves unmentioned or strains himself to find some sort of defense for the weak points in their analysis.'
6. Marshall (1920, p 757) asserts, 'Since he was the first to write a treatise on wealth in all its chief social respects, he might on this ground alone have a claim to be regarded as the founder of modern economics.'

Barber (1967, p17) observes, 'In the main, pre-classical literature had been more disposed to judge economic performance than to analyze it.' In fact, he goes as far as to say, 'Little of the content of the *Wealth of Nations* can be regarded as original to Smith himself. Most of the book's arguments had in one form or another been in circulation for some time. But this fact in no way diminishes Smith's achievement. He was the first to draw the threads together, to fit them into a coherent system, and to communicate the findings to a wider audience.'

However, the following statement by Landretb and Colander (1994, p 74), is typical of assessments of Adam Smith's contributions: 'Some historians of economic theory have attempted to rank economists according to their technical brilliance—their ability to develop new techniques of economic analysis and their virtuoso performance in applying technique. Judged by this criterion, Adam Smith ranks low. Other historians have attempted to rank past writers by originality. Judged in this way, Smith ranks behind Cantillon, Quesnay and Turgot. But viewed historically, Smith's abilities and his contribution to the flow of economic ideas represent a much scarcer resource than either originality or technical competence: his role was to take up the best ideas of other men and meld them, not with technique but with judgment and wisdom, into a comprehensive system that not only revealed the essential functioning of the economy but also provided rich insights into policy questions.'

7. ***Dupuit's Contributions:*** Until recently, Dupuit was credited only with the concept of consumer surplus, the Dupuit-Laffer Curve and the deadweight loss of taxation. Ekelund and Hebert bring to light his many additional contributions related both to 'content and method.' According to them, he developed the concept of marginal utility, resolved the 'water-diamond paradox' and provided a firm foundation for the derivation of demand. They believe that he was concerned not just with the consumer surplus but with producer surplus as well. They attribute to him the development of analysis related to monopoly, various kinds of price discrimination, product differentiation, the link between incentives and institutions, intellectual property rights and the application of mathematical methods to economic issues.

8. The methodological issues have attracted philosophers since antiquity. Redman notes that notwithstanding some fuzziness, the distinction between induction and deduction goes back to ancient Greece. She (fn. 3, p 160) states, 'Aristotle first used the word (induction) in no less than three ways to mean the passage from the individual or particular to the universal, the enumeration of all instances, and the abstraction by intuition of a general truth by considering a particular case. It is the first definition that forms the basis for the modern discussion.' The use of methodology in economics has come under attack from so many sides that Backhouse felt compelled to defend it. He (1997) devotes three chapters in its defense. He (p 5) asserts, 'The first stage is to defend the thesis that methodology matters. This involves taking on not only the "practical" objections to methodology raised by economists, but also the philosophical case made by McCloskey and Weintraub and other "postmodern" critics of methodology.'

9. Drekmeier (1962, p 189) writes, '*Dharmashastra* is of an essentially deductive nature. *Arthashastra*, by contrast, introduces inductive reasoning and a greater realism.'

    Similarly, Parmar (1987, p 14) states, 'Kautilya's method has two main ingredients—reason and experience gathered from history. The former helps him analyze the principles of politics and the latter enables him to draw sound general conclusions.'

10. ***A History of 'All Other Things Being Equal' Phrase:*** Marshall is generally credited for popularizing the phrase 'all other things being equal.' He (1920, p 36) justifies its use with the argument, 'Almost every scientific doctrine, when carefully and formally stated, will be found to contain

some proviso to the effect that other things are equal: the action of the causes in question is supposed to be isolated; certain effects are attributed to them, but only on the hypothesis that no cause is permitted to enter except those distinctly allowed for.' Similarly, Cartright (1998, p 239) asserts, 'Most scientific explanations use ceteris paribus laws.'

Daniel Bernoulli (1738) was probably the first one to use this phrase. John Stuart Mill too used this methodology. Redman (p 346) notes, 'Most frequently he uses laws to state how things would be if certain conditions hold. At least once he uses a ceteris paribus statement; and, as Hausman notes, ceteris paribus is often consistent with much of what Mill says (133).'

Ekelund and Hebert (p 12) also note, 'Already before 1850 we find Cournot and Dupuit utilizing the ceteris paribus method, as Marshall later named it.' However, Backhouse notes that a mere use of 'ceteris paribus' clause is not enough to ensure a sound scientific analysis. He (p ix) provides Kincaid's list of the barriers to good science and 'failure to investigate ceteris paribus clauses in the ways necessary to prove theories trustworthy' and lists this as number one barrier to good science.

11. *A History of Marginal Analysis*: Today, it appears that the contribution of economics would be 'marginal' without the marginal analysis. It is hard to imagine the state of economics without it and what kind of marginal analysis would there be without calculus. Faulhaber and Baumol (1988) make several points about marginal analysis. First, they note that Newton and Leibniz developed the differential calculus during the 17th century but its general acceptance in economics occurred only by the end of the 19th century. According to them, Turgot, Thunen and Cournot used the marginal analysis but Walras, Menger, Javons, Marshall and Clark are given the credit for creating the 'marginal revolution.' However, they remark, 'No one is certain just when marginal reasoning entered the economic literature, because hints of it are sure to occur in any careful discussion of the logic of optional decision making.'

Similarly, Blaug (1973, p 14)) concludes, 'Classical political economy did not begin in 1776, and the birth of marginal utility economics—marginalism, modern economics, whatever name we choose to characterize it—similarly, cannot be pinned down to any particular date.' He adds that the marginal revolution 'was a process, not an event.' Indeed, as shown by Kautilya's analysis, this process started a long time ago.

Recently, Ekelund and Hebert brought to light the contributions of Dupuit. They (p 88) claim, 'On the one hand, Dupuit's invention of marginal utility as a foundation for value culminated a long and circuitous tradition in econo-engineering. On the other hand, it was the beginning of a new tradition in economic analysis that focused on the microeconomic nature of individual markets.'

12. Fredrick, Shane, George Loewenstein and Ted O'Donoghue (2002) credit the re-discovery of inter-temporal choice to John Rae. They observe, 'Along with inventing the topic of inter-temporal choice, Rae also produced the first in-depth discussion of the psychological motives underlying inter-temporal choice.' They add, 'Inter-temporal choice became firmly established as a distinct topic in 1834, with John Rae's publication of *The Sociological Theory of Capital*.'

13. Dasgupta and Maskin (2005, p 1291) write, 'Before turning to hyperbolic discounting, we must ask the question, "Why should a DM discount at all?" A conventional answer, provided by both the economics and zoology literatures, is that, in a typical situation that an animal or human may face, future payoffs run some risk of disappearing or depreciating.'

14. Kangle (1965, Vol III, p 10-11) presents the views of many historians on the origin of the *Arthashastra* literature and concludes, 'But there does not appear to be any valid reason why the beginnings of this science cannot be placed as early as 600 BC or even a little earlier.'

Table 3.3: **Distinct Categories of Teachers**

Group I	Group II	Group III	Group IV
Manu	Bharadvaja	Katyayana	The unnamed teachers
Brihaspati	Visalakasa	Kanishka Bharadvaja	Kautilya
Usanas (Sukra)	Parasara	Carayana	
	Pisuna	Ghotamukha	
	Kaunapadanta	Kinjalka	
	Vatavyadhi	Pisuna's son	
	Bahudantiputra	Ambhiyas	

Source: Parmar (1987, p 4)

CHAPTER - 4

1. *Medema and Samuels (2001, p 299) quote Spiegel thus:* 'There are only a few ideas in the history of economics that emerged immediately in the form of a comprehensive and consistent theory. Often they first emerge as fragments, replete with contradictions and loaded with policy implications.'
2. *The Ancient Thinkers on the Law of Diminishing Utility*: Kautilya (Kangle (part. II, p 14)) stated the views of his predecessors, related to a king's behavior as: '(He should devote himself) equally to the three goals of life which are bound up with one another. For, any one of the three, viz., spiritual good, material well-being and sensual pleasures, [if] excessively indulged in, does harm to itself as well as to the other two.' And Kautilya expresses his own views as: '"Material well-being alone is supreme", says Kautilya. For, spiritual good and sensual pleasures depend on material well-being (1.7).'

    First, it is significant to note that the ancient thinkers, like today's economists, were concerned about allocational problems. Second, despite the fact they had not figured out yet how to allocate time optimally among different activities, they recommended moderation. That is, the line '[if] excessively indulged in, does harm to itself as well as to the other two' implies that they were at least vaguely aware of the law of diminishing marginal utility. Thus, their recommendation to divide time equally among these three pursuits was perhaps intended to eliminate the possibility of causing any harm. However, Kautilya recommended devoting more time to the pursuit of economic goals.
3. *A History of Ordinal Preferences*: Edgeworth is credited with introducing and Pareto for fully developing the concept of indifference curve. But Hicks (1946) may be given credit for popularizing the indifference curves. However, Morgenstern (1972) is critical of indifference curves and, in fact, predicted that they would disappear in a generation. Similarly, Cooter and Rappoport (1984) argue, 'The intuitive idea of scientific progress is that new theories are discovered that explain more than old theories. We shall contend that the ordinalist revolution was not scientific progress in this sense.' They add, 'Utility rankings were not seen as coextensive with preference orderings, nor were they derived from them.' That is, according to them, the cardinal approach of measuring utility was used only to measure 'material welfare' and not preferences.
4. *Usage of the term Precursor*: Whitaker (2000, p 387) explains, 'My

impression, though, is that usage in our field is more restrictive and the term precursor is limited to cases where the follower builds independently of the precursor and discovers the pertinence of the latter's work only belatedly, if at all. In other cases, a more neutral word such as "predecessor" might be preferred.' He singles out the most important requirement as: 'A must have proceeded to a considerable extent upon the same broad lines as B. Commonality must extend beyond obiter dicta by A or agreement on points of detail or modes of expression and must involve central ideas and general principles.'

Whitaker (2000, p 388) adds, 'However, there will sometimes be exceptional cases in which the earlier work was obscure or its full import unrecognized, and then reporting the discovery, even expost, may be regarded as credible by the community, especially if the precursor was a notable figure.'

Similarly, Groenewegen (2002, p 319) notes, 'The emphasis on core implies that a precursor of a school of thought must have anticipated the essentials of the analysis and not some of its peripheral features.'

5. *Modern History of Opportunity Cost*: Spiegel (1991, p 538) points out, 'The germ of Wieser's concept of opportunity cost was already contained in a seminar report he delivered in 1876, and although it was more fully developed in his later publications as well as by Böhm-Bawerk and other writers, it was Wieser who pioneered in this important matter.' Spiegel credits Wieser for developing the concept of opportunity cost. Although Kautilya did not provide any formal definition of opportunity cost he understood it and correctly applied it more than two thousand years earlier.

6. Barber (1967, p 174) notes, 'In general it was presupposed that alternative uses of the various factors of production were available. Firm X, for example, could not expect to acquire more land, labour, or capital for its purposes unless it was prepared to outbid other claimants for the same resources. The point at issue was described more formally in terms of "opportunity cost", ie. costs in the form of income the supplier of services was obliged to forego when committing himself to one activity, thus precluding other options. It was not always recognized within the neoclassical tradition, however, that this argument depended on conditions of full employment; otherwise some suppliers of productive services might have no readily available options. In such a situation the "opportunity costs" of employment would be zero.'

7. *A History of the Law of Diminishing Returns*: Brue (1993) provides a brief history of the evolution of the law of diminishing returns. He finds, 'The law of diminishing returns is rooted in the work of the 18th century French physiocrat Anne Robert Jacques Turgot.' He notes, 'Ricardo modestly credited Malthus and West for the discovery of the law of diminishing returns, but Ricardo developed the idea most thoroughly. Nevertheless, Ricardo's statement of the law was imprecise and mixed with the idea of heterogeneity of scarce resources.' He concludes, "Clark (1899/1956, p 201) used his modern formulation of the law to develop his marginal productivity theory of distribution. The law of diminishing returns thereafter became the central explanation for downward-sloping short-run resource demand curves.'

Adam Smith on the Law of Diminishing Returns: Samuelson (1978, fn. 13) concludes, 'Professor Stigler points out to me that I have been charitable to Smith in attributing to him knowledge of diminishing returns; and less than just to Ricardo in not crediting his Chapter 1 with having succeeded in showing that changes only in wage rates will not affect relative values. Professor Blaug also doubts that the differences between Ricardo and Smith are usefully dismissed as being merely semantic; in any case, upon review, I find no thought experiments proposed by Ricardo to which he has given a different substantive answer than would Smith's system; outright slips by Smith seem if anything less than those in Ricardo and are of secondary importance in both cases.'

Hollander (1980) finds some paragraphs in the *Wealth of Nations* in support of Samuelson's finding. He quotes from the *Wealth of Nations*, 'When the most fertile and best situated lands have been all occupied, less profits can be made by the cultivation of what is inferior both in soil and situation.'

Two remarks are in order. First, Samuelson and Hollander point to some paragraphs in the *Wealth of Nations*, which *imply* diminishing returns but Ricardo as well as others could not find those in it. However, it does not prove that Adam Smith was the originator of this concept. Second, on this issue, the level of sophistication in the *Wealth of Nations* may be only marginally lower than that in Ricardo's *Principles of Political Economy*, but both deal with declining returns from applications of fixed amounts of labour and capital to heterogeneous pieces of land.

8. Backhouse (1985, p 148-50) provides a brief history of the evolution of the concept of the production function. A production function is

defined as the minimum amounts of inputs required to produce given levels of output.

9. Negishi (1989, p 14) quotes W Petty as 'Labour is the father of wealth, as lands are the mother.' This statement is equally revealing but, perhaps, a more poetic way of indicating complementary nature between land and labour.

10. Samuelson (1978) comments, 'Ricardo and Marx were not naive observers as to believe literally in fixed proportions between capital goods and labor.'

11. *Mercantilists on Demand-Supply Framework*: Spengler (1960, p 23) characterizes the notion of competition under mercantilism as, 'The term (competition) is used to signify a rivalry of sorts, but not the price-modifying rivalry of the market place.'

    Classical School on Demand-Supply Apparatus: Samuelson (1978) asserts, 'Within every classical economist there is to be discerned a modern economist trying to be born.' On the other hand, Garegnani (1983) concludes, 'The attempt to read in the classical authors as explanation of relative prices along the lines of modern theory is not well founded.' He points out, 'The role of effectual demand is to explain the tendency of the actual or "market" price toward the normal price and not that of determining the latter. It does not therefore consist of a curve but of a single determinate price-quantity point.' In other words, there are no demand and supply schedules in the classical analysis and therefore, classical demand-supply apparatus is not a rudimentary representation or a precursor of the one developed by the neoclassicals. Similarly, Whitaker (2000, p 391) remarks, 'Or it could be argued that this stress had a more self-interested basis and was designed to throw doubt upon the claims to originality of some of his contemporaries and strengthen his own claims to authority. Most commentators have regarded his emphasis on the continuity of development from classical to neoclassical economics as overdone.'

CHAPTER - 5

1. *The Origin of Statistics*: Stephen Stigler (1986, p 361) provides a most complete history of measuring uncertainty during the 18th and 19th centuries. He provides a clear and fascinating exposition of the origins of the least squares of Legendre, error curve of Gauss, the central limit theorem of Laplace, regression (and quincunx) of Galton and the seminal contributions of Edgeworth, Pearson and Yule. He (p 361) concludes,

'The conceptual triumphs of the nineteenth century had been the product of many minds working on many problems in many fields, and one of the most striking of their accomplishments was the creation of a new discipline.' Stigler (1999, p 382) adds, 'The construction of optimal tests of significance is a twentieth century innovation in statistical theory; the early works of Ronald Fisher (including likelihood-based significance tests in the 1920s), of Walter Shewhart (including the control chart in 1924) and the joint work of Jerzy Neyman and Egon Pearson (including the Neyman-Parson Lemma of 1933) played key roles.'

2. Backhouse (1985, p 17) points out that Adam Smith would exclude the output of unproductive labour from income and the payments to labour came out of savings implying that his definitions of income and consumption were far from perfect. Adam Smith (p 430) asserts, 'Thus the labour of a manufacturer adds, generally, to the value of the materials which he works upon, that of his own maintenance, and of his master's profit. The labour of a menial servant, on the contrary, adds to the value of nothing.' Similarly, defense related services and 'churchmen, lawyers, physicians, men of letters of all kinds; players, buffoons, musicians, opera-singers, opera-dancers, etc. are unproductive' according to Adam Smith. Moreover, Quesnay is usually given the credit for developing national income accounts. Notwithstanding that, Samuelson (1977) constructs at least a rudimentary national income accounts from Adam Smith's analysis related to the 'rude' stage of society.

CHAPTER - 6

1. *Yajur Veda* on a long and healthy life free of vices: 'May we be able to live freely without being a burden on anyone. May we be able to see, hear, live, and sing your glory freely for more than one hundred years.' (Chapter 36, *mantra* 24)

    'O God, the Creator of the universe and Giver of all happiness! Keep us far from bad habits, bad deeds, and calamities. May we attain everything that is auspicious.' *Yajur Veda* (Ch 30, *mantra* 3)

2. Richard Kraut (2010) observes, 'What Aristotle has in mind when he makes this complaint is that ethical activities are remedial: they are needed when something has gone wrong, or threatens to do so. Courage, for example, is exercised in war, and war remedies an evil; it is not something we should wish for.'

James Halteman and Edd Noell (2012) explore Adam Smith's ideas on ethics. They (p 76) remark, 'The social passions are generosity, compassion, and esteem. They are inherently good and bring forth virtuous behavior, but they are also scarce and not prevalent enough in everyday life to serve as the foundation of a successful social order.'
3. Confucius 'To practice five things under all circumstances constitutes perfect virtue; these five are gravity, generosity of soul, sincerity, earnestness, and kindness.'
4. (25) Dhar (2003, p 156-157) observes, 'Our tradition recognizes certain eternal values including love, compassion and non-injury. It underscores the importance of means being right to achieve right ends.'

On the other hand, Staveren (2001, p153) asserts, 'Central to Aristotle's Nicomachean Ethics is that virtue can only be found by trial and error as a mean between efficiency and excess: virtue depends on deliberation, as I argued in chapter one. It is important to repeat Aristotle's view that virtues are not pre-given, they are not universals, nor subjectively prescribed in individual objective functions.'
5. Jim Holt (2006) asserts, 'Aristotle defined virtue as a quality of character that makes for a life well lived. Then he characterized the good life as a life lived in accordance with virtue. Circular?' However, Vedic approach to ethics does not involve any such circularity.
6. *(a) Self-Improvement:*
    Be pure and pious
    O worshippers. — *Rig Veda (10-18-2)*
    May honest earnings flourish,
    I destroy the ill-earned wealth. — *Atharva Veda (7-115-4)*
Self-discipline:
    Do not tread the path of
    Rajo (sensuous) and Tamo (destructive) impulses
    And thus thou wilt be free
    From agonies and afflictions. — *Atharva Veda (8-2-1)*
Truth:
    The earth is sustained through truth. — *Atharva Veda (14-1-1)*
Controlling Greed:
    Do not covet the wealth of others. — *Yajur Veda (40-1)*

[2] 'Better' and 'agreeable' present themselves to man:

> Considering them carefully the wise man discriminates,
> Preferring the better to what only pleasure brings:
> Dull men prefer the 'agreeable',
> For the getting and keeping [of what they crave].
> — *Katha Upanishad, Chapter II*

(b) **System Building:** The Vedas, which were composed more than four thousand years ago, emphasized charity, truth, honesty, love, harmony, nonviolence, and self-discipline. A few quotes supporting this claim are provided below.

> May all men, beasts and birds
> Be blessed with peace and prosperity. —*Atharva Veda (1-31-4)*

Charity:

> He who hoards provisions in vain
> And does not feed his elders and companions,
> Is inhuman, unkind and stingy,
> Verily he brings his own destruction.
> He who eats alone
> Is a great sinner. —*Rig Veda (10-117-6)*

> He who performs selfless action
> Accompanied by auspicious words
> Full of truth, joy and sweetness
> In the atmosphere of mutual-co-operation
> Reaches the goal. —*Yajur Veda (3-47)*

Non-violence:

> O enlightened men,
> We neither harm any one
> Nor impose ourselves on others,
> We act in accordance with
> Vedic doctrines and ideals,
> We coexist and cooperate in life
> With kins as well as aliens
> To render good to all. —*Rig Veda (10-134-7)*

Truth and Benevolence:

> They follow eternal law
> Preach and practice truth
> Extend helping hand to all

      Act as unique guide and guardian
      Bounteous, benevolent, broad-minded
      And savior from sins. —*Rig Veda (5-67-4)*

      I bless you to be free from malice
      To live with concord and unanimity
      Love one another as cow loves
      its new-born calf. —*Atharva Veda (3-30-1)*

      May we not hate any one. —*Atharva Veda (12-1-24)*
  Human Dignity:
      He who sees all beings
      In his own self
      And finds the reflection
      Of his own self
      In all beings
      Never looks down upon anybody. —*Yajur Veda (40-6)*

7. I am indebted to Ravi Prakash Arya for this and the next endnote. The contribution of *dharma* at micro level and macro level is beautifully acknowledged in *Vaisheshika Darshan* (1.1.2) as:
    yato abhyudaya nihshreyas siddhi sa dharmah
At the macro level, *dharma* is essential to abhyudaya (social and economic development or as system building). At the micro level, it is essential to *Nisshreyas* or as spiritual upliftment.
8. In *Dharmic* economics, the value of *paropakara* (helping others) has a significant role to play. Modern philosophy talks about struggle and survival of the fittest. There is another philosophy that talks about 'Live and let live.' But Vedic philosophy, based upon the ethical value of *propakara*, talks about 'Live and help others to live.'
9. *Origin of Philosophy and Religion in India*: Bolling (1977, Vol 27, p 925) notes that the origin of some of the *Vedas*, such as the *Rig Veda*, the Indian sacred scriptures, may be dated around 2000 BCE. That means that some of the *Vedas* were composed more than a millennium before the earliest of the Greek works. He explains Veda as: 'This word means "knowledge" (vid seen in Greek Ϝιδμεν "we know" Latin *videre*, Gothic *witum*, "we know", English wit), which specializes in the sense of "knowledge par excellence," "the sacred knowledge" is somewhat

comparable to the designation of our sacred Scriptures as "the Book, the Bible." He adds, 'For the oldest of these, the *Rig Veda*, the estimates of competent scholars vary from 4000–1000 BC–about 2000 B C being a conservative estimate.'

Origin of Philosophy in Greece: Brown (1977, Vol 13, p 396) points out, 'In the primitive folk culture of Greece, as in other primitive cultures, science, philosophy, literature, and art in the modern sense did not exist.' He adds, 'Until the birth of Greek science and philosophy in the 6th century BC, Greek explanations of natural and social phenomena were entirely mythical; even thereafter myth remained central in Greek religion and poetry, and philosophy and science never fully got rid of its influence.'

Evaluation of Socrates' Ideas: Rowe (2003, p 123) states, 'How should a man live, in order to achieve *eudaimonia*?' He continues, 'Socrates' own answer, which is echoed by nearly everyone else in the Greek tradition, gives pride of place to *arête*. If *arête* were equivalent to 'virtue', this could be taken as a simple assertion that the good life is, necessarily, a good *moral* life.' He (2003, p 127) states, 'But if fine or right actions matter to us, how do we come to know what fine and right actions are?' He adds, 'Socrates seems to claim neither to know himself how to give a proper account of this thing, *arête*, which he values so highly, nor to be able to find anyone else who knows about it.'

Similarly, the Greek philosophers did not explore the conflict of interest possibilities and although they did ask the question 'how a man should live?' they did not explore any substantive issues related to the question. For example, Rowe (2003, p 125) states, 'If, as he believed, we all seek *eudaimonia*, our own, not someone else's. For him too, therefore, the fact that certain types of behaviour seemed to involve preferring the interests of others to one's own was itself the problem, not the solution; and any successful case for justice and the rest had somehow to show that they were, after all, in the interests of the agent. It is in this sense that we are to understand the famous Socratic paradoxes, that '*Arête* is wisdom', and 'No-one goes wrong deliberately.' He (2003, p 127) believes, 'The rise of Greek ethics can be seen in large part as a reflection of the overlaying of a fundamentally individualistic ethos with the demands for co-operative behavior implied by the political institutions of the city-state. What the philosophers attempt to show is that there is, in the end, no conflict between the two.' He adds, 'We may deplore the fact that they expanded so much energy on exploring the foundations of the subject that they had none left for discussing the substantive issues that constitute the subject itself—rather as if a mathematician were to become so obsessed with the problem of mathematical truth as to forget to do any mathematics.' It appears that even with a considerable stretch of imagination, Greek philosophers' contribution cannot be described as a 'Greek Miracle.' See Ifrah (2000, p 360) for a challenge to the 'Greek Miracle' in another area.

10. Sen (1997) asserts, 'The tolerance of heterodoxy is not to be found here. Indeed, there is very little tolerance in Kautilya, except tolerance for the upper sections of the community.' He adds, 'Certainly, Kautilya is no democrat, no egalitarian, no general promoter of everyone's freedom.'

On the other hand, Drekmeier (1962, p 76) states, 'Now the king must concern himself directly with the common good, an idea anticipated in the *Arthashastra*.' He (p 198) observes, 'The author of the *Arthashastra* emerges as something of a champion of the Shudras, espousing their rights as freeborn citizens, and going so far as to suggest that the sons of slaves should enjoy the status of Aryans.'

He (p 201) asserts, 'There can never be a thoroughgoing divorce of politics and ethics for Kautilya; he never denies that the ultimate purpose of the state is a moral purpose, the maintenance of dharma.' He (p 201) adds, 'Traditionally, it was the religious proficiency of the *purohita* that determined the success of the king. Now, of course, the point had been reached where Brahmans must look to the state for the security of their interests.'

11. Chang (1987) explores the contributions of Confucius (551-479 BCE), a moral philosopher and Han Feitzu (280-233 BCE), a legalist. Chang remarks, 'The Confucian state is established on a set of ethical norms and rites—rules, ceremonies, and manners codified by legendry sages—and governed by men through moral influence, rather than law, coercion, or by divine spirits.' Chang adds, 'Another outstanding legalist was Han Feitzu (280-233 BC), a theoretician and a disciple of Hsun-tzu. Following his teacher, Han Feitzu believed that basically, people were motivated largely by self-interest. For the sake of social order and economic progress, Han Feitzu proposed strict and uniform application of rewards and punishments and rejected Confucian egalitarianism. In his view, chances for success under Confucianism were far less than under Legalism. In his assessment, the former would function well only

if individuals are guided by morality and rulers are sage kings, but in reality, individuals are guided overwhelmingly by self-interest and rulers are mostly average kings. On the contrary, Legalism, along with its laws and regulations designed for the good of the whole society headed by an average ruler, offers a greater chance of success.'

Similarly, Choi (1989) points out, 'Han Feitzu repeatedly argued against Confucians (moralists) and showed that proposals based on moral grounds, though eloquent, inevitably resulted in absurdity if not outright undesirability.'

12. Basham (1959, p 9), 'India was a cheerful land, whose people, each finding a niche in a complex and slowly evolving social system, reached a higher level of kindliness and gentleness in their mutual relationships than any other nation of antiquity.' He (p 153) adds, 'The humane regulations of *The Arthashastra*, probably unique in the records of any ancient civilization, are perhaps survivals of Mauryan laws, and it is therefore not surprising that Megasthenes declared that there was no slavery in India.'

13. Haddad (1996, p 77) observes, 'Admittedly, the Scottish school did not venture very far into the theory of choice. According to Campbell and Skinner (1982: 99), Hutcheson, Hume and Smith believed that moral choices or judgments were to be explained in terms of immediate sense of feelings rather than as a process of reasoning or conscious calculations.' Similarly, Sugden (2002) concludes his discussion on sympathy, empathy and fellow-feeling as: 'The account depends on hypotheses about causal relationships between affective mental states, and makes no reference to preference or choice. Thus, it cannot be expressed in the language of a theory of rational choice from which all references to affective states have been stripped out.'

14. As discussed in Section 6.1, the following observation by John M Koller does not capture the true intent behind the creation of the concept of Heaven (*Moksha*). He (1999, p 289)) states, 'However, if the discontinuity between the ultimate reality and worldly existence cannot be overcome, then it must be recognized that *moksha*, the supreme value, devalues human existence, for then it is not liberation of human beings, but liberation from being human. That is, then the value of *Moksha* belongs to *Atman*, not to embodied human existence, which ultimately is no more than the projection of ignorance.'

15. Zaratiegui (1999) does not take into consideration Kautilya's

contributions when he remarks, 'The character and content of the old ethics has little to do these days with moral behavior. Furthermore, the roles have changed: Economics is now the social science with the greater academic and cultural prestige, while it was ethics that once had priority during the first stage of the process. Ethics exercised its control with a holistic view of society, whereas the focus has now changed to analyze why individuals from different cultural backgrounds adopt similar ethical and cultural norms with respect to moral behavior.'

CHAPTER - 7

1. Kumar (1989, p xxii) observes, 'Thus a critical study of the *Arthashastra* shows synthesis in life. In his philosophy of good living, he tampers orthodoxy with rationalism, combines moderate enjoyment of pleasures and economic gains with the pursuit of spiritualism and supports self-control and not self-repression in them. We find a synthesis of all these qualities.'
2. Kautilya (Subramanian, p 13) stated, 'That mother and that father are enemies, who do not give education to their children.' Apparently, it was the parents' responsibility to get their children educated and the government's responsibility was to provide good governance.
3. Case VI has led to the harshest of criticism. For example, Sen (1997) concludes, 'Kautilya is a consequentialist of quite narrow kind.' But it is obvious that this assessment is based on this very small part and Sen totally ignores Kautilya's broad conceptual framework which has more ethical content than that in the *Wealth of Nations*.

    Perhaps that was needed at that time to maintain law and order and national security. For example, Drekmeier (p 260) writes, 'The king needed greater freedom of movement if he was to provide security and the conditions of prosperity. The state was forced to take measures that frequently ran counter to the accepted moral standards of the community. But Kautilya well knew that such policies were all that could save society from collapse. He was led inevitably to a theory approximating the reason of state arguments of sixteenth-century Europe. But he sought to emphasize the fact that such actions were not irresponsible. Indeed, it is the duty of the ruler to his subjects that compels him to take drastic steps to ensure their welfare. Survival and progress are recognized as bestowing authority.'

Similarly, Choi (1989) in expressing the views of Han Feitzu (280-233 BCE) remarks, Han Feitzu was a radical in that a little coercion, initially, is justified if the end sought is the supreme public good, the law.

4. ***Specification of the Role of Education***: Conlisk asserts, 'People spend much on human capital, in large part through schooling. The investment is partly information collection (names and dates), partly skill acquisition (typing), and partly general cognitive investment (Learning to think). The cognitive investment must be a response to bounded rationality. The part of schooling cost which goes into general cognitive development is general deliberation cost, and human capital theory is implicitly concerned with bounded rationality. The assumption that students invest optimally in schooling is an unusually strong example of optimal imperfection. Explicit recognition of the relation of human capital theory to bounded rationality might bring new insights to the theory.'

CHAPTER - 8

1. ***Mercantilists and Adam Smith on Economic Growth***: Spengler (1960, p 9) notes, 'First, disagreement persists with respect to the policy objectives of mercantilism, particularly as to whether mercantilism had power or plenty as its over-riding objective.' However, Prasch (1991) remarks, 'First, the title of the book, *An Inquiry into the Nature and Causes of The Wealth of Nations*, as well as his lengthy tracts about the mercantilists' confusion with regard to the formation of wealth, lends credence to the view that he shared the mercantilists' goals, namely the development of England's wealth and power as a policy goal. Reviewing Book 4 of the *Wealth of Nations*, one finds that Smith never raises issue with the mercantilists' policy goals, only with their attempts to achieve them.' Adam Smith (Book 1, p 394) wrote, 'But the great object of the political economy of every country, is to increase the riches and power of that country.'

In fact, Adam Smith offered paradoxical positions on the purpose of economic growth. He (Book 2, p 179) stated, 'Consumption is the sole end and purpose of all production.' But then, it might appear that Adam Smith was not concerned with growth in consumption since he believed that additional goods and services did not increase utility. For example, Prasch observes, 'These passages as well as a number of others in *The theory of Moral Sentiments* make it clear that the increase of consumption cannot stand as a justification for economic growth.' Similarly, Tribe (1999) states, 'however, Brown argues that the meaning here should not be understood as a statement with respect to the forces for economic harmony, but instead as an endorsement of the Stoic argument that material things do not contribute to the general good and therefore do not affect a person's happiness (Brown 1994, p 90). This, then, is not an argument about "trickle down", the benefits for all consequent upon the consumption of a few; it is an argument that whatever the material distribution of goods might be, this has nothing to do with the distribution of happiness.'

Prasch attempts to piece together Adam Smith's scattered thoughts on the purposes of economic growth and concludes, 'Smith initially presents us with a variety of purposes for growth, including consumption, wealth and power, and civilization. Yet these goals are not individually exclusive and in fact are subsidiary to his overriding concern—the bringing of civilization—understood as the system of "natural liberty."'

2. It seems that some technical progress was taking place. As Mokyr (1990, p 24) observes, 'The best quality steel, "seric iron" (or Wootz steel), was imported from India, although the bloomeries of the West were capable of producing some level of low quality.'

3. Mokyr (1990, p 172-173) remarks, 'In the eternal trade-off between progress and growth on the one hand, and stability and order on the other, Hindu civilization chose a position biased in the extreme toward the latter.' He continues, 'India, where daily life was conducted for millennia at the very margins of subsistence, is a *reductio ad absurdum* of the notion of an equilibrium, so beloved by economists. Yet this equilibrium was regarded as an arrangement established by the Gods, a perfect world in which everything and everyone had its place, a society in which poverty was holy and action was vanity.'

Basham (p 4), 'The great achievements of ancient India and Ceylon—their immense irrigation works and splendid temples and the long campaigns of their armies do not suggest a devitalized people.' He adds, (p 9), 'Indian character is neither lethargic nor unhappy. This conclusion is borne out by a general acquaintance with the remains of India's past. Our second general impression of India is that her people enjoyed life, passionately delighting both in the things of the senses and the things of the spirit.'

Moreover, the differences in the standard of living among nations arose only during the last two hundred and fifty years. For example, Blanchard (2000, p 195) states, 'From the end of the Roman Empire to roughly year 1500, there was essentially no growth of output per capita in Europe. From about 1500 to 1700, growth of output per capita turned positive but small, around 0.1% per year, increasing to 0.2% per year from 1700 to 1820.'

Recently, Alam (2000, Chapter 2) examines this issue in more depth. He faults the 'backward projection' method used by almost all researchers to estimate the income levels in the distant past. He concludes that around 1760, the differences in income levels between the now advanced and the developing countries were negligible if any at all. He explores the factors that might have caused the ever-widening gap between the income levels of the now-advanced and the developing countries. He (Chapter 6) carries out empirical tests and finds conclusive evidence that the loss of sovereignty by the Asian and African countries (ie. the adoption of aggressive policies of imperialism by the developed countries) caused these huge income differences.

What may be said more convincingly: foreign rule is not a necessary condition but definitely a sufficient condition for creating a stagnant economy. No country has ever prospered while under foreign rule. All those countries, which were under foreign rule during the last two-three hundred years, did not get the opportunity to choose to grow. Therefore, Mokyr has to provide more convincing arguments to prove his assertions regarding the nature of relationship between Hindu civilization and economic growth.

4. Adam Smith makes a similar assertion in his *Wealth of Nations*. He (p 112) states that machines 'facilitate and abridge labour, and enable one man to do the work of many.'
5. Adam Smith emphasizes the importance of land. He (p 195) states, 'The acquisition of new territory, or of new branches of trade, may sometimes raise the profits of stock, and with them the interest of *money*, even in a country which is fast advancing in the acquisition of riches.'
6. For example, Hall and Jones (1999, p 97-98) note, 'Two of these categories relate to the government's role in protecting against private diversion: (i) law and order, and (ii) bureaucratic quality. Three categories relate to the government's possible role as a diverter: (i) corruption, (ii) risk of expropriation, and (iii) government repudiation of contracts.'

7. According to McGuire and Olson (1996), public goods, such as law and order and other public infrastructure essentially shift the feasibility frontier upwards.
8. Kautilya (Subramanian, p 36) stated, 'He feeds on nectar, who first feeds his people and then eats the left-overs.'

   Similarly, Drekmeier (p 189) observes, 'In the *Arthashastra* literature the interests of the state, rather than the king's personal fulfillment, are of foremost importance.' According to Kautilya, a king was a paid public servant.
9. Incidentally, Olson (2000) calls this 'the second invisible hand.' He (p 12-13) states, 'This invisible hand—shall we call it as invisible hand on the left?—that guides encompassing interests to use their power at least to some degree, in accord with the social interest, even when serving the public good, was not part of the intention. This second invisible hand is as unfamiliar and perhaps counterintuitive as the first hidden hand was in Adam Smith's time, but that does not mean it is less important.'
10. For example, Kaufmann and Kraay (2003) claim that better governance leads to higher growth in income but higher income does not cause any improvement in the quality of governance. They emphatically assert that there is no 'virtuous cycle.' Kaufmann and Kraay specify their model as follows:

    $Y = \gamma_0 + \gamma_1 GG +$ (8.1A)
    $GG = \beta_0 + \beta_2 Y + \beta_4 X$ (8.3A)

    Where GG=good governance, Y=income, X=instrumental variable. It is a mis-specified model since important endogenous variables like knowledge are omitted. Knowledge is likely to affect income and that, in turn, influences the creation of knowledge.

CHAPTER - 9

1. Rebecca M Blank and William McGurn (2004), 'Is the Market Moral? A Dialogue on Religion, Economics & Justice' http://pewforum.org/events/index.php?eventID=57
2. Albert Hirschman (1982, p 1483) concludes, 'It is not just a question of difficulty of perception, but one of considerable psychological resistance and reluctance: to accept that the doux-commerce and the self-destruction theses (or the feudal-shackles and the feudal-blessing theses) might both be right would make it much more difficult for the

social observer, critic, or "scientist" to impress the general public by proclaiming some inevitable outcome of current processes.'
Also see Fourcade, Marion and Healy, Kieran (2007).
3. William McGurn (2004) [suggests], 'In short, my position is that theologians and economists need each other. Theologians and religiously-informed activists need to have some grasp of how the economy really works if their critiques are to be taken seriously. Conversely, market economists, if they are not to succumb to the same self-destructive hubris as the socialists, need a religiously informed culture to remind them that economics is made for human beings and not vice versa.'
http://pewforum.org/events/index.php?eventID=57
4. See Barr (1992) for such a distinction
5. Friedman (1980) remarks, 'To a modern economist familiar with the difficulties of maintaining a successful monopoly their concern seems if anything excessive, but that may be a reflection of improvements in the market, not in economic wisdom, over the intervening centuries.'

The problem of monopoly, in all likelihood must have been quite severe during ancient times and Kautilya considered remedying what Sen (1987, fn. 29 p 27) calls 'pull failure' and 'response failure.'
6. *Consumer Protection*: Post *et al* (1999, p 312) argues, 'This consumer movement exists because consumers want to be treated fairly and honestly in the marketplace. Some business practices do not meet this standard. Consumers may be harmed by abuses such as unfairly high prices, unreliable and unsafe products, excessive or deceptive advertising claims, and the promotion of some products known to be harmful to human health, such as cigarettes or farm products contaminated with pesticides.' It is further argued that consumers demand protection since products have become more complex, services have become more specialized, prevalence of deceptive advertising and inadequate attention paid to product safety.
7. Stiglitz (1994) analyzes the market failures, which are 'based on imperfect and costly information and incomplete markets.' Some of these are labeled as the problems of 'moral hazard' and 'adverse selection.' For example, Kotowitz (1987, p 549) notes that the problem of moral hazard is widespread and even Adam Smith was aware of it. He remarks, 'However, theoretical developments and their applications to specific problems have only proceeded over the past 25 years and are still the subject of vigorous research. While we have a considerable understanding

of the problem, we do not as yet understand fully market and social responses to it.'
8. Joseph Stiglitz (2000, p 9-10) lists four main reasons for government failure when attempting to correct a market failure: (1) limited information, (2) limited control over market responses, (3) limited control over bureaucracy, and (4) limitations imposed by political processes.
9. Robert Bradley (1990) provides an alternative explanation. He argues that Senator Sherman's intent in getting the Sherman Act passed was not to enhance consumer welfare but to settle a score with General Russell Alger, who had blocked Sherman's Republican presidential nomination. He writes, 'Upon signing the Sherman Act into law, Harrison stated: "John Sherman has fixed General Alger."'
10. According to Charles Drekmeier (1962), there was a paradigmatic shift in thinking in terms of the realm of possibilities during Kautilya's time in India. He (p 290) observes, 'New controls over the environment sharpened the distinction between physical necessity and necessity that is created by man. We may surmise that men began to conclude that remaking the world was within the realm of possibility. The ancient belief in the cyclical periodicity of time, the eternal return, was modified or displaced altogether by a sense of continuity and development approximating a historical attitude. Accumulated wealth and the military power and administrative efficiency it made possible could now be used for achieving ambitious, long-range political and social goals. The great man is, in fact, the great organizer. He creates the very conditions that make the hero obsolete, for he imposes an order that limits the unpredictable contingencies against which the hero struggles. The hero was made for his age; the organizer is the maker of his age. Man can now do things that earlier could be accomplished only by the gods.'

CHAPTER - 10

1. *Current Definition of Bounded Rationality*: Simon (1957, p 198) defines, 'The capacity of the human mind for formulating and solving complex problems is very small compared with the size of the problems whose solution is required for objectively rational behavior in the real world.'

    Magill and Quinzii (1996, p 13) define bounded rationality in the broadest way. They specify the following three limitations to indicate bounded rationality: '(i) Limitations on the knowledge that an agent has of his environment--which includes the characteristics and actions of other agents; (ii) limitations on the ability of an agent to envision (imagine) what the future may have in store; (iii) limitations on the ability of an agent to calculate optimal strategies in a complex decision problem.' They note, 'Some economists do not include (i) and (ii) in their definition of bounded rationality.'

Conceptually, it is essential to distinguish imperfect rationality from imperfect information. For example, one may not see clearly either because of an impaired vision (which may be because of cataract) or because of a dense fog. This distinction is important if we want to develop some technology to eliminate this impairment, that is, to have an eye operation or to have fog lights or both. Conlisk (1996) describes this choice as a trade-off between costly information gathering and costly deliberation.

2. Gene Bellinger (2004) defines information, knowledge and wisdom as follows:

Information relates to description, definition, or perspective (what, who, when, where).

Knowledge comprises strategy, practice, method, or approach (how).

Wisdom embodies principle, insight, moral, or archetype (why).

Vlatka Hlupic, Athanasia Pouloudi and George Rzevsky (2002) compile a list of eighteen definitions of knowledge management and provide valuable suggestions to integrate the various approaches and that might ultimately shorten the list.

3. According to Confucius (551-479 BCE), 'By three methods we may learn wisdom: First, by reflection, which is noblest; second, by imitation, which is easiest; third by experience, which is the bitterest.'
http://www.brainyquote.com/quotes/authors/confucius.html

4. Liebeskind (1996) labels this as a trade-off between protection and innovation. Similarly, Volker Mahnke (1998, p 3) writes, 'This paper suggests that knowledge-sharing might be a double edged sword in attempts to foster competitive advantage. For example, when competitive advantage partially depends on non-imitability of knowledge used in product strategies, and knowledge-sharing comes at the costs of increased leakage of knowledge to competitors, thus easing imitation, the company's competitive position might be eroded rather than improved.'

5. Marcello Basili and Carlo Zappia (2005, p 4): 'Keynes (1921, p 12) distinguished between direct and indirect knowledge. The former is

"that part of our rational belief which we know directly", the latter is "the part which we know by argument". Keynes explained: "our knowledge of propositions seems to be obtained in two ways: directly by contemplating the objects of acquaintance and indirectly, by argument, through perceiving the probability-relation of the proposition, about which we seek knowledge, to other propositions."'

6. See Maddock and Carter (1982, fn. 15) for a distinction between rational expectations and Muth expectations (all-information approach).

CHAPTER - 11

1. Similarly, Roger B Myerson (1999) remarks, 'A generation before Nash could have accepted a narrower definition of economics, as a specialized social science concerned with the production and allocation of material goods.' He adds, 'But today economists can define their field more broadly, as being about the analysis of incentives in all social institutions.'

    Ruth W Grant (2002) remarks, 'The ubiquity of the use of incentives in managing many different spheres of life is a sign of the increasing influence of the economic paradigm on the way in which we conceive of our public relationships and of our individual psychology.'

    S Todd Lowry (1987, 247) defines economics from the Greek perspective as: 'Thus their *oikonomia* or political economy was the study of the efficient management of personal and political affairs, with emphasis upon the human factor. Modern political economy, on the other hand, concentrates primarily upon the material factors of economic life and only secondarily upon human responses to them.'

    See Peter Groenewegen (2002, 68) for the definitions by Adam Smith, Marshall, Robbins and other prominent economists.

2. *Moral Hazard*: This term has two meanings. Webster's Dictionary defines it as, 'An insurance company's risk as to the insured's trustworthiness and honesty.' On the other hand, according to Wikipedia (2005), 'In law and economics, moral hazard is the name given to the risk that one party to a contract can change their behavior to the detriment of the other party once the contract has been concluded.'

    Allard E Dembe and Leslie I Boden (2000) explore the history of its two origins and two meanings. They assert, 'Moral hazard is a concept that has been employed in various ways by different disciplines for more than 200 years. There are two distinct historical pathways that have recently blended to create the contemporary environment in which moral hazard is discussed. One path originates in the literature concerning insurance and the other stems from statistical and economic analysis of probability and economic decision-making.' They give credit to Kenneth J Arrow's (1963) seminal work for the current interest in this area. According to them, 'Arrow's work thus represents an important historical turning point in which the value-neutral approaches traditionally used in the mathematical treatment of risk-bearing merged with the highly moralistic rhetoric that had previously existed in the insurance literature.' Kautilya did not make a distinction between its two meanings and tried to alleviate the problem both, due to dishonesty, and laziness.

3. See Lowry (1987, Chap III) for an in-depth analysis of Xenophon's ideas.

4. *Reemergence of the Principal-Agent Problem*: Adolf A Berle and Gardiner C Means (1932) observed that there was a separation of ownership and control in public corporations and suggested that incentives were required to induce the CEO, the agent, to adhere to the objective of the shareholders, the principal. Since then a considerable amount of effort has been devoted to explore a whole set of mechanisms to resolve the principal-agent problem. However, Joseph E Stiglitz (1987, p 966) credits Ross for coining the term principal-agent in 1973. Eric Rasmusen (1994, p209) discusses various mechanisms such as: piece rates, profit sharing, efficiency wages, bonuses, merit pay, tournaments, deferred compensation, promotions and even boiling-in-oil (ie. heavy punishments) to induce workers to supply optimum level of effort. Recently, Prendergast (1999) provides a comprehensive survey of the various incentives provided by the firms to elicit effort from workers. The survey concentrates primarily on two issues: (i) 'do incentives matter?' and (ii) are contracts designed to incorporate the trade-off between insurance against risk and incentives for effort? This is an extremely active field of investigation.

5. *Definitions (Encyclopedia)*: **Remunerative incentives** (or *financial incentives*) are said to exist where an agent can expect some form of material reward — especially *money* in exchange for acting in a particular way.
Moral incentives are said to exist where a particular choice is widely regarded as the *right thing to do*, or as particularly admirable, or where the failure to act in a certain way is condemned as indecent. A person acting on a moral incentive can expect a sense of self-esteem, and approval or

even admiration from her community; a person acting against a moral incentive can expect a sense of guilt, and condemnation or even *ostracism* from the community.

Coercive incentives are said to exist where a person can expect that the failure to act in a particular way will result in *physical force* being used against her (or her loved ones) by others in the community—for example, by inflicting pain in punishment, or by imprisoning her, or by confiscating or destroying her possessions.

Kautilya's Definition of Coercion: According to Kautilya (1992, p133), 'A decadent king, on the other hand, oppresses the people by demanding gifts, seizing what he wants and grabbing for himself and his favourites the produce of the country [ie. the king and his coterie consume more than their due share thus considerably impoverishing the treasury and the people.] (8.4).' He added that such a king 'fails to give what ought to be given and exacts what he cannot rightly take.' Thus, according to Kautilya, coercion was implied only when the rule of law was not followed.

6. *Implicit contracts:* Horne H Carmichael (1989) defines them as: 'Self-enforcing contracts are collections of promises that, while they might not be legally binding, are nonetheless credible. Everyone can be confident that the promises will be kept.' He adds, 'They are based on understandings between workers and their firms, not on legal rights.' Implicit contracts are self-enforcing.

Jeffrey Church and Roger Ware (2000, p73) define a complete contract as: 'A complete contract is one that will never need to be revised or changed and is enforceable.' They point out the possibility of opportunism and the costs of hold-up, if contracts are incomplete while there are prohibitive transaction costs to a complete contract.

7. Joseph J Spengler (1971, p74) observes, 'His analysis, of course, was implicit, not explicit; it rested upon the assumption that individual behavior could be controlled in large measure through economic rewards and penalties, particularly when these were commensurate with the action to be encouraged or discouraged. Accordingly, while Kautilya looked at economic issues through the eyes of an economic administrator, he was aware that rules must fit man's economic propensities and foster rather than repress useful economic activity.'

8. Recently, Andreoni *et al* (2003) explore the complementary role of rewards and punishments. They conclude, 'This indicates that rewards and punishments act to complement one another.' They continue, 'The

process suggested by our data is that the stick can help by getting people to move away from perfect selfishness and to test the waters of cooperation. The carrot can then take over by encouraging further cooperation, rendering the stick a rarely used but necessary tool.'
9. Kautilya did not recommend but accepted the existence of prostitution. However, he recommended the strictest possible controls over its operation. Moreover, the definition itself of what is ethical has been changing over the years and thus, making comparisons across time very difficult. Calvin G Mackenzie and Michael Hafken (2002, p 7) observe, 'An added problem is that of changing standards and then of changing laws. Some practices, once very common, would now get the practitioners indicted in federal courts.' It may also be noted that there is no such thing as national values, ie. no country is homogeneous in terms of values. Charles Kindleberger (1964, p 92) observes, 'National characteristics and values differ, but these also differ from class to class. At one time the values of one class dominate; at another, those of another. This may account for some of the contradictions in national character and the changes that supervene. We can distinguish the aristocrat, the bourgeois, the town worker and the countrymen, each with separate attitudes and beliefs.'
10. Recently, Daron Acemoglu and Thierry Verdier (2000) provide such a formal model. Joseph E Stiglitz (1998) also discusses government failures.
11. Paul Osterman (1994) finds, 'The models provide strong support for the view that efficiency wages are an alternative to supervision and that the payment of efficiency wages enables employers to provide workers with more discretion.'
12. Incidentally, see Archie B Carroll and Ann K Buchholtz (2003, p 186) for the rediscovery of the classification of individuals among moral, amoral and immoral ones.
13. Kenneth Arrow (1968) notes, 'Because of the moral hazard, complete reliance on economic incentives does not lead to an optimal allocation of resources in general. In most societies, alternative relationships are built up which to some extent serve to permit cooperation and risk sharing. The principal-agent relation is very pervasive in all economies and especially in modern ones; by definition the agent has been selected for his specialized knowledge and therefore the principal can never hope completely to check the agent's performance. You cannot therefore easily take out insurance against the failure of the agent to perform well. One

of the characteristics of a successful economic system is that the relations of trust and confidence between principal and agent are sufficiently strong so that the agent will not cheat even though it may be "rational economic behavior" to do so.'

14. Charles F Manski (1995,p 8) remarks, 'The economist presented his forecast as a likely range of values for the quantity under consideration. Johnson is said to have replied, "Ranges are for cattle. Give me a number". Similarly, President Truman preferred an economist only with one hand.'

Gerald R Faulhaber and William Baumol (1988) remark, 'Let us next examine the case of marginal analysis, remarkable because this analysis is so fundamental for neoclassical economics, while its explicit use by business and government has apparently been very limited, at least until recently.'

15. In fact, a much richer principal-agent model is implicit in the *Arthashastra*. The utility functions of the principal and agent may be specified as follows:

$$U^P (w, E (w), F (w), M, EE)$$
$$U^A (w, E)$$

Where E denotes the agent's effort, which depends on the wage package but also on its fairness, moral incentives (M) and employer's ethics (EE). The principal offers a package (w) (of wage, and supervision etc.) and ensures fairness and participation in the designing of the package and consults frequently during the execution of the task. For example, differentiating with respect to w gives

$$\partial U^P/\partial w + (\partial U^P/\partial E)(\partial E/\partial w) + (\partial U^P/\partial E)(\partial E/\partial F)(\partial F/\partial w)$$

The first term is the cost of the package to the principal and the second term captures its effect on the agent's effort, if all other things are held constant. But the third term captures the effect of other attributes of the package. If the agent considers the package to be fair, and the principal to be ethical, it is positive, that is he works harder.

16. B Frey and R Jegan (2001) provide a very illuminating survey on the possibilities of crowding out and crowding in, resulting from material incentives. R Benabou, and J Tirole (2003) offer a very rigorous and in-depth analysis of extrinsic incentives and their impact on intrinsic motivation.

Benabou, and Tirole use 'The Looking-glass self' concept in capturing the psychological effect of the material incentives on an agent's self-esteem or self-confidence. Incidentally, Kautilya was aware of the concept but not the phrase 'The Looking-glass self': For example, he (1992, p 205-6) advised a courtier, 'He shall watch carefully the king's gestures and expressions; a wise man will know the mind of another who is trying to reach a decision by looking out for the following: liking and hatred, joy and distress, resoluteness and fear. That the king is satisfied with a courtier is shown by the following: looking pleased at the sight of the courtier, returning his greeting, giving him a seat,... giving orders with a smile. That the king is dissatisfied with a courtier is shown by the following opposite indications: looking angry at the sight of the courtier, ignoring or not returning his greeting, neither giving a seat nor looking at him.'

However, A J Marr (2005) challenges the distinction between intrinsic and extrinsic distinction. He asserts, 'The intrinsic vs. extrinsic motivation controversy is a sham because *distinctive intrinsic and extrinsic motivational processes* simply do not exist.' He adds, 'The unified principle of reinforcement that is emerging from neuroscience casts doubt on many widely accepted categories of motivation due to the simple fact that they have no distinctive neural correlates, and can be more parsimoniously explained as the emergent properties of very simple neural processes that underlie all behavior.'

17. David B Montgomery and Catherine A Ramus (2003) explored whether businesses' ethical standards, environment friendliness and caring about employees attracted MBAs. They report, 'Overall they were willing to forego 11.9% of their mean expected income to work for an organization exhibiting all three characteristics.'

18. George Akerlof (1983) believes that it may be possible to move a child from being immoral to moral. He remarks, Values are not fixed, as in standard economics, but are a matter of choice. Economic theory, which is largely a theory of choice, then becomes a useful tool in analyzing how these values are chosen. Most parents attempt to choose values for their children (and perhaps for themselves) according to their economic opportunities that allow them to get along economically.' He adds, 'It pays parents to teach honesty and class loyalty because the appearance of honesty and class loyalty are beneficial; the easiest way to achieve these appearances is to be honest and loyal, even though honesty and loyalty themselves involve sacrifices.'

19. Carl Shapiro and Joseph Stiglitz (1984) analyze possibility (i), the trade-

off between monitoring (supervision) and paying an efficiency wage to reduce shirking. They find, 'The critical wage, w, is higher the lower the probability of being caught shirking.' Dilip Mookherjee and Ivan P L Png (1992) explore possibility (ii), the trade-off between monitoring and investigation. They assert, 'To regulate employees' effort, an employer could hire supervisors to monitor the workers or, instead, rely on reports from dissatisfied customers.'

20. Kautilya was a very sophisticated thinker. According to him, a king should anticipate his advisers' apprehensions in case of undesirable outcomes resulting from their advice and take appropriate measures to retain them. He (1992, p 636) asserted, 'The king becomes angry and the counselors afraid when a campaign, undertaken on the advice of the counselors, fails to produce the gain predicted by them, but leads to losses and expenses. Counselors frightened of punishment may rebel. When the king gains from a campaign, disregarding the advice of traitorous counselors, then too the king becomes angry and the counselors afraid that the successful king will kill them for giving wrong advice. This too may make them rebel. When a campaign undertaken on the advice of trustworthy counselors achieves the objective or when a campaign undertaken disregarding the advice of untrustworthy counselors fails--in both cases the net result pleases all.' Kautilya's ideas on the relationship between accepting advice from trusted or non-trusted advisers and success or failure of a campaign may be expressed by Matrix 11.2:

Matrix 11.2: **Anticipated Reactions (King, Advisers)**

	Success	Failure
Advice of Trustworthy Advisers Accepted	(Pleases, Pleases)	(Enrages, Fearful)
Advice of Untrustworthy Advisers Not Accepted	(Enrages, Fearful)	(Pleases, Pleases)

According to Kautilya, a king should be aware of the various possibilities so that he can anticipate the possible reactions of the advisers and take the necessary steps. Particularly, he should be able to differentiate between the possibility (advice of Trustworthy Advisers accepted, Failure) and the possibility (advice of Untrustworthy Advisers not accepted, Success). Despite a failure in a campaign, a king should not be angry with the trustworthy advisers. Since not only might he suffer a significant loss of men and material due to the failure, but also might lose his trustworthy advisers, who might be afraid of the king. On the other hand, despite success he should be concerned about the Untrustworthy Advisers and win them back or remove them. Incidentally, the possibility (advice of Untrustworthy Advisers not accepted, Failure) is interesting since in this case the king cannot blame the advisers for the failure since he ignored their advice. Therefore, he has no reason to be angry with them.

21. This is identical to the statement 'instead, rely on reports from dissatisfied customers' by Mookherjee and Png.
22. These conclusions are very similar to those reached by Robert Gibbons (1998). He concludes, 'We have seen, for example, how it may be useful to impose job restrictions to reduce an agent's distractions, and that reducing the agent's outside interests (such as through changing asset ownership) can play a similar role. Once such distractions are reduced, the optimal incentive contract may well have a low bonus rate. In this sense, job restrictions, asset ownership, and low-powered incentives may be complementary.'
23. On the other hand, Stiglitz (1974), after undertaking an in-depth analysis of sharecropping, concludes, 'Thus, it would appear that the main contribution of the model of risk sharing and incentives in agriculture may be more in extending our understanding of the operations of the closely held firm and the differences between it and the modern widely held corporation, than in its direct implications for the latter.'
24. Rajesh K Aggarwal and Andrew A Samwick (1999) find such evidence.
25. The classic work of Stiglitz (1974) evaluates the efficiency of sharecropping system in depth: as many as sixteen propositions are established. He concludes, 'Since there is a natural non-convexity associated with supervision, it was the larger farms which used the wage system.' He adds, 'The landlord wants the best techniques to be used. Either he must provide a strong incentive to the worker to acquire these techniques or he must supervise the workers closely.'

Akerlof (1976) also analyzes wage and sharecropping systems and sums up his findings as follows: 'Where supervision is needed for reasons other than determination of effort, the model predicts that wages rather than shares will be paid. In India, for example, as an excellent rule of thumb, capital-intensive plantation crops are grown on a wage-payment system. And these crops need supervision to insure proper cultivation.'

The works of both Stiglitz and Akerlof provide theoretical justification to Kautilya's insights.

CHAPTER - 12

1. Auerbach (1987, p 604) remarks, 'In the historical evolution of government finance, the income tax is relatively novel. It is difficult to find any evidence of a serious national income tax being used until the end of the 18th century, when William Pitt achieved the passage in Great Britain of the Act of 1799 which imposed a comprehensive income tax, complete with exemptions and abatements for dependents, on all residents of Great Britain. The tax was introduced to maintain the solvency of the British government in the face of the expense of the Napoleonic Wars.' This assertion by Auerbach may be true of the Western world, but does not hold for the rest of the world.

2. *Current State of the Theory of Income Tax*: Current discussion of income tax concentrates on: how to accomplish an intended redistributional goal with a minimum loss in economic efficiency, which results from the distortionary changes in behavior related to work-effort, savings and risk-taking. The question asked is: what should be the rate of progression or how to balance equity and efficiency [although Atkinson and Stiglitz (1980, p 360) call it an artificial distinction] for a specified amount of tax revenue? Nobel Laureate Mirrlees (1971), in his pioneering work, finds (i) 'the income-tax is a much less effective tool for reducing inequalities than has often thought', and (ii) 'the optimal tax structure is approximately linear ie. a constant marginal tax rate.'

   Recently, Diamond (1998) provides several insights into the optimal income taxation for developed countries. However, he concludes, 'There is not a simple route between the Mirrlees model and policy implications for annual income taxes levied repeatedly on families and covering both capital and labor incomes. The assumption of a zero income elasticity of labor supply and the limited information on both the shape of the skill distribution and the pattern of elasticities of labor supply by skill level would limit inferences even if there were a simple route.'

   Similarly, Stern (1987, p 83), while exploring the relative efficiencies of various designs of tax systems for developing countries, writes, 'We shall suggest that, although the theories provide valuable and important lessons for practical tax policy, they do not in general provide direct results on tax rates.'

Dahan and Strawczynski (2000, fn. 2) note, 'In Mirrlees' pioneering simulations, optimal marginal taxes decline with income. Since the shape was close to linearity, this point was stressed neither by Mirrlees nor by other authors citing his work.'

It is obvious that despite the mathematical sophistication and progress in economic knowledge, we are not any closer to answering the basic question: what should be the rate of progression in the income tax? Additionally, this is the situation despite the fact that the expenditure side of the budget is totally ignored in these explorations.

3. In recent years, the flat income tax has received some attention. For example, according to Browning and Browning (1994, p 378), 'If AGI were the tax base, a rate of 13.3 per cent would suffice' to collect the same revenue as the 1989 tax structure (USA) did.

Similarly, Hall and Rabushka (1995, p 52) claim, 'The astonishingly low 19 per cent tax rate raises the same revenue as does the current tax system.'

4. Allan (1971, p 178) notes, 'It is possible, therefore, to come to the same sort of policy conclusions by either the 'benefit' or the 'ability' argument. The rich paying more than the poor is clearly indicated by both approaches.'

5. Alm (1988) analyzes the impact of uncertain tax policies on individual work effort and savings. He distinguishes between two kinds of uncertainty: the tax base uncertainty and the tax rate uncertainty. With the income effect and the substitution effect working in opposite directions (in general therefore), it is not possible to assign a sign to the direction of change. He concludes, 'Still, the results indicate that uncertain tax policies often have a negative effect on expected revenues; tax rate risk in particular always has this effect. At present, in these cases complaints about unpredictable government actions seem well founded. Not only are individuals made worse off by the randomness, but the government itself loses revenues.'

6. Parmar (1987, p 36) remarks, 'The state in ancient India, at least in the Mauryan India, was, to use the language of modern political science, not unitary but federal and consisted of numerous principalities. However, it is difficult to ascertain the exact relationship that obtained between the imperial power and the provinces that comprised the empire. If federalism is taken to be a system in which the central authority exercises

only a limited power over the authorities beneath it, Mauryan state was a federal one; for it did not exercise unlimited jurisdiction over states under it and was in fact a loose confederation of a conglomeration of different states.'

7. In a recent work, Oates (1999) remarks on fiscal federalism, 'However, the choice of a system of governance involves other values as well: the extent of political participation, the protection of individual rights, and the development of various civic virtues.'

8. Since it assumes simultaneous moves by the merchant and the government. In fact, this could be set up as a sequential game in which government announces the policy first and the traders react to it. The tax authorities may choose the probability of detection, ϕ such that the trader decides not to cheat or the tax authorities may choose to audit a random sample (see Rasmusen 1994, Chapter 3 for a lucid exposition). Recently, Andreoni, Erard and Feinstein (1998) survey the models related to the 'interaction between taxpayers and the tax authorities.' They classify these models into two groups: (a) primarily principal-agent types in which tax authorities make commitment to audit and (b) truly game-theoretic ones in which tax authorities do not commit to auditing. Kautilya's model may be classified as a principal-agent type.

9. *Dupuit-Laffer Curve*: Atkinson (1987, p 392) notes, 'The possibility that revenue may reach a maximum has been popularized among US Congressmen by Arthur B Laffer but has been well known for many years: for example, Jules Dupuit noted in 1844, "If a tax is gradually increased from zero up to the point where it becomes prohibitive, its yield is at first nil, then increases by small steps until it reaches a maximum, after which it gradually declines until it becomes zero again" (quoted in Arrow and Scitovsky, 1969, p 278).'

10. Drekmeier, Charles (1962, p 214) states, 'Taxation policy in The *Arthashastra* and in the *Manusmriti* (as in the great body of theory culminating in the *Shukranitisara*) reflects the view that while the state has a right to the golden egg, the goose must be protected. Taxation should be gradual, increased only in times of emergency, and then only when rationalized to the people. It should be based on net profits instead of gross earnings, and an article should be taxed only once.'

11. Adam Smith (Book V, Ch II, p 350-351) listed four canons of Taxation: (1) equality, (2) certainty, (3) convenience of payment and (4) economy

in collection. He (p 350) explained the canon of equality as: 'The subjects of every state ought to contribute towards the support of the government, as nearly as possible, in proportion to their respective abilities; that is, in proportion to the revenue which they respectively enjoy under the protection of the state. The expense of government to the individuals of a great nation, is like the expense of management to the joint tenants of a great estate, who are all obliged to contribute in proportion to their respective interests in the estate.' Musgrave (1959, p 67) comments, 'Smith thus shrewdly inserted an ability element into the weak link of the benefit rule. Thereby, reliance on the protection theory of state was tempered. The two approaches were joined in one, foreshadowing a similar solution in the modern version of the benefit doctrine.' He (p 68) remarks, 'Thus the subsistence theory of wages led Smith to progressive taxation at the lower end of the income scale.' He (p 92) adds, 'For Adam Smith, the reason is simply that ability to pay was considered only as an adjunct to the more basic benefit rule.'

CHAPTER - 13

1. Table 1, which is based on able 2.4 in Sihag (1978, p 22) supports Kautilya's intuition that many regions were affected by a drought.

Table 1: **Interstate Correlations among output Levels**

	BR	MP	PB	UP
BR	1.00	0.71	0.50	0.68
MP		1.00	0.75	0.80
PB			1.00	0.83
UP				1.00

2. Ravallion concludes, 'Economic analysis can help understand famines' and he adds, 'An effective but affordable (and hence sustainable) stabilization policy in famine-prone economies with poor infrastructure will probably combine buffer stocks and regulated trade.'
3. Toshihiro Ihori and Martin McGuire (2008, fn. 13) remark, 'For individual protection and insurance, a hierarchal separation between protection and insurance decisions sounds implausible. The smoker anticipates lower life insurance rates when he quits smoking. He may think of buying more insurance at the lower rates as well. But to impute

this sort of foresight to a government, however, is not at all obvious. Thus our "complete information" case might be regarded as ideal, even utopian." Apparently they ignore the most important role of foresightedness by confining their analysis to a single period. Since no one can build buffer stocks during a drought and similarly it takes time to build irrigation facilities.

4. Ravallion (1997) remarks, 'Famines do not lend themselves to easy prediction.'

CHAPTER - 14

1. *Adam Smith and Laissez Faire*: Historically, Adam Smith has been hailed as a harbinger of unfettered free trade. However, in recent years, that view has been challenged. The change in tone may be captured by the following comments by a few writers during the last four decades. Letiche (1960, p 70) asserts, 'Smith was not a doctrinaire advocate of *laissez faire*. He recommended at least four major programs of reform: the removal of impediments to free choice of occupation; to free trade in land; to internal free trade; and to free trade in foreign commerce. Moreover, he recognized the need for government activity in such fields as public education and hygiene, public works, regulation of currency and coinage, progressive (in effect, proportional) taxation, patents, copyrights, and even moderate export and import taxes for the purpose of revenue and development.'

Tribe (1999, fn., 49) remarks, 'For example, Smith did not employ terms "free trade" or "laissez-faire", although he would have known of their use by others.'

Grampp observes that 'In the extended debate from 1815 to 1846, over the British Corn Laws, the protectionists cited Smith's statement that there should be a duty on an imported good that competed with a domestically produced good subject to a tax.' He adds, 'He expressly said domestic "industry necessary for the defense of the country" should be "encouraged". Domestic trade is superior to foreign because domestic trade gives twice the encouragement to industry that trade gives and also receives its returns more quickly (p 463, 377-78, 426, 368)' He points out that 'In the *Wealth of Nations* and in the *Lectures on Jurisprudence* there are (depending on how finely one makes distinctions) some 35 or 40 measures of government intervention of which Smith approved or which he advocated. They are of five kinds. The fourth restricts foreign trade, and the most important measures are those that contribute to defense.'

The comments from Grampp clearly cast doubt on Adam Smith's historical image. Since he did favour domestic industry over imports. Perhaps, Adam Smith went too far in attacking the Mercantilists on their obsession with trade surplus and wanted to change the focus towards domestic production.

2. Cooper (1977, Vol 26, p 910-916) describes the nature of international trade in ancient times. He observes, 'Early trade was attended by large risks—both natural risks such as storms and human risks such as piracy and brigandage—and was hampered by poor transport. Because of risks, trade was limited to easily transportable, high-value products. Trade was based largely on goods derived from natural advantages—the presence of desirable natural resources such as tin, gold, amber, or ebony—but occasionally also on the products of special technology and unique skills, as in the case of Egyptian glass beads and cloth dyed with the famous Tyrean purple.'

3. Kautilya suggested a mix of riskless and risky products: He emphasized the principle of diversification by requiring a combination of risky high value products and riskless low value goods. He classified products into two groups: the low value ones, which were safe to transport (also might have been because of their bulkiness and heaviness) and the high value ones, which were potential targets of bandits and therefore risky to transport (probably these were very light and not bulky). Therefore, Kautilya proposed a mixing of low value products and high value products. The figure (14.1) may be used to express Kautilya's ideas.

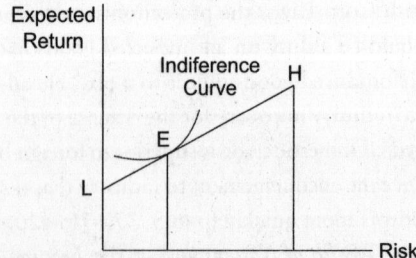

Figure 14.1: LH is the efficiency frontier.

Point L indicates a point of no risk and low return for low value products and point H represents the return and risk combination for high value products. It should be noted that these are the only points and not a Markowitz-Sharpe kind of smooth efficiency frontier as such. Kautilya suggested the selection of a point E, which indicated the portfolio-mix consisting of 75 percent of low value products and 25 percent of high value products. Kautilya did separate the decision regarding the choice of the portfolio-mix from the determination of the total size of the caravan. However, it is not claimed that he was aware of the separation theorem.

4. Caves, Frankel and Jones (2002) believe if the trade is based on 'natural advantages' then there is not much to be explained and definitely the services of an economist are not needed. They (p 13) assert, 'Some trade patterns need little explanation. If you live in the United States and like coffee, you have your coffee imported from Brazil or some other coffee-growing country because it is not produced at home.' They add, 'There would be little need for the economist either to expound on the virtues of trade or to explain trade patterns. These would be almost self-evident.'

5. Kautilya explicitly considered two countries and two commodities. Let P_x^F and P_y^F be the respective prices of products X and Y in a foreign country and P_x^H and P_y^H are their respective prices in the home country. The home country should export say product X only if after paying transport cost and security expenses for passage, C, and tariffs and gratuity to the king, T, can get more of product Y in exchange in the foreign country than could have gotten at home. Also, the phrase 'the price likely to be realized' indicates his concern for price uncertainty. Let Z captures the risk element in the price. According to him, a country should engage in trade if it is beneficial to do so, that is, a country should export product X and import product Y only if

$$P_y^H (P_x^F X - C - T - Z)/P_y^F - P_x^H X > 0 \qquad (14.1)$$

Or

$$(P_x^F X - C - T - Z)/P_y^F > P_x^H X/P_y^H \qquad (14.2)$$

Or

$$(1-\mu-t-\pi) P_x^F X/P_y^F > P_x^H X/P_y^H \qquad (14.3)$$

Or

$$(1-\mu-t-\pi) P_x^F/P_y^F > P_x^H/P_y^H \qquad (14.4)$$

Where $\mu = C/P_x^F X$, $t = T/P_x^F X$, and $\pi = Z/P_x^F X$

It is quite clear from equation (14.4), which incorporates tariffs and transportation costs that Kautilya understood, that there were gains from trade. It is ambiguous, however whether he understood the principle of comparative advantage. Never the less Waldauer *et al* (1996) conclude, 'Thus, Kautilya recognized that trade based on the principle of comparative advantage would be to the material benefit of both exporting and importing nations.'

6. Wilford (2002) reports, 'So robust was the India trade 2000 years ago that Emperor Tiberius, concerned over Rome's increasingly adverse balance of payments, complained that "the ladies and their baubles are transferring our *money* to foreigners."' He adds, 'Also, it was not an overwhelmingly Roman enterprise, as had been generally assumed. The researchers said artifacts at the sight indicated that the ships might have been built in India and were probably crewed by Indians.' He describes the archaeological trove at Berenike seaport in Egypt as: '"Mind-boggling" find: teak and metal, beads and gems, batik and peppercorns.' Of course, by the time of Adam smith, international trade had become quite significant.

7. Recently, Ken McCormick (1999) asserts, 'Specifically, this paper is about the independent advocacy of a policy of *laissez-faire* by both ancient Taoist philosophers and Classical economists. Recognizing the independent development of this idea has not only intrinsic historical interest but also provides the doctrine of laissez-faire with another substantial philosophical leg on which to stand.' He finds that 'This "hands off" approach to government is central to Taoism. There is a natural harmony in the social order, which can be achieved only by a policy of non-interference. Passivity on the part of the ruler allows the Tao to bring about harmony and prosperity.' He claims that 'Laissez-faire is simply an extension of the doctrine of "wu wei" to government policy.' He defines 'wu wei' as 'do nothing.'

CHAPTER - 15

1. Joseph J Spengler (1971) makes a special note of legal rules regarding partnership. He (p 79) writes, 'Rules for the distribution of remuneration when work was done jointly not only were laid out by Kautilya but also found expression in commercial arithmetic. When workmen, guild

members, or others engage in cooperative undertakings, they "shall divide the wages as agreed upon or in equal proportions" (3.14.18).'
2. Since Gary S Becker's (1968) seminal work, hundreds of articles have appeared dealing with a variety of aspects of law enforcement. These works also analyze law enforcement and deterrence. These may be classified as: (i) rent-seeking behavior or corruption by the enforcers and its impact on economic growth and crime deterrence; (ii) judicial fairness and the minimization of legal errors in the disposition of criminal cases; (iii) the form of punishment that whether it should be monetary or non-monetary, and (iv) the time inconsistency or the credibility problems, that is, society may not find it optimal to carry out the punishment once the crime has been committed and the related issue of judicial discretion.
3. Only recently has this issue has drawn attention from economists. Pranab Bardhan (1997) reviews the issues related to corruption and economic growth.
4. 'Early Roman law derived from custom and statutes but the emperor asserted his authority as the ultimate source of law. His edicts, judgments, administrative instructions, and responses to petitions were collected with the comments of legal scholars. As one 3rd-century jurist said, "What pleases the emperor has the force of law." As the law and scholarly commentaries on it expanded, the need grew to codify and to regularize conflicting opinions. It was not until much later in the 6th century AD that the emperor Justinian I, who ruled over the Byzantine Empire in the east, began to publish a comprehensive code of laws, collectively known as the *Corpus Juris Civils*, but more familiarly as the Justinian Code.'(Reference http://www.crystalinks.com/romelaw.html)
5. A Mitchell Polinsky and Steven Shavell (2000) survey the field on law enforcement. In the last section of their article, under the sub-heading 'future research' they recommend, 'The behavior and compensation of enforcement agents have not been examined in this article, but this topic is important and should be studied for two reasons. First, the incentive of enforcement agents to discover violations is affected by the structure of their payments. Secondly, enforcement agents may be corrupted: they may accept bribes, or demand payments, in exchange for not reporting violations. Corruption tends to reduce deterrence, and therefore its presence obviously will affect the theory of optimal law enforcement.' In the light of Kautilya's contribution their suggestion amounts to[:] 'going back to the future.'

Similarly, David D Friedman (1999) describes the various elements of an efficient system of criminal punishment, which includes 'penal slavery for criminals who can produce more than it costs to guard and feed them.' He summarizes his findings as: 'Hence imprisonment is always dominated by execution and both are dominated by fines and other alternatives. Modern legal systems do not fit that pattern. One possible explanation is that the ability of enforcers to profit by convictions can produce costly rent seeking.' Friedman believes that the real reason for the existence of inefficient system is to curb the possibility of rent seeking on the part of the enforcers.

6. For example, Thomas J Miceli (1990) remarks, 'For instance, an important question of fairness relates to the incidence of errors by the criminal process.'

7. Becker (1968) discussed only the prevention of crimes but did not suggest anything if a crime was committed. Miceli (1991) proposes a comprehensive model of fairness and deterrence, which presumably combines Becker's crime prevention model and Miceli's (1990) fairness model. However, Kautilya implicitly provided a more comprehensive approach with many additional insights. The following table captures Kautilya's conceptual framework.

Table 15.2: **Kautilya's Conceptual Framework for Defining Type I and Type II Errors.**

		Truly Guilty (G)	Innocent ($\overline{G}_C$)	
		$P(A \cap G)$	$P(A \cap \overline{G}_C)$	$P(A)$
Arrested (A)	Convicted (C)	$P(C \cap A \cap G)$ (Correct Decision)	$P(C \cap A \cap \overline{G}_C)$ (Type I Legal Error)	
	Not convicted (Cc)	$P(\overline{C}_C \cap A \cap G)$ (Type II Legal Error)	$P(\overline{C}_C \cap A \cap \overline{G}_C)$ (Correct Decision)	
Not arrested (Ac)		$P(\overline{A}_C \cap G)$	$P(\overline{A}_C \cap \overline{G}_C)$	$P(\overline{A}_C)$
		$P(G)$	$P(\overline{G}_C)$	1

Kautilya's Definitions of Judicial Errors: Let G = the number of guilty and G_c = the number of innocent. Let P_a = P (A/G) = [P (A∩G)/P (G)] = probability of arresting a guilty person, Pc = [P(C ∩ A∩G)/P (A∩G)] = probability of convicting a guilty person who has been arrested, π = $P_a P_c$ = P(C ∩ A∩G)/P (G) = probability of arresting and convicting a guilty person. The king had to compensate the victim if the criminal was not convicted and the arrest alone did not make a difference. So Kautilya's approach implied defining the probability of Type II error as, β = $(1-P_a P_c)$ = $(1-\pi)$ = probability of a guilty person not convicted, and the probability of Type I error as = α = P(C ∩ A∩G_c)/P (G_c) probability of arresting and convicting an innocent person.

8. **Miceli's Definition of Legal Errors:** A judicial process is initiated to find the guilt or innocence of a person arrested for an alleged crime. For example, Miceli (1991) defines the probabilities of legal errors as follows. He sets d = δ (G/A) = [P (A∩G)/P (A)] = probability that an arrested person is guilty; P_g = [P(C ∩ A∩G)/P (A∩G)] = probability of convicting a guilty person (ie. $(1-P_g)$ is the probability of not convicting a guilty person); probability that an arrested person is guilty and is convicted = δP_g = P (C ∩ A∩G)/P (A). Type II legal error probability = $\delta(1-P_g)$. Probability of convicting an innocent person = P_i = P (C∩A∩G_c)/P (A∩G_c), and Type I legal error probability = $(1-\delta) P_i$ = P(C∩A∩G_c)/P(A) = probability of arresting and convicting an innocent person.

Miceli's Definitions based on the numbers: Type I error probability = 5/110 and Type II error probability = 20/110. If the objective is to assess the performance of the judiciary only, Miceli's definitions are sufficient since his analysis is confined only to those who have been arrested. However, his definitions are not relevant if the objective is to deter crimes. For example, if the enforcement authorities arrest just one criminal person (out of the 1000) and convict him, that is, δ = 1 and P_g = 1. According to Miceli's definition, the probability of conviction = δP_g = 1. But that cannot be correct since the probability of conviction of a guilty person would be = 1/1000 (= δP_g A/G = A/G), which is very small to deter any crime. It means that Miceli's model did not achieve its goal of combing prevention of crimes and judicial fairness.

Polinsky and Shavell (2000) do not define the various probabilities explicitly. It seems that they define the legal errors in the following way. Let the probability of detection, P be defined as P = A/G = 110/1000, the Type I error probability (they call it Type II error), ε_2 = $(1-\delta)$ A/G

=10/1000; and Type II error probability, $\varepsilon_1 = \delta(1-P_g) A/G = 20/1000$. That means in the presence of legal errors, the effective probability of detection = $P (1-\varepsilon_1-\varepsilon_2) = \delta P_g A/G = 80/1000$. This is precisely, the probability of arresting and convicting a guilty person and is relevant for deterring crimes.

They present an alternative insightful interpretation of these errors. They consider the negative impact of Type I error (contrary to tradition, they call it Type II error) on crime deterrence. They note, 'The second type of error, mistaken liability, also lowers deterrence because it reduces the difference between the expected fine from violating the law and not violating it. In other words, the greater is ε_2, the smaller the increase in the expected fine if one violates the law, making a violation less costly to the individual.'

9. On the other hand, Miceli (1990) assumes that an increase in efforts by the prosecutor to collect more evidence shifts the distributions to the right implying an increase in the probability of Type I error. He notes that prosecutors generally try to shift the distributions to the right. That is clearly against the collective sense of justice.

10. Drekmeier (1962, p 254) remarks, 'Kautilya: holds that *danda* must be applied with justice if authority is to have the respect of the people—which amounts to saying that justice is what transforms power into "authority."' *Danda* means punishment.

11. Recently, Jennifer F Reinganum (2000) has discussed the establishment of the United States Sentencing Commission to develop the sentencing guidelines for achieving certain social goals. These are very similar, as mentioned above, to those specified by Kautilya. She states, 'The motivation for such guidelines included at least the following arguments. First, the then-current system of indeterminate sentencing with parole made it difficult for either the offender or the state to form a reasonable estimate of the actual sentence; definitive sentencing guidelines were believed to provide honesty in sentencing. Secondly, the sentencing guidelines were intended to reduce observed disparity in sentencing across apparently similar cases. Finally, the sentencing guidelines would build in proportionality in sentencing by conditioning the prescribed sentence on offense and offender characteristics.'

12. *Cost of Carrying out Punishment*: Becker (1968) reaches the conclusion that monetary fines are merely transfers and do not use real resources and therefore, are preferable. However, Becker's suggestion has been found to

be impractical and the society has to incur some cost in the collection of fines. Based on an empirical study, Robert W Gillespie (1988-89) finds, 'The relatively low enforcement success achieved for large fines, particularly drug fines larger than $1000.' Gillespie casts doubt on 'The use of fines as a criminal sanction in terms of lower social costs of punishment.'

13. Polinsky and Shavell remark, 'The implications of injurers' imperfect knowledge are straightforward. First, to predict how individuals behave, what is relevant, of course, is not the actual probability and magnitude of a sanction, but the perceived levels or distributions of these variables.'

On the other hand, in recent years, the US public has been demanding (from their respective state governments) the right to know if any sex offender lived in their neighborhood. This may serve as a warning to the parents so that they could keep a close watch on their children. Recently, some states have passed legislation requiring the registration of sex offenders. Kautilya focused primarily on the perceived probability of detecting the criminals. Doron Teichman (2004) argues, 'That such policies have limited preventive value, yet they might be justified as an efficient way to sanction sex offenders.'

CHAPTER - 16

1. ***Law and Ethics***: D'Amato (1981) lists the views of some well-known legal theorists, which vary from Bentham's extreme positivism view that there is no necessary relationship between law and morality to Cicero's extreme natural law view that there is a necessary relationship between law and morality.
2. History of *Law and Economics*: It is now almost universally accepted that the application of economic analysis to law originated much earlier than during the 50's. Mackaay (1999) provides a very detailed history of law and economics. His list includes Adam Smith, David Hume, Beccaria, Bellamy and Jerome Bentham. Medema *et al* (1999) present the contributions of John R Commons and many others on the application of economic analysis to law. Medema (2004) brings out Sidgwick's contribution to law and economics. According to Sima (2004), 'It is notable that Carl Menger, who memorably played a part in the emergence of the new science of marginalist economics, was a lawyer who contributed to the development of law.' Kautilya devoted almost one-third of his *Arthashastra* to issues related to the administration of

justice. Drekmeier (p 254) believes that Kautilya understood that 'justice is what transforms power into "authority."'

3. Bell and Parchomovsky (2005) quote Jeremy Bentham, 'Property and law are born together, and die together. Before laws were made there was no property; take away laws, and property ceases.'

4. According to Goetzmann (2006), 'When people started living in large communities like Uruk, they began to live with strangers as well as friends. It may have been possible to know everyone in a large farming village, but not in a vast city such as Uruk. What were once implicit agreements among neighbors now became explicit, contractual agreements among strangers. When everyone had the same profession and skills, neighborly help could always be repaid in kind. But when people developed different professions it must have been difficult to maintain neighborly reciprocity. Urban societies still needed cooperation, but limits to familiarity with fellow inhabitants, and difficulty with quantifying the units of such cooperation meant that people required more formal ways to insure a return on their helpful efforts. Cambridge University's Paul Millett traced this developmental relationship between urbanization and interest loans in ancient Athens in the first century BC. In Greece, the pattern is clear—urbanism necessitated explicit contracts, and gave rise to interest charges. Interest is a "sweetener" to induce someone to lend you what you need.'

5. Posner (2003, p 25) states, 'Many areas of law, especially the great common law fields of property, torts, crimes, and contracts, bear the stamp of economic reasoning. It is not a refutation that few judicial opinions contain explicit references to economic concepts. Often the true grounds of decision are concealed rather than illuminated by the characteristic rhetoric of judicial opinions. Indeed, legal education consists primarily of learning to dig beneath the rhetorical surface to find those grounds, many of which may turn out to have an economic character.'

6. Bell and Parchomovsky (2005) conclude, 'This Article has shown that property is best understood as a legal institution designed to create and protect the value inherent in stable ownership of assets.'

CHAPTER -17

1. According to Kautilya (p 741), the king, 'Shall adopt the way of life, dress, language and customs of the people [of the acquired territory], show the same devotion to the gods of the territory [as to his own gods]

and participate in the people's festivals and amusements. He shall ensure that devotions are held regularly in all the temples and ashrams. The ill, the helpless and the distressed shall be helped (13.5).'

Drekmeier (p 198) observes, 'The author of the *Arthashastra* emerges as something of a champion of the *shudras*, espousing their rights as freeborn citizens, and going so far as to suggest that the sons of slaves should enjoy the status of Aryans.'

Similarly, B R Ambedkar (1891-1956), one of the framers of Indian Constitution, a strong defender of political rights of lower classes and a vocal critic of Manu's Code, remarked, 'This country has seen the conflict between ecclesiastical law and secular law long before Europeans sought to challenge the authority of the Pope. Kautilya's *Arthashastra* lays down the foundation of secular law in India, unfortunately ecclesiastical law triumphed over secular law.'

2. Kangle (1972, part III, p 81) observes, 'There is little doubt that the *Manusmrti* in these chapters is a compilation based on many sources, the *Arthashastra* being the most important among them.' He (p 83) concludes his detailed discussion as: 'It may, therefore, be safely concluded that the *Arthashastra* cannot be regarded as indebted to the *Smrtis* of Manu and Yajnavalika and hence posterior to them in date. On the contrary, it seems extremely probable that these *Smrtis* knew and utilized this text of the *Arthashastra* are later in date than this work.'

Similarly, Patrick Olivelle (2005, p 47) remarks, 'Given the problems inherent in the dating of these two texts, it is not possible to assert with high degree of confidence who is borrowing from whom. I do agree with Kangle, however, that it is most likely that at least sections of the *Arthashastra* are older than Manu and are the source for some of the passages and vocabulary I will discuss below.'

3. Patrick Olivelle (2005, p 39) comments, 'A major aim of Manu was to reestablish the old alliance between *brahma* and *ksatra*, an alliance that in his view would benefit both the king and the Brahmin, thereby reestablishing the Brahmin in his unique and privileged position within society.'

4. For an excellent survey on social norms see McAdams, Richard H and Eric Rasmusen (2005).

5. M Stuart Madden (2005, p 835) observes, 'Ordinarily, early codes reflected efforts to gather, rationalize, and organize already extant customary law. For all that is apparent, Hammurabi himself intended that his law reconciled

wrongs and bring justice to those aggrieved. His unmistakable goal was the economic stability and enhancement of the people.'

6. For a much deeper understanding of this distinction and many others, see Benjamin Zipursky (2008). For example, he (p 106) observes, 'Wrongful injuring of another and violations of regulatory rules designed to ensure that people drive in non-injurious ways are both responded to in the law, but are responded to in different ways: the former by an individual plaintiff through tort law, the latter by the state through regulatory (or traffic) law. The moral luck problem in tort law stems, in part, from the failure to appreciate the differences between these two different modes of response within the legal system—tort liability being a holding responsible for a breach of duty of non-injury, and regulatory liability being a holding-responsible for a breach of a duty of non-injuriousness.'

7. I am grateful to Prof Peter Diamond for this formulation.

Assume penance is additive to utility from consumption and measured in utility terms the utility function is:

$U = u(I-F) - P$

Where I= income, F= fine, and P= penance.

An indifference curve satisfies

$P = u(I-F) - U$

$dP/dF = -u' < 0$

And

$d^2P/dF^2 = u'' < 0$

That is, the indifference curve for two bads is concave.

8. Guido Calabresi (2007, p 5) observes, 'Compensation to the victim was not a *necessary* part of it. And indeed, tort-like remedies that existed around the same time may not have contemplated compensation at all. The Hundred (the neighbourhood) was assessed if a thief was not caught. The Hundred was charged the amount of the thievery. But this amount didn't necessarily go to the person whose property had been stolen. Compensation was not the essence of what was going on. It was not a matter of somebody's right to recover. It was system-building, not corrective justice.'

It may be added that when a corporation is penalized, all the stakeholders may share the burden and it may be called a Thousand instead of a Hundred. Similarly, Hylton and Miceli (2005) conclude, 'There appears to be no case for multiplying damages in order to guarantee reasonable care in the medical malpractice context.' Again,

in response to higher malpractice awards, physicians are likely to resort to defensive medical practices and ultimately the cost might get shifted to the consumers through high health insurance premia.
9. Prue Vines (2007, p 15) observes, 'Apologies can be part of this corrective justice mix if one considers compensation as practical reparation and apology as reparation for the emotional and moral pain suffered for the victim.' He adds, 'Similarly, an apology might be a mechanism which reinforces the moderation of damages, on the basis that the non-economic parts of the award, such as that for pain and suffering, might be better repaired by an apology than award of *money*.'
10. Coleman (2003) explains it very aptly as: 'The rule of fault liability is efficient in the two party case in that it induces both injurers and victims to make optimal investments in safety. The rule of fault liability imposes on the injurer only if he is fault. If the injurer is rational, he will always take the cost justified precautions. We established this result above in the discussion of the one party accident case. Thus, the rational injurer will never be at fault. If people are always rational, then the costs of whatever accidents occur will fall to their victims.'
11. Ayesha (2010, p 2) points out, 'Defamation is a unique tort, especially when understood in its historical context. Until the 16th century in England, general jurisdiction over defamation was exercised by the clergy. Thereafter, the common law courts developed an action on the case for slander where 'temporal', as distinct from 'spiritual' damage could be established. This progress became too rapid for the judges who proceeded to hedge the action around with tighter restrictions. Later, the common law courts established a distinction between libel and slander on the basis that damage could be presumed in libel, but that the plaintiff would have to prove 'special damage' before an action for slander would lie.'
12. M Stuart Madden (2005, p 832) observes, 'Withal, even though the sources of contemporary civil law have changed, the needs of modern society for a similar order and predictability in human civil affair remain very similar to the needs confronting our ancestors.'

CHAPTER - 18

1. Surprisingly, Adam Smith had very similar views on foreign rule. Letiche (1960, 72) states, 'The Government of India, Smith wrote, was composed of a council of foreign merchants. "The plunderers of India", he called

them in one passage, "military and despotical", in another.'

2. Alternatively this may be specified as:
$$DE_1 = \alpha_0 + \alpha_1 Y_1 + \alpha_2 DE_2 \qquad (18.3)$$
$$DE_2 = \beta_0 + \beta_1 Y_2 + \beta_2 DE_1 \qquad (18.4)$$
Where DE_1 and DE_2 are respective expenditures on defense and Y_1 and Y_2 are the respective incomes of the two countries. According to Kautilya, national security depended not just on how much a nation spent on her defense but also how much a potential adversary spent on defense.

3. According to Tversky and Kahneman (1991), the value function has three characteristics: 'Reference dependence: the carriers of value are gains and losses defined relative to a reference point. Loss aversion: the function is steeper in the negative than in the positive domain; losses loom larger than corresponding gains. Diminishing sensitivity: the marginal value of both gains and losses decreases with their size. These properties give rise to an asymmetric S-shaped value function, concave above the reference point and convex below it.'

4. According to Tversky and Kahneman (1979), 'Any discussion of the utility function for *money* must leave room for the effect of special circumstances on preferences. For example, the utility function of an individual who needs $60,000 to purchase a house may reveal an exceptionally steep rise near the critical value. Similarly, an individual's aversion to losses may increase sharply near the loss that would compel him to sell his house and move to a less desirable neighbourhood.' Kautilya's approach would be better in this case since the price of the house is not fixed and could rise or fall, implying the use of the ratio of current assets to target assets would be more appropriate.

5. Tversky and Kahneman (1991) remark, 'Although the reference state usually corresponds to the decision maker's current position, it can also be influenced by aspirations, expectations, norms, and social comparisons.'

6. See the discussion on tort liabilities in the preceding chapter. Kautilya discussed many tort liabilities, such as accidents, defamation, malpractice etc. at length. Urbanization had [led] to the opening up of many types of services, including laundry services. Due care required washing cloth on a smooth surface stone, otherwise the washerman was liable for a tort liability.

   Building Codes: Kautilya recommended building codes to protect privacy. He (p 371) wrote, 'The doors and windows shall be so made as not to cause annoyance by facing directly a door or a window of a neighbouring house. Any window made for lighting shall be high up [so that it does not overlook a room of another house] (3.8).'

Penalties for tossing dirt in the road: Boesche knows that there is a fine if a person throws anything on the road. Pollution is a negative externality. If left to people or businesses, they would pollute the rivers, lakes and the environment. Aristotle and Adam Smith talk about externalities but Kautilya provided a solution also to handle it, a kind of corrective fine or a fee. This is explained in Chapter 16 on property rules and contract laws.

CHAPTER - 19

1. Johnston (2000) notes, 'Risk taking, for example, had a long tradition before the advent of studies in the mathematics of probability. The Babylonians had had forms of maritime insurance; the Romans had annuities (exchanges of a lump sum in return for regular payments over a long time—the risk being that the person taking out the annuity will not live to collect the lump sum); and gambling had existed since time immemorial.'

    However, Markowitz's (1952) two insights are noteworthy. (i) 'The portfolio with maximum expected return is not necessarily the one with minimum variance. There is a rate at which the investor can gain expected return by taking on variance, or reduce variance by giving up expected return.' (ii) 'In trying to make variance small, it is not enough to invest in many securities. It is necessary to avoid investing in securities with high covariances among themselves.'

2. Similarly, according to Friedman and Savage (1948), Adam Smith and Marshall did not say much on portfolio theory. They note, 'These problems have, of course, been considered by economic theorists, particularly in their discussions of earnings in different occupations and of profits in different lines of business. Their treatment of these problems has, however, never been integrated with their explanation of choices among riskless alternatives.' They comment on the incoherent views of Alfred Marshall and Adam Smith on explaining behavior towards risk. They assert, 'Choices among alternatives involving different degrees of risk, for example, among different occupations, are explained in utterly different terms—by ignorance of the odds or by the fact that "young men of an adventurous disposition are more attracted by the prospects of a great success than they are deterred by the fear of failure", by

"overweening conceit which the greater part of men have of their own abilities" by "their absurd presumption in their own good fortune", or by some similar deus ex machina.'

3. Johnston (2000) points out, 'In keeping with the legal traditions of his time, Pascal's emphasis here is on expectation and equality between the two players, the central point of his analysis, rather than on the calculation of the probability outcomes and their associated values (2). Hence, he eliminated probability from as much of the problem as possible, using certain gain and equity in its place (3).' He quotes Daston: 'Once again the modern order of reasoning regarding expectations was inverted: instead of the game being fair because the probabilities (and therefore the expectations in a symmetric game) are equal for all players, the probabilities are (implicitly) equal because the game is assumed [to be] fair—and the game is fair because the conditions of the players are indistinguishable, as shown by their willingness to exchange expectations (Daston 26).' He comments on the tension between reasonableness and prudence, exposed by the Petersburg Paradox. He observes, 'The assumption here that reasonable behaviour (the conduct of the prudent intelligent person) was a universal standard, which matched mathematical calculations of expectations was a widespread belief in the 18th century and persisted well into the 19th. This slight (although very well known) example illustrated a tension between equitable games and prudent behaviour. Equity would seem to demand a large stake from A (since the potential risk for B is high indeed), and yet, if A is reasonable, prudence would seem to insist upon a relatively small stake.'

Similarly, Wit (1997) explains it well, 'What the St Petersburg Paradox shows us is that the there is no *inherent* connection between mathematics objects and rational action. The *Paradox* only exists as a paradox if one believes that such a connection does exist. That Daniel Bernoulli understood this fact clearly demonstrate his definition of *moral expectation* as an attempt to model human moral intuitions in response to the Paradox. He argued that any gain is less than proportionately related to moral enjoyment (whereas damage possesses a more than proportional relationship). According to this *moral expectation* a *rational* (where rational is taken to be the same as acting in accordance with *moral expectation, by definition*) person would pay at most $1 for the game.'

4. Varian (1993) noted that Friedman gave a hard time to Markowitz in defense of his thesis on portfolio balancing as a part of economics.

Interestingly, Markowitz concedes the point.
5. Although Adam Smith was also worried, at least, about an underestimation of the probability of a loss, he did not incorporate it into any decision-making. Adam Smith (p 209-210) remarked, 'The chance of gain is by every man more or less over-valued, and the chance of loss is by most men under-valued.'
6. Varian (1993) points out, 'Even Keynes (1939) said, "To suppose that safety-first consists in having a small gamble in a large number of different companies strikes me as a travesty of investment policy."'
7. Interestingly, Daniel Bernoulli (1738) remarked, 'It also follows from this that a man who risks his entire fortune acts like a simpleton, however great may be the possible gain.' However, there was one significant difference. Despite the unavailability of the concepts of variance and covariance, the other developments in mathematics allowed him to show the gains from diversification and thus offer a genuine positive analysis.
8. Rubinstein (2002) remarks, 'Markowitz can boast that he found the field of finance awash in the imprecision of English and left it with the scientific precision and insight made possible only by mathematics.'

CHAPTER - 20

1. *A Brief Summary of the State of the Game Theory*: Until the seventies, control-theoretic approach was primarily used in economic analysis related to policy-making. On the other hand, during the seventies and the eighties, the focus shifted to the game-theoretic approach. However, now, both, the control-theoretic and game-theoretic approaches, are combined since both are essential ingredients of a sound economic policy. At one point, it appeared as if game theory was the only game in economic theory, since its scope appeared much broader than what actually turned out to be. The existence of multiple equilibria reduces its potential applications and similarly, the existence of multiple approaches, which advance conflicting goals of game theory, is not helping either.
Axiomatic Approach to Game Theory: Recently, in honoring the Nobel Prize winning contributions of Nash, Selten and Harsanyi, Gul (1997) remark[s], 'In the 1980s, armed with models of asymmetric information, dynamic strategic interaction and insights from the information economics of the 1970s, economists developed truly game-theoretic models of industrial organization.' He adds, 'However,

perhaps the biggest impact of game theory has been on what one might call pure theory; that branch of economics that focuses on developing tools and investigating the foundations of economic analysis.' Game theory has provided many insights into many fields. For example, it is complementing price theory in resolving the old indeterminacy of bilateral monopolies.

Varian (1992, p 282)) concludes his exposition of the game theory as 'Nash equilibrium, in its original formulation, puts a consistency requirement on the beliefs of the agents—only those beliefs compatible with maximizing behavior were allowed. But, as soon as we allow there to be many types of players with different utility functions, this idea loses much of its force. Nearly any pattern of behavior can be consistent with some pattern of beliefs.' It would appear that there are strong diminishing marginal returns to further refinements.

Behaviorist Approach to Game Theory: The above axiomatic approach is not universally accepted. The behaviorist school believes that the game theory should study the actual behavior of the individuals, and not the rational behavior. Camerer (1997) asks, 'Is game theory meant to describe actual choices by people and institutions or not? It is remarkable how much game theory has been done while largely ignoring this question.' He adds, 'At one extreme, highly mathematical analyses have proposed rationality requirements that people and firms are probably not smart enough to satisfy in every day decisions. At the other extreme, adaptive and evolutionary approaches use very simple models—mostly developed to describe nonhuman animals—in which players may not realize they are playing a game at all. When game theory does aim to describe behavior, it often proceeds with a disturbingly low ratio of careful observation to theorizing.'

Evolutionary Approach to Game Theory: On the other hand, Mailath (1998) concludes, 'However, on the positive side, important insights are still emerging from evolutionary game theory (for example, the improving understanding of when backward induction is appropriate and the formalization of strategic uncertainty). Interesting games have much equilibrium, and evolutionary game theory is an important tool in understanding which equilibria are particularly relevant in different environments.'

At present, these alternative approaches are advanced to handle strategic interactions and the challenge is to weave them into one coherent theory in which actual behavior may be allowed to deviate from the rational behavior and the evolutionary process used in restoring uniqueness.

2. *The Recent History of Time Inconsistency Problem*: The seminal work by Kydland and Prescott (1977) has ignited the current debate on rules versus discretion. According to the rational expectations school, current decisions are influenced by the perceived future policies. However, optimal control theory does not allow such anticipatory behavior. They conclude, 'There is no way control theory can be made applicable to economic planning when expectations are rational.' Since then, the problem of reneging or credibility has moved to the center stage. In particular, the credibility of the monetary authorities has come under strict scrutiny. A Central Bank may resort to expansionary policies to reduce temporarily the unemployment rate below the natural rate of unemployment, thus causing excessive inflation without any long-term gain in employment. It has been argued that in the absence of pre-commitment, whatever monetary policies are announced initially could be revised later due to a temptation to avail of new opportunities. Numerous suggestions have been offered to achieve a socially desired rate of inflation, such as, appointing a Central Bank Governor or chairman who has a reputation of being conservative (Rogoff, 1985), and linear inflation contracts (Svensson, 1997).

3. Bowden (1989, p 197) distinguishes these approaches as: 'This simply means that the maximizing π_1, π_2, are completely laid out at the start of the horizon, as opposed to *feedback* or *closed-loop* control, where the optimizing would be given in terms of the then current state variable x_1 resulting from the application of π_1.' π_1 and π_2 are the policies for period one and period two respectively and x_1 is the reaction function for period one.

4. The optimum values of A_1 and A_2 are determined as follows:
Max $G^2(r_1, r_2, A_1, A_2) = G^2_1(r_1, A_1) + G^2_2(r_2, A_2)$ \hfill (20.1)
Subject to the reaction functions r_1 and r_2 of king one
$r_1 = R_1(A_1, A_2)$ \hfill (20.2)
$r_2 = R_2(r_1, A_2)$ \hfill (20.3)
Differentiating equation (20.1) with respect to A_1 and A_2 gives
$\partial G^2_1/\partial A_1 + (\partial G^2_1/\partial r_1 + (\partial G^2_2/\partial R_2)(\partial R_2/\partial r_1))\partial R_1/\partial A_1 = 0$
$(\partial G^2_1/r_1)(\partial R_1/\partial A_2) + \partial G^2_2/\partial r_2 ((\partial R_1/\partial A_2)(\partial R_1/\partial A_2) + \partial R_2/\partial A_2) + \partial G^2_2/\partial A_2 = 0$
A^*_1 and A^*_2 are the optimum values obtained by solving these two

equations. For a very lucid exposition of the time inconsistency problem (see Bowden (p 196-199).
5. See Bowden (p 200).
6. Kennan and Wilson (1993) note, 'In this view, some conflicts stem from differing expectations due to differing information. Each party's incentive to exploit its informational advantage prevents a quick, costless settlement.' However, they add, 'The idea that private information is a prime cause of costly conflict is currently an untested hypothesis.'

References

Acemoglu, Daron and Thierry Verdier.(2000), 'The Choice Between Market Failures and Corruption' *American Economic Review* 90.1: p 194-211.

Aggarwal, Rajesh K and Andrew A Samwick. (1999), 'The Other Side of the Trade-Off: The Impact of Risk on Executive Compensation' *Journal of Political Economy*. 107. February: 65-105.

Aghion, Philipe and Howitt, Peter (1992), 'A Model of Growth through Creative Destruction', *Econometrica LX,* p 323-351.

(1998), *Endogenous Growth Theory*, MIT Press, Cambridge

Akerlof, George (1970), 'The Market for 'Lemons': Quality Uncertainty and the Market Mechanism', *The Quarterly Journal of Economics*, Vol 84, issue 3, p 488-500.

Akerlof, George (1976), 'The Economics of Caste and of the Rat Race and Other Woeful Tales' *The Quarterly Journal of Economics,* November: 599-617.

Akerlof, G A (1983), 'Loyalty Filters' *American Economic Review* 73. 1: p54-63.

Alam, Shahid M (2000), Poverty from the *Wealth of Nations*, St. Martin

Alm, James (1988), 'Uncertain Tax Policies, Individual Behavior, and Welfare,' *American Economic Review*, Vol 78, No.1 p 237-245.

Allan, Charles M (1971), *The Theory of Taxation*, Penguin, Baltimore, Maryland.

Allingham, Michael (1987), 'Wealth Constraint', *The New Palgrave: A Dictionary of Economics*, Edited by John Eatwell, Murray Milgate, Peter Newman, Vol 4, p 883, Macmillan, London, New York.

Alston, Lee and Robert Higgs (1982), 'Contractual Mix in Southern Agriculture since the Civil War: Facts, Hypotheses and Test' *Journal of Economic History* 42. June: p 327-53.

Ambedkar, B R (1891-1956), *Thus Spoke Ambedkar*, Quotations of B R Ambedkar,
http://www.ambedkar.org/babasaheb/quotations.htm

Ambirajan, S (1997), 'The Concepts of Happiness, Ethics, And Economic Values' in B B Price (Ed) *Ancient Economic Thought*, Rutledge, 19-41.

Andreoni, James, Erard, Brian and Feinstein, Jonathan (1998), 'Tax Compliance', *Journal of Economic Literature*, Vol XXXVI, June, p 818-860.

Andreoni, James, Marco Castillo, and Ragan Petrie, (2003), 'The Carrot or the Stick: Rewards, Punishments, and Cooperation' *American Economic Review* 93.3: 893-902.

Antweiler, Werner and Trefler, Daniel (2002), 'Increasing Returns and All That: A View from Trade', *American Economic Review*, Vol 92, No.1, p 93-119.

Aoki, Masahiko (2001), *Toward a Comparative Institutional Analysis*, Cambridge, MIT Press.

Arrow, K J 1963. Uncertainty and the Welfare Economics of Medical Care. *American Economic Review* 53.5, p 941-973.

Arrow, Kenneth J (1971), *Essays In the Theory of Risk-Bearing*, Markham Publishing Co, Chicago.

(1968), 'The Economics of Moral Hazard: Further Comment). *American Economic Review* 58.3: 537-539.

Ashton, T S (1972), *An Economic History of England*, Methuen & Co.

Atkinson, Anthony B and Stern, N H, (1974), 'Pigou, Taxation and Public Goods,' *Review of Economic Studies*. p 119-128.

And Stiglitz, Joseph E (1980), *Lectures On Public Economics*, McGraw-Hill, New York.

Atkinson, Anthony B (1987), 'The Theory of Tax Design for Developing Countries' Chapter 14, p 387-406, in *The Theory of Taxation in Developing Countries*, edited by David Newbery and Nicholas Stern, Oxford.

Atkinson, Leigh (2002), 'Where do Functions Come From?' *The College Mathematical Journal*, Vol 33, No 2, March, p 107-112.

Auerbach, Alan J (1987), 'Taxation of Income', *The New Palgrave: A Dictionary of Economics*, Edited by John Eatwell, Murray Milgate, Peter Newman, Vol 3, p 604-606, Macmillan, London, New York.

Ayesha (6 October 2010), 'The Tort of Defamation: An Analysis of the Law in India and the United Kingdom' http://jurisonline.in/2010/10/the-tort-of-defamation-an-analysis-of-the-law-in-india-and-the-united-kingdom/.

Babcock, Linda and Loewenstein, George (1997), 'Explaining Bargaining Impasse: The Role of Self-serving Biases', *Journal of Economic Perspectives*. p 109-126.

Backhouse, Roger (1985), *A History of Modern Economic Analysis*, Basil Blackwell, New York

(1997), *Truth and Progress in Economic Knowledge*, Edward Elgar, Cheltenham UK, Lyme, NH (USA).

Baeck, Louis (1994), *The Mediterranean Tradition In Economic Thought*, Routledge, New York.

Baker, Jonathan B (2003), 'The Case for Antitrust Enforcement' *Journal of Economic Perspectives*, Vol 17, No.4: p27-50.

Ballard, Charles L and Fullerton, Don (1992), 'Distortionary Taxes and the Provision of Public Goods', *Journal of Economic Perspectives*, p 117-131.

Barber, William J (1967) *'A History of Economic Thought'*, Penguin Books, Baltimore, Maryland.

Bardhan, Pranab (1997) Corruption and Development: A Review of Issues, *Journal of Economic Literature*, 35 (September), p 1320-1346.

Baron, James N and Hannan, Michael T (1994), 'The Impact of Economics on Contemporary Sociology,' *Journal of Economic Literature*, September p 1111-1146.

Barr, Nicholas (1992), 'Economic Theory and the Welfare State: A survey and Interpretation,' *Journal of Economic Literature*, June, p741-803.

Basham, A L (1959), *The Wonder that was India*, Grove Press, New York.

Basili, Marcello and Carlo Zappia, 2005. 'Ambiguity and uncertainty in Ellsberg and Shackle,' Department of Economics University of Siena p 460

Baumol, William J (1986), 'Productivity Growth, Convergence and Welfare: What the Long-Run Data Show', AER, p 1072-1085.

Becker, Gary S (1968) Crime and Punishment: An Economic Analysis, *Journal of Political Economy*, 76 (March/April), p 169-217.

Beider, Perry and Cary Elliott (2003), *The Economics of US Tort Liability:*

A Primer, Congressional Budget Office, www.cbo.gov/showdoc.cfm.

Bellinger, Gene (2004), 'Knowledge Management—Emerging Perspectives' http://www.systems-thinking.org/kmgmt/kmgmt.htm

Bell, Abraham and Gideon Parchomovsky (2005), 'A Theory of Property,' Cornell Law Review, Vol 90, No.3, p 531-615.

Benabou, R and J Tirole. (2003), 'Intrinsic and Extrinsic Motivation' *Review of Economic Studies* 70.3: p489-520.

Bennett, Deborah J (1999), *Randomness,* Harvard University Press, Cambridge.

Bentham, Jeremy (1789/1970), *An Introduction to the Principles of Morals and Legislation*, Ed, J H Burns and H L A Hart, London: The Athlone Press.

Bentham, Jeremy (1802), *The Theory of Legislation*, C K Ogden (Ed) Harcourt, Brace: New. York 1931.

Berle, Adolf A and Gardiner C Means. 1932. *The Modern Corporation and Private Property.* New York: Harcourt, Brace and World.

Bernoulli, D (1738/1954), 'Exposition of a New Theory on the Measurement of Risk' English translation, *Econometrica,* 22, p 23-36.

Bernoulli, N (1713). In Correspondence of Nicolas Bernoulli concerning the St Petersburg Game, available in English translation by Richard Pulskamp at http://www.cs.xu.edu/math/Sources/Montmort/stpetersburg.pdf

Bhagwati, Jagdish N (1983), 'The Pure Theory of International Trade: A Survey', in *Essays in International Theory*, Vol 2, Edited by Robert C Feenstra, MIT Press, Cambridge.

Biddle, Jeff (1999), 'Statistical Economics, 1900-1950' *History of Political Economy*, 31: 4, p 607-651.

Bilimoria, Purusottama (2003), 'Indian Ethics,' in Peter Singer (Ed) *A Companion To Ethics*, Malden, MA (USA): Blackwell, 43-57.

Blackburn, Keith and Christensen, Michael (1989), 'Monetary Policy and Policy Credibility' *Journal of Economic Literature*, March, p 1-45.

Blanchard, Olivier (2000), Macroeconomics, Second Ed, Prentice Hall.

Blaug, Mark (1973), 'Was There a Marginal Revolution' in *'The Marginal Revolution in Economics'* edited by Black, Coats and Goodwin, Duke University Press, Durham, NC.

'Kuhn Versus Lakatos, Or Paradigms Versus Research Programs In The History of Economics', in *Paradigms And Revolutions* edited by Gary Gutting, (1980), University of Notre Dame Press, Notre Dame, Indiana.

'No History of Ideas, Please, We're Economists', *Journal of Economic Perspectives*, (2001), Vol 15, No.1, p 145-164.

Boesche, Roger (2002), *The First Great Political Realist : Kautilya and his Arthashastra*, Lexington Books, New York.

Bolling, George M (1977), 'Vedic Literature,' *Encyclopedia Americana*, Vol 27, p 925-928 Americana Corporation, Danbury, Connecticut, USA.

Bolton, Gary E and Ockenfels, Axel (2000), 'ERC: A Theory of Equity, Reciprocity, and Competition,' *American Economic Review*, Vol 90, No.1: p166-193.

Bowden, Roger J (1989), *Statistical Games and Human Affairs*, Cambridge University Press, Cambridge.

Bradley Jr, Robert L (1990), 'On the Origins of the Sherman Antitrust Act' *Cato Journal*, Vol 9, No.3: 737-742.

Brannigan, A (1981), *The Social Basis of Scientific Discoveries*, Cambridge: Cambridge University Press.

Brennan, Geoffrey (1996), 'The Economist's Approach to Ethics,' in Peter Groenewegen (ed), *Economics and Ethics*, New York: Routledge, p 121-137.

Browning. Edgar K and Browning, Jacquelene M (1994), *Public Finance and the Price System*, Macmillan, New York.

Brown, Norman O (1977), 'Greek City-State Civilization', *Encyclopedia Americana*, Vol 14, p 391-404, Americana Corporation, Danbury, Connecticut, USA.

Brown, Vivienne (1994), Adam Smith's *Discourse, Canonicity, Commerce and Conscience.* London, Routledge.

Brue, Stanley L (1993), 'The Law of Diminishing Returns' *Journal of Economic Perspectives*, Vol 7, p 185-192.

Brumbaugh, Robert S (1978), 'Plato' *Encyclopedia Americana*, Vol 22, p 226-231, Danbury.

Buchanan, James M (1987), 'Opportunity Cost', *The New Palgrave: A Dictionary of Economics*, Edited by John Eatwell, Murray Milgate, Peter Newman, Vol 3, p 718-721.Macmillan, London, New York.

Calabresi, Guido (2007), 'Toward a Unified Theory of Torts' *Journal of Tort Law*, Vol 1, Issue 3: p 1-11.

Camerer, Colin F (1997) 'Progress in Behavioral Game Theory,' *Journal of Economic Perspectives*, Fall, p 167-188.

Caplan, Bryan (2000), 'Rational Irrationality: A Framework for the Neoclassical-Behavioral Debate' *Eastern Economic Journal*, Vol, 26.2, p 191-211.

Carmichael, H Horne (1989), 'Self-enforcing Contracts, Shirking, and Life Cycle Incentives' *Journal of Economic Perspectives* 3.4: p 65-83.

Carroll, Archie B and Ann K Buchholtz (2003), Business and Society,

5th Ed Mason, Ohio: Thomson-Southwestern.

Cartwright, Nancy (1998), 'The Truth Doesn't Explain Much', Chapter 13, p 233-240 in *Introductory Readings In The Philosophy of Science* edited by E D Klemke *et al*, Prometheus Books, Amherst, New York.

Caves, Richard E, Frankel, Jeffery A and Jones, Ronald W (2002), World Trade and Payments, Addison Wesley, Boston.

Chakravarti, Sitansu S (2003), Consequentialism and The Gita, http://www.infinityfoundation.com/mandala/I_es/i_es_chakr_consequence.htm

Chakravarti, Sitansu S (2006), Ethics in the Mahabharata: A Philosophical Enquiry for Today, New Delhi, Munshiram Manoharlal publishers.

Chandler, Tertius (1987), Four Thousand Years of Urban Growth: An Historical Census, Lewiston, New York, Edwin Mellon Press.

Chang, James L Y (1987), 'History of Chinese economic thought: Overview and recent works,' *History of Political Economy*, 19:3, p 481-502.

Choi, Young Back (1989), 'Political Economy of Han Feitzu,' *History of Political Economy*, 21: 2, p 367-390.

Church, Jeffrey and Roger Ware (2000), Industrial Organization, Irwin Boston: McGraw-Hill.

Coleman, Jules (2003), 'Theories of Tort Law,' *Stanford Encyclopedia of Philosophy*. http://plat.stanford.edu/entries/tort-theories/

Conlisk, John (1996), 'Why Bounded Rationality?' *Journal of Economic Literature*, p 669-700.

Cook, P (1972), 'A One Line Proof of the Slutsky Equation,' *American Economic Review*, Vol 62, p 139.

Cooper, Richard N (1977), Trade, Americana, Vol 26, p 910-916, Danbury, Connecticut, USA.

Cooper, John M (1999), Reason and Emotion, Princeton University, Princeton.

Cooter, Robert and Rappoport, Peter (1984), 'Were the Ordinalists Wrong About Welfare Economics?' *Journal of Economic Literature*, Vol XXII, No.2, p 507-530.

Cooter, Robert and Ulen, Thomas (2004), Law and Economics, 4th Ed, New York, Pearson, Addison-Wesley.

Craig, John (1699), Theologiae Christianae Principia Mathematica, London, Timithy Child.

Crimi, Steven (1984), 'The Outcome of Crisis in Hamlet and the

Bhagavad Gita,' *Moksha Journal,* Issue II.

Cushing, Barry E (1989), 'A Kuhnian Interpretation of the Historical Evolution of Accounting,' *The Accounting Historians Journal,* Vol 16, No.2: p1-41.

Dahan, Momi and Strawczynski, Michel (2000), 'Optimal Income Taxation: An Example with a U-Shaped Pattern of Optimal Marginal Tax Rates: Comment', *American Economic Review,* Vol 90, June, p 681-686.

D'Amato, Anthony (1981), 'Lon Fuller and Substantive Natural Law,' 26 *American Journal of Jurisprudence* 202, Code A81A.

Dasgupta, Ajit K (1993) *A History of Indian Economic Thought,* Routledge, London.

Dasgupta, Partha and Eric Maskin (2005), 'Uncertainty and Hyperbolic Discounting,' *American Economic Review,* Vol 95, No.4, p 1290-1299.

Davis, Donald, (2010), *The Spirit of Hindu Law,* Cambridge University Press, New York.

Deane, Phyllis (1978), *The Evolution of Economic Ideas,* Cambridge University Press, Cambridge.

'The Scope and Method of Economic Science', *The Economic Journal,* (1983), Vol 93, issue No.369, p 1-12.

De Long, Bradford J (1996), 'Keynesianism, Pennsylvania Avenue Style: Some Economic Consequences of the Employment Act of 1946', *Journal of Economic Perspectives,* Vol 10, p 41-53.

'The Triumph of Monetarism?,' *Journal of Economic Perspectives,* (2000), Vol 14, Number 1, p 83-94.

Dembe, Allard E and Leslie I Boden (2000), 'Moral Hazard: A Question of Morality? New Solutions' 10.3: p 257-279.

Dequech, David (2000), 'Fundamental Uncertainty and Ambiguity', *Eastern Economic Journal,* p 41-60

Desai, Ashok V (2002), 'A Decade of Reforms,' Chapter 2 in Raj Kapila and Uma Kapila (eds) *A Decade of Economic Reforms in India,* 2002, Academic Foundation, Delhi.

Deshpande, Ashwini (2000), 'Does Caste Still Define Disparity? A Look at Inequality in Kerala, India', *American Economic Review,* May, p 322-325.

Dhar, T N (2003), *A Portrait of Indian Culture,* Deemed University, New Delhi.

Diamond, Peter A (1998), 'Optimal Income Taxation: An Example with a U-shaped Pattern of Optimal Tax Rates', *American Economic Review,* Vol 88, p 83-95.

Dorfman, Robert (1991), 'Review Article: Economic Development from the Beginning to Rostow' *Journal of Economic Literature*, Vol XXIX, June, p 573-591.

Drekmeier, Charles (1962), *Kingship And Community In Early India*, Stanford University Press, Stanford.

Dupuit, Jules (1844), 'On the measurement of the utility of public works,' Translated by RH Barback as International Economic Papers, 1952, 2, 83-110 Reprinted in: Kenneth J Arrow and Tibor Scitovsky, eds., Readings in welfare economics Richard D Irwin, Homewood, IL, 1969, p255-283.

Ehrlich, Isaac and Becker, Gary S (1972), 'Market Insurance, Self Insurance and Self Protection,' *Journal of Political Economy*, Vol 80, No.4, p 623-648.

Economic Advisory Council (2002), 'Economic Reforms: A Medium Term Perspective,' Chapter 18 in Raj Kapila and Uma Kapila (eds) *A Decade of Economic Reforms in India*, 2002, Academic Foundation, Delhi.

Ekelund, Robert B Jr and Hebert, Robert F (1999), *Secret Origins of Modern Microeconomics*, Chicago University Press, Chicago.

Ellerman, David (1992), *Property and Contract in Economics: The Case for Economic Democracy*, Basil Blackwell, Cambridge.

Elmslie, Bruce Truitt (1995), 'The Convergence Debate Between David Hume and Josiah Tucker', *Journal of Economic Perspectives*, Number 4, p 207-216.

And Criss, Antoinette James (1999), 'Theories of Convergence and Growth in the Classical Period: The Role of Science, Technology and trade', *Economica*, p 135-49.

Encyclopedia. 2005, Incentive-definition of incentive,
http// encyclopedia.laborlawtalk.com/incentive.

Elster, Jon (1989), 'Social Norms and Economic Theory' *Journal of Economic Perspectives* 3: p 99-117.

Elster, Jon (1998), 'Emotions and Economic Theory', *Journal of Economic Literature*, p 47-74

Emmett, Ross B (1999), 'The Economist and the Entrepreneur: Modernist Impulses in Risk, Uncertainty, and Profit', *History of Political Economy*, p 29-52.

Epstein, Larry G (1999), 'A Definition of Uncertainty Aversion', *Review of Economic Studies*, p 579-608.

Evensky, Jerry (1989), 'The Evolution of Adam Smith's Views on Political Economy,' *History of Political Economy*, 21:1, p 123-145.

Faulhaber, Gerald R and Baumol, William (1988), 'Economists as

Innovators: Practical Products of the Theoretical research' *Journal of Economic Literature*, XXVI, p 577-600.

Fernald, John G (1999), 'Roads to Prosperity? Assessing the Link Between Public Capital and Productivity,' *American Economic Review*, June, p 619-638.

Findlay, Ronald (1970), *Trade and Specialization*, Penguin Books Inc. Baltimore, Maryland, USA.

Frey, B and R Jegan (2001), 'Motivation Crowding Theory: A Survey of Empirical Evidence', *Journal of Economic* Survey 15.5: p 589-611.

Fourcade, Marion and Healy, Kieran (2007), 'Moral Views of Market Society', *Annual Review of Sociology*, Vol 33: p 285-311.

Frederick, Shane, George Loewenstein, and Ted O'Donoghue (2002), 'Time Discounting and Time Preference: A Critical Review,' *Journal of Economic Literature* Vol XL, (June), p: 351-401.

Friedman, M and Savage L J (1948), 'The Utility Analysis of Choices Involving Risk,' *Journal of Political Economy*, p 279-304.

Friedman, Milton, (1956), 'The Quantity Theory of Money: A Restatement' in M Friedman (Ed) Studies in the Quantity Theory of Money, Chicago: Chicago University Press.

Friedman, David D (1980), 'In Defense of Thomas Aquinas and the Just Price,' *History of Political Economy* 12(2), Summer, p 234-242.

'Just Price' *The New Palgrave: A Dictionary of Economics*, (1987), Edited by John Eatwell, Murray Milgate, Peter Newman, Vol 2, p 1043-1044, Macmillan.

Friedman, David (1999), Why Not Hang Them All: The Virtues of Inefficient Punishment, *Journal of Political Economy*, 107 (December), p S259-S269.

Garegnani, Pierangelo (1983), 'The Classical Theory of Wages and the Role of Demand Schedules in the Determination of Relative Prices,' *American Economic Review*, Vol 73, No.2, p 309-313.

Geistfeld, Mark (2003), 'The Role(s) of Economic Analysis in Tort Law,' Law and Economics Workshop University of Berkeley, Berkeley, California.

Gibbons, Robert (1998), 'Incentives in Organizations' *Journal of Economic Perspectives*. 12.4: p115-132.

Gill, Flora (1996), 'Comment: On Ethics and Economic Science,' in Peter Groenewegen (ed), *Economics and Ethics*, New York, Routledge, p 138-156.

Gillespie, Robert W (1988-89) Criminal Fines: Do They Pay?, *The Justice System Journal*, 13, p 365-78.

Glaeser, Edward L and Andrei Shleifer (2002) Legal Origins, *The Quarterly Journal of Economics*, 117 (December), p 1193-1229.

Glaeser, Edward L, R L Porta, F Lopez-de-Slanes and A Shleifer (2004), 'Do Institutions Cause Growth?,' *Journal of Economic Growth* 9, p 271-303.

Godfrey-Smith, Peter (2003), *Theory And Reality, An Introduction To The Philosophy Of Science*, Chicago: The University of Chicago Press.

Goetzmann, William N (2006), Financing Civilization, available at www.Viking.som.yale.edu/will/finciv/chapter1.htm

Gooding, D (1985), 'He who Proves, Discovers: Herschel, Pepys and the Faraday Effect,' Notes and Records of the Royal Society, 39, p 224-244.

Gooding, D (1989), 'History in the Laboratory,' in F James, Ed, The Development of the Laboratory, London: Macmillan, p 63-82.

Grampp William D (2000), 'What Did Adam Smith Mean by the Invisible Hand?' *Journal of Political Economy*, Vol 108, p 441-465.

Grant, Ruth W (2002), 'The Ethics of Incentives: Historical Origins and Contemporary Understandings' *Journal of Economics and Philosophy* 18 April, p 111-139.

Gramlich, Edward M (1994), 'Infrastructure Investment: A Review Essay', *Journal of Economic Literature*, p 1176-1196.

Grattan-Guinness, Ivor (2004), 'History or Heritage? An Important Distinction in Mathematics and for Mathematics Education,' *The American Mathematical Monthly*, Vol 111, No.1: p 1-12.

Gray, Stuart (2009), 'Domesticating Differences: A Comparative Perspective on India's Ancient Political Thought' prepared for presentation at the 2009 Conference of the Western Political Science Association Vancouver, Canada.

Groenewegen, Peter (1996), *Economics and Ethics*, Editor, Routledge, New York.

Groenewegen, Peter (2002), *Eighteenth-Century Economics*, Routledge, London.

Grossman, Gene M and Helpman Elhanan (1991), *Innovation and Growth*, MIT.

And Katz, M (1983), 'Plea Bargaining and Social Welfare', *American Economic Review*, September, p 749-757.

Gul, Faruk (1997), 'A Nobel Prize for Game Theorists: The Contributions of Harsanyi, Nash and Selten,' *Journal of Economic Perspectives*, p 159-174.

Haddad, Louis (1996), 'Comment: Ethics, Commerce and Government: The Scottish School,' in Peter Groenewegen (ed), *Economics and Ethics*, New

York: Routledge, 68-79.

Hahn, F H (1984), *Equilibrium and Macroeconomics,* Oxford: Basil Blackwell.

Hahn, F H and Matthews, R C O (1964), 'The Theory of Economic Growth: A Survey', *Economic Journal,* p 825-850.

Hall, Robert E and Rabushka (1995), The Flat Tax, 2nd Ed, Hoover Institution Press, Stanford.

Hall, Robert E and Jones, Charles I. (1999), 'Why Do Some Countries Produce So Much More Output Per Worker Than Others?,' *The Quarterly Journal of Economics,* February, p 83-116.

Haltiwanger, J and Waldman, M (1985) 'Rational Expectations and the Limits of Rationality', *American Economic Review,* June, p 326-340.

Halteman, James and Edd Noell (2012), Reckoning with Markets, New York: Oxford University Press

Hampton, Jean (1993), 'Contract and Consent,' in Robert E Goodin and Philip Pettit (Eds.), *A Companion to Contemporary Political Philosophy,* p 379-393, Blackwell Publishing, Malden, MA.

Harberger, A (1971), "Three Basic Postulates for Applied Welfare Economics: An Interpretive Essay" *Journal of Economic Literature* 9, p 785-97

Hausman, Daniel M, and Michael S McPherson (1996), *Economic Analysis and Moral Philosophy,* Cambridge University Press, Cambridge.

Heehs, Peter (2002), *Indian Religions,* New York University Press, New York.

Henderson, James M and Quandt, Richard E (1971), *Microeconomic Theory,* II Ed, McGraw-Hill, New York.

Hicks, John R (1946), Value and Capital, Clarendon Press, Oxford, England.

Hirschman, Albert O (1982), 'Rival Interpretations of Market Society: Civilizing, Destructive, or Feeble?' *Journal of Economic Literature,* Vol 20, No.4: p 1463-1484.

Hlupic, Vlatka, Athanasia pouloudi and George Rzevsky (2002), 'Towards an Integrated Approach to Knowledge Management: 'Hard', 'Soft', and 'Abstract' Issues' Knowledge and Process Management, Vol 9, No.2: p 90-102.

Hodgson, Geoffrey M (1998), 'The Approach of Institutional Economics', *Journal of Economic Literature,* Vol XXXVI, March, p 166-192.

Hollander, Samuel (1980), 'On Professor Samuelson's canonical Classical

Model of Political Economy', *Journal of Economic Literature*, XVIII, p 559-574.

Holt, Jim (2006), 'The Bourgeois Virtues by Deirdre McCloskey', The New York Times Book Review, July 30

Hylton, Keith N and Thomas J Miceli (2005), 'Should Tort Damages be Multiplied' The Journal of Law, Economics, & Organization, Vol 21, No.2: p 388-416.

Ifrah, Georges (2000), *The Universal History of Numbers*, John Wiley & Sons.

Ihori, Toshihiro and McGuire, Martin (2008), 'National Adversity: Managing Insurance and Protection,' CIRJE-F-554.

Jamieson, Dale (2003), 'Method and Moral Theory,' in Peter Singer (Ed), *A Companion To Ethics*, Malden, MA (USA): Blackwell, 476-487.

Johnston, Ian (2000), A Handbook on the History of Modern Science, Section four, http://www.mala.bc.ca/~johnstoi/darwin/sect4.htm

Kangle, R P (2000), The Kautilya Arthashastra, Part III, Motilal Banarsidass, Delhi.

Kapila, Raj and Kapila, Uma (2002), *A Decade of Economic Reforms in India*, editors, 2002, Academic Foundation, Delhi.

Karwal, G D (1966), 'Kautilyanism', Indian *Journal of Economics*, Vol XLVI, p 369-394.

Kaufmann, Daniel, Aart Kraay and Pablo Zoido-Lobation (1999), 'Governance matters,' Policy Research Working Paper No.2196, World Bank, Washington DC.

Kaufmann, Daniel, Aart Kraay and Massimo Mastruzzi (2003), 'Governance Matters III: Governance Indicators for 196-2002,' Working Paper Draft for Comments, World Bank, Washington DC.

Kaufmann, Daniel, Aart Kraay (2003), 'Growth without Governance,' World Bank, Washington, DC.

Kautilya, Vishnugupta, (4th Century B C), *The Kautilya Arthashastra*, Part II, An English Translation with Critical and Explanatory Notes, R P Kangle, 2000, Motilal Banarsidass, Delhi.

Kautilya, Vishnugupta, (4th Century B C), *The Arthashastra*, Edited, Rearranged, Translated and Introduced by L N Rangarajan, Penguin Books, 1992, New Delhi, New York.

Kautilya (4th Century B C), translated by Shamasastry, R (1915), *Kautilya's Arthashastra*, Mysore (India): Padma Printers.

Kautilya, Vishnugupta, (4th Century B C), *Maxims of Chanakya*, by Subramanian, V K (2000), Shakti Malik, Abhinav Publications, New Delhi.

Kennan, John and Wilson Robert (1993), 'Bargaining with Private Information', *Journal of Economic Literature*, p 45-104.

Keynes, John Maynard (1921), *A Treatise on Probability*, London, Macmillan & Co.

Keynes, John Maynard (1936), *The General Theory of Employment Interest and Money*. London, Macmillan and Co.

Keynes, John Maynard (1939), 'Memorandum for the Estates Committee' Kings College, Cambridge, UK.

Kindleberger, Charles (1964), *Economic Growth in France and Britain: 1851-1950*. New York, Simon and Schuster.

Knight, Frank H (1947) *Freedom and Reform*, Dallas, Harper and Row.

Kohlberg, Lawrence (1981, 1984), Essays on Moral Development, Vols. I and II, San Francisco: Harper and Row.

Koller, John M (1999), 'Humankind and Nature in Indian Philosophy,' in Eliot Deutsch and Ron Bontekoe (editors) A Companion To World Philosophies, Malden, MA (USA): Blackwell, p 279-289.

Kotowitz, Y (1987), 'Moral Hazard', *The New Palgrave: A Dictionary of Economics*, Edited by John Eatwell, Murray Milgate, Peter Newman, Vol 3, p 549-551, Macmillan

Kraut, Richard (2010), 'Aristotle's Ethics', *Stanford Encyclopedia of Philosophy*, 2010

Krishna, Daya (1999), 'Socio-Political Thought in Classical India,' in Eliot Deutsch and Ron Bontekoe (editors), *A Companion to World Philosophies*, p 237-247, Blackwell, Malden (MA), USA

Kuhn, Thomas S (1970), *The Structure of Scientific Revolutions*, Second Ed, The University of Chicago.

Kumar, Pushpendra, (1989), 'Introduction,' in Kumar, Pushpendra Kumar (Ed), *Kautilya's Arthashastra An Appraisal*, Nag Publishers, Delhi, p xvii-xxxii.

Kydland, Finn and Prescott, Edward C (1977), 'Rules Rather Than Discretion: The Inconsistency of Optimal Plans', *Journal of Political Economy*, June, p 473-491.

Landreth, Harry and Colander, David C (1994), History of Economic Growth, III Ed, Houghton Mifflin, Boston.

Lapsley, D K & Narvaez, D (2006). Character education. In Vol 4 (A Renninger & I Siegel, Volume Eds.), Handbook of Child Psychology (W Damon & R Lerner, Series Eds.) (p 248-296). New York: Wiley.

Lazear, Edward P (2000), 'Economic Imperialism' Quarterly *Journal of*

Economics, Vol 115, February, p 99-146.

Law, Narendra Nath (1925), *Studies in Indian History and Culture*, Low Price Publications, Delhi.

Lee, Yoon-Ho Alex and Brown, Donald J (2005), 'Competition, Consumer Welfare, and the Social Cost of Monopoly', Cowles Foundation Discussion Paper No.1528,
http://cowles.econ.yale.edu

Leonard, Thomas C (2005) 'Mistaking Eugenics for Social Darwinism: Why Eugenics Is Missing from the History of American Economics,' in Steven G Medema and Peter Boettke (eds.), The Role of Government in the History of Economic Thought, *History of Political Economy*, Vol 37 (December), Annual Supplement.

Letiche, J M (1960), 'Adam Smith And Ricardo On Economic Growth', in Theories of Economic Growth edited by Bert F Hoselitz, The Free Press.

Levin, Shira B (1996), 'Economics and Psychology: Lessons For Our Own Day From the Early Twentieth Century', *Journal of Economic Literature* p 1293-1323.

Levy, David M (1999) Adam Smith's Katallactic Model of Gambling: Approbation from the Spectator, Journal of the History of Economic Thought, 21 (March), p 81-91.

Liebeskind, JP (1996), 'Knowledge Strategy and the Theory of the Firm', *Strategic Management Journal*, Vol 17, p 93-109.

Lindahl, Erik (1958) [1919], "Just taxation—A positive solution", in Musgrave, R A, Peacock, A T Classics, in the *Theory of Public Finance*, London, Macmillan.

Lindbeck, Assar (1975), Swedish Economic Policy. London, MacMillan Press.

Lingat, Robert (1967), The Classical Law of India Translated with additions by J Duncan M Derrett, Oxford University Press, New Delhi

Lipsey, R G Bekar, and K Carlaw (1998). 'The Consequences of Changes in GPTs', in E Helpman (Ed), General Purpose Technologies and Economic Growth. (Cambridge, US: MIT Press).

Locke, John (1988), Two Treatises of Government [1689] Peter Laslett (Ed), Cambridge: Cambridge University Press.

Locke, John (1689), A Letter Concerning Toleration Wootton, David (Ed) (1993), Political Writings of John Locke, London, Penguin Books.

Lohse, Tim, Robledo, Julio R and Schmidt, Ulrich (2007), 'Self-Insurance and Self-Protection as Public Goods,' Economics Working Paper

No 2007-16, Christian-Albrechts-Universitat Kiel
   Lowry, S Todd (1987), The Archaeology Of Economic Ideas, Duke University, Durham.
   'The training of the economist in antiquity,' in Economics broadly considered edited by Jeff E Biddle, John B Davis, and Steven G Medema, (2001), Routledge, New York.
   Adam Smith and the Classics: The Classical Heritage in Adam Smith'sThought, review, *History of Political Economy*, (2003), Vol 35, No.4, p 788-789.
   Lubin, Timothy (2007), 'Punishment and Expiation: Overlapping Domains in Brahmanical Law' Indologica Taurinesia, Vol 33, p 93-122.
   Lucas, Robert E Jr. (1988), 'On the Mechanics of Economic Development' *Journal of Monetary Economics*, 22, p 3-12
   Machiavelli, N (1961), *The Prince* (G Bull trans.) Baltimore: Penguin Books.
   Machina, Mark J (1982), "Expected Utility' Analysis Without The Independence Axiom', *Econometrica*, Vol 50, 277-323.
   'Choice Under Uncertainty: Problems Solved and Unsolved' *Journal of Economic Perspectives*, (1987), Vol 1, p 121-154.
   Mackaay, Ejan (1999), 'History of Law and Economics,' in online Encyclopedia.
   Mackenzie, G Calvin and Michael Hafken. 2002. Scandal Proof, Washington DC, Brookings.
   Madden, M Stuart (2005), 'The Cultural Evolution ofTort Law', http// digitalcommons.pace.edu/lawfaculty/131
   Maddison, Angus (1995), Monitoring the World Economy 1820-1992, OECD, Paris.
   Maddock, Rodney and Carter, Michael (1982), 'A Child's Guide to Rational Expectations,' *Journal of Economic Literature*, p 39-41.
   Magill, Michael, Quinzii, Martine (1996), Theory of Incomplete Markets, Volume 1, MIT.
   Mahnke, Volker (1998) 'The Economies of Knowledge-Sharing: Production- and Organization Cost Considerations' 1998,
      http:/www.druid.dk/uploads/tx_picturedb/dw1999-350
   Mailath, George J (1998), 'Do People Play Nash Equilibrium? Lessons from Evolutionary Game Theory,' *Journal of Economic Literature* September, p 1347-1374.
   Majumdar, A K, (1980), *Concise History of Ancient India*, Vol II,

Munshiram Manhoarlal, New Delhi.

Manski, Charles F (1995), *Identification Problems in the Social Sciences*. Cambridge: Harvard University.

Manski, Charles F (2000), 'Economic Analysis of Social Interactions' *Journal of Economic Perspectives*, Vol 14, No 3, p 115-136.Marcushamer, Isaac M (2005), 'Selling your Torts: Creating a Market for Tort Claims and Liability'
http://law.bepress.com/expresso/eps/513

Markowitz, Harry M (1952), 'Portfolio Selection,' *Journal of Finance*, Vol 7, p 77-91.

Portfolio Selection: Efficient Diversification of Investments, (1959), Wiley, New York.

'The Early History of Portfolio Theory: 1600-1960,' *Financial Analysts Journal*, (1999), Vol 55, No.4, 5-16.

Marr, A J (2005), 'Intrinsic/Extrinsic Motivation: The Phony Controversy'
http // www.themanager.org/HR/Motivation.htm

Marshall, Alfred (1870/1920), Principles of Economics, Eighth ed, Macmillan, London.

Marx, K (1867/1990), Capital, Vol I, London, Penguin Books

Mattessich, Richard (1998), 'Review and Extension of Bhattacharya's Modern Accounting Concepts in Kautilya's Arthasastra', *Accounting, Business and Financial History*, Vol 8, No.2: p 191-209.

Mattessich, R (2000), *The Beginnings of Accounting and Accounting History- Accounting Practice in the Middle East (8000 B C to 2000 B C) and Accounting Thought in India (300 B C and the Middle Ages)*, New York, Garland Publishing.

Matthews, Gareth (2010), 'The Philosophy of Childhood' Stanford Encyclopedia of Philosophy,
http:/plato.stanford.edu/entries/childhood.

McAdams, Richard H and Eric Rasmusen (2005), 'Norms in Law and Economics,' American Law and Economics Association annual meetings.

McGuire, Martin C and Olson, Mancur (1996), 'The Economics of Autocracy and Majority Rule: The Invisible Hand and the Use of Force.' *Journal of Economic Literature*, March, p 72-96.

McCloskey, Deirdre N and Ziliak, Stephen T (1996), 'The Standard Error of Regressions' *Journal of Economic Literature*, p 97-114.

McCormick, Ken (1999), 'The Tao of Laissez-Faire', Eastern Economic Review, Vol 25, No.3, p 331-341.

Medema, Steven (2004) Sidgwick's Utilitarian Analysis of Law: A Bridge From Bentham to Becker, www.utilitarian.net/sidgwick/about 2004.

Medema, Steven G, Nicholas Mercuro and Warren J Samuels (1999), 'Institutional Law and Economics,' in online Encyclopedia

Medema, Steven G and Samuels, Warren J (2001), 'Henry William Spiegel: historian of economic thought', Chapter 15, p 286-301 in Medema, Steven G and Samuels, Warren J (eds.), Historians of Economics and Economic Thought, Routledge, New York.

Melling, David (1993), 'Indian Philosophy before the Greeks', Nehru Lecture at Manchester Metropolitan University.

Menegatti, Mario (2008), 'Optimal Prevention and Prudence in a Two-Period Model,' Working Paper 3/2008, Department of Economics, Universita di Parma, Italy.

Menegatti, Mario (2007), 'A New Interpretation of the Precautionary Saving Motive: A Note', *Journal of Economics*, Vol 92: p 275-280.

Miceli, Thomas J (1990) Optimal Prosecution of Defendants Whose Guilt is Uncertain, *Journal of Law, Economics, and Organization*, 6 (Spring), p 189-201.

Optimal Criminal Procedure: Fairness and Deterrence, International Review of Law and Economics, (1991), 11 May, p 3-10.

Midgley, Mary (2003), 'The Origin of Ethics' in Peter Singer (Ed) *A Companion To Ethics*, Malden, MA (USA), Blackwell, p 3-13.

Miller, Gary J (1997), 'The Impact of Economics on Contemporary Political Science,' *Journal of Economic Literature*, Vol XXXV, p, 1173-1204.

Mirrlees, J A (1971), 'An Exploration in the Theory of Optimum Income Taxation,' *Review of Economic Studies*, Vol 38, p175-208.

Mital, S N (2000), Kautilya Arthashastra Revisited, PHISPC, New Delhi, India.

Mohanty, J N (1999), 'The Idea of Good in the Indian Thought,' in Eliot Deutsch and Ron Bontekoe (eds.) *A Companion To World Philosophies*, Malden, MA (USA), Blackwell, p 290-303.

Mokyr, Joel (1990), The Liver Of Riches, Oxford.

Montgomery, David B and Catherine A Ramus (2003), 'Corporate Social Responsibility Reputation Effects on MBA Job Choice' Research Paper No 1805, May. Stanford, GSB, Stanford Graduate School of Business.

Mookherjee, Dilip and I P L Peng. (1992), 'Monitoring vis-à-vis Investigation in Enforcement of Law', *American Economic Review*, 82.3: p 556-565.

Morgenstern, O (1972), 'Thirteen Critical Points in Contemporary Economic Theory', *Journal of Economic Literature*, Vol X, p 1163-89.

Morrison, Catherine J and Schwartz, Amy Ellen (1996), 'State Infrastructure and Productive Performance', *American Economic Review*, December, p 1095-1111.

Mukerji, Sujoy (1998), 'Ambiguity Aversion and Incompleteness of Contractual Form', *American Economic Review* December, p 1207-1231.

Munier, Bertrand R (1991), 'Nobel Laureate: The many Other Allais Paradoxes', *Journal of Economic Perspectives*, p179-199.

Musgrave, Richard A (1959), *The Theory of Public Finance*, McGraw-Hill, New York.

Myerson, Roger B (1999), 'Nash Equilibrium and the History of Economic Theory', *Journal of Economic Literature*, p 1067-1082.

Nash, J F (1951), 'Non-cooperative Games' *Annals of Mathematics*, Vol 54, p 286-295.

Negishi, Takashi (1989), *History of Economic Theory*, North-Holland, Amsterdam, Oxford.

Nehru, Jawaharlal (1946), *The Discovery of India*, distributed by Oxford University Press. First published 1946 by The Signet Press, Calcutta.

Nicholson, Walter (1985), *Microeconomic Theory*, Third Ed, Dryden, London, New York.

North, Douglass C (1990), *Institutions, Institutional Change and Economic Performance*, Cambridge, Cambridge University Press.

'The New Institutional Economics and Third World Development,' in *The New Institutional Economics and Third World Development*, (1995), edited by John Harriss, Janet Hunter and Colin M Lewis, Routledge, New York.

Oates, Wallace E (1999) 'An Essay on Fiscal Federalism', *Journal of Economic Literature*, Vol XXXVII, p 1120-1149.

Olivelle, Patrick (2005), *Manu's Code of Law*, Oxford University Press, Oxford, New York.

Olivelle, Patrick (1999), *Dharmasutras: The Law Codes of Ancient India*, a New Translation, Oxford University Press, Oxford, New York.

Olivelle, Patrick (2011) 'Penance and Punishment: Marking the Body in Criminal Law and Social Ideology of Ancient India', *The Journal of Hindu Studies*, April, p 1–19.

Olson, Mancur (2000), Power and Prosperity, Basic Books.

Osterman, Paul. 1994. Supervision, Discretion, and Work Organization. *American Economic Review* 84.2: p 380-384.

Pacioli, Luca (1494), *Summa de Arithmetica, Geometrica, Proportioni et Proportionalita,* Venice

Pack, Spencer J (2001), 'S Todd Lowry and Ancient Greek Economic Thought', in G Medema and Warren Samuels (eds.) *Historians of Economics and Economic Thought,* Routledge.

Palma, Andre De, Myers, Gordon M and Pageorgiou, Yorgos Y (1994), 'Rational Choice Under an Imperfect Ability to Choose', *American Economic Review,* June, p 419-440.

Pandit, Bansi (2009), *The Hindu Mind,* New Age Books, New Delhi.

Parmar, Aradhana (1987), *A Study of Kautilya's Arthashastra,* Atma Ram & Sons, Delhi.

Pearson, Heath (1997), *Origins of Law and Economics-The Economists' New Science of Law,* 1830/1930, Cambridge, Cambridge University Press.

Peil, Jan (2000), 'Deconstructing the Canonical View on Adam Smith,' in Evelyn L Gorget and Sandra Peart (eds.) *Reflections on the Classical Canon in Economics,* New York, Routledge, p 68-91.

Phlips, Louis (1988), *The Economics of Imperfect Information,* Cambridge University

Pirenne, Henri (1937), *Economic and Social History of Medieval Europe,* Harcourt, Brace & World, New York.

Polinsky, A Mitchell and Shavell, Steven (2000) The Economic Theory of Public Enforcement of Law, *Journal of Economic Literature,* 38 (March), p 45-77.

Posner, Richard A (1975), 'The Social Costs of Monopoly and Regulation' *Journal of Political Economy,* Vol 83, No.4: p 807-827.

Posner, Richard (2003), *Economic Analysis of Law,* 6th Edition, ASPEN publishers, New York.

Post, J E Lawrence, Anne T and Weber J (1999), *Business and Society,* 10th Ed, McGraw-Hill.

Ponnuru, Ramesh, (2004), Is the Market Moral? A Dialogue on Religion, Economics & Justice' Panellist, Di

http://pewforum.org/events/index.php?eventID=57.

Prasch, Robert E (1991), 'The Ethics of Growth in Adam Smith's *Wealth of Nations', History of Political Economy,* 23.2, p 337-351.

Pratt, John W (1964), 'Risk-Aversion in the Small and in the Large', *Econometrica,* p 122-136.

Prendergast, Canice (1999), 'The Provision of Incentives in Firms' *Journal of Economic Literature* 37.1: p 7-63.

Rabin, Matthew (1998), 'Psychology and Economics', *Journal of Economic Literature*, p 11-46

Rae, John (1934), *The Sociological Theory of Capital*, (reprint 1834 Ed) London, Macmillan.

Rasmusen, Eric (1994), *Games and Information*. Cambridge, MA, Blackwell.

Ravallion, Martin (1997), 'Famines and Economics' *Journal of Economic Literature*, p 1205-1242

Ray, B N (1999), *Tradition and Innovation in Indian Political Thought*, Ajanta Books International, Delhi, India.

Redman, Deborah A (1997), *The Rise of Political Economy as a Science*, MIT Press, Cambridge.

Reinganum, Jennifer F (2000) Sentencing Guidelines, Judicial Discretion and Plea Bargaining, RAND *Journal of Economics*, 31 (Spring), p 62-81.

Ricardo, David (1817/1821), On The Principles Of Political Economy, And Taxation, Third ed, John Murray, London.

Robinson, Joan (1953), *On Re-reading Marx*, Cambridge University Press, Cambridge.

Rodrik D, A Subramanian, and F Trebbi. (2004) Institutions Rule: The Primacy of Institutions over Geography and Integration in Economic Development, *Journal of Economic* Growth, 9 June, p 131-165.

Rogoff, Kenneth (1985), 'The Optimal Degree of Commitment to an Intermediate Monetary Target', *The Quarterly Journal of Economics*, p 1169-1189.

Romer, Paul M (1990), 'Endogenous Technological Change,' *Journal of Political Economy*, S71-102.

'Idea Gaps and Object Gaps in Economic Development', *Journal of Monetary Economics*, (1993), p 543-573.

'Why, Indeed, in America? Theory, History, and the Origins of Modern Economic Growth', *American Economic Review*, (1996), May, p 202-206.

Rosenberg, Alexander (1998) 'If Economics Isn't Science, What Is It?' Chapter 9, p 154-170 in *'Introductory Readings In The Philosophy of Science'* edited by E D Klemke *et al* Prometheus Books, Amherst, New York.

Ross, Stephen (1973) The Economic Theory of Agency: The Principal's Problem, *American Economic Review*, 63 (May), p 134-139.

Rowe, Christopher, 'Ethics in Ancient Greece', in Peter Singer (Ed) *A Companion To Ethics*, Malden, MA (USA): Blackwell, p 121-132.

Rowthorn, Robert (1996), 'Ethics and Economics An Economist's View' in

Peter Groenewegen (ed), *Economics and Ethics*, New York: Routledge, p 15-33.

Rubinstein, Mark (2002), 'Markowitz's 'Portfolio Selection': A Fifty-year Retrospective', *Journal of Finance*, Vol 57, No.3, p 1041-1045.

Saether, Arild (2000), 'Self-interest as an acceptable mode of human behavior', in Evelyn L Gorget and Sandra Peart (eds.) Reflections on the Classical Canon in Economics, New York: Routledge, 45-67.

Samuels, Warren J (2005), 'The Role of Government in the *History of Political Economy*: The 2004 HOPE Conference Interpreted and Critiqued by the General Discussant,' in Steven G Medema and Peter Boettke (eds.), The Role of Government in the History of Economic Thought, *History of Political Economy*, Vol 37 (December), Annual Supplement.

Samuelson, Paul A (1954), 'The Pure Theory of Public Expenditure', *Review of Economics & Statistics*, 36(4), November, p 387-89.

'Diagrammatic Exposition of a Theory of Public Expenditure', *Review of Economics & Statistics*, (1955), 37, p 350-356.

Samuelson, Paul A (1962), 'Economists And The History of Ideas,' *American Economic Review*, Vol, 52, No.1, p 1-18.

'What Classical and Neoclassical Monetary Theory Really Was,' *The Canadian Journal*. (1968), Vol 1; No.1, p 1-15

'A Modern Theorist's Vindication of Adam Smith,' *American Economic Review*. (1977), Vol 67, p 42-49.

'The Canonical Classical Model of Political Economy', *Journal of Economic Literature*, (1978), Vol XVI, p 1415-1434

'Noise and Signal in Debates Among Classical Economists: A Reply', *Journal of Economic Literature*, (1980), Vol XVIII, p 575-578.

Foundations of Economic Analysis, Enlarged Edition, (1983), Harvard University Press, Cambridge.

Sandel, Michael J (2009), Justice, Farrar, Straus and Giroux, New York.

Sato, Kazuo (1966), 'On the Adjustment Time in Neoclassical Growth Models,' *Review of Economics Studies*. p 263-268.

Sato, Ryuzo (1963), 'Fiscal Policy in a Neoclassical Growth Model: An Analysis of the Time Required for Equilibrating Adjustment', *Review of Economic Studies*, p 16-23.

Schaffer, Simon (1996) 'Making Up Discovery', in *Dimensions of Creativity* editor Margaret A Boden, MIT Press, Cambridge.

Schlatter, R (1951), *Private Property: The History of an Idea*, New Brunswick, N J, Rutgers University Press.

Schlesinger, Harris and Doherty, Neil A (1985) 'Incomplete Markets for

Insurance: An Overview', *Journal of Risk and Insurance*, p 402-423.

Schumpeter, Joseph A (1954), *History of Economic Analysis,* Oxford University Press, New York.

Seligman, Edwin (2001) Edwin Seligman's Lectures on Public Finance, 1927-28. Edited by Warren J Samuels, New York, JAI

Sen, A K (1981), *Poverty and Famines,* An Essay on Entitlement and Deprivation, Oxford University Press, Oxford.

Sen, A K (1987), *On Ethics and Economics,* Blackwell, Oxford.

'Human Rights and Asian Values,' (1997), The New Republic, 14-21 July.

Shapiro, Carl and Stiglitz, Joseph E (1984), 'Equilibrium Unemployment as a Worker Device,' *American Economic Review,* June, p 433-444.

Sihag, Balbir (1978), Economics of Foodgrains in India, PhD thesis, Cambridge: MIT.

Sima, Josef (2004), 'Praxeology as Law & Economics,' Journal of Libertarian Studies, Vol 18, No.2, p 73-89.

Simon, H A (1957), *Models of Man.* New York: John Wiley & Sons.

Singer, Peter (1972), 'Famine, Affluence and Morality' *Philosophy and Public Affairs*, Vol 1, No.3: p 229-243.

Slemrod, Joel (1990), 'Optimal Taxation and Optimal Tax Systems,' *Journal of Economic Perspectives*, Vol 4, p 157-178.

Slutsky, E (1915), 'Sulla Teoria del Bilancio del Consumatore,' Giornale degli Economisti, 51: p19-23. Translated as 'On the Theory of the Budget of the Consumer,' in Readings in Price Theory, Ed G Stigler and K Boulding, Homewood, Ill: Richard D Irwin, Inc., 1952.

Smith, Adam. (1790/ 1982), *The Theory of Moral Sentiments.* Edited by D D Raphael and A L Macfie, Liberty Fund, Indianapolis.

An Inquiry into the Nature and Causes of the *Wealth of Nations*. Edited and with an Introduction, Notes, Marginal Summary, and Index by Edwin Cannan, (1776/1976), The University of Chicago Press, Chicago.

Solow, Robert (1957), 'Technical Change and the Aggregate Production Function', *Review of Economics & Statistics*. p 312-320.

'Another Possible Source of Wage Stickiness,' *Journal of Macroeconomics,* (1979), 1 (Winter), p 79-82.

Spengler, Joseph J (1960), 'Mercantilist and Physiocratic Growth Theory' in *Theories of Economic Growth* edited by Bert F Hoselitz, The Free Press, New York.

Indian Economic Thought (1971), Duke University Press, Durham, NC.

Spiegel, Henry W (1991) *The Growth of Economic Thought*, 3rd ed,

Duke University Press, Durham, NC.

Starmer, Chris (2000), 'Developments in Non-expected Utility Theory: The Hunt for a Descriptive Theory of Choice under Risk,' *Journal of Economic Literature*, Vol XXXVIII, June, p 332-382.

Staveren, Irene Van (2001), *The Values of Economics*, Routledge, New York.

Stein, Herbert (1996), 'A Successful Accident: Recollections and Speculations about the CEA', *Journal of Economic Perspectives*, Vol 10, p 3-21.

Stern, Nicholas (1987), 'Aspects of the General Theory of Tax Reform,' Chapter 3, p 60-91, in *The Theory of Taxation in Developing Countries*, edited by David Newbery and Nicholas Stern, Oxford

Sternbach, Ludwik (1965), *Juridical Studies in Ancient Law*, Motilal Banarsidass, Delhi.

Stewart, Michael (1986), *Keynes and After*, Third ed Penguin, New York.

Stigler, George J (1980), Economics or Ethics?, The Tanner Lectures on Human Values, Harvard University, Cambridge.

Stigler, George J (1984), 'Economics—The Imperial Science', Scandinavian *Journal of Economics*, p 301-313.

Stigler, Stephen M (1986), *The History of Statistics, The Measurement of Uncertainty before 1900,* Cambridge, Massachusetts, Harvard University Press.

Statistics on the Table, The History of Statistical Concepts and Methods, (1999), Cambridge, Massachusetts, Harvard University Press.

Stiglitz, Joseph, E (1974), 'Incentives and Risk Sharing in Sharecropping' *Review of Economic Studies* 41.2: 219-255

'Principal and Agent (ii)' John Eatwell, Murray Milgate, Peter Newman (eds). (1987), *The New Palgrave: A Dictionary of Economics*. Vol 3: 966-972. New York, Macmillan.

Stiglitz, Joseph, E (1994), Whither Socialism, The MIT Press, Cambridge.

'The Private Uses of Public Interests: Incentives and Institutions', (1998), *Journal of Economic Perspectives* 12.2: p 3-22.

Economics of the Public Sector, (2000), third ed New York, W W Norton & Company.

Sugden, Robert (1993), 'Welfare, Resources, and Capabilities: A Review of Inequality Reexamined by Amartya Sen,' *Journal of Economic Literature*, Vol XXXI, No.4, p 1947-1962.

'Beyond Sympathy and Empathy: Adam Smith's Concept of Fellow-feeling,' (2002), *Journal of Economics and Philosophy,* Vol 18, p 63-87.

Supple, Barry E (1963) 'Introduction: Economic History, Economic Theory, and Economic Growth' in *The Experience of Economic Growth*, edited by Supple, Random House.

Sushruta (6th Century BCE), *Sushruta Samhita,* an English Translation by Kaviraj K L Bhishagratna, Cosmo Publications, New Delhi.

Svensson, Jakob (2005), 'Eight Questions about Corruption,' *Journal of Economic Perspectives,* Vol 19, No.3: p 19-42.

Svensson, Lars E O(1997), 'Optimal Inflation Targets, "Conservative" Central Banks, and Linear Inflation Contracts', *American Economic Review,* March, p 98-114.

Swift, Jeremy (1993), 'Understanding and Preventing Famine and Famine Mortality,' Institute of Development Studies, Bulletin 24.4.

Talreja, Kanayalal (1982), *Philosophy of Vedas,* Talreja Publication, Bombay, India.

Taylor, John B (2000), 'Reassessing Discretionary Fiscal Policy' *Journal of Economic Perspectives,* Vol 14, No.3, p 21-36.

Teichman, Doron (2004) *Sex, Shame, and the Law: An Economic Perspective on Megan's Law,* University of Michigan Law School, Working Paper #26.

Thaler, Richard H (2000), 'From Homo Economicus to Homo Sapiens' *Journal of Economic Perspectives,* Vol 14, 1, p 133-141.

Thanawala, Kishor (1997), 'Kautilya's Arthashastra A Neglected work in the history of economic thought,' Chapter 2, p 43-58 in Price B B. (ed), *Ancient Economic Thought,* Routledge, New York

Thapar, Romilla (1997), *Ashoka and the Decline of the Mauryas,* Second Ed, Oxford, New York.

Tiwari, M and Shukla HS (2005), 'Sushruta: 'The Father of Indian Surgery" Indian J Surg [serial online] 67: 229-230. Available at : http://www.indianjsurg.com/text.asp?2005/67/4/229/17005

Tobin, James (1958), 'Liquidity Preference as Behavior Towards Risk,' *Review of Economic Studies,* Vol 25, 65-86.

Trautmann, Thomas R (1971), Kautilya and the Arthashastra, Leiden, Netherlands, E J Brill.

Tribe, Keith (1999), 'Adam Smith: Critical Theorist?,' *Journal of Economic Literature,* Vol XXXVII, Vol 2, p 609-632.

Turgot, Anne Robert Jacques (1766/1774), *Reflections on the Formation and Distribution of Wealth,* London, Good.

Tversky, Almos and Kahneman, Daniel (1979), 'Prospect Theory: An Analysis of Decision Under Risk,' *Econometrica,* Vol 47, No.2, p 263-291.

Tversky, Almos and Kahneman, Daniel (1991) Loss Aversion in Riskless

Choice: A Reference-Dependent Model, *The Quarterly Journal of Economics*, 106 (August), p 1039-1061.

Varian, Hal R (1992), *Microeconomic Analysis*, Third Edition, Norton.

Varian, Hal R (1993) A Portfolio of Nobel Laureates: Markowitz, Miller and Sharpe, *Journal of Economic Perspectives*, 7 (Winter), p 159-169.

Varma, V P (1995-96), *Ancient and Medieval Indian Political Thought*, L N Agarwal, Agra, India.

Varoufakis, Yanis (1996), 'O Tempora, O Mores! Economics as the Ethos of our Times' in Peter Groenewegen (Ed), *Economics and Ethics*, New York, Routledge, p 157-172.

Vaughn, Karen I (1978), 'John Locke and the Labor Theory of Value,' *Journal of Libertarian Studies*, Vol ?, No 4, p 311-326.

Vickery, W S (1973), 'An Exchange of Questions between Economics and Philosophy', Chapter 1, in *Economic Justice*, edited by Edmund S Phelps, Penguin.

Viner, Jacob (1954), 'Schumpeter's History of Economic Analysis', *The American Economic Review*, Vol 44, December, p 894-910.

Vines, Prue E (2007), 'The Power of Apology: Mercy, Forgiveness or Corrective Justice in the Civil Liability Arena?' UNSW Law Research Paper No.2007-30; Public Space: *The Journal of Law and Social Justice*, Vol 1, No.1. Available at SSRN:
http://ssrn.com/abstrac=987424

Waldauer, Charles, Zahka William J and Surendra Paul (1996), 'Kautilya's Arthashastra: A Neglected Precursor to Classical Economics,' *Indian Economic Review*, Vol XXXI, No.1, p 101-108.

Waldegrave, Charles (1713/2007), 'The Problem of Waldegrave' by David Bellhouse, Electronic Journal @l for history of probability and mathematics, Vol 3, No.2 December/2007. www.jehps.net.

Walker, Donald A (1999), 'The Relevance For Present Economic Theory Of Economic Theory Written In The Past' Journal of the History of Economic Thought, Vol 21, Number 1, p 7- 26

Walras, Leon (1874-77/1954), *Elements of Pure Economics*, Translation W Jaffe, Homewood,Ill, Richard D Irwin.

Waterman, A M C (1999), 'Hollander On The 'Canonical Classical Growth Model': A Comment' Journal of the History of Economic Thought, Vol 21, No.3, p 311-218.

'The Beginning of Boundaries,' in Guido Erreygers (Ed), Economics and Interdisciplinary Exchange, (2001), p 42-63, Routledge, London, New York.

Weintraub, E Roy (1992), Introduction, in *Toward a History of Game Theory*, Edited by Weintraub, E Roy, Duke University Press, Durham, NC.

Weller, Royal W (1978), 'Mahabharata', *Encyclopedia Americana*, Vol 18, p 133-134, Danbury, Connecticut, USA.

Whitaker, J K (1987), 'Ceteris Paribus', *The New Palgrave: A Dictionary of Economics*, Edited by John Eatwell, Murray Milgate, Peter Newman, Vol 1, p 396-397, Macmillan, London, New York.

Whitaker, John K (2000), 'Claiming and Reclaiming the Past,' in Evelyn L Forget and Sandra Peart. (eds.), *Reflections on the Classical Canon in Economics*, p 386-399, Routledge, New York:

Wieser, Friedrich Von. (1989/1967), Natural Value New York, Augustus M Kelley.

Wikipedia. 2005. Moral Hazard: Definition and Much More. http// www.answers.com/topic/moral-hazard.

Wilford, John Noble, (2002), 'Under Centuries of Sand, a Trading Hub', Science Times, Section D of The New York Times, July 9.

Winston, Clifford (2006), Government Failure versus Market Failure, AEI-Brookings Joint Center for Regulatory Studies, Washington DC.

Wit, Ernst-Jan C (1997), The Ethics of Chance, The Graduate School Department of Philosophy, The Pennsylvania State University, www.stats. gla.ac.uk/~emst/ethics_of_chance.htm

Wonnacott, Thomas H and Wonnacott, Ronald J, (1977), Introductory Statistics for Business and Economics, 2nd ed, New York: John Wiley & Sons.

Yitzhaski, S (1974), 'A Note on 'Income Tax Evasion: a Theoretical Analysis", Journal of Public Economics, Vol 3, p 201-2.

Zaratiegui, Jesus M (1999), 'The Imperialism of Economics over Ethics,' Journal of Markets & Morality, Vol 2, No.2, p 208-219.

Zingales, Luigi (2000), 'In Search of New Foundations' NBER, Working Paper 7706.

Zipursky, Benjamin C (2008), 'Two Dimensions of Responsibility in Crime, Tort, and Moral Luck' *Theoretical Inquiries in Law*, Vol 9, No.1: p 97-137.

Index

A
Ability to pay principle 197, 204
Accounting methods 87, 96, 205, 333
Accountability 129, 158, 193
Action-oriented approach 100, 108, 111
Absolute risk aversion 303
Agent-type 175, 195
All other things being equal 34, 53, 330
Ambiguity 48, 103, 238
Asymmetric information 61, 152, 161, 172, 289, 333
Agency problem 6, 195, 332
Artha 11, 48, 51, 58, 60, 63, 97, 105, 121, 131, 179, 181, 184, 245, 329
Auditing 87, 96, 110, 112, 157, 176, 186
Axiomatic approach 69
Axiom of comparison 68
Axiom of consistency 69

B
Backward bending supply curve 309
Backward induction 61, 99, 101, 322
Backward-looking 273

Benefit principle 197, 204, 262
Benevolent man 14, 111
Birth-death-rebirth cycle 102, 114, 134
Bookkeeping 86, 155
Bounded rationality 61, 157, 161-164, 329
Budgeting 86
Buffer stock 80, 215, 227

C

Calamities 5, 60, 87, 121, 187, 222, 254, 321
Capital account 197, 212
Cardinal approach 68
Cartelisation 150
Character-building 105, 121
Choice-influencing 70
Chronological priority 46
Civic virtues 206
Classics 39
Cobb-douglas technology 179
Cognitive constraint 162
Cognitive division of labour 157
Collective property 260
Commercial man 14, 41, 111
Common property 258, 261
Comparative advantage 13, 230
Comparative risk assessment analysis 216
Concessionary loans 128
Conflict of interest 157, 335
Constrained maximization 54, 63, 104, 163
Contingency planning 55

Contractarian 123
Contractual theory 252
Corrective justice, 268, 288
Cost-benefit analysis 59, 263, 313
Corrective taxes 150
Covariance 92
Credibility problem 314
Crowding-in 184
Crowd-out 334
Crowding-out 184, 271, 334
Current account 197, 212

D

Data management 162
Deadweight loss 5, 25, 38, 199, 202, 300
Deductive 335
Deep determinant 12, 125, 132, 141, 332
Demand curve 80, 83
Demand instability 85
Demand-supply apparatus 79, 85
Dharma-based 111
Diminishing returns 7, 75, 331
Discounting 56, 85, 330
Disruptions 5, 200, 203
Distortions 199
Diversification 49, 229, 302, 309, 333
Double-entry bookkeeping 86, 96
Dupuit-laffer-curve 7, 62, 97, 213
Duty free imports 128

E

Economic analysis 7, 10, 66, 117, 161, 219, 251, 335
Economic growth 12, 27, 62, 87, 124, 216, 221, 222, 236, 279, 329, 331
Economies of scale 229
Economic surplus 92, 141
Economic thought 32, 87, 232, 328
Efficiency frontier 189, 300
Efficiency wages 62, 138, 176, 332
Endogenous 51, 122, 229, 332
Engineering approach 13, 65
Enlightened self-interest 117, 137, 330
Equity-efficiency trade-off 201
Eternal bliss 101, 134
Ethical content 13, 32, 120
Ethical environment 12, 100, 134, 175, 245, 334
Ethical grounding 103
Ethics-based 97, 111, 334
Ethics-intensive 144
Exogenous 51, 92, 139, 231
Explanation and prediction 62, 89, 96, 173
Extensive game 321
Externalities 62, 150, 273, 331
Extrinsic motivation, 13, 14, 80, 123, 138, 141, 183, 184, 195, 266, 318, 330, 334
Factors of production 7, 71, 129, 209

False accounting 90, 156
Feasibility frontier 68-300
Financial rules and regulations 88, 155
Fiscal federalism 205
Food-for-work programmes 219
Forward-looking 70, 273
Freedom from fear 15, 233, 291
Freedom from want 14, 97, 232, 291
Foundational 99
Functional classification 197

G

Game-theoretic 313
General-purpose technology (GPT) 92, 96, 333
Government failure 12, 143, 159, 237
Good governance 12, 100, 125, 127, 157, 260

H

Hidden actions 151
Hidden information 152
Hierarchical 51, 185, 317
Hindsight 36
Hindu civilization 12, 63, 130, 329, 332
Hindu growth rate 12
Historical reconstruction 35, 36
Human capital 129, 131, 231, 269
Human security 4

I

Illiquidity 82
Impartial judicial system 1, 5
Imperial 33
Import-substituting 13
Income possibility frontier 136
Income-shifting 206
Income statements 88
Income tax 197, 213, 331
Indifference curves 67, 70, 122, 273
Inductive 330
Information-based 145, 151
Information management 162
Information revolution 67, 161, 169
Inquisition 59
Internalization 104
Inter-dependent 33, 43
Inter-disciplinary matrix 58
Inter-temporal 34, 56
Intrinsic motivation 138
Invariance hypothesis 298, 333
Isocost curve 179, 184
Isoquants 67, 78

J

Judicial fairness 5, 137, 237, 239
Justice 235

K

Kama 51, 60, 105, 179, 184, 203, 245
Kautilya-curve 62, 210
Kautilya disaster relief action plan 219
Kautilya's tax system 207
Knowledge-based 296
Knowledge-intensity 163
Knowledge management 162, 335

L

Labour-augmenting 78
Labour theory of property 233, 251, 260, 266
Labour theory of value 265
Law of the jungle 148, 198, 245
Legalistic approach 100, 108, 250
Legal error 239, 240, 332
Leisure-seeking 188
Lex tallionis 283
Linear income tax 197, 204, 331
Liquidity 82, 324, 330
Lockean first occupancy theory 251
Locus classicus 36
Logic-based 13
Loss-aversion hypothesis 292, 299
Lumpsum tax 198, 201

M

Matching incentive 181
Macroeconomics 45
Malfeasance 286
Malpractice 22, 269, 281
Marginal analysis 47, 53, 63
Marginalism 330
Marketed surplus 284
Material health 11, 184

Material incentives 12, 141, 174, 195, 334
Material prosperity 32
Materialism 23, 183
Mean-variance approach 303
Mercantilism 12, 231
Mercantilist 39, 41, 87, 92, 227
Microeconomics 33, 42
Missing markets 152, 229, 242
Model specification 139
Moksha 105, 184
Monopoly 25, 38, 62, 71, 144, 177, 256, 331
Monopsony 25, 62, 148, 331
Moral anchoring 5
Moral capital 102, 105
Moral content 13
Moral degradation 103
Moral desert 103
Moral dilemma 147
Moral duty 113, 142, 222, 257
Moral fabric 272
Moral failure 14, 144, 156
Moral hazard 62, 145, 192, 330
Moral incentive 126, 175, 190, 278
Moral motivation 14, 141, 183, 184, 195, 266, 334
Moralistic approach 100, 108

N
Nation-building 62
National income accounts 87, 92
National security 28, 63, 72, 73, 119, 227, 289
Negligence-based 270, 278

Non-cooperative game 207
Nonfeasance 286

O
Optimal tax 207
Organizational design 108, 144, 159, 334
Organizational man 157
Opportunity cost 166, 265, 282, 325, 329
Optimization 34, 46, 54, 62, 77, 82, 272-325
Ordinal preferences 67, 68

P
Paradigm shift 21, 89, 169
Pareto efficient contract curve 225
Pareto static efficiency criterion 278
Partial equilibrium approach 33, 50, 63
Perceived probability 247
Periodic accounting 86, 88
Penalty-penance mix 268
Physiocrat 39, 92
Possibility frontier 68, 73, 153
Pragmatic approach 144
Principles of taxation 196, 199
Principal-agent problem 12, 49, 175, 195, 237, 332
Private marginal cost 150, 262
Private property rights 5, 124, 159, 201, 251, 260, 331
Probability distribution 243, 299

Producer surplus 62, 197, 208, 211, 329
Public goods 38, 62, 148, 209, 289, 292

R
Rational fool 126
Rational reconstruction 35, 43, 67, 181, 329
Record keeping 86, 95
Regression model 91
Relative asset hypothesis 292, 297
Relative power equation 292, 295
Relative risk-aversion 303
Rent-seeking 145, 328, 332
Restraints 104, 128
Restitutio in integrum 280
Retrospection 37
Revenue-yielding capacity 6, 95, 210
Risk-aversion 188, 303, 333
Risk management 217
Risk premium 7, 132, 255, 333
Risk-return trade-off 132, 303, 333
Risk-taking 62, 106, 176, 333
Rule of law 5, 62, 236, 332
Rules versus discretion 246

S
Safety net 118, 196, 203
Science of man 61
Second generation 12, 63
Secular law 267, 287
Self-centeredness 145
Self-improvement 102
Self-insurance 220
Separation theorem 300
Sexual harassment 111, 145, 180, 331
Sharecropping 176, 193, 194
Shirking 176, 188
Silver rule 283, 100
Social marginal cost 150, 261
Social thorns 14, 233
Sources of economic growth 12, 61, 125, 129, 142, 331
Spiritual health 11, 184
Spiritual law 267
Sovereign immunity 286
Statistical methods 10, 91, 240, 333
Substitution effect 199
Substitution possibilities 77, 85
Suo motu 248
Supply curve 67, 83, 309
System-building 47, 62, 102, 104, 274

T
Taxation power 6, 210
Tax holidays 128
Tax shifting 6, 210
Technique-based 32
Tort liabilities 268
Tragedy of anti-commons 260
Tragedy of commons 260
Theory of the gains from trade 226, 231
Theoretical skeleton 63

Thinking machines 181
Time inconsistency problem 62, 289, 312
Transaction costs 82, 132, 158, 253, 274
Transparency 193
Type I error 237, 248
Type II error 237, 244

V
Value added 95, 283
Value-neutral 181

Veil of ignorance 252
Virtues 4, 62, 101, 206, 329
Virtuous cycle 142

W
Water-diamond paradox 82, 330
Welfarism 123
Wisdom-based management 162, 165, 166

Z
Zero-sum game 299

Conclusion

KAUTILYA IS A WORLD HERITAGE

Whatever royalty is earned from the publication of this book will be donated to the Munshi Ram and Nimbo Devi Charitable Trust, which has been doing its bit in promoting quality education in rural India. The Trust built a Girls' Higher Secondary School in my village and handed it over to the Government of Haryana (India) in May 2002.

— Balbir Singh Sihag
Sisai, Haryana
January 2019

CONCLUSIONS

Acknowledgements

I have been very fortunate in getting advice and generous help from so many distinguished scholars. My graduate education at MIT was of tremendous help, it provided me with the necessary tools of analysis and the confidence in undertaking this ambitious project. Additionally, the very first thing I learnt from Kautilya was that ego is the biggest hurdle in the acquisition of knowledge and that changed my attitude to learning and opened many doors to the knowledge and wisdom of many scholars.

I owe my greatest gratitude to Professor Jagdish Bhagwati. His support was invaluable to me throughout the process of writing this book. I am grateful to Dr Manmohan Singh, Prof Robert Solow, Prof T N Srinivasan and P K Kaul for their extraordinary help in enhancing my capabilities to write this book and to Prof Avinash Dixit for encouragement and advice to minimize the role of hindsight. I am indebted to Prof Louis Haddad for advice, numerous suggestions and comments on the earlier drafts.

I am deeply indebted to late Dr Anand Chandavarkar for the superb editing and for adding both content and clarity to the manuscript. I am equally grateful to Bhoopendra Sinha, who reviewed every line of the multiple drafts and provided countless suggestions to refine, clarify, rearrange and fill the logical gaps in presentations of the manuscript. Chapter 5 was added especially due to his suggestion.

Professors Ravi Prakash Arya, Mark Blaug, John Conlisk, Jerry Evensky, Evelyn Forget, Monica Galizzi, Ruth Grant, Daniel Hammond, Daniel Hausman, V Nagarajan Iyer, Linda Kistler, Alain Marciano, Subodh Mathur, Richard Mattessich, Steven Medema, Lallan Prasad, Lall Ramrattan, Eric Rasmusen, Satyavrat Shastri, Upinder Singh, Anthony Waterman and Judge Richard Posner provided several suggestions to improve the content and presentation of various segments of the manuscript. I also benefited from the participants in the lectures and seminars at the Rajasthan University at Jaipur, the Mahrishi Dayanand University at Rohtak, the Kurukshetra University, the Kautilya Foundation in New Delhi and Transparency International in New Delhi. The figures were done by Puneet Sharma, I appreciate his help.

Dr William Hogan, former Chancellor of the University of Massachusetts, Lowell, was kind enough to grant me a sabbatical to embark on this project. I am grateful to him for providing me this precious opportunity. I am grateful to Chancellor Martin Meehan and Associate Chancellor Dr Jacqueline Moloney for supporting my project in every possible way by making available the necessary support services. Gregory Keefe, Kevin Smith and Judy Stevenson, secretary of the Department of Economics, were very helpful.

My thanks to my publisher Renu Kaul Verma, my editor Papri Sri Raman and her production team of Alok Saini and Geetali Baruah.

My wife, Neelam, has been an equal partner in this endeavour. She had to sacrifice the most. This manuscript is the fruit of her patience and faith in me. My daughters, Swati and Smita, managed all of my computer-related needs.

The generosity of L N Rangarajan and Penguin Books is greatly appreciated for giving me the permission to use the translation of the *Arthashastra* for interpretations. I am grateful to Craufurd Goodwin, Paul Dudenhefer, Kishore Kulkarni, Steven Medema, Sushil Mittal, Surjeet Singh, Hrishikesh Vind, Stephen Walker and several unknown referees for dissemination of Kautilya's ideas. I admire Dr Masudul Alam Choudhury for his courage and wisdom. I am indebted to him for publishing a special issue of *Humanomics* on Kautilya's contributions. I acknowledge with a sense of gratitude the willing generosity of the publishers of the following journals for permitting me to use my articles included in their publications earlier:

Sihag, Balbir S (2004) *Kautilya on the Scope and Methodology of Accounting, Organizational Design and the Role of Ethics in Ancient India* Accounting Historians Journal Vol 31, No.2: p 125-148.

(2005a) *Kautilya on Ethics and Economics,* Humanomics Vol 21, No.3/4: p 1-28.

(2005b) *Kautilya on Public Goods and Taxation,* History of Political Economy Vol 37.4: p 723-751.

(2007a) *Kautilya on Institutions, Governance, Knowledge, Ethics and Prosperity,* Humanomics Vol 23, No.1: p 5-28.

(2007b) *Kautilya on Time Inconsistency and Asymmetric Information* Indian Economic Review Vol 42, No.1: p 41-55.

(2007c) *Kautilya on Moral and Material Incentives, and Effort* History of Political Economy Vol 39, No.2: p 263-292.

(2007d) *Kautilya on Administration of Justice during the Fourth Century BCE,* Journal of the History of Economic Thought, 1.29, No.3: p 359-377.

(2008a) *Kautilya on Risk-Return Trade-off and Diversification,* Indian Journal of Economics and Business, December Vol 7, No.2: p 281-296.

(2008b) *Kautilya on Management by Wisdom during the Fourth Century BCE* International Institute of Informatics and Systemics Proceedings, Vol 7, p 256-262.

(2009a) *Kautilya on Economics as a Separate Science* Humanomics Vol 25, No.1: p 8-36.

(2009b) *Kautilya as a Forerunner of Neo-classical Price Theory*

Humanomics Vol 25, No.1: p 37-54.

(2009c) *Kautilya on Principles of Taxation,* Humanomics Vol 25, No.1: p 55-67.

(2009d) *Kautilya on International Trade,* Humanomics Vol 25, No.1: p 68-74.

(2009e) *Kautilya on Law, Economics and Ethics,* Humanomics Vol 25, No.1: p 75-94.

(2009f) *Kautilya on Moral, Market and Government Failures,* International Journal of Hindu Studies, Vol 13, No.1, p 83-102.

(2010) *Kautilya on Famine, Fairness and Freedom,* Indian Journal of Economics and Business, June Vol 9, No.2: p 263-274.

(2013) *Kautilya on Prudence, Protection and Prosperity,* Hrishikesh Vinod (ed.) in The Handbook of Hindu Economics and Business at :https://www.createspace.com/4224711.

(2013), *Kautilya on Ethical Anchoring as Systemic Risk Management,* Hrishikesh Vinod (ed.) in The Handbook of Hindu Economics and Business at :https://www.createspace.com/4224711.

Afterword

MY EXPERIENCES WITH PUBLISHING KAUTILYA

From 2002 onwards, I sent the proposal to publish this manuscript to a number of international publishing houses which included the Cambridge University Press, the Oxford University Press, Tata McGraw-Hill, Pearson and Penguin. By the time my manuscript was rejected for the first time, I knew none of the Western publishers would publish it, but I still wanted to get it confirmed.

The first publisher rejecting Prof Jagdish Bhagwati's strong recommendation to publish my manuscript was shocking to me. I was also particularly disappointed when Tata McGraw-Hill declined to publish my manuscript since the Tata Group is known for its independence and ethical culture and we consider it Indian.

From the rejections, I learnt that the West talks of freedom of press, but it practices the most repressive form of hidden censorship.

No stone is left unturned in suppressing non-western writers' works that challenge the writings of their icons. It is really that simple. I also learnt, subsidiaries of foreign publishers in India have no guts or souls to go against their parent companies. These subsidiaries, for all practical purposes, are foreign agents making sure the Indian mind stays colonized.

I also learnt a couple of things: The practice of myth-making in the West is quite wide- spread. For example, according to [11] Edna St Vincent Millay, 'Euclid alone has looked on beauty bare'. The irony is that there is no record of any historical Euclid and let alone seeing any beauty and still this fictitious story has been repeated a million times.

Theon, the true author of *The Elements* was looking for a 'blessed life' and not beauty, bare or clothed. Such fabrications are still continuing. For example, David E Rowe (2001) remarks, 'Euclid was reputed to have told King Ptolemy that there were "no royal roads" to mathematical knowledge (though many over the centuries seem to have thought that Euclid's Elements provided the path of least resistance).'

Another exaggerated claim: Pacioli in 1494 wrote about the accounting practices prevailing at the time and is called the father of accounting. Raju (2014, p 49) summarizes his findings on other icons as: Euclid the geometer and Claudius Ptolemy the astronomer were pure fabrications, like the stories of the Copernican and Newtonian revolutions. And these are just examples of what was obviously a large-scale and systematic effort, spread over centuries.

The first publisher's Reviewer raised several unreasonable objections. S/He said: The Author is very widely read. But, one feels arguments are often taken out of context, and redeployed in a way that subverts their meaning. Another kind of fallacy consists of not making the distinction between the availability of a theoretical concept and a particular instance of its exercise. It is obviously the case that people deployed all sorts of reasoning that we might think of as instances of evaluating opportunity costs. But it does not follow that they have the theoretical or scientific concept of opportunity cost. People can trade without having a trade theory. This fundamental confusion is manifested in the text.

This Reviewer suggested: The book would have been much more convincing *if the author made a more modest case* for Kautilya's sophistication as a policy analyst. Kautilya is too interesting a figure to be turned, with very little evidence, into an encyclopedia of economic theory. The manuscript can be revised in the light of the main criticism – there is an exaggeration of the degree to which Kautilya has anticipated modern theory. If the author concludes that Kautilya had a more compelling and analytical explanation of aspects as part of economic reality, then this is where we could legitimately begin to take up issues. To make that leap, one needs more argumentation. This could be accomplished with some rewriting *and change of tone*. The author should comb through his manuscript and ensure that such leaps are not made UNLESS he can produce a convincing argument and evidence to justify them.

I incorporated some of the suggestions but concentrated more on providing arguments in justifying that Kautilya was *a serious economist*.

When I resubmitted the revised manuscript, the Reviewer made the following comments: The author has put in immense hard work the book is clearly written and treats an important and neglected subject. I am convinced that Kautilya is a sophisticated thinker. I also think the book will generate interest. But I cannot endorse its methodology and conclusions. I still, however, have serious doubts that the case for Kautilya as a serious economist in the modern sense of the term has been made. Machiavelli knows there is a tradeoff between Christian and Pagan virtues. Does that mean he has an unfinished idea of 'opportunity cost?'

I was convinced that the manuscript already contained solid arguments and evidence to justify my claim that Kautilya was an Economist in modern terms.

The Reviewer suggested I tone it down, indirectly implying I should not challenge Adam Smith's position. Instead of ing it down, I withdrew the manuscript. Since *toning down* would make the whole effort futile.

As I understood, the word 'toning down' meant telling the lie that Kautilya was *not* an economist. I refused to lie about Kautilya's work by undermining it and the internationally reputed publisher refused to publish it. But that was not the end of the story.

The question was how to refute the Reviewer's conclusions. My wife realized that I was giving too heavy a doze and suggested a brilliant way to refute the Reviewer's conclusions. She suggested that I get each chapter published as an article. That way, I would get a third party to settle the dispute. That worked.

Although initially, some reviewers complained against the use of modern tools, but I was able to convince them that I was just following the standard practice. Several papers got published in top economic journals. The judgement came out to be in Kautilya being recognized as the first economist. My wife's smartness and my stubbornness paid off.

In my letter to the Economic Editor of the international publisher related to their Reviewer's comments on the revised manuscript, I wrote:

> I am very grateful to the referee since the quality of the MS has improved significantly. However, this time I feel quite disappointed since the referee has not made a single specific suggestion, which could be helpful in improving the quality of the MS (please see the attachment for details). His general comment: a lack of making a transition from a practice to a theoretical concept does not apply to *Kautilya's Arthashastra*. His premise is incorrect since Kautilya is not discussing any prevailing practice – rather the concept or idea is imbedded directly into his advice (to a king), which is based on sound analysis. It is also obvious from the fact that there is no reference to emperor Chandragupta or to his kingdom Magadha in *The Arthashastra* since it was meant to be a theoretical treatise. I don't understand why the referee does not appreciate the level of abstraction in *The Arthashastra* and the fact that Kautilya does not accept anything without undertaking a critical review.
>
> I take offense to the referee's comment: 'The central point is this: people can trade without having a theoretical idea of comparative advantage, they can weigh options without having a theoretical concept of opportunity cost etc.' Prof Bhagwati checked every line on the 'opportunity cost' in the first draft of the MS. He deleted a significant part of what was in that first draft. The revised draft has only what he approved.

Chapter 9 [now Chapter 14] deals with Kautilya's ideas on international trade. It is obvious that Kautilya was not a trader. He was a thinker, who was explaining the gains from trade (as David Ricardo did later). But most importantly, Prof Bhagwati has re-written the most relevant part of Chapter 9 [now Chapter 14]. You can see the language, I cannot write that well. Is there anyone in the whole world who can question Prof Bhagwati on this?

Additionally, the referee applies different and unreasonable standards to judge *Kautilya's Arthashastra* than those applied by the profession to Adam Smith's *Wealth of Nations* or Ricardo's *Political Economy* or any other classical economist. I strongly feel that any additional toning down would strip the MS of its content. As you may note I already have toned it down significantly. What would be the point in publishing a sterile MS?

I am not claiming that the MS is perfect or flawless. Also given the controversial nature of *The Arthashastra*, a few economists will strongly support my interpretations, and a few will discard them summarily, but a majority will examine them carefully and a constructive debate is likely to be initiated.

I strongly feel that at this point all that the MS needs are good editing and quick publishing. You as a publisher are not risking much (I can share the cost if you shares the profits with the Charitable Trust in my parents' name) since your reputation cannot be adversely affected by one publication but my reputation as a Ph D from M I T is on the line. I urge you to publish the manuscript, which has the potential to generate a considerable amount of interest.

I prepared the answers to the referee's observations not that I want to convince him.

I get the impression that, no matter what I do, the referee would summarily dismiss it. He has ignored all the improvements incorporated in the revised draft. I am attaching a reply to the referee's comments. I am grateful to you for your professional and courteous exchanges, patience, continuous support to me and for investing so much in this project.

With regards,
Balbir Sihag

Finally published in 2014, the book has been reasonably well received. The first print has been sold out. It has generated a lot of interest throughout the world. A few universities and colleges in India have shown interest in introducing an on-line course based on this book. Ministry of Cultural Affairs of the Indian Government has started its translation in Hindi so that a larger population of students and others can benefit from Kautilya's pearls of wisdom. Vitasta Publishing deserves a lot of credit for taking the financial risk in publishing it and designing a very insightful cover for the book that fairly represents the genius of Kautilya. The white outline of the skull denotes the purity of knowledge. The dot on the forehead (tika) signifies the pointed single-minded pursuit of subject and the key depicts ethics-based economic management as the tool for prosperity.

For further reference:

Grant, Ruth W (2002), The Ethics of Incentives: Historical Origins and Contemporary Understandings. *Journal of Economics and Philosophy* 18. April: 111-139.

Millay, Edna St. Vincent (1892-1950) Euclid alone has looked on beauty bare. http://www.poemhunter.com/poem/euclid-alone

Olivelle, Patrick (1999), *Dharmasutras: The Law Codes of Ancient India*, a New Translation, Oxford University Press, Oxford, New York.

Raju, Chandrakant (2011), *Teaching Mathematics with a Different Philosophy* - II, Calculus without Limits. Science and Culture, July-August, Vol. 77, NOS 7-8, 280-285

Raju, Chandrakant (2013) Euclid and Jesus. *Multiversity and Citizens International*, Penang, Malaysia.

Raju, Chandrakant (2014) Is Science Western in Origin? *Multiversity*, Medusa, Goa, India.

Rowe, David E (2001) Looking back on a Bestseller: Dirk Struik's *A Concise History of Mathematics*, Notes on the AMS, Vol. 48, No. 6, 590-592.